This book may be kept

SEVEN DAYS

A fine will be charged for each day the book is kept overtime.

JUN 11			
JUL			
OCT 17 '64			
NOV 24 '84			
JAN 19 '66			
AUG 10 70			
GAYLORD 72			PRINTED IN U.S.A.

by Robert Hardy Andrews

IF I HAD A MILLION

GREAT DAY IN THE MORNING

BURNING GOLD

LEGEND OF A LADY

A Corner of Chicago

Robert Hardy Andrews

A Corner of Chicago

Little, Brown and Company · Boston · Toronto

The author wishes to thank the following for permission to
use copyrighted material:

Mrs. James Thurber for excerpts from THE BEAST IN ME
AND OTHER ANIMALS by James Thurber

Holt, Rinehart and Winston for stanza from "Could man
be drunk forever" from COMPLETE POEMS by A. E. Hous-
man. Copyright 1922 by Holt, Rinehart and Winston, Inc.
Copyright renewed 1950 by Barclays Bank Ltd. Reprinted
by permission of Holt, Rinehart and Winston, Inc., and
the Society of Authors.

Published simultaneously in Canada
by Little, Brown & Company (Canada) Limited

PRINTED IN THE UNITED STATES OF AMERICA

F

To IRENE, *on our twenty-first*
anniversary, with love and faith

I keep six honest serving-men
(They taught me all I knew);
Their names are What and Why and When
And How and Where and Who.
—RUDYARD KIPLING
Just-So Stories:
"The Elephant's Child"

The name, Chicago, comes from Ind. word for "strong, power-ful," applied by Miami because of pungent garlic beds. Modern metropolis justifies orig. meaning in its vigor & bigness. City of spectacular sports, mammoth conventions, fabulous fairs, mass demonstrations & riots, it has also been country's greatest melt-ing-pot, pride of capitalistic enterprise & capital of political corruption, gangsterism & market speculation, literary capital during "American Renaissance," hotbed of muckraking & social reform. Century Of Progress, 1933-1934, flaunted miracles of science & technology.

— *The American Guide*
HENRY G. ALSBERG, editor

The name, Chicago, comes from Ind. word for "strong, power-
ful," applied by Miami because of pungent garlic beds. Modern
metropolis justifies orig. meaning in its vigor & bigness. City of
spectacular sports, mammoth convention, fabulous fairs, mass
demonstrations & riots, it has also been country's greatest melt-
ing-pot, pride of capital &c, nonsuch & capital of political
corruption, cynosure... a model population, literary capital
during "American Renaissance"; hotbed of muckraking & social
reform. Century OF Progress, 1933-1934, flaunted miracles of
science & technology.

—The American Oracle
Henry G. Alsberg, editor.

Young Man Going Somewhere

DEAR BOB ANDREWS: You sound like old times and like you are still going great guns. We are alumni of a corner of fellowship in Chicago, where our talks usually were around midnight.

—CARL SANDBURG
Hollywood
1962

Find a writer who has something American to say, and nine times out of ten you will find he has some connection with the Gargantuan abattoir by Lake Michigan — he was bred there, or got his start there, or passed through there when he was young and tender.

—HENRY L. MENCKEN
American Mercury
1933

ANDREWS: SALARY INADEQUATE IF THAT MATTERS.
—HENRY JUSTIN SMITH, telegram
Chicago Daily News
1928

IF I CAN HELP IT, and I think I can, I'll never go back to Chicago. Traveling east or west, I want clouds and smoke between me and the bawdy, gaudy old girl I loved when I was young if not exactly tender, and she showed all her hard days and rough nights. I'd sooner not see how she has changed, though it may be for the better, since they took her to the face-lifter and the psychiatrist.

Looking backward from far off and long after, I shed no tears. Some things can be wonderful only once. I had the unearned good luck to be where I wanted to be when being there mattered most. I got in free, on my press card, at a show nobody wrote, that had a beginning, a middle, and an end. Actors played their big scenes close enough to touch; lines the best of us couldn't improve came out of nowhere on cue; the curtain rose and fell with no assistance from the wings; and regularly, the scenery fell on the audience. I wouldn't care to watch a revival staged with the road company.

Chicago to me was the *Chicago Daily News*, and the *C. D. N.* was Henry Justin Smith. I thank whatever gods may be that Smith read a story I faked in the *Minneapolis Journal*, and for still mysterious reasons hired me, by wire, off of a city desk where I didn't belong anyhow at still not twenty-one; and that this occurred just when it did, in days that will not return, when all of us were rushing headlong out of the Twenties into the Thirties and cubs like me studied Smith's book, *Deadlines*, more religiously than our Church Editor conned his Bible.

3

There was faith and hope and love and charity in *Deadlines*. Especially in the chapter that Smith headed "Young Man Going Somewhere." Each of us dreamed he could be its hero if he ever got the chance, which chances were he never would. Faithfully, we slaved as *Deadlines* adjured. "Newspaper writing," Smith said, "is hard. It grinds your brains to powder. You don't burn yourself out, though. Not if you care enough. You get tempered like steel. You can temper your style, too. If you never stop working on it." We never stopped working, as hard and well as we knew how.

Most of our masterpieces wound up in the wastebasket. Day after day, we seized damp copies of the Final, scanned and suffered, slunk home vowing never to return, and ran joyfully back to the salt mine next morning. Privately, I felt rather sorry for my compeers. I claimed I had my first by-line before I was out of knee pants. And in a way this was true, though the How and Why of it were a bit peculiar.

On the Oklahoma Indian reservation where my father was the only doctor in a hundred miles, the Kiowa and Arapaho children levied war on me, a minority of one. In those times, red-skinned men and women still remembered being proud and free, before white conquerors penned them in sandhill wastelands where no one yet suspected there was oil. Old Chief Two Babies was so called because, when Chivington's Colorado irregulars massacred Black Kettle's unarmed people at Sand Creek, a trooper killed the Chief's twin brother in their mother's arms. When our young braves got drunk on vanilla extract stolen from the Agency commissary, they war-whooped as if they rode with Crazy Horse against Custer on the Little Big Horn. In the Agency school, their sons and daughters avenged the not yet distant past on me, so enthusiastically that my father decided I would last longer, and might learn more, if he taught me at home. So Kipling's *Barrack*

Room Ballads, which he treasured, was the textbook from which I learned English.

My sister died of what was then called "prairie fever." Amazing my father and shaming me, my Indian enemies came to her funeral — in a barbed-wire enclosure on a barren knoll beside the drought-dried Washita — and for love of her sang "Shall We Gather at the River?" After that, my father worked harder than ever, and was oftener away all night, delivering Indian babies or patching up their fathers, who fought each other for lack of foes they could lay hands on. Left alone, I recited "The Ballad of East and West" from our doorway at the top of my lungs, defying the coyotes that skulked and howled at the moon outside. Soon I set to making up what I thought were poems, all about the ends of the earth. When my Aunt Mary sent me a dollar for my birthday, I bought stamps secretly and mailed a sheaf of pages to the *Kansas City Star,* the only newspaper I knew of. I heard nothing whatever from this first attempt to get my words in print until a year later, when I was sent to Kansas to live with my grandmother and get civilized. She had saved a full-page clipping because the names were the same. It was headed IS THIS MAN THE NEW PRAIRIE POET LAUREATE? I had neglected to mention my age, which was going on eleven.

At twelve, I got a job on Ewing Herbert's *Brown County Weekly World,* by shoving some more of my rhymes under the office door on a Sunday. My duties included melting metal for our lone linotype, scrubbing the job presses with kerosene, pulling sale-bill proofs, correcting our hand-set mail-list galleys, sweeping out the Makeup Room, and meeting our twice-a-day trains to gather Personals. William Allen White of the *Emporia Gazette* dropped in occasionally. So did Ed Howe, the Sage of Potato Hill, from the *Atchison Globe.* I even shook hands with Walt Mason, who published a syndicated paragraph of jingling rhymed prose five days a week

5

for forty years. My grandmother said that if you could buy me for what I was really worth and find anyone to take me off your hands at my own valuation, you could pay the mortgage on the henhouse.

My salary was two dollars and fifty cents a week. When I struck for a raise to three dollars, to meet my mounting expenses for stamps and mailing envelopes, I was fired. No matter. I knew what I wanted to do with my life.

My father had hoped I'd study medicine, and tried to push me toward it by taking me along to interpret for him to Indian squaws and their husbands, and to tie stitches when he performed emergency Caesareans in sod dugouts, with a plank on sawhorses for his operating table. When I was thirteen, he gave up. By then, he was doctoring Sisseton Sioux in South Dakota. In a gesture of renunciation I had to live much longer to appreciate (I hope my son reads this), he sent me his beloved Kipling. On the flyleaf he had penciled *See him and raise him one.* This seemed possible to me then. From Ayer's newspaper directory, I culled a list of twenty small-town dailies, and wrote to all of them claiming unlimited experience around a shop and offering my part-time services while I finished high school. I got one reply, from the *Morning American* in Aberdeen, South Dakota, and showed up announcing "Here I am" before the editor had time to change his mind. I started high, but settled for thirty-five dollars a month.

Six days a week, I checked in at the *American* at 4 P.M. and stayed through to 1 A.M. or longer. My high school classes ran from nine in the morning until three in the afternoon. One of my youthful heroes, Thomas A. Edison, said four hours of sleep in any twenty-four was enough for a man who loved his job. I found no reason for disagreeing with him. The first week, a tramp printer stole my Kipling talisman. I hardly had time to miss it. Floyd Gibbons, passing through on a lecture tour, told me how he lost his eye in the Argonne and how to write a story about it, on which I put my by-line. The editor let me get away with this — and the baby tiger had tasted blood. My next self-conferred by-line was on a lengthy report of a political speech by Congressman Royal C. Johnson, who, like Gibbons, owed his eminence to deeds of daring during World War I. This brought an offer from the Congressman of an appointment to West Point or Annapolis. I couldn't very well tell him I flunked math consistently, and in any case wouldn't be fifteen for another seven months.

I decided travel would broaden me, and signed on with a promoter of newspaper circulation contests. At Thief River Falls in northern Minnesota, then in St. Paul, then at Utica and Schenectady in upstate New York, then back in South Dakota at Watertown and Sioux Falls, I wrote sales letters and page ads and what we announced as a "true-life story," which was actually a hundred thousand words of come-on that ran serially, telling how boy met girl on the campus and together they won a Pierce-Arrow for selling three-year subscriptions, and lived happily ever after. Between contests, I wrote baseball in the Class D Dakota League, where Sunny Jim Bottomley, in the twilight of his illustrious career, still hit the long one now and then. Somehow, I sandwiched in odd-shaped chunks of college. But political science charted in classrooms seemed like kindergarten stuff, to me, compared to covering the real thing in the heartland of the Farmer–Labor Rebellion.

General Leonard Wood, perhaps the only remaining American who didn't know he would never get the Republican nomination for President, came campaigning again in the dead of winter. A blizzard halted all trains. Still he insisted on keeping a Sioux Falls speaking date. On a gasoline-powered scooter borrowed from a railroad section-gang, I rode sixty miles beside the General, through a raging storm. When we reached his goal, the audience had gone home. Nevertheless, he made his speech, and I reported that his body servant, a master sergeant retired, applauded in all the proper places.

7

The General, a magnificently military figure, limped. I asked the sergeant if this resulted from a wound incurred with Teddy Roosevelt and the Rough Riders charging on foot up San Juan Hill, or with Black Jack Pershing pursuing Aguinaldo in the Philippines.

"The Old Man," the sergeant said, "never got shot at in his life. He was sitting at his desk under a ceiling fan, it being hotter than the hinges of Hades in Mindanao. Somebody gives him a 'No,' which you do not do to Generals. Up he bounces, and hits the fan with the top of his skull. This naturally busts the fan. Why it gives him a gimp I could not state with exactitude. But I can guarantee you it does not win His Nibs another medal to hang on his brass-bound bosom."

I printed this canard without bothering to look up the facts in the General's official biography. Actually, he limped because of a nerve block that was unavoidable when his life was saved by one of the great Dr. Harvey Cushing's first brain-tumor operations. Our publisher, who was a Democrat but open-minded, was justified in dispensing with my services. We needed then, as we need now, Americans larger than life to look up to, unminimized by the mocking press. And out of evil, good. Cut from the payroll on one hour's notice, I hadn't enough money coming to pay my fare any farther than Minneapolis. In those unorganized times tramp reporters, like boomer printers and itinerant copyreaders, were always showing up in strange newspaper shops, hard up or hung over or both. They were either thrown out or put to work. I was lucky. I got a week's tryout on the *Minneapolis Journal*.

My assignment was NECROLOGICS, the *Journal's* traditional slug line for death notices. Faithfully, I telephoned the undertakers, and typed what they told me, listing relatives of the deceased unto the fourth generation. Automatically, the copy desk slashed my paragraphs to sentences. I didn't dare complain. My life's ambition at that point was to stay on the *Journal,* the region's biggest afternoon and Sunday morning daily. The owner-publisher, Herschel V. Jones, had started his own career as a cub reporter on space rates. He developed a specialty: crop forecasting. His predictions of wheat yields were so accurate that grainbrokers backed him in buying the paper. It could happen again, if I could stumble onto a specialty somebody else hadn't already homesteaded. At seventeen, pretending to be twenty-five or maybe a little older, there was no impossibility whatever in climbing as H. V. Jones had climbed, until he was a multimillionaire, the Maecenas of Minneapolis, a benevolently bullying dictator who bossed the Minneapolis Institute of Arts as firmly as he ruled the *Journal,* and made its trustees and benefactors buy what he thought should be bought, whether they liked it or not.

In Europe, he committed the Institute to the purchase of Titian's "Temptation of Christ" for three hundred thousand dollars, then an incredible price to pay for any painting. This news, that set the whole town talking, came in just when I was tackling my first celebrity interview, with Efrem Zimbalist, the concert violinist (then the husband of the operatic diva, Alma Gluck), whose son has since added luster to the family name by starring in 77 *Sunset Strip* on television. I had no idea how to interview anybody. Sensing this, Zimbalist took pity on me. "What you need," he explained, "is something crazy, which is expected regarding a genius, which I am not, but we will call me one. I shall now order five stacks of pancakes for breakfast. This will please your publisher's friends, who are flour-millers, the Washburns and Crosbys and Pillsburys. I shall eat like a lumberjack, not like a violinist. This will charm your readers, to learn that to Zimbalist a recital is like chopping down trees to the Weyerhaeusers. You will also mention the Weyerhaeusers. They are big advertisers. This guarantees that your story will get on Page One." And he did, and I did, and it did, and I was on the payroll.

The dean of journalism who was temporarily holding down the city desk had problems enough without taking time out to put a leash and a muzzle on me. This left me free to invent assignments for myself. I arranged for advance notice from various cultural committees, and met and beset visiting luminaries in all sorts of improbable situations: Sol Hurok weeping in the box office because his first European importation, Isa Kremer, the chanteuse, drew an audience of less than a hundred; Mary Garden managing the Chicago Opera Company on tour, and announcing at rehearsal that Lucien Muratore sang flat and his bride, Lina Cavalieri, couldn't sing at all; Paderewski declining to receive the keys of the city from our mayor and disappearing into the railroad yards, because of a previous engagement to walk his poodle; Rudolph Valentino, just married to the exotic Natacha Rambova (whose real name was Winifred Hudnut), complaining that their honeymoon personal-appearance tour had turned out to be a sales-promotion stunt for a mud-pack preparation.

Queen Maria of Rumania and her son and daughter, Prince Nicholas and Princess Ileana, arrived on a transcontinental tour. The by-liners got the Queen. The Women's Page got the Princess. That left the Prince to second-stringers like myself. He resented this as much as we did, and knew more ways to be insulting. For the first time, but not by any means the last, I saw what reporters can do to a celebrity who treats them disrespectfully. Prince Nicholas spent most of his time changing from one splendiferous uniform into another even more like a costume for a Shubert operetta. He spoke at a luncheon at the Minneapolis Club. The Club's royal service of solid sterling silver was brought out for the occasion. The Prince's uniform tunic had enormously puffed-out sleeves. Just before the luncheon, reporters surrounded him, all talking at once while their hands were busy. When he rose to speak, thirty pieces of the Club's silverware spilled out of his sleeves. We reported this contretemps with tongue-in-cheek solemnity. And during the rest of the tour, Prince Nicholas was carefully courteous to cubs.

Gene Tunney arrived, on a vaudeville exhibition junket, following his first victory over Jack Dempsey. We took him to meet the curator at the Institute of Arts, who had once boxed genteelly at Harvard. They discussed Shakespeare and Bernard Shaw. That was to be expected. But Tunney surprised us all by saying he had heard about the Institute buying the Titian "Temptation." In front of it, he said with utmost sincerity: "I love this picture. I've always loved it. When I was a hungry youngster living in a cold-water railroad flat in Brooklyn and going to the Brothers' school, they had a chromo reproduction of the 'Temptation' at the head of the stairs. My hands were always chapped and cracked. I used to run every morning to stand in front of the 'Temptation' and warm my hands at Satan's scarlet cloak, and pray the Lord to forgive me."

We took the *Chicago Tribune* press service. In reciprocity, we filed queries now and then: "Have story thus-and-so. You want? How much?" The *Tribune* teletyped FIVE HUNDRED TUNNEY ART CRITIC. So now I was in the World's Greatest Newspaper. Or so I thought — until what the *Tribune* published came back. What I had written wide-eyed was transformed into biting satire, and signed WESTBROOK PEGLER. And when my bruised feelings healed, I thanked Pegler for a lesson: that facts are all in how you choose to look at them. Then the Managing Editor acknowledged my existence for the first time. He said my Tunney story had started people flocking to see the "Temptation." Mr. Jones was pleased. Hereafter, I would do a weekly feature on "Art at the Institute." With pictures. And a by-line.

Nobody asked what I knew about art. I joined an evening painting class. I couldn't paint, and can't. But I could look and listen. The Institute owned a little Corot, done lovingly before he became a factory grinding out nymphs and poplars. It disappeared from a gallery wall. There was consternation.

11

Police were called in, but nothing about the missing Corot got in the papers. Finally, it was found — in a laundry tub in the basement. Dust, sucked through the thinly painted canvas where it hung unwisely placed near an air-conditioning intake-duct, had darkened the picture. This had troubled a part-time guard, who was Scandinavian and liked things neat. So he took the Corot down and scrubbed it on a washboard with Ivory soap. (The copy desk cut "Ivory" out of my story: the *Journal* gave free advertising to the Institute, but not to commercial enterprises. However, if Madison Avenue can still use a testimonial out of the distant past, here it is.) The Corot was undamaged — in fact, it had never looked prettier. And the story of its bath in soapsuds did me no harm, either. Not after H. V. Jones saw crowds in front of it. The Managing Editor sent me his note: *Let's have more like this.*

The Institute, like most museums, fought a rear-guard action against benefactors who insisted on bequeathing cats-and-dogs collections on an all-or-nothing basis. One of these included nine gloomy canvases signed REMBRANDT, just one of them possibly genuine, and fifty-three portraits of Indian chiefs by a Ringling Brothers' wagon-painter. Another white elephant was a cellarful of unopened packing cases, which contained unclassified Egyptian mummies and sarcophagi in all stages of desuetude. I stumbled onto an X-ray technician who needed clients, and took a wild idea to the assistant curator. Gravely, I reported on Page One that within the wrappings of a certain mummy there were odd little bumps, which might be priceless scarabs. Problem: What if the mummy, unwrapped, should crumble into dust? Answer: We were X-raying it. So far as I know, we published the first X-rays of viscera three thousand years old. This started a new pilgrimage to the Institute. The bumps were misplaced finger-bones. But now I was the *Journal's* expert on archaeology.

Sir Philip Gibbs, a newspaperman's newspaperman, once wrote that A *successful journalist is one who convinces his*

readers he knows something about everything, without reveal-
ing that in reality he knows almost nothing about anything.
The philosophy might be cynical, and its practice quite unethical, but what was all right for Sir Philip seemed quite all
right for me, in days when less than five thousand words in any
Final was unthinkable.

I was also Education Editor, and I ran the paper's Model
Airplane Tournament. As a matter of course, when our syndicate contract for an advice-to-the-lovelorn column expired,
with a stack of letters unanswered, I was cast to substitute
for our lost Aunt Jenny Laurie. I might still be solving heart
affairs if the Managing Editor hadn't agreed to pay me space
rates.

A mother of twelve asked if she should have a thirteenth
child — Would thirteen be unlucky? I replied with an editorial
beginning: "Here is a challenge to all Americans: What are
we doing to perpetuate the large American families that used
to be? . . ." continuing for nine inches of type at fifty cents
an inch. A teen-ager torn between three undying loves — for
a football captain, a cheer leader, and her married teacher —
wanted expert evaluation. "Keep them all dangling, my dear,"
I advised maternally, in many words worth about a penny
each. "Let them fight over you: you will find this is amusing
for you and an education for them. Being male, they have
much to learn, whereas, as every woman knows, all women are
born knowing all the necessary answers." I quote from what
got in the paper. My more explicit answers didn't.

I was relieved of this assignment. But that wasn't the end of
it. A couple of bright young businessmen had set up a factory
that made kitchen appliances. Radio was the newest phenomenon; only half a dozen experimental stations perched atop
our tallest buildings, but ahead of the times these young
pioneers and their wives had decided to advertise on the air.
The same sort of laughter that greeted horseless carriages
pealed from our Advertising Department. When the foolish

four invited me to write some more advice to the lovelorn for their wives (who had acted in plays at Wellesley) to read, between sales messages, I was given an enthusiastic go-ahead. The theory was that if I couldn't kill the show, thus proving that radio was only a passing fancy, nobody could. And, as we saw it then, I was a howling success. Our first few broadcasts netted a fantastic flood of equally fantastic letters. Gallantly, the sponsors' wives plunged into the mailbags. What they read — confided to a stranger who didn't even exist — was so shockingly revelatory of sin in small towns that the startled ladies ordered their husbands to call the whole thing off immediately. That didn't, however, take me out of radio. The *Journal* opened an experimental station, maximum range two hundred miles, aptly call-lettered WBAD. After office hours, I was program arranger, stand-by announcer, and of course, publicity promoter.

Our microphones were Rudy Vallee souvenir megaphones set in telephone receivers. We went on and off the air at will. Nobody was paid but the janitor. From makeshift studios atop the Radisson Hotel, we broadcast such programs as a four-hour show presenting Henri Verbrugghen, conductor of the Minneapolis Symphony Orchestra, playing violin solos and conducting his string section; four visiting concert artists, one of whom was Robert Ringling, making his bid for success as a baritone and escape from the family circus tradition; Dexter Fellowes, the prince of press agents, on leave from the Big Top to promote young Ringling, who spent thirty minutes explaining why he'd rather talk about elephants; Charley Cordrey and His Kazoo Kollegians; and a fifty-voice boys' choir. When the choirboys were due on the air, I found them sitting on the cornice along the hotel front, leaning out over ten stories of space, dropping paper-sack water-bombs on the traffic far below. They swore they'd jump off before they'd sing for nothing. Several of them nearly fell. By the time I had cajoled them back to safety, our station engineer was through for the day and I was through with radio, I thought, for life. For once renouncing added income, I resigned from WBAD.

I had begun to hang around the composing room. I still carried an apprentice card, given to me by a tramp printer in Kansas as a joke. My fingers, broken in Ewing Herbert's job-press, convinced the *Journal's* compositors that with their guidance I might still get back on the right track. They taught me some type-juggling tricks. Pretty soon, I was not only writing pages for the Sunday supplement, but laying them out and making them up, with the boss compositor as my mentor. Also, our Drama Editor was bored, and I didn't blame him — Minneapolis theater seasons always opened with the Swiss Bell-Ringers and closed with Fiske O'Hara singing "Mother Machree." The editor let me sit in for him, reviewing Guy Bates Post in *The Masquerader,* and Florence Reed in stock at the Shubert, and Louis Wolheim and William Boyd (the William Boyd who didn't become Hopalong Cassidy) in *What Price Glory?,* and the septuagenarians, Sothern and Marlowe, as *Romeo and Juliet,* and Richard Bennett and daughters, Constance and Joan, in *Jarnegan.* The night after my critical comments appeared, Bennett halted his perfor-mance to inform the audience he had canceled all further ad-vertising in our paper because some lack-wit hiding behind the initials R. A. had set the theater back a century by his uncouth and illiterate mud-slinging at a work of art and genius. To mollify the Advertising Department, the Managing Editor assigned me to write a second review. I reviewed Mr. Bennett's harangue, which he now repeated at every show, and said that it alone was worth the price of admission. The Advertising Department reported that Mr. Bennett had forgiven me. He, too, liked his own material better than he liked the play.

Happily, our Drama Editor delegated me to cover forty vaudeville acts, every Saturday and Sunday, in our five variety houses. This was giving an infant a shotgun to play with. I scattered scornful slurs at singers, dancers, and comedians. Some of them saved their bad notices. One comedian in particular hit the top eventually, in spite of my half-column prophecy to the contrary. A time came, in New York, when a writing assignment I wanted very much was mine if this comic would agree to star in my show. Our agents brought us together. We got along so well that I told my agent "Start drawing the contracts." Then someone told the comic that I used to review vaudeville in Minneapolis. He recalled an old saying, that the three worst weeks in show business were Easter Week, Christmas Week, and Minneapolis Week. Then he said: "Some yokel out there gave me the worst panning I ever got. I wonder if you'd know him." I was positive I wouldn't. But he said, "My apartment's just down the hall. I'll get my scrapbook. Maybe when you see the review you'll remember the thus-and-such who signed it." He went to fetch his scrapbook. He never spoke to me again.

But there are brighter memories. I saw a dancing clown named Joe E. Brown succeed where then more famous stars had failed, in his first appearance as a single before a Sunday matinee audience at the Hennepin Orpheum. No one knew why, exactly, but Sunday matinees at the Hennepin were murderous for funnymen. The ticket buyers sat obstinately on their cold hands and laughed no more than if they were still in church. A pair of zanies called Duffy and Sweeney had made themselves legendary by their effort to break the never-on-Sunday jinx. Worn to a limp frazzle after twenty minutes of prat-falls and funereal silence, Duffy lay down on the stage, while Sweeney retired into the wings and returned bearing a baseball bat. "Ladies and gentlemen," he announced, "my partner, Mr. Duffy, and I are about to do something very amusing. Before we do it, permit me to warn you that after we have done it, if you do not laugh, I shall come down the aisle and beat the living bejasus out of you." All he got for that, I

reported in my review, was a wire from the booking-office:
CANCEL DUFFY AND SWEENEY IMMEDIATELY FOR THREATENING
THE CASH CUSTOMERS.

But young Joe E. Brown had his own ideas, and they shattered the spell. Suddenly, he leaped headlong from the stage into the orchestra pit. The startled audience screamed involuntarily. Then he bounced up from the trampoline on which he had landed, and went on performing remarkable feats through several well-earned encores. I said next day, in close to two thousand admiring words, that he was the first single who ever stopped the show cold on a Sunday at the Hennepin. While I was reading my favorite author, the Managing Editor came by, and said I was to write something new and different in the way of a Christmas sob-story. I said there hadn't been anything new and different to write about Christmas since the *New York Sun* said, "Yes, Virginia, there is a Santa Claus." Then my phone rang. Joe E. Brown was calling, to thank me for what he said was the finest notice he ever had. He'd like to buy my lunch.

So I lunched with a stranger who has been my friend ever since. He was bound for Hollywood, and wondered how moviegoers would take to his style. (They took to it so enthusiastically that he starred in more successful film comedies than any other comedian ever made.) He reminisced about his beginnings in show business, as a boy acrobat stranded in San Francisco by the earthquake and fire in 1906, and about being stranded again on Broadway by the Actors' Equity strike. (Though he wasn't yet a member of Equity, he walked out of his first starring role on opening night in loyalty to his profession.) I wound up with material for a three-page Sunday spread. Then, when we were about to part, I mentioned my Christmas Story assignment, and he told me about a dream he had that didn't come true, when he was a hard-up youngster selling papers in Toledo.

We went out into a snowstorm, and on Nicollet Avenue

found a newsboy shivering, gallantly shouting his wares, selling none. For three dollars, most of which Joe E. provided, we bought all his papers. Then, as Joe E. had wanted to do long ago, the boy went shopping for Christmas presents in the Five- and Ten-Cent Store. He spent only twenty cents on himself, for a pair of mittens. With twenty-eight dimes, he accumulated fifteen small packages to carry home and stuff in stockings he'd hang up after Mom and his little brothers went to bed. We bought a little imitation Christmas tree, which he didn't think he should accept since he couldn't pay for it, and put him in a taxicab despite his protest that we were squandering our money. "As long as he lives," Joe E. Brown said softly while the boy rode away with his Gifts of the Magi, "he'll never be a prouder man than he is tonight." And the Managing Editor said the story wasn't bad, but asked if I was doing publicity for a vaudeville actor on the side. I said "No. For Santa Claus." And he pardoned my impertinence, since it was Christmas Eve.

Then on Christmas Day a tipster called and said a squad of Prohibition enforcement officers, captained by a newly appointed chief who was out to make a record, was staging a big raid, and if I got there in a hurry I might see some fireworks. I found the chief dry agent waiting, armed to the teeth, annoyed because I hadn't brought along a photographer. I called for one, while a dozen agents loafed on fire escapes and rooftops. The photographer arrived, and got his camera lined up. The commander of the raid fired off his six-shooters and crashed through a door shouting "Stand where you goddam' are!" Then he looked slightly sheepish. All this melodrama had produced a single cringing captive, ninety if he was a day, and his homemade still, which took three hours to produce a pint of moonshine, drop by drop.

I went on another raid that wasn't as easy to write about. This was a strictly business affair, at a warehouse where Scotch trucked in from Canada was mixed one to five with local rotgut, then rebottled and sold for premium prices to our leading citizens. In the dry agent squad was an earnest, upstanding young fellow, a divinity student who had quit school when his young wife told him she was going to have a baby, their second in two years. He said he had looked for work for weeks, until God's mercy led him to the right place. He believed in Prohibition. He told me how fortunate he was to be able to earn a living for his family while fighting the Demon Rum, a job he could be proud of. On this, his first raid, he ran in ahead of the other agents. A moronic hoodlum shot and killed him with a twelve-gauge shotgun.

On my way back to the office, I stopped at his address to get a picture for the paper. He lived upstairs at the back, over a Chinese laundry. I heard a baby crying. I knocked. The door was opened by the dead man's fragile, pregnant wife, who had just picked up her year-old first child from its crib. The ill-heated, cheaply furnished two-room flat was spotlessly clean. She thought I was a bill collector, and told me breathlessly that she and her husband were ashamed to have run into debt, but finally their prayers had been answered: he had a new job, working for the Government. If I'd trust them a little longer, they'd never have to owe anybody again. Could her husband call me somewhere, as soon as he got home? Their wedding picture was on the wall behind her. I couldn't tell her "He's never coming home." I turned and ran down the stairs, and back at the *Journal* the City Editor told me to take the sob out of my story. Who, he asked, felt sorry for Prohibition agents?

Then a chance arose to play detective, like a reporter in the movies. Police were called to a loan company's office. The woman manager had recently been discharged, supplanted by a man, formerly her assistant. A package came for him, Special Delivery, Registered. Opening it, he stared at a box of expensive chocolates. Candy was his weakness. He was about to start eating when a customer called him away from his desk. While his back was turned, his secretary ate two chocolates. Almost at once, she was deathly sick. Rushed to the hospital, she showed symptoms of arsenic poisoning. The police were busy when I arrived. While they built up a case of attempted homicide, the wall clock ticked toward deadline time for our afternoon Final. If I waited for the police toxicologist to analyze the chocolates and report, we'd lose the story to tomorrow morning's Opposition. Surreptitiously, I borrowed several chocolates from the box, while the police were looking the other way, questioning the intended victim. Hotfooting it back to the office, I passed a pet store, and ran in and bought three white mice in a small wire cage. We set the cage on the city desk, focused a camera, and dropped in bits of chocolate. The mice weren't hungry. Minutes passed before one of them nosed a piece of the suspected candy, then nibbled, then gulped, then rolled on its back and died with tiny toes pointing up at the camera. No picture ever got through Engraving and onto Page One faster. We scooped not only the Opposition but the Homicide Bureau, and were also ahead on the final pay-off, which was that the apparent target for murder most foul had sent the chocolates to himself. He had embezzled forty thousand dollars, and hoped that by eating one of the chocolates and almost dying, but not quite, he would divert suspicion from himself to his predecessor in charge of the loan company's funds.

Thus, on the swings and roundabouts, a very young reporter got more and more words in the paper, and added five dollars and five dollars there to a paycheck that never quite supported him in the style to which he wished to become accustomed. I substituted for the Music Editor, reviewing Alexander Brailowsky's first piano recital in the United States, and though I didn't know Rachmaninoff's Prelude in C Sharp Major from a Franz Liszt rhapsody, informed our readers, from my heart, that Brailowsky was greater than Vladimir de Pachmann, a name I chose at random out of the *Musical Courier.* Then de Pachmann came to Minneapolis, and, when I went to interview him, said he couldn't talk without a glass of vodka in his hand. I obliged, on my expense account, and the Managing Editor okayed it because, in the speakeasy, de Pachmann suddenly produced half a dozen uncut rubies and emeralds and tossed them in the air "to make a rainbow." He lost one, and insisted on having the floorboards torn up while we searched for it. This brought in what de Pachmann insisted on calling the Cossacks: a couple of Prohibition agents who didn't really want to close the joint, but had to under the circumstances. We found the missing ruby in de Pachmann's shoe, which he had taken off to swat a cockroach.

« 2 »

Memories, like trees, grow taller with the years. Branches and tendrils thicken; vagrant vines attach themselves, further obscuring the overburdened trunk of truth. But it is still there somewhere. I believe I see very clearly the gentle little old lady in her wheel chair, on a pleasant front porch in a backroad Minnesota town, who described the horrors of the Sioux Uprising in 1862 (that ended when President Lincoln's reluctant order sent thirty-six Indians to hang simultaneously on an enormous scaffold, in the greatest mass execution in American history) with such circumspect detail that finally I said: "It sounds almost as if you were there." She said simply, "I was," and lifted her snowy white wig. She had been scalped and left for dead when she was six years old, and lived to tell about it on her seventy-first birthday.

I see a lone mine shaft looming against the stormy night sky, on a barren hilltop along the Minnesota Iron Range. Again, a bell tolls. Three hundred feet down, forty-one miners drowned when a new drift they were opening, under protest, tapped the bottom of a lake. One of them reached the ladder at the bottom of the shaft, and drowned there with his hand entangled in the rope that signaled, too late, for the elevator. A corpse's weight kept the bell ringing urgently until someone, cursing, cut the rope. Gene Fox, our photographer, crept closer through the darkness, while I kept watch for shotgun guards who had orders to run reporters and photographers off the mining company's property. We were the first to arrive. We had no flash bulbs for night picture-taking then; Gene used powder spread on a triggered tray, set off by a percussion cap. He had forgotten to bring his flashgun, and we were two hundred miles from Minneapolis. I lost sight of him, but saw guards approaching. He reappeared, out in the open. He had found a miner's lamp and a washtub in the change-room near the shaft. The guards yelled and came running. Gene dumped six bottles of flash powder in the tub, drew back and lined up his camera, and tossed the miner's lamp. The powder exploded thunderously. The tremendous flash lighted up a scene of shawled Finnish and Lithuanian women, widows since four hours ago, spaced in a circle surrounding the shaft like the standing slabs at Stonehenge, and as still and lifeless. Stunned and blinded, the guards recoiled. The mourners never moved. The blast sent me reeling backward into a snowdrift. Gene was down, but he came up running. He thrust the plate from his camera into my shaking grasp, and turned to face the guards, stabbing at them with the spiked legs of his tripod. That gave me time to crawl through a barbed-wire fence, leaving behind most of my new and unpaid-for overcoat. By car, and on foot through the snow after it stalled in a drift, and finally on a freight train, I traveled all night, and started writing as soon as I stumbled into Editorial at the *Journal* in the morning. Gene's picture filled six full columns, top to bottom, on Page One. Wrapped around it and running on from there were nine columns of copy I wrote in a daze, before I passed out quietly at my desk. The Chinese were right. Gene's grimly eloquent photograph had much more impact than my thousands of words towards forcing official inquiry that revised the system of state mine inspection. There was talk of recommending us for a Pulitzer Prize. Nothing came of that. More important to us, anyhow, were the ten-dollar bonuses we found in our pay envelopes that Saturday.

Then there was the time when every reporter who could be rounded up on a Sunday was rushed to Chippewa Falls, Wisconsin, where a train carrying passengers home for the holidays had jumped the tracks while crossing a railroad bridge. The last car, hurtling down into the river, drowned or crushed thirty-four men, women, and children. I wish I could claim I solved the problem of how to get that story out ahead of the Opposition, in a town where there was only one telegraph operator on duty. Miss Lorena Hickok did that. Forbiddingly large, she was surprisingly kind to cubs, and placid even when she covered a story in competition with men who mistakenly thought they could out-report a lady. She smoked a pipe, swore softly but stunningly, and carried a New Testament which she read between bursts of unflurried activity.

In the telegraph office a step ahead of us, she handed the operator her Testament and a twenty-dollar bill, and told him "Start sending with Matthew, and don't stop." That gave her the wire, and we couldn't cut in. The operator was well along into Luke, and her Managing Editor was on the verge of apoplexy because he couldn't stop the sending from his end, and I was the youngest but loudest of a dozen rival reporters threatening to lynch the operator, when Lorena steamed in majestically to interrupt the Parable of the First and the Last with her lead on the story of the wreck. All we could do was wait helplessly for her to finish in her own sweet time; and she didn't hurry. She beat me on the street with the story by an hour and eighteen minutes, and it took me seventeen years to forgive her. When she went to the White House as Mrs.

Eleanor Roosevelt's personal press advisor, I sent her a pound of the very best pipe tobacco, and my card with one word written on it: *Peace.*

Back in Minneapolis, word came across the bridge from St. Paul regarding an aristocratic newcomer with an overpowering Oxford accent, who had found employment in the James J. Hill Reference Library, cataloguing scientific and technical publications in German, French, and Russian. The job called for extraordinary erudition, and he handled it extremely well. He was called plain Dmitri Obolensky, but rumor whispered that in fact he was a refugee Russian nobleman, incognito. An heiress, who was not named in the papers then and will not be named here (since she is now a distinguished and admirable grandmother), accused the mysterious stranger of being a prince. He didn't exactly say "No." She announced she was going to marry him, and be a princess. He protested politely. Her trustees had police arrest him, alleging he was a fortune-hunter. He denied this with well-mannered indignation. Too much the gentleman to say "The lady pursued me and I retreated with dignity," which I found was actually the case, he would go no farther than to state that she was much too grand to waste herself on him. Released, because there was no trace of legality in any charge against him, he was crossing the lobby of the St. Paul Hotel, crowded with railroad engineers and brakemen gathered in convention, when the matronly immigrant wife of one of them saw him and ran to embrace him. She called him her long-lost foster-child in one breath, and "Your Highness" in the next, and claimed that she had been his nursemaid in Scotland. He was gentle with her, but got away as quickly as he could, and kept on traveling. Much later, when as Prince Michael Romanoff he attained a special sort of headline notoriety, and New York newspapers and magazines agreed that actually he was Harry Gerguson or Ferguson, an American-born impostor, I wondered; and he let

24

me go right on wondering. Still later, when he became proprietor of Hollywood's imperially elegant restaurant by the same name, I ventured one night to ask if he remembered a boy reporter in Minneapolis who may have written the first of at least a thousand stories in which his true identity was still left in the realm of Maybe. Mike grinned, and answered by buying me a drink.

And there was a strange gathering at the University of Minnesota, attracting a handful of professors who told me they were "colloidal chemists." The classification was as new to our copy desk as it was to me. Their solemn assertions that in the not distant future their weird laboratory experiments would lead to the making of artificial rubber and substances they spoke of as "plastics," and even women's stockings and men's shirts, from oil and air and water, were so obviously fantastic that though I quoted them with earnest accuracy, the chief copyreader tacked on, under the slug line INDENT PRECEDE: *The reader is advised to have a saltcellar handy while reading this, the writer having forgotten to take his along.*

Undaunted, I came in with an equally wide-eyed interview with another oddball visitor, whose handmade rockets fizzled and fell apart when he tried to demonstrate them in the Minneapolis Millers Ball Park, yet who assured me soberly: "Within your lifetime, young man, scientific progress will land man-carrying rockets on the moon." Such H. G. Wells-type tomfoolery, our wiseacres decreed, deserved the mocking feature head it got: *FOURTH OF JULY (OR APRIL FOOL?) COMES EARLY WITH "SPACE CONQUEST" PROMOTER.* The man was Dr. Robert Hutchings Goddard, pre-nuclear physicist, whose pioneering researches probed high-altitude secrets and thus helped clear the way for current events at Cape Canaveral. But if newspapers were put together by prophets, there would be no need to buy another Final tomorrow.

Neither satire nor space was wasted often on a Swedish-born country lawyer in Little Falls, who had been a Congressman from Minnesota for ten years, and never earned a headline until he voted with Senator Robert M. LaFollette's Little Band of Willful Men against declaring war on Germany in 1917. Because Charles A. Lindbergh Sr. didn't agree that war would make the world safe for democracy, his house was rotten-egged and painted yellow, his fifteen-year-old son and namesake was ostracized by high school classmates, and he was finished politically. Still he kept on making speeches to farmers, and running for office, and was mentioned in the papers only when he lost again. He had been dead a year when his son, an air-mail pilot, put the family name back on Page One by announcing that he proposed to win the twenty-five-thousand-dollar Orteig Prize by flying nonstop across the Atlantic from New York to Paris.

I had met the father only once, and found him not so much unfriendly to reporters as afraid of them — which was scarcely surprising, all things considered. The son distrusted and disliked us, and made no bones about it. Whatever other reasons he had for this attitude, a recent incident had sharpened the edge of his resentment. In Chicago, he was hired to fly reporters and a photographer to an Illinois town where pickets and strikebreakers battled bloodily. He was ordered to wait beside his plane in a pasture. A man he didn't know came running, handed him a set of photographic plates, and told him to get these back to Chicago immediately. He complied so efficiently that the paper to which he took the pictures scooped the town. The trouble was that he had been fast-talked into delivering them to the wrong paper. The wily reporter who put this over on Lindbergh embroidered the joke, and in fact lived on it, for years. Naturally, nobody paid Lindbergh. The theory was that if he was that dumb, he deserved to go hungry. Oddly, he didn't see it that way.

He was impenetrably aloof except when tinkering with engines and mingling with mechanics; then he was likably relaxed. I tracked him down at Wold-Chamberlain Airport, named for two Minneapolis pilot heroes in World War I. He was enthralled by an experimental low-wing monoplane, whose designers were trying desperately to raise enough money to put it into production. They could hardly believe their luck when he insisted on giving their plane a flight test. Stunting it with a master's recklessness, he landed volunteering to write and sign a testimonial to the effect that its then radical design, scoffed at by experts, was actually a long step forward. I wrote at length about his kind deed. Next time we met, he looked straight through me.

Not long afterward, I was sitting in as temporary editor (for ten dollars extra per week) of our Baseball Green Sheet, which was wrapped around the Final for street-sale in the early evenings, to cut in on the morning Opposition's territory. Deadline was 6 P.M. At 5:50 our time, on May 21, 1927, "Lindbergh the Lone Eagle" was somewhere over the Atlantic, or in it. I took my own wild solo risk, and sent the Green Sheet to press with a screamer line: *MINNESOTA HERO LANDS IN FRANCE,* and a boldface bulletin, uncredited: **Charles A. Lindbergh Jr. of Little Falls, Minnesota, tonight successfully completed his history-making lone flight across the Atlantic from New York to Paris in his "Spirit of St. Louis."** We didn't beat the Opposition. They also gambled, with an Extra. Our Managing Editor said he ought to fire me for printing what wasn't confirmed by the Associated Press until twelve minutes after we were on the street. Then he grinned, and said he'd have fired me if I hadn't done it, and gave me a five-dollar bonus, with orders not to mention it in the newsroom.

Then along came another murder. This one occurred in the Northwest Angle, which was and is a story by itself. Commissioners running the boundary between Canada and the United States, in dead of winter, erred slightly in their surveys, and decided it wasn't necessary to correct the error since the area involved was worthless wilderness. That left a triangular segment of Minnesota, the northernmost point in the United States, separated from the rest by an arm of Lake of the Woods. Not even noted on most maps, the Angle had no registered inhabitants but a few hunters and trappers, and no law enforcement agency to take charge and feed facts to the papers in Minneapolis, three hundred miles away, when a woman was found dead in an isolated cabin, frozen stiff, with a butcher knife driven through her heart. Nor, as our Opposition soon discovered, was there any way to get a reporter through a blizzard that never stopped, fifty miles across ice floes in the storm-lashed lake, to the scene of the crime from which the *Journal*'s Special Correspondent was busily filing Exclusives.

We identified the murdered woman as principal heiress to an Oklahoma oil well empire. We revealed that she had eloped a few months before with an itinerant rodeo rider, and then that a one-thousand-dollar reward for information as to her whereabouts — offered by relatives with whom she had quarreled first about her inheritance and then about her romance — had gone unclaimed and suddenly been withdrawn. Then our Special Correspondent picked up her trail toward the Northwest Angle at Warroad, a jumping-off town on the southern shore of the lake. There, our Exclusive reported, she and a man who called himself her husband, and another man who said he was their guide, used one-hundred-dollar bills (whose serial numbers we listed) to buy a motorboat and supplies for a winter's stay in the Angle, including the butcher knife with which the murder was done.

We named and described two men sought for questioning. According to us, trackers and bush pilots hunted them deep in the wilderness. Then we switched locale to Baudette, another frontier hamlet, where one of the wanted men walked in and surrendered, denying everything. Then the other wanted man appeared, also denying everything. Then a relative of the victim appeared at Warroad, offering five thousand dollars for arrest and conviction of the murderer. Then the three principals in the story went their ways, whatever those were, and the story died. We closed out our Exclusive serial, without revealing to the Opposition that our Special Correspondent had never left our warm and cozy newsroom. He was me, talking twice a day on long-distance with backwoods telephone operators, snowed in and bored, who whiled away the hours listening in on all the party lines and were only too glad to gossip with a friendly stranger in the city. The arrangement saved a lot of time and trouble, and as far as I could see harmed no one, least of all the murderer, whoever he may have been. (I think I know who he was. If I am right, he would be long dead by now.)

There was always more to write about, if writing was all you wanted to do. On the Far North Side of Minneapolis, I interviewed three Greek girls who had won first prize in so many Amateur Night contests that they were turning professional, and said if I didn't object they'd call themselves "The Andrews Sisters," since it would look so nice in lights. I subbed on City Hall and County, and made sure of free lunches on Thursdays and Fridays (when my money always ran out) by electing myself to cover Kiwanis and Rotary. (I have loathed chicken and green peas and inspirational speeches ever since.)

Dropping in, one no-news afternoon, at Probate Court, I heard a clerk make a casual remark that set me to searching in his files. I turned up many wills whose makers left bequests to establish and maintain free beds in hospitals. Meaning to write a Sunday filler about Good Samaritans still aiding the needy from beyond the grave, I checked hospitals mentioned in the wills. I was startled to learn that no free beds were available. Still meaning to be nice about it, I asked if the large amounts bequeathed for this specific purpose had been diverted to other worthy uses by decision of executors. I was told this was none of my business. I ventured to disagree. So did my paper. Bureaucratic high-handedness, not actual dishonesty, was the answer; and even to allege that much might be construed as libelous. But under our lawyer's tutelage, I learned that there are ways and means of getting the truth across to readers, while keeping the paper out of court.

I had an acquaintance, a minister who was determined to get ahead in his profession. Being a reformer helped in this laudable effort. It made him foreman of a Grand Jury then in session, investigating whatever might make headlines. I buttonholed him privately. In exchange for a promise to feature his sermons on our Church Page, he entered my story in the Grand Jury record. This made it what the law calls "privileged," and therefore publishable. Our banner line read *GRAND JURY PROBES MYSTERY OF "FREE BEDS" THAT ARE NOT THERE THOUGH PAID FOR.* Actually, no official action was taken. But a lot of changes occurred in certain hospitals. (I suspect similar inquiry might be made today in almost any city, and that the answers would still make news.) And after this, I was delegated informally (putting it in writing on the assignment sheet might tempt me to ask for a raise) to keep on looking for necks that might happen to be sticking out. I found these in unlikely places. Even in the Public Library.

According to the legend I chose not to doubt, although no two informants agreed on the details, an eccentric physician who died after a bout of fever (that might have been delirium tremens) had left property that became enormously valuable when the city boomed, in trust in perpetuity, to endow a library on which he placed some most peculiar restrictions. No income derived from his bequest could ever be used to buy anything written by a woman, or by a preacher. And a stated percentage must establish and support a natural history

30

museum, devoted principally to the care and study of snakes. And this weird will, I was told, could not be broken.

Indubitably, the top floor of the Public Library was the feudal domain of a strong-minded lady named Grace Wylie, who displayed much less interest in human beings than in her numerous and proliferating reptilian charges. Because I feared snakes dreadfully, I took to walking amongst them, cold sweat standing on my forehead — and in penance, not for pleasure or expecting to get copy for the paper (pictures of snakes, even in "Tarzan," which was one of our cartoon strips, were *verboten* in the *Journal*), spent much time talking with Grace Wylie, forcing myself to pick up and fondle her writhing pets, falsely assuring her that this cured me of my phobia. One day, she was unwontedly brusque. Belowstairs, feminine custodians of the book stacks huddled in whispering groups that dissolved when I approached. My thumbs pricked.

My father always held that curiosity is the faculty that distinguishes man from the other animals (with the exception of Cousin Ape). I was born with an oversupply of it that has made me a pain in the neck to many people. I pained the librarians, until one of them, to get rid of me, whispered a startling secret. Two recent additions to Grace Wylie's herpetological treasury, king rattlers some six feet long, had escaped from their glass cage, and were loose somewhere in the building. It hadn't been reported to the authorities. If it was, Grace Wylie might be accused of negligence. So she, and her friends, were trying to find the venomous things, without warning the public of the danger that might lurk coiled behind any book stack. I kept their secret until next day, when we could beat the morning Opposition with an Extra. That got me a by-line, under a screamer head: *DEADLY SNAKES LOOSE IN PUBLIC LIBRARY.*

The snakes were found in the children's reading room. Grace Wylie said I had betrayed her trust. The rattlers, she said, were harmless. She proved it, to her satisfaction, by picking them up and draping them on her shoulders. I got a picture of this, but felt a little ill, and couldn't write the follow-up immediately.

Through the years, I read about Grace Wylie now and then. She was famous as the Cobra Woman at the San Diego Zoo, until one day, while she was posing for another picture, fondling one of her pets, it struck her, and she died. I didn't have to write that story. I had written too much about her as it was.

Deadlines said the way to learn your trade is to work at it. I worked. Meanwhile I showed up on a convenient campus now and then, accumulating snatches of more formal if less immediately useful education. (My English thesis, save the mark, was called *The Truth About Daniel Defoe*.) At the *Journal*, we experimented with color printing on newspaper stock, and by trial and error got some fairly good results.

Then one cold afternoon the Managing Editor invited me to go for a ride, during which he asked me to tell him about myself. This took minimal urging. I remember his expression when I confided that in Oklahoma, where a king rattler broke its fangs in the heel of my copper-toed leather boot and never touched my skin, I nearly died with all the classic symptoms of snakebite, and subsequently the Indian children gave me a name, *Ch'takah Ch'hungh'ah*, that can be translated as "Little Big Mouth." I poured out this past history as confusingly as I capsule it now, recollections racing ahead of my tongue as they race ahead of my typewriter.

We rode around for an hour, while I wondered increasingly why the ride began, and probably he wished more and more that it hadn't. Finally, he said: "With the world at peace, Mr. Jones thinks people are tired of reading about foreign affairs. They want to read more about what happens where it matters to them: here at home. Mr. Jones wants the paper to be, as he puts it, all-American. He thinks you have a way of making local events sound interesting." He paused. I've never been sure how optimistically he continued. "Beginning Monday, Bob," he said, "you're the new City Editor."

« 3 »

Being twenty, posing as past thirty, was load enough to carry without falling over my own feet. Being pitchforked into the driver's seat, over the heads of startled wheel horses twice my age and older, was a challenge nothing had prepared me to cope with. I cannot pretend, however, that modesty prompted me to demur, once a guest card and an incautiously unlimited charge account at the Athletic Club were thrown in, to compensate for the extracurricular income I must now forego. I bought a derby that kept falling over my eyes, and started smoking nickel cigars that gave me heartburn, and unveiled a mustache that came out pink; and fooled nobody, not even myself.

The staff had seen other morning glories bloom, and fade. The prize, before me, had been a dean of journalism who thought it might be stimulating to see how the lower classes lived, instead of attending a summer seminar at Columbia. Portly, ponderous, pedantic, he talked a great fight but was putty under pressure. He edited not by sharpening — improving impact whilst saving space — but by interpolating interpretive asides, apparently addressed to mongoloid morons. Criticism from hairy illiterates on the copy desk strengthened his frankly expressed conviction that our newsroom's I. Q. level would bar its inmates from his Freshman classes. This went on until the slot-man (who had flunked out of Eighth Grade and started on a Tennessee throwaway) charged at him brandishing a foot-long pair of scissors, shouting: "You couldn't write a l-head on the Second Coming of Christ. Get out of my sight, before I amputate you from your blankety-blank M. A.!" I had no M. A. to lose.

I tried to use *Deadlines* for my road map. *Truth and reader*

33

interest, according to Henry Justin Smith, *are equally a newspaper's responsibilities.* "News" *means fact, not fiction, just
as "freedom of the press" means liberty to tell the truth, and
all of it, but not to twist it.* How well you make truth come
alive in type is the test. *No first page is first-rate unless it has
stories on it that are true, and yet put novels in the discard.*
In theory, this is the Golden Rule for all newspapers. In
practice, it is highly impractical. I believed I grasped what
Smith was driving at. Making it work was quite another matter for (according to *Editor and Publisher*) "the youngest
City Editor of a metropolitan daily thus far on record."

Desperately, I studied by-line pieces clipped from the *Chi-
cago Daily News*, which reached us two days late. Names became familiar: Robert J. Casey, Leland Stowe, Edward Price
Bell, Ben Hecht, John Gunther, Wallace Deuel, Edgar Ansel
Mowrer, Paul Scott Mowrer, Carroll Binder, Carl Sandburg.
I extracted What, Why, When, How, Where, and Who.
Rearranging these, I retouched them with my own inimitable
words. I have some Irish in me, so for a time I concentrated on
Bob Casey's Chicago Irish fantasies. All I learned about his
technique was that if I touched a line, the Gaelic gossamer
disintegrated.

John Gunther's style was at the other extreme. *Forty-two
miles from Casper by flivver and mule pack, midway between
the Laramie Rockies and the Montana border, in the heart of
the desolate Wyoming wasteland, lies Teapot Dome, actually
a shallow basin with a hundred million dollars in it,* read one
of Gunther's leads. I gave up trying to improve on it. Gunther
says the style makes him shudder nowadays. On the other
hand, regarding *Inside Europe*, he has said he wakes at nights
sometimes and thinks: "My God, suppose I hadn't written it!"
Comparisons are not in order, but I have a similar nightmare
occasionally, regarding a piece of writing I did when I thought
the Lord had forsaken me.

Donning my derby one bright morning, chewing a cigar

34

that cost a quarter, I marched belligerently into the newsroom and thumbtacked to the bulletin board my first official ultimatum. No Page One, I decreed, was worth my *Okay* unless it was built around a feature, preferably with picture, about a dog, a child, somebody's mother, or some sad but not too sad small human predicament, subtly dramatized to make the reader feel "There but for God's grace go I." I put the staff on notice. Each member of it must produce, at least one a week, in addition to his assignments, "a self-originated special, aimed to elicit not a worried *Wow!* but a heart-warming *Gee!*" I called this a blueprint. What my sullen subjects called it was blue but unprintable.

Silently, they handed me short takes tagged MORE 2 KUM, blandly burying the lead, if there was one, where I couldn't dig it out in time for a rewrite. Stubbornly, I scheduled a hole a column deep on Page One every day, and fought all morning to get it filled. One noon, only a single typewriter clacked. Its two-finger operator was Joe Jepson (whose name I change slightly, as I shall alter others, to protect the guilty). Joe capitalized himself as A Character. In his leisure hours, he cleaned up traveling-salesman jokes, which he contributed to *Captain Billy's Whizz-Bang*. He wore tortoise-rimmed glasses on a velvet ribbon, claimed to have won the Croix de Guerre at the Marne but lost it during an amour in Paris, owed alimony to four former wives, kept a Siamese cat on a leash to lead him in and out of speakeasies (the Volstead Act was a Minnesotan's claim to immortality), and belched four-letter words as naturally as he breathed. Using several of these, he exhorted me to hold my horses, while he finished a feature I'd never forget.

He hunted and pecked, while the clock hand raced toward press time. With less than fifteen minutes to go, he scattered pages before me, with the manner of one casting pearls. Then everyone died laughing. Everyone but me. His "feature" was a report, in phrases that would have made Lady Chatterley

35

blush, that our nine leading advertisers were opening a coast-to-coast chain of drive-in brothels, Charge Accounts Solicited. And he met my fury with a smirk. "No likee?" he leered, playing the Idiot Chinee that was one of his best impersonations. "So solly. Can happen." Then he let me have it, venomously. "You're the *Deadlines* kid. Let's see you wiggle out of this one."

Collecting his cat, he set forth on a pub crawl that ended as usual in the drunk tank, and guessed no more than I did that he had transmuted a dream into reality. All that mattered, at the moment, was that I had to fill twenty inches of white space on Page One, and fill it fast or never, and there was absolutely nothing to fill it with. I dug through galley proofs on the Overset spikes. No luck. I beavered in baskets filled with Northwest News Bureau flimsies. And with the devil at my heels, I ran head-on into salvation.

Died, at an upstate county poor farm, its oldest inhabitant, aged 104. Claimed he was a Civil War drummer boy. No living relatives. Picked up in a hobo jungle, half frozen, half starved. For fifteen years, a charity charge. The last twelve, bedridden, partially paralyzed and speechless. That much and no more; but I was off and running at a hundred words a minute.

Methuselah [I wrote] *lived nine hundred years, and died revered and mourned. Today at Bemidji, another very old man, about whom nobody cared, who had nothing to be proud of but his age, was buried in a pauper's grave, with no pall-bearers, because all he managed to do with his life was to out-live anyone who ever knew him when he was a human being, not just a freak of purposeless longevity.*

Joe Jepson had a standing bet in money or marbles that touch-typing was the only trick I knew that he couldn't top with one hand tied behind his back. I admit the only medal I ever won was first prize in a typewriting speed contest I entered purely for show-off reasons, after my Commercial teacher flunked me for failing to turn in *fghj* practice exercises. I didn't have time to practice. I was too busy typing. Part of my job after school, on the *Aberdeen American* back in South Dakota, was taking the Associated Press pony service over long-distance wires straight onto the typewriter, from a bureau man in St. Paul who talked faster than Floyd Gibbons.

That noon in Minneapolis, I broke my record. I also broke Smith's rule that nothing belongs on Page One if it isn't true. All I knew about the late unlamented was capsuled in four lines. Editorializing, philosophizing, fictionizing, I gave him a wife, children, a family tragedy, secure in knowledge nobody could contradict me. I put him at Gettysburg, marching off in search of whiskey, oblivious to immortal words which I quoted extensively. I made him another Ishmael, wandering to nowhere. I almost made myself weep, while I filled the Page One hole to overflowing. Then there was silence in the newsroom, if not awe. And the following Monday, I stared at a telegram to CITY EDITOR MINNEAPOLIS JOURNAL that had to be a hoax. I checked. It was real.

INTERESTED REPORTER WHO WROTE METHUSELAH STORY. IF ALL RIGHT WITH YOU PLEASE HAVE HIM GET IN TOUCH WITH ME. THANKS. FRATERNALLY, HENRY JUSTIN SMITH CHICAGO DAILY NEWS.

Helplessly, I realized I couldn't possibly wire: AM COMING. ANDREWS. I knew from *Deadlines* how Smith scouted the out-of-town dailies, even weeklies, on the lookout for any Young Man Going Somewhere. I also knew my story was a fraud. I couldn't imagine he'd forgive a City Editor who wrote a fake and plastered it on Page One. Not journalistic integrity but shame kept me busy all that night, editing and re-editing a confession that filled three pages, single-spaced.

I was out of the office, across the street, sharing my self-pity with a bartender, when Smith's reply arrived. Joe Jepson, squatting on my property as he always did when I wasn't there to protect it, read the telegram, doubted his eyes, spewed four-letter words, and read aloud to all concerned:

ACCURACY CAN BE TAUGHT IMAGINATION CANNOT. WE CAN USE BOTH. OFFERING YOU JOB START IMMEDIATELY. CONFIRM. SMITH C. D. N.

When I appeared, walking a tightrope that wasn't there, the Send Andrews to Chicago Committee had almost finished taking up a collection to buy me a traveling bag, and the Managing Editor had Joe Jepson throwing hard in the bullpen. Chilled by congratulations that ended hopefully "How soon are you leaving?" I stalled, wiring Smith YOU NEGLECTED TO STATE SALARY. Word about this got me summoned to the publisher's office by his eldest son and second in command. A noted amateur magician, Carl Jones made my handkerchief disappear while he warned me, for my own good, that I wouldn't last a month in Chicago. Then he offered me a ten-dollar raise. I blurted "Make it twenty dollars!" He asked who I thought I was, Ben Hecht? Back at my desk, I read Smith's final words: SALARY INADEQUATE IF THAT MATTERS. Suddenly it didn't. I wired: COMING. BE THERE FRIDAY.

At 4 A.M., on a Friday I won't forget, the send-off committee lifted me into the four-passenger Fairchild that was then about all there was to Northwest Airlines. I slept all the way to Chicago, my considerable weight propped against the unlatched cabin door. Propeller backwash kept the door closed until we touched down at Cicero. Then the door flew open, and I fell out. I lay in the mud looking up at an unfriendly sky, shocked out of my hangover but in no haste to rise and walk. I managed to waste two hours before I stood at last outside the ramshackle rabbit warren on Wells Street under the El, that was then, as it had been for more than fifty years, the home of the *Chicago Daily News*.

4

When I entered, finally, the worn, uneven floor sagged under my lagging feet. Warily, I skirted a convention of alley cats meowing around a white-clad milkman who set bottles down in a row and was paid in small change by an aged but briskly efficient cashier wearing a green celluloid eyeshade, alpaca sleeve-protectors, and the sort of starched shirtwaist and ankle-length black skirt that were standard equipment for business girls when she and Emmaline Pankhurst were teenagers. Kipling, when he was a sub-reporter on the *Civil & Military Gazette* at Lahore in British India, or Charles Dickens, in his Fleet Street days in London, would have seen nothing unusual at 15 North Wells. But I stood there wishing I had never read *Deadlines*.

The *Daily News* started doing business at this stand soon after Christmas Eve in 1875, when a trial run of "the West's first penny daily" tickled the town but infuriated Joseph Medill, who had taken charge of the *Tribune* only the year before, by proposing with mock seriousness: *"For President of the United States, Alaska, the Western Islands, and perhaps Cuba*: Hon. Joseph Medill of Illinois. We have good reasons for believing, that if the office of Chief Executive were tendered to Mr. Medill by unanimous vote of the country, on a silver platter, he would accept."

By the time I arrived, the publishing plant developed by Victor Lawson during half a century of uninterrupted prosperity had spread like a propped-up banyan tree. Doors broken through walls of buildings that withstood the Great Chicago Fire in 1871 connected half a dozen odd-shaped structures, all condemned as fire hazards so often that inspectors no longer bothered to serve summonses.

An obsolete actuarial clause, "The Habit of Standing," was invoked in dealing with insurance companies. From what I saw, it appeared to apply as well to *Daily News* employees.

Naked electric bulbs dangling from Victorian gaslight fixtures, countinghouse desks polished by the elbows of two generations, iron grilles like those in Grant's Tomb, a single cell-like elevator hauled up and down on frayed ropes, were not incongruous here. The anachronisms were typewriters and adding machines operated by the Advertising, Accounting and Circulation serfs, who should have been using quill pens and an abacus. The paper was still being printed from type fonts cast in 1900. Presses installed by R. Hoe & Co. before the first Chicago World's Fair in 1893 shook the whole establishment when they rolled. And rocking with the roll, at the Information Desk, was a whiskered Cerberus who looked like Horace Greeley after he ran for President, and sounded like Donald Duck.

He gave me both barrels. "No jobs open. Won't be any. Step aside, now. Next!" I protested, brandishing my dossier: "Mr. Smith expects me." He doubted that. "Smith don't see anybody anyhow 'til after he goes out for his cigarette." When would that be? "When he gets around to it. No smoking on the premises. . . . Next!" Crumbling the last cigar that ever touched these lips, I headed for the elevator. A lumbering behemoth beat me into the car, which was barely big enough to cage him. In lonely days that followed, I learned he was Honest Abe Lincoln Mahoney, who covered Labor. He was the only reporter I ever knew who drove a Rolls-Royce. It was presented to him, somewhat the worse for wear and tear, by heirs of the original owner, who had put too much faith in its bulletproofing. He kept a gun and a set of handcuffs in it, in case of emergency, which he would be happy to arrange, and often did.

When the car came down, it disgorged another rhinoceros on the run. Cerberus identified him as Jim Mulroy. "He won the Pulitzer Prize." My awe made him briefly loquacious. Once upon a time, he said, there were two cubs on the paper. When police found a little boy, Bobby Franks, sadistically murdered and stuffed in a culvert, the cubs brashly assigned themselves to the story. At the scene of what came very close to being the perfect crime without passion, they dug up a broken spectacle-bow, which trained investigators had heedlessly trampled in the mud. Convinced that not many of these were made of 18-karat gold, but afraid to ask the city desk for carfare, they trudged endless miles from optician to optometrist. This earned them their nickname, "O'Connor & Goldberg," for the shoestore chain. Their thousand-to-one chance paid off. They traced the spectacle-bow to Nathan Leopold, then aged nineteen, who along with Richard Loeb, then eighteen, was about to be cleared of suspicion by the police, for lack of connecting evidence. That broke Chicago's most publicized murder mystery. "Naturally," Cerberus told me, "Mr. Mulroy was 'O'Connor.'" I asked, "Who was 'Goldberg'?" He shrugged. "I forget. He don't work for us any more." To Cerberus, as to just about everyone else on the paper, if you left the *Daily News* you ceased to matter. Eventually, I learned that Mulroy's partner prizewinner had been Alvin Goldstein. Why he left, or where he had gone, nobody seemed to know. But the legend that proved cubs could be kings, at least for a day, was told and told again.

I launched a legend of my own that day, by stealing the elevator from a hurrying, well-dressed personage who didn't impress me with the announcement that he was Walter Strong. (I thought Victor Lawson still owned the paper. Actually, he had been dead three years; Walter Strong was the new publisher.) I left him standing there, and was glad the car crawled up so slowly, stopping twice while the groaning block-and-tackle machinery rested for another try. *But men at whiles are sober And think by fits and starts. And if they think, they fasten Their hands upon their hearts.* Hesitantly, I emerged on the fourth floor, and faced a rat the size of a Pekinese. It judged me, dismissed me, and darted, flirting its tail, under a Noah's Ark rolltop desk at which a double for Justice Holmes wrote sedately in Spencerian longhand. He, I would learn, was Mr. MacMillan (I never presumed to ask his first name), who had been on the *Daily News* since he put out the World's Fair Souvenir Edition in 1893.

Some weeks later, he fled from the outpost he had defended when McKinley was in the White House, because the clatter of my typing disturbed the naps he took between segments of his daily stint for Opposite Editorial. By then, I felt such deep respect for him that I made matters worse by offering to stop typing any time I saw him nod. He knew I meant well, and was kind. But he said it wouldn't help. He'd still know the machine was there. Machines, he told me, meaning nothing personal, were ruining a once honorable profession.

And perhaps some premonition nagged, the first time he appraised me, before he broke long silence by calling quietly: "Boy!"

This brought an ambassadorial dignitary, at least ten years my senior. Like the rat, he took my measure at a glance. "Over there by the washroom."

Yesterday, I gave the orders. Today, a copy runner commanded, and, meekly, I obeyed. Consigned to Coventry, I discovered why the washroom was known as the Black Hole of Calcutta. Slivers of some petrified substance were chained to its walls, beneath placards warning EMPLOYEES STEALING SOAP ARE SUBJECT TO DISCHARGE. I felt Big Brother watching, and stepped softly, going to a battered desk, out of the way of strangers who were putting the Final to bed. Nobody shouted. Phones rang gently. Teetering on a rickety kitchen chair, I puzzled over a humpbacked Oliver typewriter dating from circa 1910. Afraid not to seem busy, I picked out variations on NOW IS THE TIME and THE QUICK BROWN FOX. The I-key stuck.

Then I saw Smith. He appeared unobtrusively from beyond the city desk, where the City Editor and his assistant and the two top rewrite men were cutting cards for partners in a bridge game. Lean, slightly stooped, rimless glasses balanced insecurely on the arched patrician nose that dominated his pointed, patient face, Smith wore the neat dark suit, high collar and apologetic manner of an English essayist about to read selections from Andrew Marvell at some denominational college. Halting near the city desk, he stooped to pick up pins, and added them to a row bristling in his lapel. *See a pin and pick it up, All the day you'll have good luck* was said to be Smith's only superstition. It was supposed he didn't suspect that a junior office boy was detailed to scatter pins where they would stop him when something went on that shouldn't be interrupted.

I didn't know this then. I didn't even know he was Smith. The bridge players paid no apparent heed to him, nor did he intrude on their politely brutal bidding. He came on in my direction. "Andrews?" I stood up, nodding like a Christmas tiger in a toy shop. "I'm Smith. Do you smoke?" I managed "Yes, sir," and followed him down creaking stairs to the cashier's cage on the first floor, where he presented me to Miss Harriet Dewey, a venerable lady as formidable as her surroundings. "This is Bob Andrews. Here's his start-slip." So at least I was on the payroll, though at five dollars less than they paid me in Minneapolis. Visibly, Miss Dewey thought this was too much. Smith asked, with obvious embarrassment, "Do you need to draw an advance?" I did, but I couldn't say so. I gulped "No, thank you." Relieved, he led on, out of the building, along under the El, into the shabby smoke-shop that *Deadlines* called the Cave of Winds.

Men I'd seen in the newsroom were there, and others entered. They nodded to Smith, but looked past me. We smoked together, silently, for precisely seven minutes. Then I trailed Smith back to Editorial, where he left me abruptly. Not a word had been spoken about what my job would be, or what he thought of me, or didn't think. And nobody else came near, while I fiddled with the Oliver until I got the I-key working.

The bridge game ended, and the players left. The newsroom

emptied out. The office boy who had assigned me to Coventry went around turning off lights. When he approached, I said, "I think I'll stay awhile and write some letters." He said, "That's not allowed," and clicked the last light-switch. I asked his name. "I am Louis Mariano."

He was called "the World's Oldest Office Boy," and was proud of being just that. He liked being around reporters, but didn't choose to be one. Their lives were too disorganized. Louis earned as much as most of them, had his days off to be with his family, never had to work nights, didn't have to drink unless he felt like it, and yet was an important citizen in his community because he worked for the *Daily News* and had inside information on everything that hit the headlines. He ruled the younger office boys with their best interests in mind, fired some, encouraged others to finish night school and then ask Smith for a tryout, and treated Smith and was treated by him as an equal in the business of giving guidance where it was needed and deserved.

I wasn't one of Louie's boys. And on the evidence up to that point I wasn't one of Smith's, either. I followed, through echoing catacombs. When we emerged on Wells Street, I asked, "If you were me, a stranger in Chicago, where would you go now?" Louie answered succinctly: "Home." Then he ran to catch the Diversey Express, and there I was, alone in the big city. I wandered west, and flinched from the Chicago River. I wandered east along Madison, to Michigan Boulevard, and turned north. There was the river again. The drawbridge was up. Cars and double-deck buses waited fender to fender, while a string of garbage scows waddled back from dumping their cargoes in the lake. Everybody was going somewhere. Everybody but me.

The bridge closed. I drifted with the tide, past the white-tiled Wrigley Building that was built on chewing gum. Beyond lay Tower Town, Chicago's Greenwich Village. Exploring hopefully, I found only a succession of speakeasies. On

Chicago Avenue, I circled the pseudo-Gothic water tower. I had read that Louis Sullivan, father of modern architecture in Chicago, was sorry it survived the Fire in 1871. Mutely, I agreed with him. Then I had to talk fast, to get a room in the Allerton House. I was informed it was official Intercollegiate Alumni Association headquarters, and had guests representing a hundred colleges, 95 per cent of them permanently in residence, and that if I trespassed on the floors reserved for ladies I would be evicted instantly. I said I'd done my trespassing for the day. Neither this remark nor the record of my college career endeared me to the management.

I left a call for seven, was wide awake before six and back at 15 North Wells before eight, but couldn't get past Cerberus at the downstairs postern gate until nine, when Miss Harriet Dewey arrived and rather reluctantly admitted I had squatter's rights in Editorial.

For two weeks, my physical presence was my total contribution, and all I learned was what Pablo Katigbak told me, out of pity for a fellow foreigner. A moon-faced, toughly amiable Filipino, he had let his parents send him from Manila to study Business Administration at Northwestern in Chicago, but quit school after a month, and grinned himself onto the payroll at 15 North Wells. "Reporters," he told me, with the ambiguous modesty that masked his clicking mind, "they can get a dime a dozen. Another pushing nobody like me, this don't come along very often."

Pushing nobody, he did well wherever an extra hand was useful. He never asked for a raise, or a title. He had an encyclopedic memory for the contents of *Daily News* Foreign Bureau background reports, unlisted telephone numbers, clipping classifications in the Morgue, past performances of film stars, politicians, Founding Families, and hoodlums. "My brain," he said, "is maybe not for big thinking. So I make it a large sponge. Squeeze, and who can tell what comes out?" What

45

came out least obviously was his charitable comprehension of the fiscal and feminine problems besetting by-liners who might bark "Boy!" at him when they were riding high, but murmured "Hi, Pablo, pal," when trouble flared. His parents in the Philippines thought he demeaned himself as some sort of servant in Chicago. He was nobody's servant. He was getting an education. When he was ready, he would graduate himself.

A lot of us tell ourselves we pursue this course. But something happens. We stay put, until suddenly one day the rest of the way is all downhill. Not so for Pablo. Every move he made angled onward and upward. But he shoved no one aside, clung to no coattails, and remained as amiably tough and as warmhearted toward many people, in many places, as he was to me. He stopped suddenly at my desk, one afternoon when (he confessed eventually) he was really no surer than I was how much longer either of us would be around 15 North Wells, and announced, "Once upon a time they lose Floyd Gibbons." Eagerly, I said, "I know Floyd Gibbons." Pablo's frown shut off my South Dakota recollections. "Naturally," he proceeded, "they yell 'Boy!' They tell this office boy, 'Find Floyd Gibbons wherever he be. Give him in his hand, personally, this envelope.' The boy says, 'But . . .' Then he has sense to shut his fat mouth. Okay. He finds Floyd Gibbons, who happens to be in London. This takes one month. Then this boy cables to the Managing Editor in Chicago, collect of course: ENVELOPE DELIVERED. SEND MONEY. So they send it. What else can they do? While this boy waits, Gibbons introduces him to the King and Queen. His pictures are in the papers. This boy, he travels ten thousand miles almost, which costs the paper maybe ten thousand dollars, and what is in the envelope he must give personally to Gibbons? Why, it is a nasty note from the Business Office because in his last expense account before he returns to Europe, Gibbons charges the paper $11.40 for what he calls reciprocal courtesy by which he means whiskey."

46

Thus Pablo embellished what Gibbons himself had told me differently in South Dakota. It happened on the *Tribune*, not on the *Daily News*. If it ever happened at all. But I thanked Pablo for talking to me, and we went on from there. Between jobs here and there in Editorial, he took time to squeeze out information for me, from the brain he called a sponge. Victor Lawson, he said, didn't actually found the *Daily News*. He was originally only its landlord, but took over from Melville Stone, Great White Father of the Associated Press — after the paper had lost money its first seven months — and within ten years had more subscribers than the *Tribune*. Lawson never took orders from an advertiser, Pablo said, or fired a reporter for being drunk. An immigrant's son, he financed free schools for the children of immigrants. A millionaire from birth, he established and supported the first Fresh Air Fund for children from the slums. Personally modest to the point of painful shyness, whenever the paper had a victory to celebrate he hired a battery of artillery and fired cannonades along the lake front. He backed Melville Stone in developing the Associated Press; but finally, fed up with domination by New York papers that had run things for half a century, led what the *Daily News* history called "a final uprising against the proprietary evils which threatened to disrupt systematic news-gathering." Out of this, "the Revolution of 1893," emerged the first worldwide nonprofit co-operative news service; and Victor Lawson was its president. Yet almost immediately he initiated the *Daily News* Foreign Bureau, and instructed his correspondents to scoop the Associated Press anywhere, any time they could manage it. Childless, he made the paper his life. Dying at seventy-five, he left an estate of twenty million dollars. Typically, he made no bequests to old employees, but assured them of jobs as long as they cared to work.

"This," Pablo said, "was a kind of publisher we don't get much any more." He set me to studying the C. D. N. stylebook, and its roster of writers who began to write at 15 North

Wells: Harry Hansen; John V. A. Weaver; Keith Preston; Wallace Smith; Will Irwin; Ray Stannard Baker; Colonel George Harvey; Will Payne; Vincent Starrett; Henry Blackman Sell; and, farther back, George Ade; Eugene Field; L. Frank Baum, who wrote *The Wizard of Oz*; "Mr. Dooley," who was Finley Peter Dunne. And I could identify, thanks to Pablo, the by-liners who joined Smith on his daily pilgrimages to the Cave of Winds.

One of them was Howard Vincent O'Brien, who wrote *War Birds*, and was our new book reviewer. Pablo said he would run Fannie Butcher of the *Trib* right off the book-reviewing bandstand. And the handsome, courtly gentleman was Lloyd Lewis, who planted publicity for Paul Ash and the Balabans and Katzes. He was writing a play with Sinclair Lewis, no relation, and was going to edit Drama for the *Daily News*, succeeding Amy Leslie, who was a Floradora Girl before she came on the paper. Had Pablo told me what Amy Leslie answered, when they asked why she married a bell-hop at the Sherman Hotel, a fellow named Frank Buck? She said, "I'm tired of sharpening my own pencils." Then when the marriage broke up, and Frank Buck went off to chase tigers in the jungles and write *Bring 'Em Back Alive* and *Fang and Claw*, Amy Leslie said, "The coward didn't dare to say 'Good-by!' " Seeing Amy Leslie, as I did once or twice, I didn't blame Frank Buck.

As a matter of fact, the *Daily News* collected possessors of colorful peculiarities: a relapsed revivalist who quoted the Psalms while he took orders for excellent bootleg bourbon manufactured in a homemade distillery by his former organist; a part-time astronomer who kept trying to prove Einstein was wrong; a yoga practitioner who demonstrated during coffee breaks; a British-accented Iowan who claimed lineal descent from the Ten Lost Tribes of Israel; a come-down-in-the-world aristocrat so accustomed to being waited on that when she wanted to know the time, she summoned the World's Oldest Office Boy to look at the clock on the wall behind her back;

48

an otherwise average citizen who firmly believed a leprechaun lived on his shoulder, and sometimes, cold sober, argued with it. If you lacked a little oddity, you were labeled "odd" at 15 North Wells. Crotchets and quirks, to Pablo, were perfectly natural, where all but he and I were geniuses.

Pablo said: "Some we lose. Not many. Some, after ten or fifteen years, they become foreign correspondents. This is very nice work if you can get it. Victor Lawson loved foreign correspondents more than anybody. Them, only them, he did not mind paying much money to, and no trouble about expenses." He caught the gleam in my eyes, and threw cold water quickly, telling me about Raymond Gram Swing, who said the *Daily News* opened Foreign Bureau offices "to advertise the paper, to provide a reading room and convenient waterclosets for visiting Chicagoans, and to get names which must be cabled daily, but not for the purpose of disturbing the readers back home." When Swing wrote a series of articles, early in 1914, which claimed war clouds were gathering over Europe and predicted that armed conflict was inevitable before the end of summer, they went in the wastebasket. "Mr. Lawson didn't believe it is polite to frighten the customers," Pablo explained. "And besides, everybody in Chicago knows then that there will never be another war, so who is this Raymond Gram Swing to argue with them?" Then he grinned. "You are crazy if you believe me. I do not believe myself."

Fondly, Pablo pointed out his friend and defender, Hal O'Flaherty, who headed the *Daily News* Foreign Service, which was, of course, biggest and best on earth. Pablo said Hal owned maybe two thousand neckties, each worn only once. Whenever anything went wrong, he'd take off his tie, don a new one, never wear the unlucky one again. And he wouldn't give away his cast-offs. That might put the curse on someone else, and Hal, being Irish, was sensitive about such things. Why the necktie phobia? Well, when Hal was a correspondent in London during World War I, he pulled strings for months until he got exclusive clearance to go to sea on the first British Q-boat, a seemingly unarmed schooner actually packed with guns and bombs and suicide volunteers. The Q-boats were supposed to lure German submarines into surfacing and opening fire with deck guns to save torpedoes. Then the target dropped its false bulwarks, and blew the U-boat out of the water. Maybe.

"Hal is hurrying to catch the train to where he sails, when he sees a spot on his necktie. Can't face the proper British looking like a sloppy American. He stops in Savile Row to buy a new tie. This makes him miss his train. Everybody else on it boards the Q-boat. What happens? It blows up in the harbor, killing all hands but Hal, who is not there because of a necktie. Naturally he believes if he changes his tie it breaks the spell of the banshees."

And Pablo said the elegant gentleman joining Smith and Hal was Edward Price Bell, who really wrote the Kellogg Pact and organized the Disarmament Conference, which had ended wars forever; but he was modest about it. Oh, and did I know about Hal O'Flaherty and Edgar Wallace? I didn't. Well, Edgar Wallace, too, worked for the *C. D. N.*

According to Pablo, racetrack losses kept Wallace broke. He wheedled Hal into handing him an advance, out of London Bureau funds, against serial rights to four new mystery novels, none of which were written. But since Wallace could write a book in seven days if he had to — that was all right. The difficulty was to get him to write at all, with the world so full of a number of things he found more enjoyable. Hal had to hound him for chapters, which he turned over only when he ran short of funds, demanding additional advances until Victor Lawson said "No more." Then Wallace sent in a chapter that ended with his hero trapped in a hole a hundred feet deep, surrounded by a hundred hamadryad cobras.

Frantic yelps finally reached Wallace on the Riviera: HORRI-

FIED YOU KILLING HERO STORY JUST STARTED. THIRTY MORE
INSTALLMENTS DUE. READERS COMPLAINING. Wallace cabled collect: SO AM I. STRANGELY UNABLE THINK WHEN STARVING. LARGE
REMITTANCE IMPERATIVE. He got his remittance, and cabled
the next chapter, also collect. It began, with majestic sim-
plicity: "After I got out of the snake-pit . . ." Or so Pablo
swore, and however much fable and fantasy I swallowed, I had
room for more, and went on listening.

And this won a second ally: of all people, Miss Harriet
Dewey. Pablo said that although Walter Strong was surprising
his partners by treating reporters like people, a mistake Victor
Lawson avoided lest it encourage them to ask for more money,
even Walter Strong knew better than to infringe on Miss
Dewey's fiercely defended domain. She could fire you, or have
you fired, for any one of a long list of offenses against the
status quo. She was perfectly capable of refusing to give me
my paycheck, which we both knew I hadn't earned. But there
was a chink in her armor. Pablo told me what it was. Dubiously, I tried what he suggested. Miraculously, it worked.

Sidling into her dragon's lair downstairs, I declared I came
only to ask her about Eugene Field. I said I felt his presence
all around the *Daily News*. Glibly, I recited Pablo's summary
as my own: that Field came to the C. D. N. from Denver in
1893, to write Chicago's first casual column, "Sharps and
Flats," and in it, for not one extra dollar, cheerfully gave away
his copyrights on "Wynken, Blynken and Nod," and "Little
Boy Blue" and other verses I had looked up and memorized
for this occasion. "They shouldn't," I told Miss Dewey, "be
covered with dust and forgotten in the attic of Americana."
My studied phrasing didn't impress her. In fact, she said Field's
poetry was only an idiosyncrasy. What mattered was his devotion to the *Daily News*. In detail, and not for the last time,
she told me how, just out of ladies' business college, she saw
something worth while in Field, and despite his objections
took it upon herself to hold back his pay, doling out just

enough to meet his bills, investing the rest in *Daily News* stock, and thus making him the only reporter who ever got rich working for Victor Lawson. Spying the pitfall just ahead, I stammered that of course she wouldn't do such a thing for anyone who hadn't proved himself. Maybe, sometime in the future, I could impose on her for wise advice. I reached for my check while I asked her to tell me more. This worked, too.

She never married, because she was wedded to the C. D. N. She, too, owned stock in the paper, which she refused to sell when the new owners came in. They tried to put her on retirement pension, and retreated in disorder. She disapproved of Walter Strong's determination to house the paper in a new building, with all new presses and type-faces. Outvoted, she was still an intransigent minority. What was good enough for Victor Lawson was imperishable to her. She guarded the heritage he left, including the high moral tone that was traditional inside 15 North Wells. In the lunchroom, she required female employees to sit en masse on one side, males on the other, and no fraternizing. Such laws as LIGHTS OUT AT SIX and EMPLOYEES STEALING SOAP ARE SUBJECT TO DISCHARGE were imposed and enforced by her.

She also administered the Cat Milk Fund, which she started when Mrs. Lawson picked up a starving kitten in Newsboys' Alley and commanded someone to feed it. This was one item on the daily cost-sheet at which the backers boggled. After one session with Miss Dewey, Walter Strong marked it "Must." It stayed that way, until three years after we moved into the new building and 15 North Wells became a parking lot. Altogether, milk was provided, courtesy of the *Daily News*, to feed an ever-growing army of feline freeloaders seven mornings a week for thirty-seven years.

Miss Dewey saw nothing odd in this, though the reporter who padded his swindle sheet by the price of a bottle of gin would rue his recklessness. In more than half a century, only one expense account had her ungrudging approval. That was

52

Stanley Washburn's. Covering the Russo–Japanese War in 1904, he carried blank checks signed by Victor Lawson. At Chefu on the Korean Peninsula, he cashed one of these, for sixty thousand dollars, with which he bought a seagoing tug for fifty thousand and a deckload of coal for what was left. Then he vanished. Not a word came from him until he reappeared at Chefu on January 10, 1905, with only one story to show for four months at sea and Lawson's sixty thousand dollars. That happened to be the only eyewitness account of the fall of Port Arthur. And the *Daily News* Cable Editor, in haste to begin his Saturday night on the town, spiked the scoop of the generation without reading it. The flimsies hung there for forty-eight hours before someone noticed them. Even then, the *Daily News* had a worldwide Exclusive.

What counted to Miss Dewey was not the story, but the aftermath. Washburn sold his tug to the Japanese Navy for more than it cost him, and remitted the full amount to Victor Lawson, who gave him a hundred-dollar bonus. She pointed the moral for me: Youngsters should thank their stars for the privilege of catching at the coattails of a great tradition; in gratitude, they should beg for the chance to give more than they got. She didn't tell me, however, what to offer for which the *Daily News,* or Smith, had any present use.

The days continued to crawl like empty boxcars in a slow freight through South Dakota. After two weeks, I was still an outsider in Editorial, and a stranger in Chicago.

« 5 »

Being on the *Daily News* wasn't something you boasted about. You took your brahminical caste, and its responsibilities, for granted. I read the Opposition papers, front to back, and found nothing in them to lessen my willingness to accept Pablo's tale of the Chicago reporter who begged a visitor from back home: "Please don't tell Aunt Nellie I'm working for Hearst. She thinks I'm playing piano in Hinky Dink's saloon."

As for the *Tribune* calling itself "the World's Greatest Newspaper," I learned that the proper question, if you carried a C. D. N. press card, was "Greatest in what?" You answered your own inquiry: "Not in concentrated circulation. Not in news coverage. Not in reader respect."

I hadn't written as much as a NECROLOGIC since I arrived from Minneapolis, but by osmosis I acquired the *Daily News* attitude of calm superiority. At 15 North Wells we referred to the *Tribune*'s trumpeted "More Than a Million Copies Today" as the "Salute to Scatterville," and annoyed colleagues from the pseudo-Gothic citadel on Michigan Boulevard by citing the record, which showed that when the *Tribune* began calling itself The W. G. N. in 1911, both the *Daily News* and Hearst's *American* had larger circulations. They retorted by reminding us that things changed in a hurry when Robert Rutherford McCormick, not yet a Colonel, was elected president of the *Tribune* Company in 1912, and that by 1918 the *Tribune* was far out in front. We couldn't deny this, but we asked if at least some of the credit shouldn't be given to Moe and Max Annenberg.

The Annenbergs had in fact done yeoman service for the Opposition. (Neither ever worked for the *Daily News*.) Moses L. Annenberg was with Hearst, having begun in 1900. By 1907, he had exclusive distribution rights in Milwaukee for all Chicago dailies. By 1917, he was publisher of Arthur Brisbane's *Wisconsin News*. In 1920, he was named circulation director of all Hearst publications. He attributed his success to a chance remark by his wife, who said one day that what she wanted most was a plentiful supply of teaspoons. He started selling subscriptions with advertisements which said that if you subscribed, you had only to fill out a coupon and send along an additional 15 cents to cover cost of mailing, and you would receive not only the paper but a genuine silver-plated teaspoon. Circulation boomed. Annenberg disposed of literally millions of spoons, including the State Seal spoon, which he is

54

said to have invented. Even people who couldn't read had use for teaspoons. And once they accumulated a set of these, other premium offers kept them renewing their subscriptions. A member of the Hearst executive council until 1926, Moe Annenberg left then only because his *Daily Racing Form* and other popular publications called for his undivided attention.

His brother, Max, was never known as a teaspoon salesman. When the *Chicago Journal of Commerce* sued the *Tribune* Company, claiming interference with its newsstand distribution, Max Annenberg testified that he had worked for The World's Greatest Newspaper since 1910. Asked if things were peaceful between publishers and carriers at that time, he answered "I will say they were not." Asked what the trouble was, he said that Nick O'Donnell, Nick Altman, Dutch Gentleman and eight or ten others "were instructed to go around in automobiles and slug any boy who cut their order or had their order cut or would permit the *Tribune* to replace an *Examiner*, and to give them to understand that they were not only through with the newspaper business, but that they were through on this earth."

The reader who pays a nickel or a dime for the paper he buys from Joe on the corner may wonder why mayhem and the threat of murder should result from dispute over which dailies Joe sells or doesn't sell. But nickels and dimes multiplied by hundreds of thousands become Big Money. Newsstands were sold in Chicago for prices that would amaze the uninitiated. Stands were wrecked, and their former owners disappeared, whenever another circulation war broke out. What did Max Annenberg do to keep Hearst's *Examiner* from crowding out Colonel McCormick's W. G. N.? According to clippings in the Morgue at 15 North Wells, Annenberg testified "I knew the newsboys pretty well and I went around and told them that the *Tribune* Company would protect them in every way." And Colonel McCormick said "There was a great amount of open lawlessness and many flagrant violations of the law. Twenty-seven newsdealers and boys were killed and others injured." Max Annenberg was asked "Did you hire any sluggers?" He said: "Let's see. I had Mossy Enwright working for me, Jim Regan, Walter Stephens, and Arthur McBride. Four well-known sluggers." He added that "At one time, in that battle, there were sixty men employed. By both of us." Asked, "Was anyone arrested in connection with the struggle?" he answered, "Not that I know of."

That was Chicago newspaper history, which made it seem a little strange to me when editorial pages discoursed on Chicago gangsterism as something new resulting solely from the Prohibition Amendment.

On Randolph Street one evening, Pablo Katigbak stopped me and pointed. "You see that old newsstand? Very historical." He drew me into a doorway. "Wise not to talk too loud some times, some places." He wasn't pretending; he was serious. "Once upon a time," he confided, "very fine old immigrant man, foreigner like me only come to stay, for a long time is selling papers there. Immigrant from Poland, very proud he is naturalized American citizen. Works hard, saves hard, puts three sons through school, owes nobody. He thanks America. Comes the Circulation War. Come the gangsters, breaking legs, smashing skulls. This old man, he said, 'I sell papers for Greatest American. If he know what gorillas do, he make them stop. I go tell him.' Everybody says, 'Don't be a damn' fool.' He says, 'Why shall I be afraid? This is America.' Dressed up like for Mass, or for his funeral, he goes to tell what gorillas do not wish to have mentioned. He is found at the bottom of an elevator shaft, very dead. 'Accidental,' it says in the paper."

That didn't happen at 15 North Wells. We had no elevator shaft down which a man could fall far enough to hurt himself much. But our Newsboys' Alley was nothing to be proud of. I saw one of its gang bosses in action. In place of a right hand, he wore an iron hook, filed razor-sharp. Another gang boss tried to muscle in. The hook widened his mouth two inches on either side. Who sold what paper and where was still decided by jungle law: *He may take who has the power; he may keep who can.* Sluggers rode the delivery trucks, showing off their skills, hoping scouts for the Syndicate would see them and sign them up for bigger things. Al Capone himself, I read, bragged proudly that he was once mere Al Brown, "a bum from Brooklyn," when a circulation hustler imported him to improve the efficiency of a Chicago newsstand goon-squad. "That's how I got my start. And look at Big Al now!"

I looked at his pictures in the papers, and then at the *Tribune* Tower, thirty-six stories of hyperbolic grandeur, built after an international architects' competition in which the winner, Eliel Saarinen of Finland, didn't get the contract because his design was too functional. What rose instead was a sort of cathedral pulled out to a point, into whose elaborately carved gray granite the builders set stone from less publicized monuments such as the Parthenon, the Great Wall Of China, the Alamo, and Notre Dame de Paris. According to the *Tribune*'s historian: "Homer would have liked to work here. So would Horace, with his wealth of incident. So would Addison, Samuel Johnson, Dickens, Hardy, Kipling, and Mark Twain." For myself, I was quite content to work in a fire trap at 15 North Wells.

The *Encyclopædia Britannica*, the Great E. B., had been printed by Donnelley in Chicago since 1909, and owned by Chicago's Sears Roebuck since 1920. It still gave considerable space to such *pukka* British publications as Berrow's *Worcester Journal* and to the *Northern Whig* (and in fact still does so in 1962), whereas we were disposed of in a breath — "Since 1900 the trend of journalism in the United States has been towards consolidations and extensions of chain newspapers. Those under publishers like Ochs of the *Times*, Nelson of the *Kansas City Star*, Lawson of the *Chicago Daily News*, etc., were simply exceptions to the general tendency." Being an exception to

57

the rule was itself a rule at 15 North Wells. If the paper clung to quaintly restrained and sometimes rather too grammatical headlines, this was not solely because Victor Lawson had declined to buy new larger-sized type until what was in the cases wore out completely. Circulation turned down subscriptions because our superannuated presses couldn't grind out any more copies. But the *Daily News* had never given away teaspoons, or put on any other kind of circulation contests. Uniquely, I think, in the annals of big city dailies, paid advertising wound up in our hell-box because the presses couldn't even print more pages. But also, there were strictures on what went into the *Daily News*, and what didn't, that made me proud though I had nothing at all to do with it. Doom-shouters predicted shocking changes when the new regime acceded. Walter Strong's financial backers expected it. He had been a cub reporter once, though only briefly, on his home town daily. He went where the money was, and took charge of the *Daily News* as another profit-making investment. But around the shop, it began to be believed that holding a C. D. N. press card made a new and different man of him.

His insistence on a new building startled his partners. They had expected another and less expensive sort of modernization, beginning with the recruitment of a whole new staff, composed of sober, sensible, well-born, well-bred young gentlemen who would handle news like stocks and bonds or yard goods or any other merchandise. Walter Strong invited them to dinner in the unfinished new building, and arranged to have an apparent murder interrupt the speeches. Then he called on the critics to write their own reports of what they had seen. He started reading these aloud. The authors begged for mercy, which he gave. No more was said about new wine in old bottles. Even after Walter Strong, when Colonel Frank Knox became publisher while he waited impatiently for the Grand Old Party to put him in the White House, change was so slow as to be almost imperceptible. Smith went on hiring and firing, and deciding what to print.

Death-house executions were played down, on inside pages. Adoptions went in the files, not in the paper. This applied also to most contested divorces. Abnormal offenses got minimal space. Crime stories were coldly clinical. We carried no gossip columns. On the other hand, doctors and teachers and preachers caught where they had no business being, or doing what they shouldn't be doing, could never cajole the *Daily News* into killing the story. If it couldn't be proved, Smith wouldn't print it. If it could be, and it belonged in the Paper That Goes Home, he printed it in spite of hell, high water, or the front office. If, that is, it was well enough written.

Gene Fowler said, years later, in the back room at Dave Chasen's in California: "There never was and will never be again such a collection of real newspapermen who could really write as Henry Justin Smith put together and held together, Heaven knows how, on the *Chicago Daily News.*" Sharp young Newspaper Guild shop-foremen and radio-commercial spielers, sea-changed into television news interpreters, asked "Who was Smith?" or said with vague politeness to their elders "The name rings a faint bell," and resumed discussion of how to wangle a Nieman Fellowship. But in the Golden Days, no newspaper had a longer list of applicants for any job that might be open, or more complaining but contented galley slaves who turned out books and meanwhile wrote their hearts out for a quiet boss who (as Ben Hecht recalls) "loved our paper with an interest that ignored circulation figures, and saw it as a daily novel written by a wild but willing bunch of Balzacs."

Hecht had orbited onward and upward before I bought my copy of *Deadlines*. Out of sight, he was not for a moment out of mind. Pablo Katigbak pointed out that when Hecht and MacArthur peopled *The Front Page* with seedy rapscallions,

59

they had to go to the Opposition for their prototypes, and use Hearst's Walter Howey, not Smith, as model for a Managing Editor you could hate to love. Actually, Howey once had a try-out on the *Daily News*. Smith asked "How well do you know Chicago?" He said, "Like the back of my hand." Smith asked, "How long would it take you to get from here to the intersection of Washington and Jefferson Boulevards?" He said, "Ten minutes." Smith showed surprise. Howey said, "I'm fast." Smith said, "If you're that fast, Mr. Howey, we can't do without you." So away went Howey to the nearest policeman, who informed him that Washington and Jefferson Boulevards met nowhere. "So," said Pablo, "Howey keeps right on running, to Hearst, and is hired, and they are very happy together, and so he gets into *The Front Page*." He said the names used in Hecht and MacArthur's play were real: Hildy Johnson, Jimmy Murphy and Buddy McHugh were still on the job at Central Police, and doing their drinking in Joe Stein's place on South State Street. But Pablo didn't think I'd get anything but a headache out of meeting them in the flesh. After all, they worked for the Opposition.

Continuing regarding Hecht, he said that when postal authorities raised a rumpus about Hecht's *Fantasius Malaire*, because of the back-fence words in it, Smith wouldn't read the book, but started a collection for a Hecht Defense Fund, because if you worked for Smith nobody was allowed to push you around. In times to come others repeated as dubiously accurate gossip what Pablo told me as gospel: that *1001 Afternoons in Chicago* would never have been published if Smith hadn't forced Hecht to write a daily piece "about anything just so it's about something" and edited the results with a surgeon's dispassionate precision, in spite of Hecht's loud cries of pain. It was no myth that another Young Man Going Somewhere, John Gunther, published a novel somewhat in the Percy Marks *Plastic Age* manner, called *The Red Pavilion*, but stopped writing fiction the day Smith hired him.

"John," Pablo explained, "was okay on the facts but nervous on names and addresses. This way you get sued for libel. So Mr. Smith makes John a foreign correspondent, where mistakes don't matter because who knows the difference in Chicago?" Pablo also wanted me to believe that Smith heard a shock-haired Scandinavian from Springfield reciting improvised unrhymed poems to pay for his supper of stale paper-thin chicken sandwiches in Jack Jones's Dill Pickle Club in Tower Town, and put him on the *Daily News* payroll, ostensibly to furnish fillers for Amusements but actually because Vachel Lindsay was then the only hobo minstrel who could make a living at it. "That," Pablo said, "is how we get Carl Sandburg." Both yarns were as full of holes as a slab of free-lunch cheese. But then, Ben Hecht himself was on record as saying that he discovered Sandburg, and induced Smith to give him a job, in 1914.

All mountains have many discoverers, who forget that the mountain was there all the time. In fact, Sandburg wrote news on the *Manitowoc Tribune*, the *Milwaukee Sentinel*, and the *Milwaukee Journal* and was writing editorials for the *Milwaukee Daily News*, while Hecht was still a circus acrobat. After being secretary to Emil Seidel, first Socialist mayor of a major American city, Sandburg started on the *World*, the Chicago Socialist daily, as a by-line feature writer, in 1912. He drew twenty-five dollars a week, big money then for a reporter anywhere, from the *Day Book*, the no-advertising daily that E. W. Scripps founded for fun, in 1913. When Scripps dropped the *Day Book*, Sandburg wrote for *System* Magazine. He didn't go to the *Daily News* until 1917. That year, Hearst's *Chicago American* put him under contract, at a hundred dollars a week, to write editorials. He stayed less than a month. "The stars I was under," he says, "said I wasn't fated for a Hearst career." He got his own job with Smith and was satisfied with half the salary his Hearst contract guaranteed.

And if this chronology disagrees with Hecht, and spoils the

myth of the shaggy stranger declaiming in the Dill Pickle Club, it doesn't diminish Smith. I thought at first that since it was manifestly absurd for Carl Sandburg to be called the Movie Editor. The title must be kindly subterfuge. Nothing of the sort. Whatever he did, he did it as a pro. Smith kept him on the news staff as long as possible, because he was one of the shrewdest, sharpest reporters the *Daily News* ever had. His first Exclusive was a by-lined interview with Big Bill Haywood, locked up and facing deportation to Bolshevik Russia, accused of "ten thousand crimes of sabotage aimed at hindering the war effort." His copy on the coal-mine war in Harlan County earned banner lines for days. He wrote in defense of Eugene V. Debs and in cold criticism of A. Mitchell Palmer. He was angry, but he was accurate, and his copy ran as written. Smith saw to that. Victor Lawson hated Socialists, and suspected the State Department of being bossed by Bolsheviks. But if Smith hired you, you stayed hired.

Sweating it out in my slum alongside the Black Hole of Calcutta, I got the World's Oldest Office Boy to bring me some Sandburg clippings from the Morgue. His style was as terse and evocative as his *Chicago Poems*, even when he described a Coming Event at a State Street movie palace.

It is certain, Smith wrote in *Deadlines, that our days would be gloomier were it not for the leisurely, genial, enigmatic being who moves about among the shades. To find him at one's elbow, unexpectedly, furnishes a moment of novelty and warmth. There is nearly always — at least, during our Poet's variable office hours — a knot of young reporters listening to his wisdom. The Old Man is wont to boast: "I've managed to keep that man on my staff all these years." A rightful boast. It is no joke to keep a poet anywhere.* I saw the Poet only from a distance. But I couldn't have flipped a paper clip, from where I sat, without hitting some other published author I had heard of, who never heard of me, and wasn't about to show any interest.

Thirty-one men, altogether, had manuscripts on their desk or at the publishers'. Victor Yarros, Wallace Deuel, Frank Smothers, Harry Beardsley, Paul R. Leach, Eugene Stinson and others Pablo identified were deep in treatises on subjects as various as the fallacies in Henry George's single tax, the decadence of the Chicago Opera, and Joseph Smith and the Mormons in Illinois. Even back in the Art Department, where photographers dressed and talked like Wheat Pit brokers, a future Pulitzer Prize winner blocked out backgrounds with an airbrush. He was already signing his occasional cartoons HER-BLOCK. And another Art Department minion bothered everybody but me with a comic strip he hoped to sell. I proved my genius for missing the boat by agreeing with Pablo that the strip didn't have the ghost of a chance. The cartoonist was Chester Gould. The strip was "Dick Tracy."

Pablo and I were more concerned about Charlie Mueller, who consulted us because nobody else seemed to have time to look at his comic strip about a couple of black-face characters who owned a one-cab taxi company. He called this "The Adventures of Amos 'n' Andy." The jokes were provided by a team of vaudevillians, Charles Correll and Freeman Gosden. They had been on Colonel McCormick's radio station, WGN, with an act called Sam 'n' Henry, which set no rivers afire. Demonstrating the fallibility that humanizes greatness, the Colonel let them go. They tried again, on the *Daily News* station, WMAQ. As anciently as 1923, Billy Jones and Ernie Hare sold Hap-hap-happiness on the air, and the National Broadcasting Company had been in business since 1926. But radio's first fantastic saga of success began in August 1929 when NBC and Pepsodent put Amos 'n' Andy on the network. Almost instantly, they were famous everywhere but in our cloistered catacombs.

Several office boys owned hand-built crystal sets. Under pressure from readers, the *Daily News* gave space to program listings. But the newsroom majority voted thumbs down on

63

radio, another transitory fad like coonskin coats or the Toddle. Strangely, Amos 'n' Andy were heard on all floors at the Allerton House. A chambermaid told me I mustn't miss them. "Those two men all by theyselves they do the voices, just so natural." Then she added, mystically: "I always says, 'Familiarity breeds confinement.'" Correll and Gosden and I have tried for thirty years to make sense of this *sequitur*. When I heard it, I wasn't wasting thought on Amos 'n' Andy. All I cared about was that I was at the *C. D. N.* but I wasn't on it. And finally I risked leaving the newsroom, not at all sure I'd be permitted to return to it, and roamed the Loop praying for a miracle to rise up and hit me.

Then, in a pawnshop window, I saw a gangling, lop-eared puppy, forgotten and locked in by its owner, who had hung up a crudely lettered sign: CLOSED ON ACCOUNT OF ILLNESS. Hungry, thirsty, quivering with loneliness and fear, the puppy leaped against the glass, barking desperately. A crowd congealed. Somebody said "Call a cop." There was no policeman in sight. People moved together. The window broke. A wild old woman in a charity-bazaar flowered hat and moth-eaten coat too large for her clutched the puppy to her bosom and scuttled around the corner. Now the Law appeared. "Whata you mean, nobody saw nothing?" There were rings and watches and cameras and guns inside the shattered window. I was sure there were thieves in the disintegrating crowd. But I would have sworn, if the Law had asked me, that nothing of value was stolen.

I almost ran back to 15 North Wells, past Cerberus at Information, up the dark stairs, past Mr. MacMillan dozing at his desk, past Pablo Katigbak reading Maxwell Bodenheim's *Replenishing Jessica*. I couldn't do a hundred words a minute on the humpbacked Oliver, but I didn't do much less. While I hammered, fighting the I-key, Smith passed, bound for the

Cave of Winds. He didn't stop, nor did I. I wrote about the abandoned puppy, as well as I knew how, for a column and a half. Then, circling the bridge game at the city desk, I put my pages on the table at which Smith worked, and slunk back to Coventry as if fleeing from a burglary. Smith returned, and disappeared into his office. I waited. Smith reappeared, and went home. The newsroom emptied. The lights went off, one by one. I walked around the Loop, in the rain, until long after midnight.

Next morning, Pablo lay in wait, with another tale to tell. Had I heard of the cub Smith once sent along to run errands for Vincent Sheean, or maybe it was Negley Farson, covering a local war in Southern Illinois, or maybe it was Kentucky? Anyhow, the cub saw bloody corpses in the dust, and forgot everything but how to pound a typewriter. He wrote four thousand words, mostly adjectives, including thirty-two invocations of the Deity, and filed his bid for immortality straight telegram, never having heard of press-rate. "And Smith doesn't fire him. Smith doesn't do anything until the Final is gone to bed. Then Smith sends a night letter: NEVER MIND THE MASSACRE. INTERVIEW GOD. GET PICTURES IF POSSIBLE."

I asked him "Why tell me?" He grinned inscrutably, and went back to *Replenishing Jessica*. Obviously, my story about the puppy in the pawnshop was the day's best joke in the newsroom. Grimly, I typed several versions of a dignified note to Smith, telling him we had both made a mistake and I would save him the bother of discussing it. Finals came up, and were passed around to all desks but mine. Then Pablo brought me a copy, opened to Opposite Editorial. About a third of my story was there, under my by-line. It had been edited with a scalpel, not with a meat-axe. "Pretty good stuff," Pablo said. I knew better. But I was in the paper.

Next morning, I entered the newsroom as if I belonged there. On the Oliver, I found a scribbled note: ANDREWS: *The lead on the Creation story was only ten words long.* SMITH. I was still digesting that when the World's Oldest Office Boy appraised me speculatively, before he said "See Smith." I went braced for the guillotine, and found Smith blue-penciling a delayed dispatch from Junius P. Wood somewhere in Siberia. He said "Sit down, Bob," without looking up. I slumped in a chair, and tried to calm my nerves by reading Wood's dispatch. (Handling type and makeup had taught me how to read upside down and backward. The trick came in handy, subsequently, in Madison Avenue advertising agencies and Hollywood film studios.) Wood reported his success in importing two dozen Made in Missouri corncob pipes, in which he smoked makhorka, "the cheapest and foulest tobacco the Russians know how to produce." He told gleefully of puffing makhorka fumes in the face of Vladimir Ilich Ulyanov, "alias Nikolai Lenin," until "under my poison-gas attack, his arrogance wilted and he talked almost honestly."

The Bolshevik censors had passed Wood's copy untouched, apparently afraid it might bite them. Smith felt no such fear. Methodically, he turned the story upside down, putting the lead where it should be. Meanwhile, he meditated aloud. "Everybody hates editors. Writers especially. They give editors stuff they can't possibly print the way it is, and when the editors make it printable, the writers curse them instead of thanking them." He looked up suddenly. "It takes meanness to be an editor." If he found it this hard to fire me, I felt sorrier for him than for myself. "Editors," he said, "can't be kindhearted. They can't mind being damned and detested." He rose and glared out at ugly rooftops beyond the soot-streaked window. "An editor can like a writer as a brother, and still say 'No' to what the writer thinks is his masterpiece. If he can't do that he's cheating. Unless he spends his own money, in which case he's a fool to be an editor." He turned on me. "How many friends have you made in the newsroom?" I started to say "None but Pablo Katigbak and the rat that's raising a

66

family under my desk" — but he went right on: "What's your opinion of *Midweek?*" And I was out on a swaying limb.

The Opposition put out enormous Sunday editions. As for us, Victor Lawson refused to publish on the Sabbath, as righteously as he rejected advertising for burlesque shows, massage parlors, firearms, tobacco, or patent medicines containing alcohol. He questioned the ethics of giving subscribers anything they didn't pay for. Time and again, he said "No" to Smith's proposals for a literary supplement, a showcase for spare hours' writing by the staff, free with the *Daily News* on Wednesdays. But Walter Strong thought it might be worth trying, at least for a few issues. "Sink or swim" was all right with Smith. What he hadn't counted on was that good intentions are not enough to keep a magazine afloat.

He expected a flood of manuscripts, a plethora of prose and poetry, from his crew. It didn't materialize. Twenty-four pages yawned, and advertising filled only 30 per cent of the space although 46 per cent was break-even on production cost. National advertisers held back, because *Midweek* publication wasn't guaranteed past the first three months. Local advertising was spotty. The State Street stores said Chicago's uncertain weather, matched by Chicago women's whims, made it too much of a gamble to give firm commitments more than forty-eight hours ahead of publication. Such problems were outside Smith's purview, and he wanted them kept that way. But he couldn't help knowing that from the start the Damoclean sword hung on a fraying thread.

Six *Midweeks* had been put together, largely with scissors and paste, when Smith wired to me in Minneapolis about the Methuselah fable. Originally, he intended to hire another reporter. But it stuck in his mind that I credited myself with experience in laying out and making up magazine pages, and in working with colorprint on news stock. My actual knowledge didn't qualify me to comment helpfully on what a lot of Doubting Thomases, including the publisher, were already calling "Smith's First Folly." So while I stammered and stalled, he went on thinking out loud. Facing the window again, he said: "Good writing must be around somewhere. The problem is to find it, capture it, and be able to pay for it. Good writers are usually hard up. I can't help them. You can't. *Midweek* could. Not much, but some."

He turned on me. "No charity, you understand. A newspaper isn't a charitable institution. Mr. Strong has to make the *Daily News* pay. The new building is costing millions." His eyes were shadowed momentarily. The prospect of leaving 15 North Wells frightened old-timers on the staff. It saddened Smith. He hurried on. "We have to remember at all times that *Midweek* must pay its freight. It can't be used as a means for giving back-door handouts to the needy and deserving." Suddenly, he demanded: "Can we buy good stuff — for fifty dollars a page?"

My God, I thought, he's not firing me — he's saying "We." For once, Little Big Mouth was silent. "Fifty dollars a page," Smith repeated wryly. "That's almost worse than paying nothing at all, like the little magazines that bloom in May and die in July." Then, again, he challenged. "That's all we can spend, as long as we're a losing venture, and don't expect me to ask Mr. Strong for more." He buttoned his vest and coat. "Can we get quality that cheap? We can't unless we go out and look for it, instead of waiting for it to walk in with its hat in its hand, which it won't. Where should we look first?" I had absolutely nothing to offer. He said, "Let's smoke on it."

So we went to the Cave of Winds, and finished two cigarettes each out of my package, and returned to the catacombs, neither of us having said a word. This time, we didn't part in the newsroom. Eyes followed us as he led on past his office, along a series of disjointed hallways, up a flight of creaking steps, into a maze I hadn't entered before, whose occupants had charge of such arcane activities as "Childrens' Pen Pals" and "Of Interest to Homemakers" and the annual *Daily News*

68

Almanac. All at once, I saw where he was taking me. Carl Sandburg sat alone in a glass-walled cubicle, engrossed in publicity sheets from Hollywood.

The figure before us, Smith had written, *with its luxurious bangs of hair, with the military shoulders and the careless drab clothes, is familiar, yet remote, inexplicable.* I knew now this was understatement, like everything Smith said when he wrote about what he loved. Sandburg to me, at that moment, was three times larger than life. (He has shrunk very little since.) His look at me was not encouraging. It didn't change when Smith said, "Carl, this is Bob Andrews, from Minneapolis. He's going to edit *Midweek.*" Sandburg indicated a desk on the far side of the room. "Make yourself comfortable," he said. Then he went back to his work, and so did Smith, and I sat in the corner the rest of the day with nothing to do and no typewriter to do it on. My only friends, Pablo Katigbak and the rat, were three buildings away. We might never meet again. Or so I thought, until at lights-out time Pablo appeared, exchanged a comradely "Good night" with Sandburg, and told me "Come on. I'll buy a beer."

He took me across Wells Street, under the El, to Hy Green's speakeasy, which was pretty much a private club for inner-circle members of the *Daily News* family. The draft beer was bad, the Syndicate gin was worse, and only a starving Eskimo could stomach the blubber Hy put in his roast beef sandwiches. But Bob Casey and Hal O'Flaherty and John Drury were at the bar, with Paul Leach, who covered Washington, and Wallace Deuel, just about to join the Berlin Bureau, and Clark Rodenbach, the jockey-sized Dartmouth *cum laude* who covered Police. After thoughtful inspection, Drury said "Hi, Andrews," and Deuel nodded. Pablo nudged me. "Play it slow and easy." I made my schooner of foam last, until he nudged me and muttered, "Okay. Let's blow."

Outside, he punched me in the short ribs. "You're in!" he said. My lack of comprehension surprised him. "You don't get it?" I didn't. He said: "Your neck is out — oh, yes; oh boy, but you got problems! Who cares? You're on your way." I was still a disappointment. "Smith pins the label on you," he elucidated patiently. "Now it stays until somebody knocks it off. Go read *Deadlines* some more. About the Young Man Going Somewhere. This is what you have today become." But if that was what I had become, even Pablo, who had answers for almost everything, was silent when I said, "If I'm going, tell me where."

« 6 »

Henry Luce was a Young Man Going Somewhere, until he left to launch *Time*, which Pablo said wasn't likely to last because Luce didn't stay at 15 North Wells long enough to absorb the full meaning of Smith's First Commandment. I learned what this was the first time I drummed up enough courage to show Smith an unsolicited article that I thought was too good to turn down, even though parts of it quarreled with *Daily News* Editorial Page policy. Having seen Charles H. Dennis, Victor Lawson's Editor, still enthroned — a noble old Roman who hadn't changed his mind since he voted against a second chance for Grover Cleveland — I took it for granted that Smith wouldn't think of crossing swords with him; but I said I could do a rewrite, eliminating the controversial elements, if that would save the piece.

Smith read, frowned, nodded, and scrawled *Okay* SMITH. "The day we slant to fit policy," he told me matter-of-factly, "I'll cease to be a part of this organization." And he meant it. He truly believed Saint Peter would ask for no other credentials if a knocker at the Pearly Gates showed a *C. D. N.* press card. Like a father who trains up sons in the way they should go, always aware he must lose them as soon as they can travel alone, he made reporters out of cubs, writers out of reporters, and asked from them no more than he gave: pride in our profession, honesty, and decency. Except for *Deadlines*, and *Chi-*

cago: The History of a Reputation, which he wrote in collaboration with Lloyd Lewis, Smith's own published work had at most a minor audience. But if he wrote less successfully than he taught, I do not think it flaws the image. Rather, it confirms his singularity: that he was glad, not envious, and hopeful, not hurt, when his Young Men Going Somewhere arrived at the discovery he wanted them to make, that by luck or by God's grace they were endowed with talents he was well aware he lacked. Which is one reason why not many *Daily News* alumni are fond of a certain words-merchant, who had a hit play on Broadway and a contract in Hollywood, and stopped over between trains to accept congratulations. Smith arranged a luncheon honoring him — at Schlogl's, just beyond the Cave of Winds, where Sherwood Anderson (or it may have been Raymond Gram Swing) once declared that no matter what the thumb-marked menus called it, the *specialté de maison* was always actually boiled owl with toadstools.

Passing my cubicle, Smith asked, "Would you like to join us at Schlogl's?" Bells rang. Flags flew. I followed, expecting something rich and rare, into a shadowed *bierstube*, with sawdust on the floor and GENTS ONLY over the door. If ladies wanted what Schlogl's sold, they had to go upstairs and keep their voices low. What attraction the place had for Smith and his friends was arguable. Probably it was Richard Schneider, the literary headwaiter. After he got used to me, Richard let me look at his copy of Harry Hansen's *Midwest Portraits*, signed by the author, embellished with drawings by Gene Markey and the autographs of William McFee, Konrad Bercovici, Arthur Brisbane, Gilbert Seldes, Horace Liveright, Heywood Broun, Upton Sinclair, H. L. Mencken, George Jean Nathan, Paul De Kruif, Edgar Lee Masters, Opie Read, Ford Madox Ford, and others too numerous to catalogue. All were introduced to Schlogl's, and to Richard, by regular, devoted patrons, all of whom claimed the food was frightful.

Smith told Richard: "This is Bob Andrews. He edits *Mid-*

week." Richard didn't ask for my autograph. I hadn't published a book.

The honor guest was late. While they waited, his former colleagues, with Richard's assistance, settled such literary questions as the accuracy of Riq Atwater's new translation of *The Secret History of Procopius,* and what Paris and Gertrude Stein were doing to young Ernest Hemingway from Oak Park. Then the honor guest arrived, and proved he was no Hemingway.

Customarily, Smith lunched on two poached eggs, toast, and tea, then sipped yellow chartreuse liberally laced with soda, and listened, while others talked. On this occasion, he ordered beer, and raised his stein, proposing a toast to a Young Man Going Somewhere who had gone clear to the top.

Responding, his erstwhile pupil jeered. "Smith," he said, "it's time you quit smirking coyly and stealing bows. You're no creator of geniuses. You merely have the privilege of being present, while they create themselves."

Smith smiled. We joined him, in pretense that the ingrate was trying to be funny. But if this specialist in published self-examination wonders why his name is missing from the roll I call, I remind him of a day when he showed his size by seeking to make small of Smith. The man to whom we all owed more than we could pay never had to fight a libel suit, never faked a story, never took his coat off in the office, never called a reporter anything he wouldn't call the publisher to his face; he stopped to pick up pins on his way to order an Extra re-plate when the *Daily News* beat the town on the Valentine's Day Massacre in 1929. But there was steel behind his gentleness.

Big Tim Murphy, whose sun was setting because he was a mauler, not a murderer, stormed into Smith's office with a pair of brass knuckles on his massive fist. So huge that he had to bend to get through the door, he bellowed that he was there to pulverize the s. o. b. who libeled him by mentioning him in the same paragraph with Jim Colosimo and Johnny

Torrio. Smith looked up from the copy he was editing, and said: "Go outside. Take your hat off. Come in quietly. Then we'll discuss your reputation." And Big Tim, staring, did as he was told. Five minutes later, pounding Smith's frail shoulder, he announced: "You're okay, Henry. And I'll pulverize the s. o. b. that ever lays a finger on you." Yet when it came to *Midweek*, Smith was strangely shy.

Smith wished Bob Casey would write for the magazine. So did I. Now and then, Bob wearied of gangsters and politicians, even of the Chicago Irish. Then without warning he went away for a while, traveling alone to the farthest possible destination. Once it was Angkor Wat in Cambodia, where he broke his leg, and crawled two miles through jungle teeming with snakes and tigers, being too Irishly independent to yell for help. Again, he sailed to Easter Island from Tahiti, on a hell-ship schooner whose half-caste skipper had to be Irish-charmed out of robbing him and dropping him overboard, as prelude to turning pearl-pirate. Whatever Bob did, he got a book out of it. Smith felt it would be presumptuous, and unfair, to ask Bob to waste saleable stuff on *Midweek*, at our prices. Personally, I was more concerned by the probability that Bob would bash me with a brick, if I had the impudence to add to his very small collection of rejection slips. On the other hand, I had begun to feel my oats.

Meyer Levin, preparing himself for his novels about Israel and his eventual dramatization of the Loeb-Leopold case of compulsion, filled space daily under a standing head, "A Young Man's Fancy," with exotic tapestries of prose that prompted Theodore Ellis, the Demon Proofreader, to label the column "A Fancy Young Man." This was unjust, but Mr. Ellis was a classicist, a contributor to academic journals, whose lightest reading for pleasure was Aristotle in the original. Even to *Midweek*'s holder of uncertain power, Meyer was like a budding ballet dancer doing practice leaps and pirouettes. I didn't have to ask him to write for *Midweek*. He needed more room for his flights into the blue.

Through Smith, he sent me several of his carefully plotless pieces. I admired them. I had them set in type, pulled proofs, sent these down to Miss Dewey so she would issue checks. But somehow or other, my layouts sometimes forced me to leave Meyer in the *Overset*. If he minded, he rose above it. And Smith, having told me editors need meanness, was too much the gentleman to list exceptions from the rule. Anyhow, before long, Meyer left us. On his own, he went to Israel. Trouble erupted there. Smith cabled asking for coverage. Meyer sent three words: I AM SAFE. And Smith was not put out. Ringmaster of a menagerie of ill-met mesomorphs, only one weakness in writers surprised and saddened him: if you lacked enthusiasm, or lost it, Smith gave up on you.

This led, however, to miscalculation. He knew how reporters lie, not to the public but to each other, not in the paper but at bars where they foregather to renew the confidence that City Editors and copyreaders chip away in working hours. Arching eyebrows, winking confidentially, inventing to outdo each other, they insist they know the story that can't be printed behind whatever published story may be mentioned. Quite often, they tell the truth. But at least once, those who foregathered at Hy Green's wished they didn't know quite so much about the truth that couldn't be written. This had to do with the last days of Shirley Short.

Shirley Short wasn't a newspaperman, but anyone on the *Daily News* was proud to buy him a drink, any time. Shirley, whose weathered willingness to battle anything that walked or flew belied his feminine-sounding name, was a seat-of-the-pants pilot, who had a saying that "Eagles never die." "Nobody ever shoveled dirt on an eagle's corpse," he told me. "Nobody ever saw an eagle's skeleton. When an eagle knows it's his last time up, he sets a course and flies as high as he's able, and he never comes down. If you doubt me, go watch an eagle long enough. You'll see it happen."

Shirley was at the controls the day the once-famed Omer Locklear, who taught him to fly, was cut in two by a propeller blade during a wing-walking exhibition at a county fair. "Before I took him up," Shirley said, "he told me 'I won't be coming down this trip.'" Shirley was in and out of the newsroom, bringing confidential reports of progress in a top-secret project. One of his pupils, Clarence Chamberlin, set a world's record in 1927 by flying a Bellanca monoplane nonstop from New York to Germany, 3911 miles in 42 hours, 31 minutes. In 1931, Russell Boardman and John Polando, flying an improved Bellanca, set a new nonstop record, 5011 miles from New York to Istanbul in 49 hours and 20 minutes. Bellanca thought he could build a plane that would fly nonstop around the world, from Chicago to Chicago, in under 80 hours. Other aircraft designers said this was impossible. They said his plane — a sort of tail-less flying boxcar, with both puller and pusher propellers synchronized to rotate in opposite directions, yet smoothly and simultaneously, at front and back of a single power-plant — would never get off the ground. But somehow or other, the *Daily News* became the backer of the first and last aircraft ever financed by an American newspaper.

Pablo Katigbak was positive that this was due to Shirley Short, not to Bellanca. No other pilot would sign on to test the cranky contraption. Shirley, having flown everything else, said "I'll go along for the ride." It was he who convinced the publisher that another fifty thousand, and then another hundred thousand, would finish the job and provide the *Daily News* with a promotion stunt topping anything ever tried by the *Tribune*, or even by Moe Annenberg for Hearst. But finally the publisher demanded more than hope for his money. That day, a hurricane hit Nicaragua. There was tremendous loss of life and damage. I saw Bob Casey and Charley Ford, the paper's top photographer, hurrying out with Shirley Short.

When I saw Casey again, four days later, he looked and felt ten years older. He and Charley Ford never reached Nicaragua. There was so little spare space in the engine room, which was also the pilot's cabin, that Casey and Charley had to lie flat on their stomachs on top of the gasoline-tanks. Lying there, choked by fumes and spattered by leaking oil, Casey saw something swinging back and forth outside a porthole. A chunk of the rudder had broken off and was hanging by a fraying wire cable. Charley tried to snap a picture of it. Casey yelled. Shirley Short called up to him: "I know. I know." Vibration, that snapped the rudder, sheared heads off of rivets. These flew like bullets, while Casey prayed, and Shirley crash-landed in a Florida swamp.

The Opposition heard nothing about this. The badly crumpled Bellanca was shipped back to Chicago. Bellanca, the builder, worked frantically to repair the plane. He was on notice, now, that no more money would be forthcoming until the thing checked out as soundly, safely airworthy. Shirley Short marked time, waiting for the showdown test. Studying Shirley, the one time we saw him, Pablo said what I was thinking: "He knows. He knows." The Bellanca was going to kill him. He couldn't say so; wouldn't. He had made his bet, and the paper had backed his play. He couldn't cure the ineluctable flaw in Bellanca's calculations: which was that the puller and pusher propellers could never be perfectly synchronized, and therefore rivets and welds were subjected to vibration no metal could stand past an unpredictable breaking-point. But at the start he had said, "I'll go along for the ride." *Who rides on a tiger must ride to the end.* Shirley chose his own time for the final test. Just as dawn broke over Lake Michigan, he took the Bellanca up, as high as it would fly. It fell apart in the air. There was no corpse to be covered over with dirt. Not even a skeleton.

And there was no talk of eagles in the brief and factual story we published.

Smith let the Opposition boast of publishing "All the News That's Fit to Print." A lot of this never saw daylight in the *Daily News*. As a result, his reporters had more cause than their less circumscribed colleagues to blow off steam wherever they could. This ought to have made them write for *Midweek*. But what they turned in was strangely disappointing. As one example out of many, six separate yet strikingly similar off-the-cuff contributions labeled "Fiction" came to my desk within a week after Jake Lingle was shot and killed in the pedestrian underpass leading to the Illinois Central station on the lake front, while on his way to the races, on June 9, 1930.

Lingle, who worked for Colonel Robert Rutherford Mc-Cormick's *Tribune*, was the only newspaperman slain during the gangster wars, though scores of them walked unarmed in greater peril than policemen who were paid to risk their lives. The day after the Lingle shooting, Colonel McCormick called a meeting of the Publishers' Association, at which he volunteered to pay all costs of finding and convicting the murderer, above the usual County allowance for homicide investigations. The offer was accepted. A *Tribune* attorney became special prosecutor. An out-of-town hoodlum named Leo Brothers was arrested, and quickly convicted. He went to prison for fourteen years, and the *Tribune* announced that the Lingle case was closed. This did not, however, end discussion of it. "The *Tribune*," Colonel McCormick finally felt forced to say, "has treated the nagging by two little evening contemporaries with silence born of contempt. The fact is that those newspapers are so deeply in debt that whoever may be held up as editor or publisher is little more than an office boy for the creditors."

As for the six stories submitted for *Midweek*, they read like pulp-magazine exposés. All dealt with a character out of the stock bin: the smart operator who outsmarts himself. He was described as a fourth-rate legman, illkempt, illiterate, not entitled to call himself a reporter, who hung around the Vice Squad, tagged along on raids, phoned names and addresses to the rewrite desk: in sum, a shabby tipster, nothing more. Despised, and barely tolerated in the company of his betters, suddenly he burgeoned into a blustering exhibitionist whose display of wealth awed even foreign correspondents home on leave. His pockets bulged with greasy currency. Proudly, he bragged of having become collector of payoffs for a detective captain. Dives and call girl bureaus closed or opened according to who paid him how much. But though his income pyramided, he lost in the market and on the races faster than he could extort cash from his growing clientele. To get more dirty dollars faster, he corrupted hitherto decent reporters, hard-pressed to meet alimony payments or family doctor's bills, and enlisted them as subcollectors. They let him convince them that newspapermen were untouchable, and that anyhow they did no wrong since they weren't being paid to keep crime news out of print. He leased two hotel suites for poker parties and girl parades, made the down payment on a cottage in the country, bought two big automobiles on the installment plan. His debts to tailors, nightclubs, bookmakers, madames and brokers mounted astronomically, but for a while no creditor pressed him. Then there was a changing of the guards at City Hall, and his "connection" was transferred to the suburbs. Another payoff system left him out in the cold. Now creditors closed in, and he didn't know which way to turn. Drunk, he slept. Sleeping, he dreamed of a certain stock that was sure to shoot sky-high. All he needed was twenty-five thousand dollars. That would square his debts and get him out of town with a bankroll.

Waking, he went to a disbarred lawyer, employed by the Syndicate to ride herd on its more reputable attorneys, and proposed a deal that he said couldn't miss. The Syndicate owned a dog-racing track that was closed by the police before it opened, because the State Legislature, while it legalized horse racing, with interesting ambivalence outlawed dog tracks. "I have a judge in my pocket," the corruptionist declared. "He's due to retire. He wants to buy a house in Florida. Price, twenty-five thousand dollars. Okay. You give me twenty-five thousand dollars. I'll give it to my judge. You'll announce you're opening the dog track. The papers will howl. I'll handle that. The cops will warn you. I'll handle that. We'll have the whole town talking. Then you open. The cops close you. You're in all the headlines. A million bucks' worth of free advertising. You go before my judge. He'll make a big thing of it. He'll say it's a complicated legal issue, and grant a thirty-day restraining order, pending trial. Then the cops can't touch you, and you run wide open for a month. Then you're back before my judge. He gives you hell for thumbing your nose at Law and Order. You're padlocked. But you're off the nut — with a profit. The papers print editorials: What a shame, to lose a judge with such pure principles. He's got his house in Florida. And you and the boys laugh all the way to the bank."

And according to all six stories, he walked out with twenty-five one-thousand-dollar bills, and instead of buying the judge took a taxi to La Salle Street and bought all he could, on margin, of the stock he had dreamed about. And it didn't go up; it went down. He was wiped out. Meanwhile the Syndicate invested another one hundred thousand dollars in painting and refurbishing the dog-track, lodging whippets in its kennels, advertising the Grand Opening. The corruptionist begged and borrowed frantically. He couldn't come up with anything like twenty-five thousand dollars, and the judge couldn't be corrupted for a dollar less. The reporter panicked, then summoned a trapped weasel's crazy courage and defied the Syndicate. "Okay. So my foot slipped. So what? You can't touch a newspaperman!" A phone call contradicted him. "Hello, Sam. The boys on the papers say you're a nothing. We say a thief is a thief. Good-by, Sam." And he ran, with nowhere to run to. And a tommy gun cut him in chunks. THE END.

I made six copies of a single rejection note: *Sorry. Not for* MIDWEEK. I told Smith that, with so much Page One competition, I was sure he'd agree we could do without any gangster fiction. He agreed, but with odd hesitance. Finally, he showed me half a dozen stories, typed any old way on copy paper. "The boys," he said apologetically, "have been dropping these on my desk." He got up and looked out the window. "They don't have much time to shape and polish," he said after a moment. "Writing for more than just today's Final takes patience. It's hard to be patient when you need fifty dollars." He wasn't downgrading anybody. Nor could I, even if I wanted to. After all, the only thing I had ever sold to a magazine, up to then, was a Sophomore English quatrain imitating Swinburne, for which H. L. Mencken paid me $2.75. That must have been what it was worth. He never printed it.

Smith sat down again. "If there's anything in this stuff," he said, "that you think might be fixed up with more work, give me your suggestions, and I'll pass them along." That made it worse. I wasn't going to hide behind his signature on a memo. I confess I wondered if it wouldn't be simpler, and in fact plain common sense, to hold the stories a few days, then give them back saying only that I had no suggestions. Perhaps he half-expected this. In any event, I read the stories, and told him the truth as I saw it. He sent them back to the writers, with a note that said *Midweek* was unfortunately overstocked just then, and it might be wiser if, in future, writers discussed their ideas with Bob Andrews before submitting manuscripts.

This did not, of course, enhance my popularity in the newsroom, where I hovered whenever I could leave my cubicle, hoping for some catastrophe that would force the City Editor to push the panic button, recruiting all hands including me. The news-getters I envied were calloused against outrageous editing of their output for the Final. Few cared to ask a twenty-one-year-old intruder to tell them what to write, and how to write it, for *Midweek*. I don't know if small, shy, brilliant William Shawn had to sweat it out similarly, when he first went on the *New Yorker*. I rather doubt it. Bill dealt with published authors, and had the taste and integrity to earn and keep their respectful admiration, while he became the calming force behind Harold Ross and eventually Ross's meek but mighty successor. It may just be, though, that he got some ideas, about what not to do, from watching how I blundered.

When we met at 15 North Wells, Bill showed no signs of interest in being an editor anywhere. He had a job, and liked it. His pretty wife, Cecile, worked in Features across the hall from my corner. Dropping by now and then to walk home with her, Bill let me tell him the trials of running a magazine. Almost agonizingly considerate, as self-effacing as he was shrewd, he shook his head when I hinted he might do something for *Midweek*, and said with some ambiguity: "You have the best in the West to call on." I called, but got few answers. I scratched for what I could find, wherever it could be found.

A windfall dropped out of a bulging manila envelope that came Postage Due. Jacques Chambrun, a New York literary agent, offered American rights to an assortment of short pieces already published in England and France. He was the first literary agent who bothered about *Midweek*, and the only one for a long while. What he sent was not out of the top drawer. The manuscripts were finger-marked and coffee-stained from many previous unsuccessful submissions. Otherwise, I was sure he wouldn't have settled for fifty dollars apiece for work by "names" as impressive on my covers as André Maurois and one of the numerous Princess Radziwills. But thanks to him, I began to build a backlog.

Then I felt as Balboa must have felt, struck dumb on a

peak in Darien. MacKinlay Kantor's mother sent me some casual, nostalgic sketches of small-town life in Iowa. She wrote warmly, truthfully. Her letters, discussing her sketches, were chapters for a novel her son must write when it is written. More than she may have realized, she drew her self-portrait, which was that of a truly remarkable personage. Entering a field invaded by few women when she was young, Effie Kantor conquered with calm determination. She edited county-seat weeklies, printing what people had a right to know about their neighbors, leaving out local scandal that wouldn't help anybody. She was unaware of her own importance. "My son," one of her letters began, "was a writer before he could spell. I think he was writing stories in his mind before he could talk. I wish I had his imagination. But the Lord decides what we shall be, and I have never felt competent to criticize His judgment."

I featured her name on our *Midweek* covers before her son came to us on a blustery January day. He was a practicing, publishing professional, the first of his standing who offered to accept what we were paying. I had read his Chicago novels, *Diversey* and *El Goes South*, and his short stories, for which Edwin Baird at *Real Detective Tales* paid him a cent a word. *College Humor*, printing one of his poems, a narrative in rhyme, told how, when he lived in Webster City, Iowa, before he was eighteen, he won the *Des Moines Register*'s short story contest. I thought he thought he was slumming, selling anything to *Midweek*. He tells it differently:

One day in 1929 I walked through the slush on Wells Street, entered a dark old building, and reached a messy office crowded with desks, newspapers, and miscellaneous junk. Here was Henry Justin Smith, who would live through only seven more Januarys. I had called on the telephone and haltingly inquired whether, if, by any chance, the editors of *Midweek* had reached a decision concerning my story, "A Guest at Dinner." Smith snapped over the telephone, "Come on over!" and hung up with a crash. So here I was, in the role of supplicant author and not liking it at all. "You're Kantor, eh?" said Smith, as if he didn't like my looks. Icy eyes peeked at me through his glasses. "How much do you want for this?" I said my last story was ten thousand words, and Edwin Baird paid me a hundred dollars for it. "Nonsense! That's practically a book! What did they pay you for your last short story?" "Fifty dollars." "I'll pay you seventy-five for this. Now please get out of here. I'm busy." The next thing I knew, I was back in Wells Street, wading in the slush, but not what you would call unhappy.

So Mac was Smith's discovery, not mine. That summer, he drove up from Boone, Iowa, with his wife and their baby, and dropped in on Smith, and grandly invited him to lunch at Schlogl's. ("The year before, I ate at a dairy lunch on a side street, where it was cheap, which Schlogl's wasn't.") More: Mac insisted on driving Smith to lunch in his green Chevrolet with yellow wheels, and with the baby's bed in the back seat. Smith brooded all during the *Kaffeeklatsch* that involved Carl Sandburg, Bob Casey, John Drury, Lew Sarett, Charles Layng, and other notables. I sat back studying Smith, who studied Mac. Smith, not I, had turned down four of Mac's stories in a row. Outside, Smith glared at Mac's car. "You really brought a baby four hundred miles in that?" Mac answered with some resentment: "Yes. Why not?" Smith answered: "Write us a story about that." And Mac came up with *And These Went Down to Burlington*, and got one hundred dollars for it, which was the most we ever paid any author for anything.

But James T. Farrell was my problem. Hardly anyone had heard of him at that time, as he told me defiantly while I studied him more than his stories, in my office one grim afternoon. He was my age, resentful, overconfident, lonely, hungry for more than food. Smith would not have snapped at him as he snapped at Kantor. Smith would have pitied him, and shown it in spite of himself. Then, reading his manuscripts, Smith would have suffered. For he would feel he had to say we couldn't print them. He despised censorship in all its manifestations, but he owed a duty to the publisher and the Paper That Goes Home. Farrell wanted Smith's verdict, not mine. If I tried to explain why he was better off not meeting Smith just then, he would think I was stupid, or cowardly, or envious, or all three. And because there might be just a modicum of truth in this, I bought two of his stories without consulting Smith.

I had to have them set in type to get Farrell a check, which he needed desperately though he wouldn't beg for it if he starved first. There were out-of-work men in droves huddling around trash cans filled with burning newspapers, on the loading platforms under Wacker Drive. Hard times coming were more than a black cloud on the near horizon, though the *Daily News* continued to agree editorially with Calvin Coolidge, and with Herbert Hoover waiting in the wings, that the cloud would blow away if they continued to ignore it. Smith had said we couldn't give handouts. All right. I could tell him honestly that to me, at least, Farrell's stuff was worth a lot more than we could ever pay for it. But discretion was the better part. For the time being, what Smith didn't know couldn't worry him. So I mixed my galley proofs, making sure he missed the ones he needn't see just yet. Eventually, crossing my fingers, I put the least startling of Farrell's stories in the magazine, and set myself for fireworks. There weren't any.

Pointing at the Farrell page, Smith said, "This fellow Farrell, whoever he is, can Write." The capital belongs — his tone put it there. Then, looking out the window, he said, "But we can't go too far too fast. You know that, Bob." That was as far as he would let himself go, about a man who could Write. So in Makeup, while the compositors were at lunch behind the lockers, I broke Union Law by touching type. I dumped Farrell's much stronger and far better story in the hell-box, and informed him in a stiffly formal letter that rights had reverted to him, and he was free to sell it elsewhere if he could. I expected him to despise me for this. If he did, he sees it differently nowadays.

"I never forget the buying of my stories by you," Farrell wrote recently. "I gave you other stories, that make people shudder to this day. You paid me the most I had earned, for the first stories I sold. But you did more than buy stories. I was almost wrecked by a *Studs Lonigan* myth. The refutation of that myth is in *Helen I Love You*, which you let me re-sell. I came back from Paris, by charity of Travelers' Aid, in April '32. I learned Mencken had bought it. O'Brien reprinted it, and it is in his permanent *Best Short Stories*. If I have a place in American literature, *Midweek* has a connection with it, and you have, too. And Smith, too. I didn't know he was behind it. I wish there were a *Midweek* now. There are no Smiths, however, any more."

But when there was a Smith and a *Midweek*, almost anything could happen. Next time I overspent my budget, and had a blank page to fill, I juggled with more confidence. The result, from which I managed my next Big Leap Forward, was a head-on collision with Carl Sandburg, or at least with his "Notebook." He gave it to us for nothing, but that wasn't why it was MUST in *Midweek*. Consistently, it was the best thing in the magazine. He wrote it in short takes, jotting lines or paragraphs when they occurred to him. Some pieces were poems; some were essays; some were jokes Abraham Lincoln liked. Sometimes, he took off his shoes, wiggled his toes in heavy home-woven wool socks, wrote a few sentences, then tuned his guitar and half-sang, half-talked, softly so as not to disturb his office mate, some ballad that might or might not be found in his *American Songbag*.

When the *Songbag* came out in 1927, it went almost ignored, except amongst people with whom he had swapped yarns, hummed and strummed. (It is missing today from most lists of his published works.) He went to professional composers with an amateur's squiggles, which he said looked "more like a shivaree than a respectable wedding." But he got the musical arrangements he wanted, from contributors as various as Rupert Hughes ("author," he noted, "of remarkably free and independent inquiries into human credulity") and H. L. Mencken (who contributed the harmonization of *The Drunkard's Doom*). He gave credit to everybody but himself. Pablo said he heard Sandburg, sitting alone in the corner he shared with no one then, speaking his *Songbag* dedication aloud, "like he's saying a prayer," before he put it in type. "This book was begun in depths of humility, and ended likewise with the murmur, 'God be merciful to me, a sinner.' It is a book for sinners, and for lovers of humanity. I apologize to them for the sins of this book, and that it loves much but not enough." I never worked in any other newspaper office where that word *love* could be used without a sneer or a snarl.

I had a first edition of the *Songbag*, which I had bought the morning after Smith said "Carl, this is Bob Andrews." I wondered if I'd last long enough to know him well enough to ask for his autograph under the Foreword: "To those unknown singers who made songs out of love, fun, grief, and to those many other singers, who kept those songs as living things of the heart and mind, out of love, fun, grief." That word, *love*, again. All over the country, people stood in line to buy tickets for his lectures that always ended in songs. I got in free. But that didn't admit me to his friendship. He wasn't unfriendly. He had America to think about. And thinking tall thoughts, not always somber, he wrote or pondered or sang to himself, while I pretended to read manuscripts and lay out another *Midweek*. There was no fellowship between us then.

Though he sat only six feet away, I doubt if he spoke more than thirty words to me during the first month after Smith had put me in his corner and he had raised no objection. I caught him considering me, infrequently and briefly. I won his undivided interest only when, endeavoring to seem at ease with a loud lady author who insisted on selling me ten poems for ten dollars each, I leaned back magisterially in my chair, clasping my hands behind my head, forgetting the big electric fan at my elbow. Its blades bit into my bare arm, to the bone. Blood spurted on the lady author. She shrieked and fled. Sandburg says now he was tempted to tell me there are easier ways to get rid of a poet. At the time, he merely called First Aid, and told me where to get my arm stitched up.

But then one midnight he put away his guitar, put on his shoes, dropped some copy paper on my desk, and, for the first time, said "Good night" audibly. He started out, then stopped, and remarked that Pixley & Ehlers, at 22 South Clark Street, sold a sound old-fashioned supper — a pot of baked beans with crisp salt pork on top, brown bread, and coffee — for twenty cents. It was information, not an invitation. He disappeared, leaving me with a totally unexpected addition to his "Notebook." It told about two composers, each of whom claimed he wrote the "Livery Stable Blues." They took it to court. The defendant testified, in toto, as follows: "A lady dancer started cutting up, so I corneted some horse laughs at her. The trombone come in with some pony neighs. Then the banjo and sax and cowbells made their comments. And the 'Livery Stable Blues' was born." He won, which was fine with me. But the way Sandburg told it would eat up four inches in 10-point type, two columns wide.

Most weeks, I welcomed any space-eater. This time, I had already scheduled the page on which the "Notebook" was MUST so tightly that I'd have to pull slugs, and cheat at top and bottom, to make room for Sandburg's sentences already set, plus a Marshall Field ad and a short story by a new *Midweek* discovery, Douglas Hardy. I hadn't told Smith that, for no reason I can think of unless my parents foresaw that some day I might need a choice of aliases, my name in full is Charles Robert Douglas Hardy Andrews.

Smith said, after reading the galleys, that the Douglas Hardy story seemed quite good, to him. He was sorry I'd only been able to pay twenty-five dollars for it. I didn't tell him twenty-five dollars was just enough to buy me a Homburg hat and what Von Lengerke and Antoine called a "whangee": a bamboo cane made in India, the kind Kipling may have flourished when he, too, was out to make a showing, on the *Civil & Military Gazette*. Unlike James T. Farrell, I cannot recall with pride the first short story I sold to *Midweek*. Still I bled while I cut it in type next morning. The Marshall Field ad was late. When it came up, it was three inches deeper and a column wider than Advertising had told me. Grinding my teeth, I cut three more paragraphs out of Douglas Hardy. Then I balked.

I knew from experience what happens when Scandinavians are annoyed. In Minneapolis, during the Norse-American Centennial, we had no by-liners with Swedish or Norwegian-sounding names. I invented Lars Bjornsen Andersen. I ran supposedly funny features, so signed. The Swedes blamed them on the Norwegians, and vice versa, until they formed common cause and sent a posse to deal with Lars Bjornsen Andersen. The ensuing contretemps left scars. But in Chicago, for Douglas Hardy's sake, I butchered Carl Sandburg's "Notebook." Then I waited, giving my best impersonation of Sidney Carton bound for the guillotine.

Copies of *Midweek* came up. The World's Oldest Office Boy passed them around. Pablo Katigbak, from whom I had no secrets, whispered that Sandburg was very busy at the Horner Library, re-checking his research for *The War Years*. Temporarily reprieved, I wandered in on Smith. He hadn't noticed that the "Notebook" was shorter than usual. Or if he had, he let it pass. He said it was the best *Midweek* yet, and showed me a note he was sending to the publisher. "By trial and error, which it seems is how these things have to be done, you will see we are getting closer to a readable literary publication, something Chicago should have a place for." Wistfully, he added: "If Advertising and Circulation could be induced to admit this has some slight value in strengthening home-readership, production costs might become a somewhat lessening consideration." That was as far as Smith would ever go towards asking lesser departments to show respect for Editorial.

I left Smith, feeling better. Then I saw Sandburg, sitting at his desk, with his shoes off, studying the "Notebook" page. Seeing me, he got up in sections, and came padding softly on large sock-clad feet. Incredibly, he pointed not to his murdered paragraphs, but to the Douglas Hardy story. "It reads easy," he said. "And there's sense in it." He nodded gravely. "Snappy and sensible." Then he dropped a new piece of "Notebook" copy on my desk. He had just written it.

Among the best definitions of poetry in simple words, I enter as an exhibit the remark of a character in a story by young Bob Andrews in the last MIDWEEK. *"It is easy to write a poem. There is the matter of a word that will ring, and another word that goes after it and rings also and rings against it. Not so much the idea. That will take care of itself. But words." This is better than Wordsworth's definition, "Poetry is emotion recollected in tranquility."*

He knew all about Douglas Hardy. And all about Bob Andrews. And having made this clear, he tuned his guitar, strummed and hummed for a while, then put his shoes on, tucked *Midweek* under his arm, and went away without a word. But a few nights later, he said, "If you're not editing anything urgent, let's walk around and look at what we might stumble onto." So we walked in the fog for an hour, and then ate pork-and-beans and brown bread, two orders each, and deep-dish apple pie à la mode to top the feast, at Pixley & Ehlers. I called him "Sir" and "Mister" until he growled: "I'm not that old, and you're not that young." Then, of course, there was no stopping me.

I knew he had been a volunteer in Puerto Rico in the Spanish–American War. I said my father was a *Cuba Libre* patriot, too, who got there just in time to miss San Juan Hill and catch the yellow-jack. I told how my father intended to travel to India and be a poet like Kipling, but became a doctor instead, and ended up taking care of Indians in Oklahoma and the Dakotas, where the braves and the squaws believed the Indian Bureau sent him to cut them up and kill them off the bounty rolls, and their children threw rattlesnakes at me and named me "Little Big Mouth." He was such a satisfying audience that I was still giving him my autobiography and opinions at 4 A.M. He called me "Bob," and paid the check. Before we parted he said, "Keep on, keep on." And it shows the measure of the man that, having accepted me as equal partner in our corner, he was philosophical about it when Smith informed us apologetically that he was presenting me with two assistants, not because I needed helpers, but because there was no place else to put them.

« 7 »

First came lanky Jack Lawson, in green-and-yellow checkered Mackinaw, crimson flannel shirt, bright blue copper-riveted stag-pants, and knee-high hobnailed logging boots. Smith said Jack had promise, but didn't say of what. Jack said that dressing like a lumberjack about to invade Skid Row, and chewing Copenhagen snuff, put him in the proper mood to write like James Stevens, who sold Paul Bunyan allegories to the *American Mercury*. With what tact I then possessed I suggested that ours was more of a Somerset Maugham ménage. Next morning, Jack appeared in Harris tweeds and fringe-tongued brogues. In place of the figure studies of burleycue belles he had planned to post above his desk, he arranged a display of Balinese half-nudes. We worked this out, while Sandburg held his peace. Then we were hit by a hurricane from Paris named Claude Caspar-Jordan.

The *Daily News* Foreign Bureau sometimes shipped more or less promising young men to 15 North Wells, theoretically to learn newspapering at the summit. In practice, this produced a passing parade of scapegrace sons whose prominent parents were being repaid for favors done to our correspondents overseas. Generally, they came with loud reluctance, and departed as soon as foolishly forgiving mothers sent return fare. But Claude Caspar-Jordan came because he wanted to come, and arrived prepared to scalp red Indians on State Street and spit right in Al Capone's eye. Chicago, to Claude, was his chosen oyster. And he proceeded to open it with astonishing lack of judgment for a Frenchman.

A tap on his jutting but fragile jaw would drop him in his tracks, but he had the feisty belligerence that was born in poodles until Park Avenue popularity bred it out of them. Work was for peasants. Play was pointless unless it built up to a brawl. The battered beak of a dissolute Napoleonic eagle hung crookedly in his pale, old-young face. His sparse blond hair stood up like uneven bristles in a worn-out bathbrush. Under the slightest provocation, or none, he forgot the fractured Oxfordian English he had learned at the Sorbonne, but not the Anglo-Saxon fighting words he had memorized in Harry's American Bar. He lavished these on anyone, of any size, who challenged his incurable conviction that a C. D. N. press card gave him diplomatic immunity.

In Hy Green's speakeasy, he drained a waterglass of gin in one great gulp, and gasped that he much preferred it to his father's best Courvoisier. Then he passed out cold. But ten minutes later, he was up and roaring for more. For Claude, the party was always just beginning. He neither asked nor waited to be told what his function was on *Midweek*. He was too busy barging into and being bounced out of all the bars he could locate. That I wouldn't join his Pilgrim's Progress distressed him. He lectured me, bilingually, on the silliness of slaves who cherish their chains. Aware of Sandburg listening unreadably, I stopped Jack Lawson's struggles with entries in a short story contest I wished I hadn't started, and sent him out to represent me as Claude's companion in adventure.

The natural result was that I had to go hunting both of them, along a battle-blazed trail that led finally across the river and the Chicago and Northwestern Railroad yards to Madison and Canal Street, where the new *Daily News* building was under construction but a long way from completion. In Minneapolis I had read Herbert Asbury's articles for the *American Mercury*, later embroidered into his *Gem of the Prairie* (still a perennial seller in paperbacks luridly subtitled *The Story of "The Wickedest City in the United States"*). I had even waded through W. T. Stead's piously prurient *If Christ Came to Chicago*. But nothing I had read or heard about Chicago prepared me for Canal Street.

The men and women who lurched across the sordid paths I trod had squandered wickedness until the devil closed out their overdrawn accounts. Not yet quite eligible for Potter's Field, they drank a witches' brew distilled from alky-cooker garbage, purchased with pennies panhandled from flinching Chicagoans, who rushed home and wrote to *Pro Bono Publico* demanding eradication of all such creatures, Chicago's uninvited and unwanted guests, and then salved their indignation by telephoning rush orders to the corner bootlegger. We had a public inferno of sorts near the Falls of St. Anthony in Minneapolis, where police on patrol walked two by two, spotting stiffs in the gutters, and ambulance interns marked their charts DEAD ON ARRIVAL before they picked up passengers. In Chicago I saw no police, then or ever, on Canal Street.

All doors stood open wide. Passing, glancing in, I felt I walked a Kafka treadmill, hurrying yet standing still. Within each narrow, crowded, odorous room, rag dolls lined one wall, unblinking empty eyes fixed on the unattainable. At counters, arrogantly wealthy buyers surrendered their wealth to sellers, all cast from the same flawed mold, who doled smoke-colored liquid from gallon jugs into unwashed tin cups. In the seventh of these dives, I found my problem from Paris. "Bob! Here is

Claude!" he shouted happily. "Look! Here is me!" His coat was split. His pince-nez lacked a lens. He had been hit on the nose again. "Stand back, bums!" His sweeping D'Artagnan gesture almost floored him. Recovering, he pounded with his cup. "From the bottle of the house, a double double for my boss! Also the same for me! He do not pay, I do not pay! We are gentlemen of the press! We go first-class, for free!"

Audace, toujours l'audace! failed Marshal Ney at Waterloo. It worked magically for this far-wandering scion of his Old Guard, on Canal Street. Sipping the owner's un-cut Scotch, I asked Claude, "What happened to Jack Lawson?" He shrugged and giggled. "I lose him somewhere." He banged with his emptied cup. "Anozzer for my boss! Also 'nozzer *pour moi!*" I said, "What you need is bed." He scoffed. "For why? The evening, she is yet a pup!" Then he folded forward, and I lugged him to a Checker Cab, in which the eagle rested for all of forty winks. Then he sat bolt upright, blinking, hiccough-ing. "Poor Bob. Too bad. Poor Bob." He clung to my lapels to keep from toppling on his face. "You worry all-a-time where you go. I worry where you been. Not Chicago. Only in your corner. What's-a-matter, Bob? You scared or somesing?" He suffered for me. "Poor Bob. Too bad. You got such halova lot catching-up to do!" Then he snored, while I said in sudden realization: "Claude, my fine French featherless old bird, you're right, you're absolutely right!"

Claude had made me see the forest beyond the trees. You didn't have to be called a reporter to be what Smith meant by a newspaperman. What Claude knew by instinct was revela-tion to me: that when your choice is sink or swim, there are better things to do than yell for the lifeguard. Fobbed off on the Paris Bureau, shipped out to Chicago on a one-way ticket, cast away on a hostile shore at 15 North Wells, did he whim-per and hide in the underbrush? *Au contraire*, Claude Caspar-Jordan charged the cannibals — bugles blaring, and a foot-high chip on his shoulder. What about Bob Andrews from Minneapolis? Smith had asked, "Can we get quality? Go out and look for it." I hadn't gone out — until I had to look for Claude.

There was story stuff on Canal Street. Not news. Not small human predicaments to be ballooned into features, banged out to fill empty white space or written in desperation to remind Smith of my existence. There were people on Canal Street. I hadn't talked to them. Claude had. He called them "bums" and made them back off while he bullied the bartender. But they knew him and he knew them. After two weeks, he knew Chicago like a book. I hadn't turned the second page. Whose fault was that? John Craig and Luke Hunt on the city desk had all the news-chasers they wanted. But as long as *Midweek* gave Smith an excuse to keep me on the payroll, I had a *C. D. N.* press card. Claude was getting a lot of mileage out of his. Maybe I'd better do some traveling on mine. Maybe Smith, as well as Claude, thought I had halova lot catching-up to do. All right. I'd start, and see what happened. And I did. And it did.

Young Man Catching Up with Chicago

"The impulse to write springs from a curiosity about human beings, pushed to such an extent that it becomes affection."
—THORNTON WILDER
Interviewed in Chicago
1929

BOB: You write excitingly, but you have a tendency to put HORROR in your stuff. We don't want to give *Midweek* readers the shivers.
—HENRY JUSTIN SMITH
Interoffice memorandum
1929

DEAR ANDREWS: Unfortunately I can't take anything in the form of fiction. . . . Keep trying, please. I'd like very much to have you in the *American Mercury*.
—HENRY LOUIS MENCKEN
In a letter
1930

Down dark Chicago alleys, where I showed my C. D. N. press card at guarded doors, I wasn't surprised to be told, "As long as you're not from the *Trib*, I guess it's okay to let you in." *Tribune* veterans have told me this was because the World's Greatest Newspaper was feared by evildoers, whereas the Paper That Goes Home was not. This may have been so. In any event, wherever my press card got me admitted I immediately established myself as a strictly cash customer by insisting on paying for my standard drink: a double Old Rarity with Perrier. This stamped me as both a spendthrift and a connoisseur. Continuing the imposture, I tipped carefully chosen waiters a dollar, even if all I ordered was a pot of black coffee. The theory was that, unlike barbers, waiters suffer from pent-up conversation. They can never be sure the customer won't quote them to the management, which is invariably their enemy. Now came a naïve youngster who would listen to anything, and keep it to himself.

Further lulling suspicion, I claimed close friendship with Richard Schneider, waiter and resident critic at Schlogl's, who was widely admired by waiters generally, even if they couldn't spell "cat" without two tries. "This must be some rich guy's kid playing like he's Ben Hecht. How else would he get the scratch to throw it away, which reporters don't got and if they got it they wouldn't spend it, the chiselers?" I didn't discourage this guess. And whatever they chose to confide, I was careful not to say, as reporters are wont to do, "You're wrong and I'll tell you how I know."

97

My father did his best to teach me that a gentleman insults only his superiors. He went out of his way to discuss life's disappointments with people most people ignore. He would have gotten on famously with Steve Giadapolous, who waited on tables and pushed drinks, and did some bouncing when the situation called for it, at the Club Alabam, a shabby speakeasy where the featured attraction was Evelyn Nesbit Thaw. She performed every hour on the hour, from 10 P.M. to 4 A.M., re-enacting her Broadway debut in 1905 as "The Girl in the Red Velvet Swing," and telling how and why her husband, Harry K. Thaw, murdered Stanford White on the Madison Square Garden Roof in 1906. I wasn't intrigued by this resurrection of a past much better left buried. Steve was more my speed.

He wanted to own an Athenian Palace ice-cream parlor, but couldn't because he had twenty-eight godchildren depending on him. Whenever one of his compatriots had a first son or daughter, Steve was sure to be chosen as its godfather. He never said "No." By immemorial Old Country custom, he took the child from its mother, who wasn't allowed to attend the christening, and in exchange gave her a twenty-dollar gold piece. He bought the christening robe and paid the priest. During the ceremony, when he announced the baby's name, a messenger ran to the mother with the news. That cost Steve another ten dollars. Thereafter, he was expected to keep the child supplied with shoes, caps, and mittens, and of course send gifts on birthdays and saint's days and at Christmas. It was his bounden duty to see his godchildren through school, find jobs for the boys, arrange good marriages for the girls, and make sure they didn't intermarry. So no matter how industriously Steve cadged tips, cheated the house, rolled drunks, and otherwise augmented his earnings, he was always in debt to the neighborhood loan shark, who also worked for the Syndicate. But when I asked why he didn't stop being such an easy mark, he said, "Tell me what I get out of life can be better than have a big family and still I got no wife to give me trouble?"

And then there was Michael Terence Bloom, a waiter in a Chinatown speakeasy called the Purple Pheasant, where Clyde McCoy played his wah-wah trumpet. Mike was born in Dublin, where his father was cantor in a synagogue. He grew up arguing Irish literature with Oliver St. John Gogarty, knew and disliked George Bernard Shaw, and met and was mystified by James Joyce. One of his first jobs was hawking programs in the Abbey Theater. He had the rarest, rollingest brogue I ever heard. He sent a tithe of his tips to Dr. Chaim Weizmann and the Zionists, and an equal amount to help De Valera harry the Sassenach out of Ireland. He said De Valera mustn't be judged too harshly, for having been born in Brooklyn, not on the Ould Sod. He debated union tactics with Jimmy Petrillo when the future czar of the Federation of Musicians was still a drummer in an orchestra "and missed more beats than he hit," and argued that there's no money in music with Dr. Jules Stein when the future founder of the Music Corporation of America was a part-time violinist "and not too bad for a dentist" — before these two between them controlled just about all the orchestral din in the United States. He was fluent in Gaelic, Mandarin, and Hebrew, and had no regrets about anything. I wish he had lived to have Brendan Behan at one of his tables.

Mike, like most Chicago waiters in those times, carried Old 86 in a convenient pocket. This was the code designation for a Mickey Finn, which itself was Chicago-invented slang for an inexpensive and easily obtainable purgative. Nine customers out of ten, male or female, drank too much and then got too obstreperous, which was no wonder considering what the Syndicate sold. Bouncers were likely to play too rough, and now and then an ejected customer was maimed or killed, and sometimes this caused a little commotion. But powders dumped in

99

a glass, presented by a beaming waiter saying "This one's on the house," sent undesirables packing and were hardly ever lethal, although if you were 86-ed you might long for death until the effect wore off.

Nobody gave me a Mickey, even when I overestimated my capacity. This favoritism, noted by the management, usually resulted in an invitation to sit in the "Amen Corner," the table or tables reserved for Syndicate partners and other distinguished guests. Introducing myself, I would explain that though I was an editor, I had no city desk connections. I guaranteed that nothing I observed, overheard or surmised would show up on Page One. (I didn't feel constrained to explain that this was because I was *non grata* in the newsroom.) Perhaps I overplayed the country boy, but it really didn't matter. The hoodlums were method actors themselves. They played Cops and Robbers for keeps, and their cap-pistols killed, but they clung to Let's Pretend. In point of fact, they were the only inventive melodramatists the papers could rely on. Joe London, crime specialist for *Le Matin* in Paris, was amazed by the ease with which I arranged for him to take notes enrapturedly while Al Capone impersonated Paul Muni impersonating Capone in *Scarface*, with touches of George Raft. In fact, any new audience was more than welcome.

Joe's articles, collected in a book that became a best seller all over Europe, were dedicated "To my Chicago pal Bob Andrews, the *bien ami* of *les gangsteurs*." I was nothing of the sort. So many writers I saw nowhere around at the time have since emerged as declared eyewitnesses to what happened in Chicago that if they hold a convention, it will have to be in Soldiers' Field or the Los Angeles Coliseum. I don't belong to their club. But as for mingling with *les gangsteurs*, if you were there you did that whether you wanted to or not. Gangsterism in Chicago then was an evil you had to live with, like leprosy in the Dark Ages. If you caught the contagion, it was your own fault. If you watched your step, it was possible to walk through the lazaretto uncontaminated.

I still encounter survivors of the Syndicate, at least officially retired from the rackets — income taxes paid up in full, loot invested in blue-chip stocks, daughters married into the *Blue Book* — who know they knew me somewhere. Once I asked one of them who he thought I was. He said, "I used to think you was Mickey Walker with a shave and a haircut and a cane and a Homburg hat." Oldsters who saw the Toy Bulldog in his prime, battling joyously in the ring or in the closest convenient alley, will understand why I took this for a compliment, as it was intended. That does not, however, give me any urge to mix and reheat leftovers from *Rattling the Cup on Chicago Crime* or *X Marks the Spot*.

Walter Winchell, Jack Lait, Lee Mortimer, Robert Stack and his Untouchables, and a lot of others more or less widely known, have already proved to the public's pleasure that Chicago became synonymous with gangsterism because of Al Capone, or the Mafia, or the city's inherent sinfulness, or all three combined. The solution seemed simpler to some of us who were there at the time. Chicago was central. The network of railroads and highways covering the country's heartland, that made Chicago hog-butcher to the world, was also available to the illicit but not at all unpopular bootleg industry. Canada was close. Boats plying the Great Lakes landed cargoes easily and cheaply. There were a lot of gipsy fliers around who flew World War I biplanes by the seat of their pants and could land on a dime in a cow pasture. One enterprising pioneer lined Jenny fuselages with copper, thus creating tanks that held a thousand gallons each of uncut Scotch from Toronto. When dry agents caught onto this dodge and called in Coast Guard patrol planes to intercept the Whiskey Squadron, the pilots executed evasive tactics. If they landed loaded with Scotch, the government would confiscate their aircraft. They could get more whiskey. So they opened petcocks, and sprayed a town below with enough Johnny Walker and Old Smuggler to float a small battleship. Citizens crowded the streets, heads tipped back, thirsty mouths wide open. Next morning, the whole town had a hangover. And the Whiskey Squadron flew north for another cargo.

Such successful free enterprise naturally encouraged hundreds to join the new Gold Rush. Then, just as they did in California in 1849, Big Operators moved in. Let it be noted that all of them came from elsewhere, mostly from Back East, where neither distribution channels nor the buyer market were as satisfying. Italians running little neighborhood stores, members of Unione Siciliana, had sugar in stock and permits to buy more, and sugar was an essential in alky-cooking. They did business with the Syndicate, or were bombed out of business. Murders of Nails Morton and Dion O'Banion made it "Gang War between the Irish and the Jews." But there was no more justice in blaming Chicago's gangster era on one racial element or another in Chicago's seething melting-pot than there was for allegation by San Francisco Vigilantes that Gold Rush crime in California in 1849 was exclusively the fault of Sydney Ducks from Australia. Some of these were lynched and more were deported; and crime was worse than before. Then the burden of guilt was cast on the Chinese. Then fashion changed, and civic leaders philosophized that the Hip Sing and On Leong Tong hatchet wars were really private quarrels and shouldn't be worried about anyhow, since by killing each other the antagonists saved police the bother of arresting them and taxpayers the expense of trying and convicting them. This comforting argument was adapted by Chicagoans, including editors, who said that the more gang murders there were, the sooner gang rule would crumble. Somehow, it didn't seem to work out that way.

Chicago had always been a city for conquest, for immigrants who knew what they wanted and went after it. While Anton Joseph Cermak was mayor, it was pointed out that 20 per cent of all the Czechs in America lived in Chicago, more than in any other city but Prague. We also claimed, at various times, more Irish than Manhattan, more Germans than Frankfurt or Hamburg, more Greeks than Salonika, more Italians than Venice. But Murray Humphries was no more English, despite his assumed name and the accent he thought went with it, than Machine-gun Jack McGurn was Irish, or Willie Bioff a Sicilian. In the empire erroneously described as "Chicago's Underworld," the humpty-dumpty game was up Jim Colosimo, down Tim Murphy and Spike O'Donnell; down Big Jim, up Johnny Torrio; down Torrio, up Al Brown alias Al Capone; and finally, down Capone, destroyed not by the hunters but by his own wolf-pack of all nations. The gelt was up for grabs, and everybody tried to get into the act. Including amateurs.

They were the expendables. Determined to get their share, these slum-reared Horatio Alger climbers set forth to win fame and fortune armed with eight-dollar guns bought or stolen from the neighborhood pawnbroker. Most of them made their first mistake, which was also their last, by poaching on the preserves of established professionals. A few moved up the ladder, though seldom very far. Each echelon in the organization was ruled suspiciously and ruthlessly from the next step above. This had not always been so. Time was when a pioneer could stake a claim and shoot at trespassers until he was left in undisputed ownership. But in the late Twenties, the Syndicate owned everything.

It was not, as far as I could learn, controlled by a board of directors holding regular meetings, keeping office hours, issuing profit-and-loss reports, harkening to minority stockholders. Rather, it was a confederation of utterly conscienceless dictators bound together by two things: their total distrust of each other, which was totally justified, and their adaptation of Benjamin Franklin's maxim that hanging together is preferable to hanging separately. Always, just below, there were thrusters reaching up for more of the loot. Always, there was Mr. Whiskers — the Government at Washington — which could do nothing about purely local crime, but had G-men, T-men and who knew what else eager to throw the book at violators of the Mann Act, income-tax evaders, and even bootleggers. To avoid this called for the best legal advice, which was very expensive, so the Big Guys pooled resources and hired the very best. I talked with mobsters, who insisted seriously that the Syndicate was no more than a businessmen's protective association, formed to improve trade practices and eliminate unethical competition.

I saw how the Syndicate system worked when word went around that the bookies, all of whom worked for the Syndicate, were bleeding and squealing. The first loud squealer was a piglike character called Iffy, because of a talent he had for teasing two-dollar horse-players into doubling their bets with "If it comes up mud at Saratoga . . ." or "If you'da took my yestiddy tip on the fifth at Tanforan . . ." He operated in a candy shop, behind a counter at the back on which there were four telephones. Three were for taking bets from charge-account customers. The fourth connected directly with the Syndicate's layoff bureau. Iffy couldn't read or write. Runners brought slips and called the totals, which he memorized. He reported to the Syndicate at twenty-minute intervals. Its experts balanced the odds and spread the load around the country on long-distance. Police gave the place a wide berth. A couple of loungers out in front kept their eyes on everyone who entered or left, and also on Iffy.

The inside pockets of Iffy's coat were his cash register. On an ordinary day, they held several thousand dollars. One particular morning, the Syndicate's whisperers fed a fixed-race rumor to the suckers. It snowballed, while Iffy stuffed his pockets. Then one of his customer-telephones rang. Answering, he heard a muffled voice. His caller was speaking through a handkerchief, held over a mouthpiece somewhere. "Iffy? That pink necktie don't go nice with your pasty face. Yeah, Iffy. I see you. But you can't see me. Don't hang up, Iffy. That could get you killed. Just listen, Iffy. Listen and look. Two punks just walked in the front door. You see 'em, Iffy? One's out of his pants at the knees. The other should change his shirt and wash his neck. I say they're full of hop. I say they're wearing rods and don't care who they shoot at. Could be I'm wrong. You can find out, Iffy. You can yell. Then either you're dead, or you're not. But you don't play long-shots. Not you, Iffy. So what you're gonna do, you're gonna reach in your pockets and bring out the moolah. All of it, Iffy. Slow, now. Slow and easy. Attaboy, Iffy! Now put it all in that envelope right by your elbow under the house phone. You're stalling, Iffy. The punks are jumpy. Look at 'em, Iffy! They blow quick when they blow. And from where they're standing, they couldn't miss. Attaboy, Iffy! Now hand the envelope to the punk in the dirty shirt. That's right, Iffy. Now just sit there."

Iffy sat. The messengers sauntered out to the street. A wildcat cab pulled up. They got in. The voice on the phone anticipated. "No, Iffy. You can't catch the license number. The cabbie lost his plates somewhere. Still, Iffy. Still. Hold your breath, now, while I count. One, two, three, four, five. . . . They're gone. You can yell now, Iffy." Iffy yelled. And nobody believed him. Syndicate cross-examiners pounded him into quivering pulp. He died still insisting he had been robbed by telephone. A few hours later, the holdup was repeated, far out on the South Side. Then it happened again on the edge of Tower Town, and again in Rogers Park. How it worked was anybody's guess. The caller could have been miles away. The messengers, a different duo for each holdup, might have been hired for a couple of dollars to pick up an envelope and drop it off somewhere, and run out of town when their job was completed. Whoever was working the racket had nothing to fear from the Law. Thieves can't cry "Help, police!" when they're robbed. However, the Syndicate had its own operatives and enforcers.

The secret adversary toyed with them. More and more, it was obvious that he must be on the inside. Suspicion spread. Guards at a bookie joint on Halsted Street shot and killed a suspect who turned out to be a Syndicate agent sent to check on them. The take fell off, not because the crop of suckers lessened but because bookies were quitting in terror both of the voice on the telephone and of being third-degreed after the fact. Then an informer named a name. He couldn't be believed. The man he accused was only a step from the top in the Syndicate. Another informer was used, to bait a trap. He whispered, "Eddie Garth says to meet him at the Old Bohemia. He says you better be there. He says he's got something to sell. He says if you don't buy it, the bookie bosses will." By the act of going to keep the rendezvous, the accused convicted himself to the Syndicate's satisfaction. A single tommy gun burst took care of him, and of the informer against him. It was probably the same Syndicate gunner who killed the go-between that same night. This, in the gangster code, was tying up the package with a bow on top.

But nothing discouraged the strange desire of hangers-on to mutter secrets to outsiders. One furtive fellow haunted me, because no one else would humor his delusion that he was an undercover reporter. He had been born and brought up on what the papers called Death Avenue. Every gang of juvenile delinquents had its tag-along patsy, mocked and kicked, cowardly, cringingly grateful if one of his idols deigned to send him on an errand. This particular patsy, grown up and married, clerked in a West Side neighborhood grocery store, employed by his father-in-law because no one else would hire him. He spied on hoodlums, old acquaintances, not for pay but because to him they were still D'Artagnans ten feet tall, and he could tell me, "I knew them when . . ." He brought tales about his heroes until the evening when one of them stabbed him to death with an icepick, because his adoration caused him to blurt out: "I told the guys at the papers they don't know you like I know you."

And there were others who hung around too long where they didn't belong to begin with. One of them died in the Valentine's Day Massacre. He wasn't a hoodlum. He never did anything illegal, or even sly. He had a nice wife, a nice office, a nice practice. But he fell into the habit of dropping by for coffee with Bugs Moran's beer-runners, so he could listen to their lies, which he believed implicitly. The last time he dropped by, he was putting sugar in his coffee when the alley door of the garage slid open and three policemen entered. At least they wore police uniforms. They lined him up with six mobsters, faces to the wall, and played their tommy guns back and forth like garden hoses, hemstitching the seven with several hundred slugs. The innocent lived the longest, not long enough to say anything to detectives (who were strangely slow in arriving), but long enough to gasp while he died, to Charley Ford from the *Daily News*: "They were cops. Real cops. Real cops."

That left one living witness. A dog. Chained to the wall, bleeding from a bullet-crease along its back, maddened by shock and the smell of blood, it was one of fifty German shepherds a schemer sold to the Syndicate as night guards for the beer-drops. Selecting dogs for size and savagery, he fenced off a rented section of forest land in Wisconsin, inside of which he turned the animals loose to live off the wilderness and each other through four winter months. During this time they reverted to wild beasts. In the spring, he rounded up the survivors and collected five hundred dollars each for these prize specimens. With his profits, he built a hideaway for hoodlums on the lam, and charged them one thousand dollars a week. (One of his later customers was John Dillinger. The last I heard of him, he had gone home to Czechoslovakia, just in time to be caught, robbed of his fortune in Yankee dollars, and thrown into a concentration camp by Communists taking over the country.)

The dog in the North Clark Street garage was a magnificent creature, and Charley Ford was a dog fancier. So he finished shooting pictures that were much too ghastly to be printed in The Paper That Goes Home, and then risked being chewed to shreds, muzzling the dog with his trench coat, tying its legs together with his belt and necktie, before he unsnapped its chain. When detectives and Opposition reporters and photographers arrived, Charley and the dog were gone. He sat on his Exclusive for ten days, while he kept the dog caged in his bathroom, bathing elsewhere because gentling the animal was a very slow process. At last he could touch its head with his hand, without being bitten. Even then, he chained the dog to the steering-wheel of his stripped-down Kissel Kar roadster when he started downtown to 15 North Wells, bringing in his Exclusive. As far as he could, he drove on quiet side streets. Turning finally into the Loop, he came to a corner where a policeman, just transferred to Traffic from Homicide, saw his Press *insigne* and waved him through a red light. The dog saw the policeman. It lunged. The chain snapped. The dog did its wild best to kill a cop. Whether it attacked an enemy seen before, or only a uniform, it was shot. And so there was no story.

That is how things went in Chicago. At a bar whose operator never wholly recovered from shock that stunned him the first time I said that, though I carried a press card, I insisted on paying for my Old Rarity with Perrier, I sat four stools away from three thugs who would have been fired for hamming it up if they played the scene the same way in a Grade C movie. It was hard not to laugh outright at their hoarse stage-whispered imitation of Hollywood. FIRST HENCHMAN: *"Yeah.*

That Frankie, all of a sudden he makes like little Caesar." SEC-
OND HENCHMAN: *"Yeah. Somebody should talk to Frankie."*
THIRD HENCHMAN: *"Yeah. First they should break his arms
and legs, the louse, like in a movie I see last night."* FIRST
HENCHMAN: *"Yeah. You see the one where the Mob shoots
Nails Morton's stupid horse because he falls off of it and
breaks his stupid neck?"* SECOND HENCHMAN: *"Yeah. I always
thought Nails was maybe pushed."* THIRD HENCHMAN: *"Yeah.
I wonder what those Hollywood muzzlers smoke in their
pipes?"* FIRST HENCHMAN: *"Yeah. So let's go see Frankie."*

So they went, and two mornings later, Frankie MacErlane
was fished out of the Drainage Canal. They had broken his
arms and legs, one at a time, before they stood him on his
head, still alive, in a barrel of cement. This wasn't particularly
new or novel. But Frankie got his start fixing out-of-state dog
races and cheating the local bookies. So beside his barrel on the
muddy bottom lay a racing greyhound, shot between the eyes.
This inspired touch of the macabre gave the murderers many
clippings for their scrapbooks, which like most mobsters they
kept proudly. In fact at least three Big Shots besides the Big
Guy subscribed to New York's most honored clipping bureau,
and pasted every item and editorial, no matter what it called
them, in volumes one of which (I handled it) was bound in
human skin.

They had a special fraternal feeling for outsiders who, like
them, thrived on publicity. For some time, they feted a visitor
they dubbed the Texas Terror. He took their adulation seriously, and to a degree they were sincere. They called Louie
Alterie "Billy The Kid" after he invested some of his loot in
a ranch in Colorado. They quarreled boastfully about their
trigger prowess compared with that of Wild Bill Hickok or
Jesse James, though most of them couldn't hit a barn door at
ten paces. They called the Texas Terror a nutty old creep until
he showed them the notches on his gun-butt. Suddenly, they
realized he wasn't lying. To me, he was as fraudulent as Buf-

109

falo Bill or Al Jennings . . . until I checked his clippings. He was a killer, all right. If not a homicidal maniac.

He had been a Panhandle farmer, retired and living in town from royalties from an oil strike on his land, when seven swindlers working out of Chicago ganged up on him. He had been honest until then, only because he wasn't smart enough to steal. They showed him how. With eyes wide open, he plunged into a crooked scheme. Then when the cheaters cheated him, he couldn't comprehend why local authorities declined to hunt them down and hang them out of hand. He got a back-country sheriff to deputize him, bought two hogleg .45s, and embarked on a personal vendetta, paying his way by lecturing on his quest and shooting his guns at tin cans. He didn't mind his meager existence. For the first time in his life, he enjoyed the luxury of being feared.

He caught one of the swindlers in Florida, and killed him "trying to escape." He repeated this when he caught another of the seven in Louisiana. Twice, his story got him off. Tears choked him while he dramatized how his poor wife died in his arms, of shock and heartbreak, after the scoundrels robbed them. Actually, she was dead of abuse and overwork before his oil wells came in. But the man no longer knew he lied. In Chicago's dives, he fondled four notches in his gun-butt and giggled "Three more to go!" The mobsters grew uneasy. No telling when the crazy old creep might shoot off his cannons. So they bought him a ticket to Kansas City, where they said their connection would finger another of his enemies. The man he shot in the back this time was actually an East St. Louis hoodlum who had never been near Texas, but was in wrong with the Syndicate. Intermittently thereafter, crime magazines, which all literate mobsters read, reported the progress of the Texas Terror's manhunt. He was still at large, and had six notches in his gun butt, the last I heard of him. "The crazy old creep," the hoodlums said, "he's nuts, but, baby, has he got that old moxie!"

Moxie, to them, is what makes a youngster bite his lip until it bleeds, but refuse to cry, when he gets his skull laid open with a shinny-stick. They knew they didn't have it; so they praised yet patronized its possessors. Another facet of their weird juvenility caused them to take delight in the offstage misadventures of Milton Berle, who has made a vocation of being accused, and accusing himself, of being "The Thief of Bad Gags." Other comedians yearn to play Hamlet. Berle longs to be hailed as a card-trick wizard. In a Tower Town club that fronted for a gambling room in which every game was rigged, Berle bucked the tiger at blackjack, betting twenty-dollar bills. The dealer stacked his deck too clumsily to fool others at his table. They dropped out. Finally, it was Berle alone against the house. After five hands, the dealer knew the location of every card in the deck. So did several watchers. It would, however, have been bad manners, not to say asking to be hit on the head, to tell Berle he was beaten before he placed his bets. He doubled up, and went on losing. Then, as the dealer shuffled awkwardly, arranging his aces and tens in sequence, Berle's hand shot out and closed on the dealer's wrist. "I'll take those cards!" Berle grated. I looked for the nearest exit, realizing I'd be trampled in the rush. Two hoodlums with bulges under their starched shirtfronts moved in. Berle didn't notice them. He was showing the dealer a card trick, the kind the life of the party performs at the P. T. A. election supper. I doubt if he ever had a more selective audience. His trick completed and applauded, he handed the cards back to the dealer, said "Lay 'em out!" and went on blissfully being robbed.

And there was the orchestra leader, Guy Lombardo. With his Royal Canadians, he played for dancing at Al Quodbach's Granada on the South Side. I listened to their slightly off-key saxophones on radio one night. Suddenly, the Sweetest Music This Side of Heaven was drowned by loud hubbub. Tables crashed over. Gunshots popped. Women screamed. The broadcast stopped. A studio stand-by pianist struck up my friend Jimmy McHugh's "Sunny Side of the Street." Page One next morning banner-lined 3 *SLAIN IN SOUTH SIDE SHOOTING FRAY*. One of the Syndicate's gunmen, annoyed because his girl said he was too drunk to dance, spied three other hoodlums on the far side of the floor. He had no quarrel with them; or, if he had, no one ever found out what it was about. But he pushed past the dancers, opened fire, and pumped lead until his Luger was empty. Then, sobered, asking loudly, "Now why did I do that?" he threw his gun at the bar mirror, smashing it, and walked out, unmolested.

There were three hundred customers in the place. All of them, they told police, were in the powder room when the shooting occurred. Lombardo and his Royal Canadians, however, were indubitably on the orchestra stand. It was very embarrassing. Embarrassment ended when the Lombardo orchestra accepted a contract to play at the Roosevelt Hotel in New York. "This Lombardo," I was told, "is smart. He's very smart." Another accolade. Incidentally, the triple murderer was not arrested, or even interrogated. He was, though, killed a few weeks later, not by the police. The Syndicate frowned on hired hands who went trigger-happy.

Those days, in Chicago, you had to dream up some new gimmick to get yourself well known. Unless you were Pete Penovich. He couldn't improve on the simple fact that all of his seven sisters were cloistered nuns. Even after he called Al Capone "yellow" to his face, in an argument in Cicero, the Syndicate kept Pete on the payroll, because no one doubted what he told me about himself, the first time we discussed each other: "I ain't honest, but I'm honorable." His business was crooked gambling, but his personal code was "Pete don't lie." All mobsters stole from each other. All but Pete. He couldn't go to Confession, but he never missed eight-o'clock Mass. He kept a missal and a rosary in the safe with his marked cards and loaded dice.

Some Ivy League college graduates with M.A.'s in economics joined forces to gamble on futures, on the Board of Trade. According to their Ten Year Plan, they would be millionaires at thirty-five. They would then select wives who passed tests already charted, settle in Winnetka, enter politics, and clean up Chicago. And the first part of their program progressed perfectly. Soon they were giving statements to Financial Editors, explaining how easy it was to get rich in competition with illiterates. But departing from their plan, they leased and lavishly decorated penthouses atop two tall adjoining apartment buildings facing Lincoln Park, connected these with a covered bridge, issued gold keys to unlock ground-floor doors of the private elevators they installed, and celebrated success from market closing to market opening.

Life was a bowl of cherries, until their elegant eyries palled and they went out on the town, and made the mistake of bucking Pete Penovich's games. When he called on them to pay or else, one loser fell or jumped from the covered bridge. The others signed their penthouse leases over to Pete. The following Monday, he opened his games at his new address. One penthouse offered food, drink, and entertainment by violins, along with blackjack, chuckaluck, dice, and roulette, ten-dollar limit. Across the bridge, all betting limits were off. But in both departments, Pete demanded quiet decorum. Six feet two and stronger than Sandow, he needed no bouncer to enforce house rules. In his youth, he served two stretches for felonious assault with intent to do great bodily harm. Now, pursuant to a vow to his saintly sisters, he walked as softly as he spoke, courteously called all women "Ma'am," prohibited profanity, and ran his place so well that his customers hardly minded being robbed.

I sat with him one midnight, discussing a *History of the Popes* I had located at his request. The alcoholic only son of a

Detroit potentate burst out in obscenities at the blackjack table. Pete went to him quickly, and suggested *sotto voce* that apology to ladies present was in order. The offender, his match in size and weight, described the probable profession of those he saw from where he stood. Suddenly, Pete's hand gripping his necktie and shirtfront half-lifted him, bore him backward to an open window, held him helpless over a twelve-story drop. He knew no Latin, but in a few seconds Pete had him reciting the *Confiteor*. I never heard *Mea culpa* cried more fervently. At last, Pete personally frog-walked the culprit to the elevator, and threw him into it in a sobbing heap. He said, and I believed, that he gave his cut of that night's take to one of Cardinal Mundelein's youth charities, in atonement for the venial sin of losing his temper.

"But you can't print that." Nobody had to tell me this. The *Daily News* glorified no home-grown Robin Hoodlums. Smith left it to the Opposition to print such stuff as a lady reporter's breathless exclusive interview with Al Capone, at the Lexington Hotel on the edge of the South Side Levee, where he lolled in a thronelike chair under framed portraits of his three favorite Americans, George Washington, Abraham Lincoln, and Mayor Big Bill Thompson. "*Why, lady,*" Beauty quoted the Beast, "*I'd rather the papers didn't print a line about me. No brass bands for Big Al. There's nothing but grief, to be in the spotlight like I am. If I was plain Izzy Polatski, you wouldn't catch me standing in the gutter hoping to get a peek at Big Al. I'd tend to my business and let him tend to his. All I do is supply a demand that's pretty damned popular. The very guys that make my business good are the ones that yell so loud and make a laughingstock of the city. They claim I'm not on the legit. Why, lady, nobody's on the legit, and everybody knows it.*"

Smith disagreed. Progressively less wide-eyed as my Chicago After Dark research continued, I talked with him sometimes about the half-world he never entered, and soon got over being surprised by his knowledge of its geography, *mores*, and inhabitants. Copy came to him about Capone's fan mail: letters, cables, Valentines, from Europe and Africa and the farthest Far East. "A woman in London offers to pay his passage to England if he'll run over and kill off her noisy neighbors." Not for the *Daily News*. Nor was he impressed by Capone's alleged generosity. "He never gives hat-check girls less than ten dollars, newsboys less than five dollars, waiters less than one hundred dollars." Smith said dirty money doesn't care who owns it. In 1928 Capone circulated a press release in which he announced that since arriving in Chicago from Brooklyn, in 1920, he had "fooled away seven million bucks." Some of this went for gem-encrusted solid gold cigarette cases and diamond-studded belt buckles, presented to hangers-on somewhat as King Arthur conferred the badge of knighthood. But Smith, who blue-penciled such reports as this, exploded finally — when city desks were notified that "Again this year, Big Al has arranged for Cicero merchants to supply all needy families with clothing, groceries, and coal, as his annual Christmas gift."

Unofficially, Smith let me look into this. I wandered in strange streets. Nobody wanted to answer questions. Nobody threatened me, but I did not walk alone. Playing cat-and-mouse with my escorts, I lost them for a while, and found a grim little neighborhood grocer who spat when I mentioned Capone. From him, and from a very few others, I gathered my own story behind the story. I swore to name no names, since reprisal would follow if I did. I went back to Wells Street shivering, not only because the winter wind bit deep. Smith didn't put my by-line on what I turned in, and for once that was all right with me. For it told how Big Al worked his Christmas charities. His mobsters simply passed the word to poor little storekeepers whose profits were pennies at best: "You got a choice for Christmas. You give to the Big Guy's party, or we plant a pineapple in your crummy joint." Proof that Capone took all the credit, for not one cent in cash, was no surprise to Smith. But he pointed out what I had been too stirred up to take into account. Printing the truth wouldn't hurt Capone. It would just get some Mom and Pop stores blown up, some old women and cripples sent to the hospital, to illustrate the folly of speaking anything of him but praise. All we could do was let the Opposition hang holiday wreaths on him, while we gave him no publicity, *pro* or *contra*, to paste in his foot-thick scrapbook.

He was also cheated of *Daily News* acclaim when the Syndicate went collegiate. I told Smith that Murray Humphries, alias "The Camel," was sporting a Phi Beta Kappa key, actually acquired from a pawnshop, and Machine-gun Jack McGurn had a new coonskin coat lined in crimson satin. Frankie Nitti and Greasy Thumb Guzik lectured intimates in the Amen Corner on the intricacies of the Minnesota Shift. Bottles Capone predicted his nephew would be a Notre Dame halfback. (He wasn't.) All this, I told Smith, because the Mob had taken over the football betting pools. I thought *Midweek* should blow the lid off. I had a cover-page layout ready, featuring WILL GANGSTERS CAPTURE COLLEGE SPORTS? My idea was to hit with this the Wednesday before the Big Ten's Big Game. But Smith said, "No, Bob. No." What I proposed, he said, was advertising the Syndicate couldn't buy and we wouldn't sell. "The readers it would shock don't gamble anyhow. The ones it won't shock will steal the school-lunch money from the sugar bowl, and run around begging somebody to take it away from them." Smith sighed. "One of the things a newspaper can never hope to do," he said, "is convince its readers that nobody beats the odds but the odds-makers."

Then ticket scalpers held out a block of box seats on the fifty-yard line, alongside those reserved for regents and deans and distinguished guests including senators and judges, at an otherwise sold-out college game. After play got under way, during a time-out on the field, the Syndicate's overlords, en masse, entered on the far side of the stadium. Parading across the chalk-lined turf, shouldering ushers and police aside, passing bottles around, swearing at their women, they swarmed into their boxes. In his own good time, the Big Guy signaled, like another Caligula, for the gladiators to resume the fray. The show, according to the Opposition, was better than the game.

Smith was not amused. Nor was the *Daily News*. Our story dramatized deliberate insult to decency, and pictured the Big Guy as exactly what he was: a swaggering, insufferable boor. It listed aliases and summarized the criminal records of his guests of both sexes. And as Smith predicted wryly, this raised no rumpus whatever in Chicago. As far as I know, the spectacle was not recalled by any reporter covering Capone's income-tax-evasion trial in 1931. But I have it from Pablo Katigbak, who was there, that among the judges at the game was one who sat in judgment when counsel for Capone cried bitterly in Federal Court: "If this defendant's name was anything else, he would not be on trial here. But because of what it is, Chicago and the Government will hear of nothing but *'Delenda est Capone!'* "

« 2 »

Chicago hardly heard of Dollie Wedburg, and not at all from me. I change his surname somewhat even now, because he was my friend. The neatness that got him dubbed "Dollie" in boyhood summarized the man. He was born with a faculty for always looking as if he had bathed, shaved, put on fresh linen and a suit delivered by his tailor only half an hour ago. His mind was as fastidious as his manner, except for his habit of leaving certain phrases uncompleted. A peculiar person, to him, was simply "a peculiar." That he was this himself suggests no inhibition or inversion. It was part of the lifetime

117

plan he pursued as thoughtfully as he dressed for the role in which he had cast himself.

In the Sixth Grade in East St. Louis, he knew more mathematics than his teacher. A hophead gunman killed his father, who ran a cigar store as front for a bookmaker. Dollie had to leave school, but went on educating himself. He worked first as runner for a policy racketeer. He was never arrested, or even questioned by the cop on the corner. He never touched a gun. He had total recall for figures, and simplified comlicated accounts so quickly and accurately that soon the Syndicate's representatives put him in charge of both sets of their books: those on the basis of which they paid their income tax, and the others that told the truth. Somehow, he convinced them that honesty, at least with Mr. Whiskers, was plain common sense. Before long, he set up as a consulting expert. Working for clients whose criminal records were as long as his arm, he continued to keep his own hands clean.

It was said he could walk into any mob-owned speakeasy or bookie joint and walk out ten minutes later with a mental chart showing to the penny how much the place should be making, and how much its operators were stealing. It was a perilous way to earn a living. However, nobody bothered Dollie. He had too many powerful clients who needed him. Bribes budged him no more than threats. He was offered all sorts of silent partnerships. Always, he said, "No." In the profession he had created, he had to be, and was, above suspicion. He walked alone. His fees, already high, went higher, while his reputation spread. His success, and the man himself, fascinated many women. None entangled him. "The ones that want me, I can't use," he told me in Chicago. "The ones I'd want, I'm wrong for."

Initially, he was brought to Chicago to arbitrate between two high-ups in the Syndicate, whose running feud had contributed considerably to the count of four hundred and ninety-seven gang murders between mid-1926 and late 1929. A

118

dapper Daniel in something worse than a lions' den, Dollie
went about his business as calmly as if he were merging a
couple of country banks. The trouble he ran into was not with
the two antagonists. He handled them so smoothly that each
was convinced the other was going to get the worst of it. But
if he could bring about a truce, there would be a consolidation
of forces, and that meant unemployment for some thugs
whose only gainful trade was mayhem. One hoodlum loudly
declared he would personally run the intruder out of town.
"This phony pretty boy" — he vowed — "I'll make him crawl
all the way back to East St. Louis!"

Dollie's employers saw no percentage in protecting him. In
their philosophy, the man in the middle put himself there,
and it is up to him whether he fights or runs. Dollie did
neither. The hoodlum hounded him, insulted him, threatened
him. Dollie seemed to pay no heed. His imperturbability drove
the persecutor to reckless lengths.

Harry Richman was opening at the Chez Paree, for
his thirty-ninth engagement, having earned more than six
hundred thousand dollars from his appearances there. While
Richman was putting on the Ritz before a packed house, and
in the presence of many witnesses (some of them respectable),
the hoodlum accosted Dollie, who sat alone at a ringside table.
Yanking Dollie to his feet, flicking a switch-knife within inches
of Dollie's unreadable eyes, the persecutor swore: "If you're
anywhere in Chicago twenty-four hours from now, I'll carve
my initials on your pretty face, so deep they'll never come off!"
The management broke this up, and Dollie returned to watching and listening to Richman doing "Shake Hands with a
Millionaire."

It was his custom to go to the theater two or three nights a
week, always buying two seats on the aisle, halfway back. He
put his coat and hat on one, and dozed in the other, rousing
only if something on the stage appeared to merit brief attention. The night after the knife threat, he came out of a big

vaudeville house, at the end of a bill so usual that he had slept clear through it. Under bright marquee lights, he saw his Nemesis, who came at him cursing, shoving men and women aside. Many of them saw the switch-knife flash, just before Dollie drew a snub-nosed .38 and fired five times. Then he walked a block to Police Headquarters, told the Desk Sergeant, "I had to kill a man in self-defense," and handed over his gun and his permit to carry it for personal protection, which had been issued to him four weeks before, when the hoodlum first threatened him publicly.

He was not even booked. His record stayed spotless. The Coroner's verdict had to be "Justifiable Homicide." And he never needed to carry or use a gun again. Word went around that, for a month, he had practiced an hour every morning in the basement at his apartment house, pumping bullets at varying ranges into a plywood cutout the size and shape of the man he knew he would have to kill. A small target was painted on it. The bull's-eye was precisely where he had put five slugs in the hoodlum's belly, so neatly that the palm of the police surgeon's hand covered all five bullet-holes. And, hearing of this, Dollie's dissident employers accepted his verdict settling their dispute, with no further argument. In fact, they offered him a bonus. "Anything, pal. Name it and you got it." He said he would take a loan, and told them how much he wanted. They backed off precipitately. "With me," Dollie said, "a deal is a deal." They thought about the hoodlum, and the target on which Dollie practiced. Undoubtedly it also occurred to them that he knew more about the ins and outs of their setups than they knew themselves. "You're rough," they told Dollie. "You sure do figure. And you don't ever miss. Okay. You got your money. Now what are you gonna do with it?" That, Dollie told them calmly, was his business, not theirs.

Then he built a super-speakeasy, which he called "999." I met his erstwhile employers in the place, the night it opened.

"That Dollie," they told me, "he could have anything. And what does he wind up with? A saloon!" Then Dollie joined us, and quietly ordered them to get out and stay out. "I always wanted," he said, "to know nice people. That's the only kind this store will let in. There will be one joint in Chicago where the clean don't have to mingle with the dirty. This is it." And against all precedent, he also banned unescorted ladies of the evening, and reporters, in that order.

He made the top floor his home, the first he ever had. Bookshelves and closets, both filled, lined the walls. Windows were iron-shuttered. The doors were backed with sheet steel. He entertained no guests. When he closed 999, on the dot at 3 A.M., he went upstairs alone. He was down again at nine, when he checked meat and sundries delivered for the kitchen, and bar supplies from the Syndicate. His agreement called for nothing but the pure McCoy. Of course the Syndicate tried to cheat. He sent back the bootleg stuff, and demanded, and got, the best liquor sold anywhere in Chicago. His prices made first-time patrons gasp. If they complained, he tore up the check and said pleasantly: "Please don't come in again." Brawls were part of the show in most speakeasies. He employed no bouncers, and none of his waiters carried Mickey Finns — but in Dollie's store you behaved as a guest should or out you went, so quickly and quietly that no one noticed your departure. No policeman, in or out of uniform, and no Prohibition enforcement agent, ever got in, or drew a bribe for going away. In sum, 999 was a peculiar, the proper setting for its proprietor.

After seven weeks, Dollie sent his financial backers certified checks for what they had loaned him, plus 20 per cent. They claimed their *droit de seigneur*: to go on sharing the profits, as they did from all other enterprises in which they invested any money. Dollie said again, "With me, a deal is a deal." They sent hoodlums with veiled warnings. These never got past the front door. They decided to bomb the place, but then thought better of it. Leading representatives of Chicago's Founding Families, the nice people Dollie always wanted to know, were regulars at 999. Some of them were also members of the newest Clean Up Chicago Committee. Showering them with pineapples, just to square accounts with Dollie, could be going a bit too far. People might talk.

So someone sent for a former Broadway producer who had been making money for the Mob, running its hot spots in New York. He rebuilt three Tower Town brownstones, spending four times what it cost to open 999. The resulting Gold Coast Club was as brassy as the throng of free-loaders invited to its private preview. Reporters were welcomed. So were all the others on Dollie's No ADMITTANCE list. The owners proclaimed that their new joint would beat him down to Nickel Number One in no time. Then they got drunk, and started shooting each other. Next morning, headlines screamed. Pressured by Dollie's regulars on the Reform Committee, the police had to padlock the Gold Coast Club before it ever had a cash customer. That night, business was better than ever at 999.

The baffled Big Guys gave up. Dollie, they said, had the devil's luck. He said the secret was Danger at his heels. He was not being literary. Danger was his dog. Dollie's only outdoor exercise was a daily thirty-minute constitutional that never took him more than a dozen blocks away from 999. He knew a tommy gun might chatter at him any time, from any alley's mouth, but he never looked back over his shoulder. One day, he had taken a new turn, and had come to a pet store. Through the window, he saw a lean, austerely handsome white pit-bull that stood oblivious to the yapping of a litter of puppies in the adjoining cage. Dollie and the dog considered each other. Something strange occurred. I like to think they decided simultaneously that they were two of a kind.

Flourishing Kennel Club papers, the pet store owner asked for twice what the pit-bull was worth. Dollie paid, in hundred-dollar bills. He opened the cage. The white dog's cropped ears flattened. It growled softly, through bared teeth. "He's mean," the pet store owner warned. "He's been hit by people. Lay a hand on him, you'll lose it. I tell you, Mister, that dog's dangerous." Dollie asked, "Who likes to be hit?" and told the dog: "Okay. So your name is Danger. Come on." The dog didn't move. He reached to take hold of its spiked collar. The dog snarled. He slapped its sensitive pink nose, back and forth, hard, with his open hand. Then he turned away. The dog's leap at him froze. The pet owner whispered, "My God, my God!" Danger stepped out of the cage. Dollie chose a chain-leash, and snapped it on. Danger neither growled nor strained against the chain. They went back to 999 side by side.

A week passed before any of us knew Dollie no longer lived alone. Late one afternoon, when like other regulars I had dropped in for a decent Scotch and some conversation, man and dog came downstairs together. I never saw Dollie again, but once, when Danger was not at his heels. As far as I could tell, the dog chose the vantage point on the second floor landing from which, from then on, it inspected everyone entering below. Foolish women, though they had learned not to thrust themselves at Dollie, cried, "Oh, the beautiful dog!" Danger neither snarled nor fawned. But teeth showed, if a man's hand went toward him. I caught Dollie watching the dog when first-time customers came up the stairs. I became convinced he trusted Danger's intuition equally with his own.

Twice each evening, the dog left his post, went behind the bar, selected an egg, and ate fastidiously. A bus-boy, for a joke, put a spoiled egg in the box. Danger bit into it, and then calmly bit the bus-boy. Dollie paid damages out of Danger's bank account, in which he deposited one hundred dollars every Saturday "in case the animal outlasts me." He called me at the office one morning. "Let's have lunch." Any invitation from Dollie was unusual. I expected almost anything. It turned out that he wanted my expert comment on the man-styled coonskin coat he had just had made to Danger's measure. The dog's opinion was clear. It loathed the thing. The Windy City's winters are cruel to man and beast, but Danger wanted no sissified wrapping covering his sleek hide.

"I buy him something even Mrs. Rockefeller McCormick's hounds don't have," Dollie said, "and what happens? He hates me. What kind of a dog is that?" He was grinning. This in itself was a rare sight. "Well, he lets me know where he stands, and where I stand. Would I get that from a woman? Or a man?" That was as close as I ever heard him come to overt sentimentality. Cynics called Dollie and His Dog the season's best New Act. It may have been that to begin with. But nothing that had to do with Danger was aimed at the newspapers. I suggested that Charley Ford, the top C. D. N. news-cameraman, would be happy to put the dog and his coonskin coat on Page One. Dollie simply looked at me. "All right," I said immediately. "Forget it."

That night, Dollie showed me what was left of the coat. "We met some mongrels on Clark Street," Dollie said. "They gave my boy a bad time. He yanked the leash loose, and took care of them. It did his wardrobe no good, but he feels fine." Next day, Dollie ordered two new coats, "one for a spare," of much more expensive short-haired white beaver. "We've worked out a deal," Dollie told me. "We meet a dog, the dog makes cracks, my boy waits while I take his coat off, I hold it while he chews up the wise guy, he comes back, I put the coat on him; he gives me no argument. He's enjoying himself. He don't know it yet, but he's due to run out of opposition any day." Then, on another night, Danger was missing from his post on the second floor landing. It was late, but Dollie was away, none of his people knew where.

Leaving, I met him in front, getting out of a taxicab. "The stupid animal," he said. "The stupid, stupid animal." Customers, coming or going, called "Hi, Dollie!" For once, he was discourteous. "The dog," he told me harshly, "the damned.

fool dog chased a mongrel out in the street. And got hit by a car. It didn't stop. I took the stupid animal to the vet's. Look at me." There was blood on his overcoat, and on his hands. "The damned fool dog," he said, "it's dying." Suddenly, he ran from me, into 999. I followed, in time to see him disappearing up the stairs. Whitey, the head bartender, asked, "What hit Dollie?" The best advice I could give was "Don't ask him." In fact, for the next ten days no one talked much to Dollie about anything. We saw little of him, until he appeared one evening carrying Danger in his arms.

"The stupid vet gave up on him," Dollie told me tersely. "He says 'I fixed his bones but I can't make him walk.' He said, 'If you don't take the animal home, he'll think himself to death.' How do you like that? This is 'home'?" He had a mat and pillows placed on the second floor landing. Danger lay there, seemingly lifeless. But when a first-time customer entered below, the sleek head lifted. Dollie saw this. He told Whitey, "Give the animal an egg." Danger wasn't interested. The egg lay there untouched, at closing time. Dollie started up the stairs, not looking back. The gaunt white body arched and steadied. Each step was a mountain, but Danger neither whimpered nor stopped climbing. And 999 was back to normal, for a while.

Then we had the incident of the Prince, who made a profession of being a White Russian refugee. Officially, he was a sculptor. Actually, he had talent. The portrait heads he made were idealized but recognizable. However, he had to play the social game to get commissions. Also, he was lazy. One night, when Danger's limp was almost gone, Dollie stopped the sculptor on the stairs. "You owe me a big tab," Dollie said. Volubly, in three languages, the Prince promised payment as soon as he finished and collected for a bust he was about to start. "We're talking about now," Dollie said. "I want a head of the animal, in white marble, to put over the bar. If it's good enough, your tabs are on the house." The sculptor objected indignantly. "I am an artist for people, not for animals. If I do a dog, the people will laugh." Dollie said, "I won't laugh." The sculptor turned from Dollie's eyes, to stare at Danger. "I'll try," he said finally. "I'll try."

He tried so hard — at first in fear, then suddenly seized by an honest fervor new in his experience — that his head of a dog got him a dozen commissions from prominent people. Danger in marble above the bar, Danger on duty at the stairs, brought curious customers who stayed to spend much more than they had intended. Cynics scoffed admiringly: "That Dollie. Always there with the angle." Surprisingly, Dollie said the store was getting too crowded. During Danger's convalescence, he had been reading even more than usual. He told me, "I think I'll travel." He added, oddly thoughtful: "The way I figure it, there comes a time when it's time to move." I couldn't imagine 999 with Dollie and Danger away. I asked if the Syndicate was crowding him again. He left me without answering. Whatever he had on his mind, a woman pushed him to decision.

Fifteen years before, she had married an ambitious immigrant. She was Old Chicago Family, but penniless. He had a little money, and a promoter's flair. She taught him table manners, improved his English, introduced him to the heirs of earlier immigrants, now in the *Social Register*. Their marriage was all business, and she planned policy for the firm. In ten years, they were rich. Using the connections she arranged, he pyramided holding companies. All at once, they headed committees, were in the receiving line at exclusive affairs lengthily reported in the Society Pages. She told her husband on their fifteenth anniversary: "Well, here we are, where I told you we'd be if you listened to me." He said, "And I'm sick of listening to you. I'm in love with a girl who's young and pretty. She can give me what you never gave. I want a divorce."

Her heart didn't break. But she said she had earned exactly

half of all he owned, and unless she got the full amount, in cash or bankable equivalent, she would take him into court, and that would cost him a great deal more. Overweening conceit would not permit him to admit he was a woman-made success. So the newspapers were presented with a contested divorce case that even the *Daily News* could not dispose of in a few staid paragraphs buried in Section Three. Despite all his attorneys could do, she turned the trial into a circus, with her husband as chief clown. On the witness stand, naming names, she coined a phrase that crackled like Chinese firecrackers in the Opposition's headlines. Chicago, she said contemptuously, had only a sausage and sauerkraut aristocracy.

Within twenty-four hours, I had four hastily written articles on my desk, with the lady's testimony for text. Each told a slightly different version of the legend that when the Infanta of Spain was invited to the 1893 World's Fair, more properly called the Columbian Exposition, it was taken for granted that Mrs. Potter Palmer, Chicago's challenge to New York's Mrs. Astor, would be her official hostess. But the Infanta asked, "Why should I be the guest of an innkeeper's wife?" Proceeding from this, the writers juggled Armours, Swifts, Leiters, McCormicks, Medills, Pullmans, Ryersons, Wentworths, Bordens, irreverently if not libelously. Smith didn't have to tell me that scurrility stemming from an angry woman's fleer was not for *Midweek*. I told him. He chuckled, and showed me two more pieces cut from the same cloth, just delivered to him by special messenger. We sent them back, the same way.

As for the lady, she got part of what she wanted. The case was concluded in chambers. She would have been pushed off of Page One anyhow. Schemer Drucci, arrested for creating a disturbance at a polling place, by a young policeman who didn't realize he was manhandling the Big Guy of the late unlamented Dion O'Banion's gang, went berserk while being booked, and tried to seize a detective's gun. The detective shot him four times. He had a fine funeral, and left an estate appraised at half a million. No divorce case could compete with that. And the next night, I saw the lady in a booth at 999, talking earnestly with Dollie.

You might not have believed him, but I did. He said she laid it right on the line. She had three million dollars and could buy anything she wanted, and what she wanted was to buy him, and take him to Paris with her. I started to laugh, but thought better of it. Something had happened to Dollie. He said, "She's a lady, but they've put her on the outside and she'll never get back in. So she and me, we start even." Then he repeated, really to himself: "There comes a time when it's time to move." I couldn't say anything. Nor could anyone else. As for Danger, he watched his rival unreadably. She was too intelligent to offer any overtures. Not many nights later, her new Rolls-Royce waited outside at 3 A.M. She came out and got in the car. Then Dollie appeared, with Danger at his heels. The three of them rode away together.

A month passed. The Paris Bureau filed a query. French papers were full of stories about a mysterious Chicago billionaire who caused furore wherever he went, because a white dog, a savage beast, was always with him. When the guard at the Louvre said animals were not allowed to enter, the mystery man and his white shadow turned away. At the Folies-Bergère, man and dog occupied two seats on the aisle, halfway back, and attracted more attention than the nudes on stage. Who and what was "D. P. White?" The reply, I understood, was "Forget it."

The lady was never mentioned in connection with Dollie and Danger. The Opposition carried a Sunday story about her. She had joined the International Set. Her escorts included a duke, an *avant garde* poet, and a bicycle racer. She was being called "the Countess from Chicago."

Dollie returned, with Danger at his heels. He had changed, imponderably to me. Perhaps he had seen too much to see himself as important any longer. Perhaps, having reached for the stars, and felt them cold and crumbling in his grasp, he had run out of things to reach for. We still talked, but not as often or as long. He said once, looking at the dog, not at me: "The animal's getting old. He backs off from all the women." Their walks together were infrequent now. Dollie was busy downtown, bucking the stock market, and losing. He let the Syndicate lend him bail-out money. That brought in a Syndicate house man, who cut the Scotch and raised the prices. Business fell off. Dollie didn't seem to care. His luck was running out. You could feel it, and see that he felt it, too.

Danger died, in the night, at the foot of Dollie's bed. Dollie said, "The stupid vet says the animal's heart just quit. The animal wasn't that old." Soon after, he announced, "I'm selling the store." I asked, foolishly, "Why?" He asked, "Why not? What do I win if I win?" I had no answer for that. He invited me to his farewell party, and I said I'd come if I could. As it happened, I couldn't, so I didn't have to watch what I'm glad I didn't see. The few who were there said that suddenly Dollie ripped the dog's head down from above the bar, smashed the long bar mirror and all the bottles and glasses with it. Then he ran out into darkness, and never entered 999 again. He carried the dog's head with him. What became of it, nobody knows.

I was long gone from Chicago when the police arrested what was left of Dollie for a senseless murder of which he probably wasn't guilty. The story was that the Syndicate framed him. Either his code wouldn't let him sing to save himself, or he really believed he wasn't born to burn in the electric chair. Anyhow, he was convicted. All his money gone to lawyers, from the death cell he wrote to bartenders, taxi drivers, waiters, enclosing worthless personal checks, none for more than one hundred dollars. "If I beat this thing," he said, "you know I'll make the check good. Even if I lose, you won't." Thousands of dollars came in, mostly in tens and twenties. That financed his last appeal. He lost.

When the Warden came to walk him down the last mile, Dollie lay dead on his bunk. His insurance paid what he owed. With Dollie, a deal was a deal.

<< 3 >>

I'm glad I wasn't in 999 the night Dollie said good-by to the part of his life that went according to his plans. I wasn't there because Smith sent for me that afternoon, and kept me waiting, wondering, while he re-shaped sentences in John Gunther's correspondence from Berlin, in which John predicted that Adolf Hitler's *Mein Kampf*, just published, would raise more hell on earth than Karl Marx's *Das Kapital*, unless Stalin stepped in to halt the Nazi rise. Sharp eyes hemstitched my back. They belonged to Simon Milacco, "Simon the Hunchback."

Walter Strong had insisted Smith must have a secretary. Smith shuddered at the prospect of some officious female bringing order and the scent of Chanel No. 5 into his monastic cell. He respected Hazel Flynn and Carol Frink, by-line woman reporters for the Opposition; they knew their job and did it, asking deference from no male rival when the chips were down. The *Daily News* was proud of June Provines, who could model for a cover on *Vogue*, but whose femininity was never a weapon; she could beat your ears off covering a story, any story. But Smith wanted no woman sitting in his office. And his problem had solved itself one night when he was walking alone around the Loop, in the rainy darkness, as he often did. From a doorway a drenched, misshapen dwarf leaped out at him, croaking unintelligibly, brandishing soaked newspapers. Smith bought them all, for a dollar. Clutching this, the dwarf scuttled like a crab toward an alley's mouth. Smith followed. His quarry turned at bay, spitting insults in Italian.

Smith wouldn't be repelled. Obliquely, soothingly, he calmed and questioned.

Simon, Smith learned, was brought from Naples as a baby. Crippled from birth, orphaned before he could talk, abandoned on the doorstep of a shelter for cast-off waifs, repeatedly rejected for adoption because of his deformities, he was finally expelled by welfare workers for what they called "incorrigible ingratitude." He found a sanctuary in the Newberry Library. He went there at first to warm his twisted body. Then he began to read, and a world opened up in which he could lose himself unafraid. His gargoyle's back and stunted legs hurt constantly. Warped, sick, he survived however he could, hiding his misery behind spite and hatred. But he couldn't hate Smith, and he couldn't run away from Smith's undramatic, unstinting benevolence.

Smith bought Simon his first decent clothes and shoes, that had to be specially made, and got him a room, and entered him in night school to learn shorthand and typing. Smith's own salary was less than the guaranteed minimum wage of a middle-bracket Newspaper Guild timeserver in the socializing Sixties. Still he protested when men on the staff claimed their right to contribute to what they called the Smith Secretarial Foundation. Soon Smith ensconced Simon the Hunchback at a roll-top desk facing his own. It became Simon's watchtower, from which he spied only enemies. Smith picked up strays and coddled them. Smith must be protected from this, his only bad habit. And also from anyone who might become important to him, thus menacing Simon's own self-assumed importance.

So rubbed-raw sensitive that if you smiled he was sure you laughed at him, Simon had to be forgiven, and almost always was. Nobody objected too seriously when he appropriated theater passes intended for the working press, or even when he set up a loan-shark side line: two dollars on Tuesday, for three dollars payable on Saturday, and a dollar a day for delinquency. He didn't have to stand in line at charity dispensaries any more. He went to the publisher's doctor and paid with his own money for expensive treatments and medicines. These did little good. He suffered, but thought he hid his pain. He wouldn't let himself fall ill. He wouldn't take a vacation. If he did, Smith would find out he wasn't irreplaceable.

Of course Smith knew, and of course he did the best he could to ease Simon's fears. I am positive it was he who located a girl whose sad deformities matched Simon's, and improvised a job for her in the Almanac office down the hall. Simon and Martha became a devoted couple. They lunched together apart from us, left the building together at quitting time, met at the entrance in the morning, accepted overtures from no one. Simon had a listener at last, to whom he dared to tell his secret. He dreamed of being as tall as anyone on earth, of looking down on the world and all the people in it from a mountaintop. He had never seen a mountain. But much of his reading in the Newberry Library had been of books about the West. The Rockies, and particularly Pike's Peak, were clearer in his mind than the faces of Smith's Young Men Going Somewhere.

He snapped and sneered at us. He knew, if Smith did not, that we were all liars, schemers, chiselers. By devious maneuverings, he managed to usurp control of Editorial expense accounts, which had been Miss Harriet Dewey's prerogative since the days of Eugene Field. He slashed mine gleefully, and delayed my *Midweek* checks, which were routed through Smith's office. He would have said, and I am certain he believed, that in doing this he protected Smith.

Now he glared at me balefully, accusingly, until Smith looked up at last from John Gunther's correspondence, and handed me a note he had ordered Simon to type. "That's the name and address of a fellow I happen to know in advertising. He'll pay you three hundred dollars for a ten-thousand-word prospectus to butchers, about a new line of packaged pork his company is putting on the market."

Embarrassed as he always was when money had to be discussed, Smith rose and headed for the Cave of Winds. "Of course you're fired," he said over his shoulder on the way out. "I won't have a man working for us who's doing publicity on the side." I turned on Simon. He didn't explain; he excoriated; and I had it coming to me. Catching up with Chicago, the way I was going about it, called for a bankroll I didn't have, and couldn't earn no matter how fast I pounded my typewriter. H. N. Swanson at *College Humor* and Edwin Baird at *Real Detective Tales* paid higher than *Midweek*, but thus far my stories hadn't charmed them. Among other things I didn't need but couldn't do without, I was buying a coonskin coat on the installment plan, from experts in dealing with cockeyed optimists. They sold what they knew the buyer couldn't afford, on conditional sales contracts whose fine print few buyers read until too late. Total price, plus collection costs and attorney's fees, became collectible if a single payment was overdue. The game was to garnishee the hapless victim, wring a settlement out of him, then repossess the property and sell it over again. And it didn't matter at all to them that, though Victor Lawson was gone to his reward, his stern system lingered on at 15 North Wells.

Reporters might be excused for living beyond their salaries; if they had any practical common sense, they wouldn't be reporters. But anyone listed as an executive, who got himself garnisheed, lost his job forthwith. The chart called me an executive. The garnishment papers said I owed just under three hundred dollars. Miss Dewey might have covered for me, in memory of my veneration for Eugene Field. But nothing escaped Simon the Hunchback. That morning, he had informed Smith that the coat-skinners had tied up my paycheck. He had my dismissal notice ready for Smith's signature. But instead of signing it, Smith negotiated a three-hundred-dollar loan from the Printers' Bank, instructed Simon to pay off the garnishment in full, and got busy on the phone with his friend who advertised packaged pork.

Simon told me this in sharp, staccato bursts of speech. Finished, he chuckled. There was not a spark of malice in his grin. Unbelievably, he said, "Good luck." Those were the only kind words he ever uttered to me. (Not long afterwards, he grew so ill and weak that, practically by force, Smith got him to go away and rest. He took a train for Colorado and the Rockies. En route, he mailed postcards at every stop, to all of us, that were full of the affection he hadn't allowed himself to risk revealing while he guarded his temple in which Smith was God. Then the teletype clattered. DENVER. SIMON MILACCO CHICAGO NEWSPAPERMAN COLLAPSED DIED HEART ATTACK WALKING UP PIKE'S PEAK. NEED ANY MORE? Nobody wanted to show the query to Smith. Somebody had to. Watching while he read it, I couldn't see his eyes. He filled in a few words, just enough to make it a brief for inside. He seldom wrote a head. He wrote this one. Just one line, 12-point bold. **He Died Climbing Mountains.** Sentimentalism? Of course. Smith was one man who never felt he had to be ashamed of being a sentimentalist.)

The day Smith fired me, I blundered back to my corner, told Jack Lawson I was called away on personal business, and tried to be brisk and bright when I faced Smith's friend in his office Back of the Yards. It turned out he was a part-time poet, thus far published only in Richard Henry Little's "Line o' Type or Two," and on some greeting cards. He wanted to discuss Edna St. Vincent Millay and Elinor Wylie. I wanted three hundred dollars as fast as the Lord would let me get it. My mercenary attitude caused a certain coolness, to which I added when he said he couldn't pay me for the prospectus until thirty days after delivery and acceptance. But then he said he'd give anything to meet Thornton Wilder, who had won the Pulitzer Prize with *The Bridge of San Luis Rey* and come to teach a graduate class at the University of Chicago.

That was Thursday. Simon blinked unbelievingly, then applauded silently (bless and rest him), when I handed Smith my three-hundred-dollar check right after the Final rolled next Tuesday. On our way to the Cave of Winds, we stopped at Miss Dewey's cage. Beaming, she put me back on the payroll. While we smoked, Smith asked if I'd had any time to think about the next *Midweek*. As guilelessly as might be, I said I thought of trying for an interview with Thornton Wilder. "All the big magazines are bidding for his name on their covers. We might be able to get it free." Smith said that sounded like sharp practice. Then he relented. "Well," he said, "I don't suppose it would hurt to ask him."

I telephoned asking for Wilder's secretary. He didn't have one. The voice I heard was his. And he said, "Come on over." I went, and for once Simon didn't object to my expense account for taxi fare. I told Wilder all about *The Bridge*, which I'd read that morning. He said he was much fonder of *The Cabala*, of which I'd never heard. Why? "Because I knew how it would come out when I started it. I was halfway through *The Bridge* before I knew who should be the fifth to fall off it. The obstinacy of an author's arrogance had prevented me from admitting until then that of course it had to be The Boy." The mystique in this was beyond me. But when Saturday came, I kept my part of the bargain with the brief employer for whom I had rhapsodized about packaged pork chops. I introduced him to Thornton Wilder, in the inner circle at Schlogl's, to which I hadn't been admitted myself until that day, when I brought Wilder to lunch on my expense account.

He sits down, [I wrote] between Henry Justin Smith and Lloyd Lewis, and lights a cigarette, and listens. Richard, the literary waiter, tells him "The boiled tongue is very good today." He says

135

"I think I'll just have a salad." Richard says, "Listen, Mr. Wilder. I read *The Woman of Andros*. You need nourishment. Take the boiled tongue." He eats obediently, and writes in Richard's book of autographs: "The boiled tongue was just what I needed." He likes not being bowed down to. He has a terror of the possibility that he might come to enjoy being lionized. He has a conscience, but doesn't let it worry him. He goes to church every Sunday, and joins in all the hymns, but one of his favorite friends is Texas Guinan. He knows Shoeless Joe Jackson's batting average, and Christy Matthewson's pitching record. He wishes he had worked on a newspaper. He doesn't care to live in Europe and hobnob with fugitives from America, although he likes beer and thinks Munich is probably the second best city on earth. (Courteously, not condescendingly, he ranks Chicago first.) He says when he has walked across enough vacant lots and been in enough bus stations at 3 in the morning and eaten enough ham and eggs and heard enough people agree to disagree, he'll write his American novel; not before. He feels entirely at home in the visiting preacher's quarters at the University. He was missionary bred. Students in his 'most promising' class of fifteen wonder how a man who writes best sellers can scan their compositions with more than perfunctory tolerance. He says, "The academic life is good for me. It helps me to forget I, too, am an author."

When the galley proofs came back from Smith, I found he had crossed out Lloyd's name and his own, with a scrawled note: *Can't advertise ourselves in our own paper*. He substituted the names of Lew Sarett, who wrote "The Ode to Illinois" and taught at Northwestern, and of Phil R. Davis, a lawyer who tried to write like Dorothy Parker in *Sunset Gun*, and headed the Elizabethans, a literary drinking club that opened its by-invitation-only sessions with readings from Mark Twain's suppressed erotica. Smith also penciled a proofreader's exclamation mark alongside each of several quotations from Wilder: "I have a New England conscience which makes duty and routine, not in the ugly sense, necessities"; and: "The Victorian-Protestant upbringing sends writers either into flippant though sometimes brilliant protest, or the reverse, retaining in them what the radicals call sentimentalism. I don't mind being called sentimental"; and: "The thing that saves me from intense, bitter self-preoccupation is the buoyancy of health of an unfatigued believer"; and: "The unexpected in human hearts finally becomes more constant than their conformity. All beings have a capacity for rewarding a writer's affectionate interest"; and: "I am still green. There is always so much more for a writer to learn." I put the words in type. Smith, in his way, suggested: "Think about them."

That *Midweek*, with Thornton Wilder on the cover, was a milestone. It earned a memorandum from Walter Strong that was also a reprieve: *Fine. Let's have lots more like this.* Smith was even more pleased by praise from Robert Maynard Hutchins, then president of the University of Chicago, who was president of their class when he and Wilder were freshmen at Oberlin. It was no time to tell Smith that another contribution to the issue came from a writer who had gone about as far as he could from Wilder's clean, uncluttered path. His style of speech aped Dos Passos crossed with Ezra Pound, he covered his complexes with a patchwork of pretense, and he had imitations of everybody from Samuel Putnam to Jean Cocteau in his bulging, battered briefcase, along with copies of *The Perfumed Garden* and *The Memoirs of Fanny Hill.*

Though, like Wilder, he was born in Wisconsin, he despised all things Midwestern. A country boy, he walked miles into town, and by arrangement with the spinster librarian checked out a dozen books a week, all by Europeans or American expatriates. She helped him convince his family of his rare qualities, so effectively that his father mortgaged the farm and sent him to Paris, where he lived in a garret with an artist's model, drank Pernod, had delirium tremens, and was stranded when the bank back home foreclosed on the farm and his father hanged himself in the hayloft. He badgered his brothers and sisters for remittances. What they sent was insufficient to free him from worldly cares while he wrote, wrote, wrote. In desperation, he came back to Chicago.

He was walking dogs to earn his meals, in Tower Town, when a job printer took him into very private partnership. Working nights, they ran off hundreds of copies of *Perfumed Garden* and *Fanny Hill* on the cheapest paper obtainable. He Americanized such subtleties as there were, in these classics of a kind, doing this shabby job shabbily. Then in a rattletrap Ford, he went on the road. In small towns, he sought out the male social center: usually a pool hall, with a blind pig and a poker game in the back room. He would introduce himself as a traveling salesman specializing in ladies' lingerie. Taking a paper-backed book out of what he called his sample case, he would sit pretending to read it, sniggering. Always, and usually soon, someone asked, "Whatcha reading?" Then he pretended startled caution. "I'd better not show you. Hot stuff. Smuggled in from Paris." Then he yielded. "But I can see you've been around, so I guess it's all right to let you read a page or two."

He sold copies of *Fanny Hill* for fifteen dollars, a clear profit of $13.75. *The Perfumed Garden* cost more. He claimed he had translated it from the Persian. His best customers, he said, were doctors. Morticians came second, then clergymen. He never sold more than half a dozen books in any town. Then he departed, after solemnly warning his clients that possession of pornography is a Federal offense. He felt no guilt or shame. On the contrary, he said his artistic dedication was strengthened by recurring proof of the grossness of Americans. He stopped his sowing of erotica, back and forth across five states, only when his printer partner was arrested for counterfeiting revenue stamps for the Syndicate, which paid him to keep his mouth shut and serve a three-year sentence. The peddler had saved six thousand dollars, which he figured would support him for a year while he did nothing but write, write, write. That ought to be time enough to make him greater than Julian Green or Glenway Wescott.

All he needed now, he told me, was publication, to stimulate his creativeness. So he would let me take my pick of his work in progress, any two items for two hundred dollars. He would throw in copies of *Fanny Hill* and *Perfumed Garden*, of which he happened to have a few left in stock. I was intrigued, but said, "Let's keep it clean," and paid him twenty-five dollars for a Paris sketch which I rewrote for the Travel Page. Apparently, that was the only thing he ever got published under the Frenchified pen name he adopted before he escaped from Wisconsin. The last I heard, he was turning out "how to" pamphlets for a correspondence school, specializing in *You Too Can Make Big Money Writing for Profit in Your Spare Time.*

Frank Rosengren, another once-only *Midweek* contributor, was an utterly different and infinitely more admirable bookseller. He hated to sell books. I have seen him glimpse a potential customer approaching, run to the door and lock it, yank down the blinds, and strike up "Turkey in the Straw" on his banjo, while muttering, "The thing that's wrong with this country is free education. Too many monkeys can read." His tumbledown store on Michigan Boulevard occupied frontage valued at a million dollars, whose owner was holding out for three times that much. It delighted Frank that his magpie's nest was an eyesore to Colonel McCormick, who glared down at it from the Tribune Tower across the street. Entering, you were likely to fall through the floor, which Frank never got around to repairing. He was too busy prowling the city, buying up castoff libraries. He insisted there might be treasure in this trove, but never found any, and really didn't care. He bought books as compulsively as fat women gobble sweets. His forever dismayed but always forgiving wife moaned softly, then lent a hand, when he appeared with another purchase piled in their old car. Each time, he declared he would start disposing of the stuff tomorrow. He never got around to that, either.

Mrs. Rosengren ran the rental library, which supported the store. It was kept well-stocked by the editor of a Chicago magazine, not *Midweek,* who notified all the Eastern publishers that their new books would go unmentioned unless they sent two review copies, not one. Surplus copies went to Rosengren's at publisher's wholesale less 5 per cent. This same profit-minded editor sent me some stories his contract wouldn't let him buy for his own magazine, signed with transparent pseudonyms. At Frank's suggestion, we met and talked it over. This led to a working arrangement, interrupted intermittently over the years, but still a source of occasional mutual satisfaction. In further proof of friendship, Frank let me read the letters he got from Fred Allen.

In town in a show, Allen wandered into Rosengren's, intending to buy a pocket *Thesaurus.* He left Frank carrying an eleven-volume Glasgow printing of Frazer's *Golden Bough,* plus two historical novels by Maurice Hewlett. A fifteen-page commentary, written in his dressing room at the next stop on his tour, seemed wittier to me than any monologue he gave for pay in a theater or on radio. In a postscript, he commissioned Frank to select what he should read, and ship it to him collect. Thereafter, Fred Allen was the only book buyer Frank respected. He shipped a bundle of books every week. Checks came by return mail. Between them, in chapter-length letters, they left few balloons unpricked. Later, when Colonel Frank Knox was our publisher, Cecil Jensen did cartoons in the *Daily News* that lampooned a certain "Colonel McCosmic." This invention, which Colonel McCormick of the *Tribune* took personally, has several claimants. I saw it first in the Fred Allen–Frank Rosenberg correspondence.

It was attached to an apocryphal tale attributed to an unnamed attorney, who was supposedly somehow concerned in the struggle between Colonel McCormick and Joseph Patterson, his cousin, for sole control of the *Tribune* Company. Stock holdings were so evenly divided that neither could oust the other. According to the fable, they flipped a coin. It is on the record that McCormick got the *Tribune*, while Patterson took *Liberty*, a colossal money-loser, and the *New York Daily News*, which at that stage was no gold-mine either. Then, Allen and Rosengren chose to imagine, the victor arrived to begin his reign as undisputed monarch of all he surveyed, clad appropriately in British riding kit, complete to burnished boots and riding-crop. Alongside his baronial desk, in his manorial office, there stood an electric horse, a contrivance on which he bobbed up and down as if he rode to hounds, while he dictated the day's decrees. This morning, he found the corridor crowded with silent serfs who hid their smirks. He opened his *sanctum sanctorum*. Surrounding the electric horse and covering all the vast floor space of imported English oak, brought in at heaven knows what great expense and with what conspiratorial connivance, was the departed co-owner's parting remembrance: a layer, two feet thick, of tightly packed manure.

I told Frank, "It never happened." He said, "No, but I wish it had." I tried to get some of Fred Allen's letters, not including the one about Colonel McCosmic's last ride, for *Midweek*. Frank said if he let me print them, Allen would never get another booking, and he, Frank, would lose his only cash customer. He consented, finally, to sign an article we called "Gold on Your Bottom Shelf," which told our readers that collectors are crazy, and therefore neither age nor quality was necessarily the criterion of their taste. For example, according to Frank, a copy of Admiral Byrd's first autobiography with the dedication, *To the wife of my youth,* was worth twenty dollars, while a copy with the hastily revised dedication that added *who still abides with me* could be found in his store, marked down to fifty cents. His wry irreverence glinted through the pedestrian prose I thought the subject called for, but he lost money on the article. It brought a rush of house-wives who demanded cash for rarities unearthed in their base-ments and attics. So he bought more books, until his wallet was empty. Then he locked the front door, hung a GONE FISHING sign in the window, and wrapped up another shipment for Fred Allen.

Dixon Wecter, in his *Age of the Great Depression,* con-cludes that at summer's end in 1929 hardly any American saw anything ahead but a limitless vista of upward-spiraling pros-perity. *Time's* Man of the Year was Walter P. Chrysler. Ivar Kreuger and Samuel Insull appeared successively on *Time's* covers. But Frank Rosengren had his own barometer of the times, which signaled trouble: people had not only stopped buying books, they no longer even rented them. His landlord sold out to bolster his margin betting in the market. The new landlords refused to renew Frank's lease. They pro-posed to put up a forty-story skyscraper on the property with their profits from Insull Utilities. Heaping old books on tables out in front, Frank displayed wistfully hopeful placards, rang-ing from ANYTHING HERE FOR TWO DOLLARS down to ANY THREE FOR FIFTY CENTS. Passers-by browsed, having no work to go to, but they didn't buy.

One afternoon, in the middle of a banjo serenade, Frank mentioned over his shoulder that he would be shutting up shop tomorrow. I asked about his future plans. "I plan to catch up on my reading." Ignoring the wolf on the doorstep? "We have an old family recipe for 'How to Cook a Wolf.'" (Someone used this title later. I heard it first from Frank.) Next day, he roamed aimlessly around the tables, leafing pages of books with which he hated to part, though he had long for-gotten where he bought them or why. His wife heard him cry out, and ran to him, fearing the worst. He brushed past her and went to the telephone, which was due to be disconnected at noon. Incredulously, she heard him place a person-to-person call to a man in Indiana he had never met, who was noted equally for millions amassed by marketing a household remedy, and for a miser's parsimony in bargaining for the rare books he collected.

Frank had found, bound into one of three old volumes he couldn't sell for half a dollar, the third known First of Edgar Allan Poe's *Murders in the Rue Morgue*. He demanded thirty thousand dollars for it, and swore he wouldn't take a penny less. The landlords who had put him out of business now hurriedly proposed to let him stay if he'd buy stock in their skyscraper promotion. He said worrying about wealth would interfere with his banjo-playing, and bought a pedigreed Irish stag-hound that could eat a wolf for breakfast, and left with Mrs. Frank for their first visit to Europe. He was prowling along the Left Bank in Paris, buying French books he couldn't read but couldn't resist, when the only man to whom he ever really tried to sell a book lost two million dollars in the market, on Black Friday, 1929.

« 4 »

In the whole United States, no manipulator of millions that weren't his'n ran faster in all directions on Black Friday, and farther past it before he fell, than Samuel Insull, of whom his subordinates maintained that in his prayers he told God, "Mind your business and I'll mind mine." *Tell him too much money has killed men and left them dead years before burial; and quest of lucre beyond a few easy needs has twisted good enough men sometimes into dry thwarted worms.* Carl Sandburg didn't say he had Insull in mind when he wrote that for his "Notebook" in *Midweek*. Anyhow, Insull was not the man to take warning from a poet. Or from anyone, for that matter. He was indignant when Senator George W. Norris, the father of T. V. A., had the audacity to question his admitted investment of $237,925.10 in the Illinois primaries in 1926, of which $172,925.19 went to support Frank L. Smith's campaign for the Republican Senatorial nomination, while Smith retained chairmanship of the Illinois Commerce Commission. "As being responsible for six hundred and fifty million dollars of investment in Illinois," Insull snapped, "I have every right to take part in these affairs."

Donald Richberg, the lawyer-reformer, started a series of articles in the *Daily News,* declaring his intention to prove that a chain of command ran directly from Insull's office to that of Mayor Big Bill Thompson. A weirder alliance could hardly be imagined. Insull came to Chicago to be a king. Big Bill came to play football for the Chicago Athletic Club. Insull was an immaculate miniature, a perfect model for the groom on a wedding cake. Big Bill was untidy, obese, so short of breath from high living that he couldn't begin a campaign oration until he unbuttoned the two top buttons of his trousers. Insull spoke with undisputed authority on any subject whatever. Big Bill bragged, "I ain't bright, but I'm smart enough to hang out with who is." He had entered politics originally to win a fifty-dollar bet. He claimed he hadn't opened a book since he turned hobo to keep his family from sending him to Yale. Yet somehow he had collected a set of quotations from English authors that served wonderfully in his shouting, sputtering speeches. One of these was Kipling's "Having seen Chicago, I urgently desire never to see it again. It is inhabited by savages." Another was Arnold Bennett's "Chicago: A mushroom and a filthy suburb of Warsaw."

This was the man Richberg accused Insull of keeping at Chicago's helm. And an ultimatum was served on Victor Lawson at the *Daily News.* Richberg's articles would stop, or half a million dollars would be spent to bury William E. Dever under a landslide and re-elect Big Bill, who had no platform but *Shall Your Taxes Be Spent to Make Your Child Hate George Washington?* This was the title of a pamphlet supposedly written by Big Bill. The excuse for it, and for his internationally headlined threat to "punch King George of England in his royal snout," was the presence in Chicago's Public Library of many books published in Great Britain, some of which bore Queen Victoria's bookplate. Big Bill, and certain editorialists who endorsed his Anglophobiac fulminations (never in the *Daily News*), chose to forget why the British books were there. The explanation was that although the Chicago Fire in 1871 caused great financial loss to British insurance firms and to private English investors in Chicago companies, a spontaneous wave of sympathy for the stricken city prompted public subscriptions not only of cash for immediate relief, but of thousands of books to replace those destroyed by the holocaust. Having felt no need for one before, Chicagoans had to build a Public Library to house the books they hadn't asked for. Fifty-eight years later, while Big Bill howled for a book-burning and Samuel Insull never said him Nay, not a dollar of city tax revenues was available to the Library for the purchase of new volumes. In fact, when the Century of Progress World's Fair opened in 1933, no funds had been allotted to the Library, for any purpose, in three years.

As for Richberg's articles, they came from the front office, and Smith had no voice in whether they should run or be dumped in the hell-box. They stopped. Dever lost. Big Bill the Builder — shouting "Throw away your hammer and get a horn!" — celebrated his victory by suspending William McAndrew, the Superintendent of Schools — an educator Smith admired — and having him tried on charges of being "a stoolpigeon for George Five of England." Samuel Insull himself was English, born within the sound of Bow Bells. But he had outgrown more than his Cockney antecedents. In his self-made world, there was room for only one ruler. He was it.

He was never interviewed. He issued proclamations. "We are trying to develop the idea among the newspapers that public utilities offer a very fertile field for developing regular, prompt-paying customers for their advertising columns. When that idea penetrates, we will have less trouble with the newspapers than we have had in the past." An underling said it, but publishers knew who planned the policy. Even *Daily News* by-liners awaited official approval before attributing attitudes or actions to Insull. He looked no more regal than Soglow's Little King, but no cartoonist caricatured the stumpy, dumpy, strutting climber, once Thomas Edison's part-time secretary, who rose so fast and far that when I first laid eyes on him — of course from a respectful distance — he was president of at least fifteen gigantic holding companies, board chairman of some sixty corporations, unquestioned master of seventy or eighty more. It was Samuel Insull, not Al Capone, who said (to the Illinois State Committee on Defense, which he headed during World War I): "I can do whatever I want in this State."

Certainly, no one was going to assign me to write any words about Insull. Still, I went through his day-to-day biography in many boxes of clippings in the Morgue, and added notes recording what I saw and heard and guessed at. This proves no mystical prescience. It was just that if you were trying to catch up with Chicago you had to study the city's most powerful, most domineering, most feared citizen. And that, with due allowance for their difference otherwise, was Insull, not Capone. Money, not gangsterism, took the Page One banner line the day Insull's magical maneuverings pushed Middle West up to 570, Commonwealth Edison to 450, Public Service to 435, Peoples' Gas to 404. He was credited with a personal fortune of a hundred and seventy millions. With a flick of his diamond-flashing hand, he could cut off electricity, gas, heat, water and ice from Illinois east to Maine and New York, south to Alabama and the Carolinas, west to Nebraska and the Dakotas, north to Ontario and beyond. And the symbol of his almightiness, his forty-two story Taj Mahal, rose on the river front at Madison and Wacker Drive: the new home of the Chicago Civic Opera Company, of which, of course, he was president.

He decided who should sing opera in Chicago, set all fees, sent up or shot down singing stars on impulse. Then he decided whether the fees should be invested in Insull Utility, or Corporation Securities, or some other of his myriad companies. European divas fought for the opportunity to come to Chicago, where good, kind Mr. Insull would make them billionairesses. A few cashed in and fled back to La Scala. Most stayed on; and more came over.

Beginning in early September, 1929, *Midweek* carried articles about the opera season soon to open, by Mary Garden and her *protégé*, Barre Hill, who would co-star in Debussy's *Pelléas et Mélisande,* and by Marek Windheim, the only tenor I ever knew who thought tenors are ridiculous, whose specialty was the village moron in Smetana's *Bartered Bride.* Writing these, I decided they made me an expert in another field of the arts, and bought my first Tuxedo (we had not yet learned from the Prince of Wales to call them dinner jackets). Seven nights after Black Friday, I watched a procession of shiny hearselike limousines crawl out of the gloom on Wacker Drive and disgorge their cargoes of chinchilla and ermine and emeralds and top hats and white ties and tails on the threshold of Insull's monument to Insull.

Across the river, floodlights bathed the austere lion-pawed white building, only half as tall as Insull's pride, into which the *Daily News* would move before much longer. Water already plashed in the Victor Lawson Memorial Fountain. Daily guided tours took sightseers to the Lawson Memorial Room, eighty feet long, sixty feet high, paneled in carved oak from the old Lawson mansion, its fireplace large enough to roast an elephant. From WMAQ's radio studios atop the building, Amos 'n' Andy were broadcasting another chapter of their trials and tribulations with the Fresh Air Taxicab Company, and the larcenous Kingfish, to fifty million devoted listeners from coast to coast. But Chicago was tuned in that night on Samuel Insull's defiance to Depression's tidal wave.

It was a cold, cold night. That afternoon, Middle West closed at 295, which was 275 below the high for the year. Commonwealth Edison was down to 285, Public Service to 272, Peoples' Gas to 255. Inside the building, too, everything went wrong with utilities. The costly curtains, designed to be managed by push-buttons, refused to separate until stagehands yanked them apart by main strength. *Aïda* began forty-five minutes late. Instantly, shocked surprise spread across the whole middle third of the cavernous auditorium. Someone had hashed up the acoustics. I was one of buzzing hundreds who could barely see, and couldn't hear at all, the proceedings on the far-off enormous stage, where electric lights kept winking out. Perhaps it was just as well.

Singing that night were men and women whose whole gainful years were spent with the Chicago Opera, whose life savings were invested in Insull's holding companies. Listening were men and women no younger and no better off, also Insull investors, also pretending unsuccessfully that they were not burdened by doubt and dread. At intermission in the pressroom, champagne flowed. None of us toasted our unwontedly generous host. Too many had suffered from calls to their City Editors by Insull spokesmen, who appeared to earn promotion according to how many reporters they tomahawked and scalped for writing news they said Insull didn't like. But it was inconceivable that he could fall. If he did, then nothing was sacred any more; we might as well let the Democrats run the country, if the Indians wouldn't take it back. (At 15 North Wells, you were either Republican or silent.)

Our music critics concentrated on *Aïda* as written, not as heard. Our business reporters wrote about the building: *Revenue from rental of offices on upper floors guarantees a permanent endowment making this the richest Opera Company on earth.* Whole floors of offices were empty, but no one mentioned this. *Observers found Mr. Insull quietly pleased but modest as always, amidst tributes to this latest demonstration of his unique financial acumen.* Nobody quoted Mrs. Insull, and it was still a while before her husband would say starkly, "I've got a melancholy wife," and burst into tears.

Our society reporters, as usual, concentrated on Mrs. Edith Rockefeller McCormick, who arrived punctually as always in her plum-colored Rolls-Royce, with chauffeur and footman in plum-colored livery. She was wearing the diamond dog-collar and matching tiara that cost a million dollars, and her ermine cape of three hundred matched skins from Ishima. John D. Rockefeller's daughter, who bought Peter the Great's bedroom rug for one hundred and twenty-five thousand dollars, Catherine the Great's emeralds for one million five hundred thousand, and a pearl necklace for two million, was resigned to what was in the stars, by which she believed herself to be guided in all things. "We are in the pains of childbirth," she told the newspapers, "and in proportion to the pain is the severity of the suffering. Each one of us is being uprooted, so that we face in the opposite direction to that which has been the direction for two thousand years. This change is inevitable, and no one can escape it. For this reason, there is no fear."

It may have eased the fears of others less endowed with occult inspiration to read next morning that her dinner guests that night, before the opera, were given menus printed in French in raised gold letters, and served on the set of gilded silver — sixteen hundred pieces of it, weighing almost seven hundred and fifty pounds — that belonged to Napoleon's brother-in-law and bore the Borghese arms, a dragon and a crowned eagle upon a ducal mantle, surmounted by the imperial crown of France. As usual, our photographers did their best to get pictures of her without including her *cavaliere servente,* a small bounding Swiss named Edwin Krenn, whom we called Eager Eddie. She had granted James Joyce a pension of one thousand Swiss francs per month, until he sent her a portion of the manuscript of *Ulysses.* Then she canceled his pension, without comment. Back in Chicago, she financed Krenn in real estate ventures that seemed reckless even to rival speculators. Each morning, he was at the door of her palace on Lake Shore Drive bearing a little bunch of wildflowers. It was said they talked for hours on end about the teachings of Dr. Jung, whose clinic in Switzerland both had patronized. Krenn stoutly supported her belief that she was the reincarnation of King Tutankhamen's child bride, Seti.

James Keeley, also present, had once told a Congressional committee "Over the *Chicago Tribune* my power is absolute in all departments." That finished him at the *Tribune*. But while he passed his declining years as spokesman for the Pullman Company, he held daily conferences with Insull, and was the only newspaperman Insull respected. According to Keeley, Edwin Krenn had a secret pocket in his tailcoat, in which he carried a tiny jeweled pistol, with which to defend Mrs. McCormick in the event of a Bolshevik uprising. Even Keeley couldn't explain why the weapon was where it would have to be drawn with the left hand, though Krenn was right-handed. But he said it might be needed, before *Aïda* was over. And if even Keeley admitted obliquely that the opening of Insull's Opera Building was a disaster, small wonder that those who loved Insull less made increasingly cruel remarks during that long funereal evening.

For myself, I was more interested in a distinguished stranger, impeccably turned out, about whom everyone whispered, wondering what noble rank he held. Actually, he was a butler, just arrived from London, looking for a Chicago connection. Hazel Flynn, covering crowd angles for Hearst, suggested a scheme borrowed from Harry Leon Wilson's *Ruggles of Red Gap*. In the audience, snoring, was a graduate hoodlum who had struck it rich in the garbage-disposal racket, in time to import three entire cellars purchased from the same number of indigent English lords just before the Volstead Act went into effect. In spite of this, he had thus far failed to crash the guarded gates of Chicago "society." So after the second act of *Aïda*, we waked him, introduced him to the butler, and let nature take its course.

Later, when his new employer went to Florida for a conference with other racket operators, the grateful butler gave a party for selected representatives of the press. One of us, seeing a lavish display of exotic liqueurs such as no Chicago bootlegger had heard of, let alone attempted to counterfeit, announced that he alone in all humanity could build a fourteen-layer *pousse-café*. We jeered, but the butler said grandly: "Be my guest." The adventurer began measuring dollops of Danziger Goldschwasser, Vielle Curé, Créme de Violette, Triple Sec, Grand Marnier, *et cetera*, into a foot-high crystal goblet. A rainbow grew, then dissolved into a poisonous-looking purplish potion. Rather than waste this, he drank it, and started over from the bottom. He repeated this performance every ten minutes, until he stiffened where he stood, so rigidly that we couldn't bend him when we carried him out at daybreak. When he recovered, he took the pledge, and kept it until payday. The rest of us did business with the butler, when we could afford it. A bottle of veritable Napoleon brandy was twenty-five dollars on his price list. I bought one, the next time Douglas Hardy had a story in *Midweek*. By no coincidence, this was about a gentleman's gentleman whose employer knew he was a thief but couldn't bear to fire him because he was so elegant. The brandy had turned to vinegar in the bottle, but I couldn't complain. The story wasn't much good, either.

A more profitable result of my first night at the Opera was an introduction to Mrs. Courtney Borden, of a Founding Family, who consented to contribute some articles to *Midweek*. I was also introduced to Mrs. Austin Young, smartly social, who invited me to tea. I lectured her on what and how to write. (Neither of us foresaw that this traumatic experience would eventually impel her towards becoming "Lydia Lane," syndicated in two hundred newspapers.)

I told Smith that in just a few hours I had picked up enough gossip, new and old, to give us a sensational series. He agreed I had the material. "But," he said, "I'd like to go on publishing *Midweek* and I doubt if Mr. Strong's patience would survive the libel suits you'd get us into."

So I looked for another market, and settled on the *Chicagoan*, a slick-paper magazine that copied the *New Yorker's* format but unfortunately had no E. B. Whites and James Thurbers and Robert Benchleys and Peter Arnos to make the mare go. The editor, William Weaver, let me try my wings anonymously, with a no-names fleer at Chicagoans on dress parade, based rather too obviously on the opening of Insull's operatic mausoleum. I stepped on some tender toes, whose proprietors complained in letters which Weaver printed, thus bringing in more letters and starting a paper storm that boosted circulation noticeably. He didn't print one letter. (It was from my dentist, who recognized my style, having listened often to Little Big Mouth, and asked Weaver to remind me of a bill I owed him. Paying it was almost a pleasure.) My check from Weaver, the first I ever got from any editor but myself, totaled twice what I dared to collect from *Midweek*. And with it came an order for more of the same, "and signed," which Weaver blurbed in advance in an ad that ought to have carried the disclaimer prudently affixed to Hollywood movies: *Any resemblance to actual persons living or dead is purely coincidental.* Pablo Katigbak agreed that no one would recognize me from what Weaver wrote: BOB ANDREWS *is our nominee for the fool-killer's mantle of Ben Hecht, or Charles MacArthur, or both. He looks like a* SATURDAY EVE-NING POST *drawing of a Rhodes Scholar turned pugilist, edits* MIDWEEK *in a madcap way, has the strange idea he wants to be a book reviewer, writes five thousand words an hour, and would be our town's most-read drama critic if the* DAILY NEWS

*would let him fry the audience along with the actors. He is re-
puted to have arrived from Minneapolis by airplane. If he
lambasted the high and the mighty in Minneapolis the way he
scarifies Chicago's elite in our next issue, we can see why he
chose such a fast and altitudinous vehicle for his getaway.
Don't miss "Those Trying Tower Town Teas."*

I braced for comment from Smith. None was forthcoming.
Nor had he anything to say when he read the article, which
began:

Drop in any afternoon. Bring gin. We'll drink it while we tell
you what your best friends won't; and a gentleman doesn't interrupt. We will talk about us and James Joyce and the girl who
just left and the one who is coming in and why is Nathalia Crane
and Cabell and how to pronounce him and us and the novel we
have been giving birth to for three years and five hours and the
ninth verse of "Willie the Weeper" and how to smoke muggles
while dancing and us and the girl in the blue dress that fits in
all the worst places and *The River Amour* and who borrowed it
last and why is Hemingway and Hart Crane but not Stephen
and us and don't get the idea we invited you over to listen to you
for if you had anything to say we have already said it and anyhow who do you think you are when all you do is what you do
and you get all that money for it God knows why; and next
time, bring more gin; and now about us. And us. And us.

It went on and on and on like that.

All new to me, and passing peculiar. All old to Smith, I'm
sure, and sad. Hobohemia was not for him. Once, when Maxwell Bodenheim appeared in Editorial, with his arm in a sling
to attract attention though there was nothing wrong with it,
Smith shut his office door and telephoned. "Bob, Bodenheim is
here again. Talk to him. I can't. I can't face him and forget
what he could have been if being what he is wasn't easier." I
remembered this while I waited and Smith read:

The high spot in this one's career was achieved the day he had
eleven drop-ins all bringing something to drink, and he wore

153

tight trousers and no shirt and flexed all afternoon, sitting on the window-sill with his canary perched on his forefinger or walking up and down belly-in chest-out, all the while saying that this musician is a fake and that painter is a pal but he'll never learn how to mix oil and that writer ought to take up tatting and that dancer can't deny a rumor he wouldn't vouch for but he'd tell it anyhow. After a while he took off his trousers. He wore bright blue shorts monogrammed on the right hip and I think he thought he looked like Jack Dempsey but he didn't even look like Maxwell Bodenheim.

Smith let me wait a few days for his opinion. Finally, changing the subject from a story I brought in for his comments, he said, "Bob, if the copyreaders form a union, and I'm afraid they will eventually, they'll outlaw the kind of writing you're doing for *Chicagoan*. There's no place to put a full-stop period so the reader can catch his breath." I said weakly, "It's sort of a change of pace from *Midweek*." He let that pass. Nor did he indicate that he even read my next piece in *Chicagoan*, which earned enemies even Ben Hecht might have envied me:

I went where the elite meet to eat. Their sleek heads dipped low in unison, as if their plates were troughs. Right arms crooked, mouths opened wide, food popped in, jaws snapped like beartraps, teeth crunched, lumps danced up and down behind distended cheeks, while they talked as loudly as they ate. I saw a lady from Lake Shore Drive prop a mirror against her wineglass, smack her nose with a tattered puff on which I wouldn't shine my shoes, rub her face with a grimy chamois I wouldn't use to polish my car if I had one, and meanwhile never miss a bite. I saw a bank's board chairman who also heads the blackball committee at an exclusive club dig meat from between his molars with his personal gold toothpick, add up his check on a damask napkin, flip a quarter into the *sommelier's* tasting-cup, and exit with Madame following like a Kiowa squaw, both still chewing as they went. And I went out onto Randolph Street and walked along peeping in through windows at other elegants dining out, their elbows on the tables, their faces in the fingerbowls, and wondered why Chicagoans bother to go to the Lincoln Park Zoo to watch the keepers feed the animals.

For this, an Opposition columnist noted, *Bob Andrews received a packet of used razor blades as a hopeful hint from his other reader.* Another columnist, Ashton Stevens, who wrote for Hearst, was kinder. At least he classed me as a fellow story-teller. *Julius Rosenwald, Bob Andrews confides, contributed a lot of money to Admiral Byrd's South Pole expedition. On inspecting the outfit, the head of Sears Roebuck was something less than delighted to find that Byrd had bought everything from Montgomery Ward.* I didn't know Julius Rosenwald from Admiral Byrd. The tale was borrowed from John Maloney, who had written for *Midweek* about Rosenwald's Museum of Science and Industry. But my motto was "Try and Stop Me," long before Bennett Cerf adopted it. And it was wonderful wine for a twenty-two-year-old — being noticed by columnists, even if they wrote for the wrong newspapers.

We yawn at yarns of the prodigious productivity of Lope de Vega, one of them announced, *since hearing about Bob Andrews. He began a long short story at 4 P.M. on Friday, and wrote until 5:30, when he had to hurry to a cocktail party. He resumed at noon on Saturday, and hangover or not, rang the rafters with his typing until 3:05, when he wrote* THE END *after 15,000 words, having hung up a record of 55.5 words a minute, or almost a word per second. Whereupon he ran down the stairs, raced off in a taxicab, and nine and a quarter minutes later sold his latest to* REAL DETECTIVE TALES. *The check he collected lasted him until almost midnight.* Only part of this was true, but it led to the beginning of a treasured acquaintance with Lloyd Lewis.

Out of fondness for Smith and also, I chose to think, in kindness to me, the author of *Myths After Lincoln* came as close as Quaker reticence would allow to lecturing me on the perils of trying to become a myth too soon. He did this at

155

Schlogl's, where he volunteered casually a story about Wilton Lackaye, a fine old Shakespearean trouper who drank as flamboyantly as he acted, and Frank McGlynn, who for years played nothing but Drinkwater's *Abraham Lincoln*, on stage and off. McGlynn walked the streets bewhiskered like the Great Emancipator, wearing a rusty stovepipe hat and black Prince Albert and a mien of sorrowful contemplation. He was never seen without one hand clutching his heart, the other knotted behind his bent back, and his head bowed as if he weighed words for the Gettysburg Address. Inadvertently, he entered a Loop saloon, where Lackaye was downing his tenth Irish whiskey of the yet young evening. Lackaye froze, staring at the apparition of McGlynn as Lincoln. "You this-and-that," he roared, "you won't be satisfied 'til you're assassinated!"

I got Lloyd's point. But writing too much too fast was harder to stop than a snowball rolling down a mountain. I had turned out, in Minneapolis, Sunday pages adding to some two hundred thousand words, called "The Truth About Pirates." No one who watched me type believed it, but these were painstakingly researched. To dig out the facts, I had to teach myself to sift sense from passages in old Spanish and older French, neither of which I could read. (Science can prove a bumblebee can't fly. Nevertheless, it flies.) In Chicago, I began to get driblets of royalties, from a New York syndicator who sold the series wherever he could for whatever it would bring. I followed my "Pirates" with a bolder venture, "The Truth about Artists." In writing this, I had the assistance of Harold Van Doren, a collateral of the noble clan that included Mark and Carl and Irita and Dorothy, and Charles. He had been Williams Lecturer at the Louvre, was assistant curator at the Minneapolis Institute, translated Vollard's biographies of Renoir and Cézanne, and knew a lot about painters and sculptors even if I didn't.

I claimed I applied a reporter's tests of probability, in inventing what I made my chosen subjects think and desire and do. I expected the *Journal's* readers to be fascinated, as I was, by my portraits of Mrs. Patience Wright, who modeled Benjamin Franklin's bust in colored wax and whose son designed the first coins on which our newborn nation declared IN GOD WE TRUST, and of Anton Joseph Wiertz, who proclaimed "In me are combined the virtues of Homer, Michelangelo, and Christ!" and got the burghers of Brussels to believe him, and of Gustave Doré, who according to me sold more pictures than he could count but died lamenting, "I was never an artist!"

The syndicator found few buyers for "The Truth About Artists." But it occurred to me that between pirates and painters, I had a lot of used clay on hand that would bear reworking for *Midweek*. Tentatively, I tried romanticizing such seagoing murderesses as Mistress Ching-yih, who commanded a hundred thousand Chinese buccaneers, and Alwilda of Denmark, who married all her handsomest prisoners and drowned them when the honeymoon was over, and Maria Cobham, who pinned lace-trimmed targets over the hearts of her masculine captives and shot darts at them from what she called her Cupid's crossbow. These were signed by Douglas Hardy, but Smith's note read: BOB: *You write excitingly, but you have a tendency to put* HORROR *in your stuff. We don't want to give* MIDWEEK *readers the shivers.* Very well; I would write about artists, whose gentler trade should make them more acceptable in the Paper That Goes Home. What ensued from this decision produced reactions that were, as the film trade press reports diplomatically after certain Technicolor previews, somewhat mixed.

We already had an Art Editor, designed by Helen Hokinson, and numerous aspirants waiting in line should she tire, as seemed unlikely, of "Society"-sponsored exhibitions for the benefit of this or that. For her, Art began with Murillo and went downhill after Rosa Bonheur. She lumped Van Gogh and Dali with "all those other crazy Frenchmen." Matisse, she was comfortably positive, couldn't draw a horse as well as her grandchild, aged four. She changed the subject, delicately — as Emily Post recommends when a *faux pas* is committed — if any Chicago painter was mentioned in the same breath with John Singer Sargent. Regularly, she brought me enough about Art as she saw it to fill three *Midweek* pages. Brashly, I cut this to a column and a half. Tearfully, she appealed to Smith. Patiently, he smoothed her ruffled feathers. Then we went through it all again.

But now I poached, which I had no business doing. In a page headed "We Had Nowhere Else to Go," I fictionized about a group of "We Girls from Winnetka," fleeing a sudden cloudburst that interrupted shopping for Stylish Stouts on the Boule' Mich', and seeking shelter behind Lorado Taft's stone lions that guard the portals of Chicago's Art Institute, only to find upper floors already overcrowded with refugees from the rain. My fugitives wandered down to the basement, and for the first time in their lives were confronted by Modern Art in the raw, in the Birch-Bartlett Collection. I had just discovered it myself, and decided (and have never changed my mind) that Van Gogh's "Room at Arles," with its sad chrome-yellow bed and patch of aching cobalt sky, is one of three paintings on earth for which I would almost trade my hope of heaven, such as that may be. I transferred my discovery to the Girls, and had them leave the gallery miserable, because they were no longer shielded by "I don't know anything about Art but I know what I like."

"You Don't Know What You Like" grew naturally from this. " 'Modern Art' baffles you? Why let it? I remember an experiment conducted several years ago, when about a thousand school children were asked to select, with no guidance from their teachers, the paintings that most impressed them in a large museum. Their instructors expected them to vote for the academic, representational classics that crowded most of the walls. Instead, by a stunning majority, Cézanne came in first, Renoir second, Monet third, Rousseau (no, not the writer) fourth, Rembrandt a rather poor fifth, Delacroix sixth, Mary Cassatt seventh, Winslow Homer eighth, Titian a bad ninth, and Gainsborough tenth. The answer? Simple, actually. The young viewers, briefly freed from the prim and proper conventions which we insist on imposing under the guise of 'art appreciation,' looked with their minds and their emotions, and saw clearly, as their 'educated' elders do not. If you will look with as little prejudice implanted in advance, at any of many paintings not now 'liked' in Chicago, I don't believe you'll find them ugly, or fraudulent. If only you don't insist on an answer to 'But what does it mean?' The error lies in demanding explanation of a bird's song or a cloud, or music or poems, or paintings, pursuant to rules decreed in schools or anywhere else. As it has been said of climbing mountains, what matters is: It is there."

And long, low hoots rose from the newsroom, indignant schoolmarms penned fiery letters to the Editor, and Smith looked at me and shook his head. Chicago then had C. J. Bulliet, who wrote *Apples and Madonnas,* the first appraisal I had read of the apothegm attributed to Cézanne: "All Art can be expressed in the cube, the cylinder, and the cone." Bulliet had credentials as a critic. I had none. Meštrović's stone horsemen in Grant Park, which didn't look much like real Indians, were modernism enough and to spare in the opinion of the arbiters of taste in Chicago who placed or controlled the placement of newspaper advertising, and collected nothing painted or sculptured after 1893. Walter Strong was asked point-blank, "Who is this Andrews? Where does he get off, plugging Modern Art?" I heard this from Pablo Katigbak, who had heard it from the World's Oldest Office Boy. I could only hope Smith would let me go on getting away with it.

I knew, of course, that I wasn't as all-knowing as I liked to think I was. Smith knew the rest: that though I wrote nothing

159

I couldn't get paid for, I would have written as much, as recklessly, for nothing, as long as it got in print. Writing hadn't yet become what you did for your living; it was how you lived. I told Pablo there is more than one profession in which enjoyment along with the fee is lagniappe to be cherished. This didn't impress him as much of an epigram. But in his mercy, Smith withheld the lowering of the boom. And my jejeune essays introduced me to some more discoveries, in the process of catching up with Chicago.

« 5 »

In *Midweek*, I told the story of Helen West Heller. She began trying to paint when she was five years old. Her parents were dismayed, because nothing she painted looked like a dog or a horse or a tree. She got little formal schooling; she was needed to help on the farm. She was young when her parents married her off to a neighbor, a widower. One of his two mules died during the first week of their marriage. He yoked her to the plow, beside his other beast of burden. She rose at dawn to milk the cows, hurried back to the farmhouse to cook breakfast, then dug in the kitchen garden, then worked in the fields with the mule and her husband. He let her keep one fifth of the egg money. When she saved enough (it took almost a year), she sent away to Sears Roebuck for a box of primary paints, a Children's Holiday Special, the first Christmas gift she ever received. Thereafter, she hurried breathlessly through the final chores of her daily servitude, until at last she could hurry out to the west side of the house. Then, straining her eyes while the sun died and twilight darkened, she mixed colors on a broken plate. Then, in the kitchen, in the circle of light from a kerosene lamp, she painted. Like a pianist transposing a score for violin, she tried to paint colors as she remembered them by daylight, not as she saw them at night. She did this for six years, until her husband said he was sick of her silly wastefulness. She could no longer keep any of the egg money to buy paints. When she protested, he whipped her with a harness-strap. That night, while he slept, she left him, walked five miles to town, and caught the train for Chicago.

She had just enough money to pay the rent in advance for a cellar room, and to buy a barrel of oatmeal, wholesale. Then she locked herself in, ate oatmeal and nothing else if she ate at all, and painted and drew until she had nothing left to work with or to keep her alive. Then she found part-time work as a charwoman, and went on slaving, mixing colors as sunset ended, painting by lamplight. Shyly but never apologetically, she watched school-trained artists at work. But her self-schooling had gone too deep. She had to paint in her own way. When a dealer finally gave her a show, to fill an empty week in his schedule, she had one dollar to her name, owed two weeks' rent, and was hungry. She bought fifty two-cent stamps and mailed notes to people whose names she found in the Art Institute yearbook, asking them to come and see her pictures. She sold three, for forty dollars. "She dreams," I wrote, "of going abroad if some day, before she is too old, people will buy enough of her oils and woodcuts and watercolors and lithographs and drawings to pay for her one-way ticket to France or Italy. She doesn't want to look at pictures; she wants to see sculpture and tall medieval churches and the tracery of stone on façades from Rome to Rheims. She doesn't want to visit galleries; she feels it's too late for the sight of others' painting to do her good or harm. She realizes she will never be able to see color as it is by sunlight; transposition to twilight tones is automatic with her now. She knows she will never reach the stars she started reaching for when she was five years old. She isn't sad about it. She pulled a plow, harnessed beside a mule; she went a step at a time then, and still does, and will until the last sunset." This seemed profound to me, but not to Helen West Heller. Rather incredibly, while she struggled with the stone for a lithograph she called *Jain*, in which I saw nothing but strange shadows, she quoted Kipling: *But each for the joy*

of the working, and each, in his separate star, Shall draw the
Thing as he sees It for the God of Things as They Are!

And there was Raymond Katz, who called the paintings he couldn't sell "experiments in dynamic symmetry," and signed SANDOR to striking sketches in white on black that sold well enough to support him in a studio in the old Auditorium Building. It was so cluttered with work in progress that when, later, distinguished gentlemen representing the Century of Progress, the 1933 World's Fair, came to hire him to paint the murals for their Hall of Religions, they shouted his name from the doorway rather than risk getting lost in his studio jungle. Ray was a double rarity: an artist who punched a time-clock, albeit it was his own, and put in precisely nine hours a day at his easel, with thirty minutes off for lunch, and morning and afternoon coffee breaks; and one who could laugh about himself, and did, sincerely, not merely to cozen possible customers. He was chuckling when he telephoned and said something had occurred that I wouldn't believe any more than he did, but if I came over he would prove it to me.

Thumbtacked to the tilted rectangle of planks taller than himself, that he used for a drawing board, there was a life-sized sketch on butcher's brown paper, in swift black strokes with the effective economy of Hokusai, of a pretty, pudgy girl, stark nude, seated in posture that made her body's curves identical with those of the bass-fiddle that stood beside her, its throat clutched in her outstretched right hand. "I was working," Ray said, and showed me a study in gouache (which he sold to me eventually for twice what I expected to pay.) "Comes a knock at my door, which is most unusual. I open. Here is this girl, young, terribly serious, very brisk. 'Do you make pictures of people?' 'Yes.' 'I would like to see how I look with my instrument.' She refers to her bass fiddle. No mention of money. Such naïveté must be respected. 'Come in.' She enters. I prepare my equipment while I say, 'In the corner, behind the

162

screen, is a mirror if you wish to fix your hair as young ladies always do.' She disappears. She reappears. I turn. She is clothed like Eve before the Fall. Such clean sincerity is fantastic. 'What do I do now?' 'You sit there. You sit so.' I pose her, and her bull-fiddle. I am very human, but this is strictly business. I draw, while she is motionless, silent, utterly without expression. I finish. She looks. 'Is that me?' 'It is you to me.' 'Thank you.' She goes behind the screen. She reappears in her going-to-music-class clothing. She looks once more at my drawing. She smiles secretly. This is what puzzles me the most. She says, 'Good-by,' and is gone. Now what do you think about that?"

I thought it was not for *Midweek*, but excellent for telling. He was disappointed. "In the paper, people read it, and if you include my address, maybe I sell a picture. In conversation I talk only with competitors, who say 'You think that's funny? Wait till you hear what happened to me!'" As I have indicated, Ray had a practicing professional's point of view. But the following week, he telephoned. "Again you won't believe it. Come on over." And he showed me another sketch: this time of a willowy lady, nude, sawing gracefully on a violin. When he told me who she was, I said, "You must be lying." He wasn't. "By accident, somehow, I get invited to a tea she gives for culture. Only tea; no whiskey. Bored, and nobody knows me, I make conversation to strangers. I tell about 'Me and My Bass Fiddle.' No laughs. I am leaving, when the hostess catches me. 'I,' she says, 'I play the violin.' Today, she comes to my door and it is like with the little girl before, only somewhat more interesting, although I assure you, strictly business."

Suddenly, he was dining out three nights a week. He made a production of "Me and My Bass Fiddle." He asked me not to drop in at his studio without calling first. His collection of sketches grew. Concurrently, so did his sales of studies in dynamic symmetry. I cannot say his employment at the Century of Progress resulted from his sudden success in "Society." His murals were quite magnificent designs developed from the vowel-less ancient Hebrew alphabet. Rabbinical scholars praised them. I recall much more vividly Ray's orchestra of nudes, which grew and grew while his career progressed. The last time we talked, he told me happily that he had just dined out as guest of a well-preserved dowager who wondered how she looked playing her accordion. I wonder, too.

And there was Sol Greenberg, who loved beauty and loathed violence, but fought four-round prelims in outlying towns to pay for his paints and lessons in landscape; and David Bekker, who took the subjects for his woodcuts from the Torah, and invited me to my first Seder Night. One day, they auctioned their work and their belongings, and went off together, arguing their irreconcilable interpretations of Art, to fight for Zionism, and died before Israel was free. And Edgar Miller and Edgar Britton, who painted Wild-West-with-Indians murals, Styles A, B or C, in hotels and coffeeshops from coast to coast, working at this six months a year so the rest of the year they could paint what they liked, which nobody bought. And Aaron Bohrod, a rare exception, whose artistic ambidexterity put his paintings in museums, and on the covers of *Time*. And Paul Trebilcock, an accomplished portraitist, whose shows were "High Society" events. His large, expensively framed oils-in-many-colors were being unloaded from a van and carried into a North Michigan gallery, when an anonymous tipster of my acquaintance reported to Chicago Avenue Precinct police that "A naked woman is crossing the Boulevard and stopping traffic." Sirens screamed. Blue-coated guardians of public morals converged. The naked woman was there, all right, life-size, on a canvas by Trebilcock. The Opposition photographed the lady and put her on Page One, four columns wide, and set a street-sales record, but judiciously pulled her out of the Mail Edition. More police had to be called, to control the biggest crowds that ever attended an art show in Chicago.

And there was Robert Lee Eskridge, lineal descendant of both General Robert E. Lee and General George Washington, who described himself shamelessly as the only professional beachcomber produced by a First Family of Virginia. His beachcombing was a special kind. With no means of support but his sketch pad and paint box, he roamed into the Sahara, encountering wild desert Arabs who waged *jihad* against other *farangi*, but made Bob their honored guest. They love storytellers, and he told tales at oasis campfires so marvelously well that they would have made him a *mullah* or a *shaikh* if he had stayed a little longer. He looked like Salah-al-Din exhumed. His eyes were hypnotic when he talked of ghosts and weirds; his hands wove spells. A prized pupil of Lhote in Paris, he painted abstractly by preference, but could be representational when he chose. The supernatural fascinated him, Discussing the imponderable intangible, he made it believable with inflections, pauses, gestures, as artfully as if he composed a canvas with evocative strokes and shadings. His ancestry, his manners, his travels, his gifts as raconteur, were sufficient to make him a guest wherever he chose to be one. But between whiles, he worked hard and honestly, and at more than his painting.

He went to Tahiti before *White Shadows in the South Seas* spoiled that Pacific paradise with a flood of fugitives who had run away from everything but what made them run. He met Gauguin's half-caste son. They swam and fished together. Gauguin's by-blow lived by yarning to tourists about a father about whom, really, he knew less than pundits in Paris who wrote the treatises from which Somerset Maugham extracted portions of *The Moon and Sixpence*. Tahiti hummed with rumors that somewhere on the island there was a lost treasure of Gauguin paintings that had escaped the idiot bureaucrats and reformers who burned or stole and smuggled back to Europe whatever they could find after — according to them — the devil caught up with Gauguin finally in 1903. His son confided to Eskridge, "I have pictures by my father." Bob says he thought, "I'll be rich," but has never said whether in gold or in finer metal. His guide led him secretly, by hidden tropic trails, up jagged orchid-covered heights, to a *nipa* hut that was all his property on earth. Bob entered, and stood trapped between laughter and tears. The walls were papered with cheap chromos from European magazines, crudely reproducing Gauguin originals that were already in collections and museums before Gauguin's son was born. "How could I tell him they were worthless?" Bob asked me in Chicago. "They were all he had of his father."

Through one Chicago winter Bob lived, alone, immured in a huge old mansion heated only by fireplaces for which there was no wood, loaned to him as caretaker by its owners, who always wintered in the South of France. Suddenly, he was off to Palm Beach, as the guest of some wealthy Chicagoans to whom he sold decorative, technically masterful Hawaiian scenes painted with cold-stiffened hands in Evanston, and told South Sea tales entertainingly at dinners. One was about leaving Tahiti because it was getting too crowded with imitators of Charles Nordhoff and James Norman Hall, and drifting down the Pacific to the Marshalls, to atolls no beachcomber reached before him. By chance, he came to one, a dot on the sailing-chart, a coral reef thinly covered with white sand in which perhaps a hundred palm trees groped with questing roots, where not more than a hundred gentle brown people managed to subsist and smile. They welcomed him shyly, gave him coconuts and breadfruit and fish speared in the lagoon, built a thatched cottage for him where the painting light was best. He worked in water color at that stage. (Subsequently, he was a judge on international water-color juries.)

"I never felt better painting," Bob always said at this point in the story. Yet slowly he realized there was something wrong in this tiny Eden. Behind their smiles, the people were afraid. He asked "What frightens you?" in sign language, their dialect being unlearnable. Instead of answering, they fled, and hid, as much as they could within the square mile or so that comprised their universe. Then he woke early one morning, and went out on the beach, hoping to catch the sunrise in a water color. And he saw strange markings in the white sand, coming out of the ocean, crossing the atoll, going back into the ocean: the large, deep prints of a giant man's bare feet, and beside them, the pad-marks of an enormous dog. "Understand," Bob said, "there was no human being on that island whose feet were half the size of the footprints. And there was no dog on the island. The people had never seen a dog. I tried to describe one. They recoiled from my gestures showing size and shape, and covered their eyes against sight of it when I did a drawing of a dog. What I pictured was a hideous monster, to their eyes. Their fear was not for themselves. They had lived with this immemorially. They knew, as their forebears knew, that it forewarned of sudden death impending, when Something with Something Walking Beside It came out of the depths and crossed their world and returned into the depths. Their fear was for me, the intruder, their guest. Sensing this, I tried to convince them — and myself — that the prints in the sand were put there by the wind. But there was no wind. The sand was white. The prints were black. And magically, they were erased. But next morning, there they were again. This time, they crossed the atoll past my door. Now the people begged me to leave, and I tried to convince them — and myself — that if I did so, it was only to free them from their fear. But if I ever return, I know I will watch the white sand at sunrise, and one morning I will see where Something with Something Walking Beside It came out of the depths in the night, and, looking up, I shall see Death."

And Bob told me that when, according to his custom, he rose suddenly as he spoke these words, and pointed for effect at a shadowed doorway behind the other dinner guests: "I saw Something beckoning, and knew that this time I hadn't told a ghost story. This time, I told the truth." But back he went, to the Marshalls, to the Marquesas, but not to the atoll where he saw black prints in white sand. He was strangely deterred from this by the eerie pull of another lost island, where ruins of a mysterious walled city glimmer fathoms deep in a blue lagoon, and ashore a renegade priest gone mad enslaved the people and forced them to build a cathedral and a fortress for him, and prisons for themselves. Bob wrote a remarkable book about this, *Manga Reva*, that deserves another publication. Because of it, before he returned to Chicago I had him writing for *Midweek*, illustrating his own stories. Then a telegram came: PLEASE MEET MY TRAIN. MUST TALK. IMPORTANT. BOB.

On a grim March afternoon, in the ill-lit, reverberant Dearborn Street Station, Bob emerged from the last car. His painting arm was in a sling. He struggled with suitcases, painting kit, a portfolio of drawings, a padlocked manuscript folder, and some heavy object wrapped in a strip of tarpaulin. Two redcapped porters bustled to relieve him of his burdens. He let them take everything but the object he carried under his useful arm. Unveiling this, he showed me a squat, scowling Polynesian *tiki*, a household idol, carved from a block of driftwood by an artist whose art was ancient, not primitive. Its queer square head was stained. "I brought this for you," Bob said. "It's real. At least two centuries old. I don't know how much blood has been poured on it."

Suddenly, the station felt like an overpopulated catafalque. I said, "Thanks" — without enthusiasm — and asked "What happened to your arm?" Bob said "I was cursed." We were walking along behind the porters. Their heads half-turned toward Bob. "I stayed too long," he continued. "An old priest warned me to leave, and I wouldn't. So he showed me the Dark Power." The porters were going faster. "I walked on the beach," Bob said. "There was absolutely no one in sight. Then I saw prints form in the white sand: the black footprints of a barefooted giant who wasn't there, and of a dog that wasn't

168

there either. Then Something lifted me up and flung me down. Only my arm was broken. But I knew that was the last warning." The porters had broken into a shuffling trot. We kept pace automatically. "The curse is with me still," Bob said. "If I let it master me, it could strike you dead. You or anyone." And at that moment (this I swear), out of the baggage coach ahead disembodied hands shoved two coffins silently onto waiting hand trucks. And the porters froze. Like mechanical toys out of kilter, they wheeled to face Bob and the *tiki* brooding in my hands. They set Bob's belongings down, and disappeared before either of us could shout "Hey!"

We laughed about this, last time we met. Nowadays, Robert Lee Eskridge is a settled citizen. He roams no more to the islands, but lives sedately with his wise and pleasant wife, in a solid white house that the first Territorial Governor of Washington built, on a pine-shaded knoll overlooking the State Capitol at Olympia, with the blue Pacific beyond. There is no *tiki* in this sanctuary. The furnishings came from New England with the pioneers. When he isn't painting abstractions, Bob gardens or writes or cooks. His pictures bewilder the neighbors, but they admire his begonias. Altogether, he is as far as human planning can arrange from places where Something walks beside Something in the night, leaving black prints on white sand. But recalling the past while we sipped sundowners on his veranda, Bob and I fell silent, looking out at the ocean stretching endlessly. We told each other we really should go inside, out of the sudden twilight chill. Then we talked louder than need be, about the Albright Twins.

If they hadn't been born, surely Walt Disney would have invented the Albrights. This is said in awed affection. Ivan Le Loraine Albright and Malvin Marr Albright could play two more of Snow White's doughty defenders, in street clothes and without makeup. They were, and are, however, much more than impish but cuddlesome gnomes. Amused by their eldritch eccentricities, suddenly you realize they are laughing, too — at you. They worked like beavers, round the clock, weeks at a stretch, at Warrenville, the sleepy town toward which Chicago's suburbs leap, in the abandoned Presbyterian church their father bought for a studio, and which they shared with him under mutually satisfactory agreement that they didn't have to argue Art with him and look at his paintings, or vice versa. When they appeared in Tower Town, it was only for some small shenanigan. Then off they went to work again.

Thomas Brown Albright averaged twenty-five thousand dollars a year when that was a tycoon's take-home, turning out barefoot boys with cheeks of tan, and blushing maidens under the harvest moon, for Brown & Bigelow calendars. He earned, I was told, one hundred thousand dollars while his sons were completing a meticulously realistic portrait of a weather-beaten door eight feet tall, with a draggled funeral wreath hung on its rusted iron knob. They titled this "That Which I Should Have Done I Did Not Do." Staring at it, I hoped the door wouldn't open, revealing what lay just inside. The canvas caused a great to-do at the Carnegie International exhibition, not only because of its haunting strangeness but because the Albrights priced it at one hundred thousand dollars, since their father had mentioned this amount and it struck them as a nice round figure. Another of their works was "Into the World Came a Soul Named Ida." At first glance, "Ida" was Everywoman of a certain age, alone in her bleak bedroom, free to remove her girdle, to sag, to surrender, to trim her toenails and invite her soul. Then what the Albrights did (and do) uniquely in their paintings made men as well as women shudder.

I say "the Albrights," though only Ivan signed these canvases, and others since shown in the best museums — purchased for more than the twins' father earned in several years; reproduced in *Life*. Malvin, born four minutes and twenty seconds after Ivan, accepted his elder brother's seniority before they walked and talked. I cannot recall any occasion when Malvin put himself forward. Painting was as essential to him as to Ivan, but Ivan was there first, so he called himself a sculptor. When he found it impossible to exist without making pictures, he signed them Zzissly, "as far as I can get from Albright." Ivan did oils. Therefore Malvin stuck to water colors. After watching them at work for years, I gave up trying to decide who painted what. It was no use asking them, because they really didn't know.

Nor have they admitted or refuted a guess I made in *Midweek*. Old-fashioned doctors like my father, who had no miracle drugs to lean on, worried about what they called "proud flesh." This was not an attribute of arrogance, but the fulsome growth produced by granulation in suppurating wounds or sores. I said in an article about the Albrights that "Into the World Came a Soul Named Ida" was "a blob of proud flesh," and pontificated that "Real artists as well as true physicians comprehend that what matters about proud flesh is not its substance but its cause." Smith asked what this meant. I explained by telling him the story I hadn't written because he didn't want HORROR in *Midweek*. Ivan Albright, I said, was the last man who ought to put on a uniform and shoulder a gun, but that didn't keep him out of the Army in World War I. He drove drill sergeants berserk. Then some file clerk noted his civilian occupation: "Artist." Nobody bothered to tell him why he was suddenly yanked away from peeling potatoes on K. P., rushed onto a train, hustled aboard a troopship, hurried ashore in France, shoved into an ammunition camion going to the Front, and dumped in a communications trench in the Argonne. Someone thrust a box of paints and brushes into his hands. Whistles blew. He was swept along across No Man's Land, in a surprise attack, that didn't surprise the Boche. Then at last he learned what he was there for.

War was fought less scientifically then. A wounded man might lie unattended for hours, before he could be moved back by slow transport to a hospital at Base. The holes in him, torn by shrapnel or grenades or bullets or bayonets or barbed wire, changed appearance radically as gangrene set in. Medics needed a record on wounds at the moment of first incidence, for comparison with what was brought to them. There were no combat correspondents armed with color cameras and flash-guns. An artist, however, could do a useful job with water colors, and with a corporal to center an electric torch on what he pictured. So a little, agonizingly sensitive man who had never pulled a trigger, who hardly knew where he was except that it was hell, worked under fire, day and night for weeks on end, painting numberless sketches, realistic to the last searing detail, while his subjects writhed and choked and cursed him for the outward callousness that kept him sane, and often the corporal said: "Knock it off. This one's *kaput.*"

If painters must learn how to mix colors that put HORROR in humanity, I told Smith, there was never a school like that. Then I wished I hadn't been so sure of myself and, unsure of him, said I'd cut the offending lines. He said: "No. Leave them in. I was just curious. Not about the Albrights." Then he asked "Is your father living?" I said, "No, sir. He died four years ago." Smith said, "He must have been still quite young." I said, "Yes, sir. But he was tired. He told me once he was too tired to climb even golden stairs." Then again I wished I wasn't Little Big Mouth. Smith said, "From the way you see things sometimes, I'm surprised you're not a doctor like your father." I said honestly, "I wouldn't be any good at it." He waited for me to finish my confession. "I tried to paint," I said. "I'm no good at that, either." He smiled, not laughing. "We ought to talk oftener," he said. "Not about *Midweek.*" Then he busied himself with copy that really didn't need any more editing.

Next day, Simon the Hunchback brought me a note Smith had him type, with copies for all concerned including our Art Editor. BOB: *Let's try some more Art features, for the news side. I suggest as by-line,* THE PREVIEWER. *It's harder to sue a pseudonym.* SMITH. Nobody sued, though I laid about me with a bludgeon, offending some pretty-pretty portraitists then fashionable with the Founding Families. I managed, if not with Smith's approval at least with his consent to help make the Albright Twins, who hadn't sold a canvas, more talked about than their father, who had sold a thousand. In gratitude, they sold me two pictures for twenty dollars each, marked down from one hundred thousand. When we meet these days, they sigh reminiscently. "It would be nice to be back where we were young and foolish," Ivan says (or maybe it is Malvin).

<h2 style="text-align:center">« 6 »</h2>

In Chicago there is the mysterious something that makes for individuality, personality, charm; in Chicago a spirit broods on the face of the waters. You might expect that from Carl Sandburg, but hardly from Henry L. Mencken, who wrote it. He called Chicago "the literary capital of America." (His only other illusions were that Baltimore is beautiful, and beer is nonfattening.) Before my time, he foregathered at Schlogl's with Smith and Sandburg and Hecht and Bodenheim and Gunther and the Mowrer brothers and Sherwood Anderson and Robert Morss Lovett and Arthur Davison Ficke and Lewis Galantiere and others saluted in Harry Hansen's *Midwest Portraits.* Richard, the literary waiter, let me look at his copy of Hansen's book, embellished with caricatures by Gene Markey and the signatures of William McFee, Konrad Bercovici, Arthur Brisbane, Gilbert Seldes, Heywood Broun, Upton Sinclair, Ford Madox Ford and others he served and whose writings he criticized to their sometimes reddening faces. Mencken had a whole page to himself.

I heard my seniors and superiors mention to each other with obviously affected carelessness: "Oh, by the way, I had a letter today from Mencken." Sherwood Anderson notes in his memoirs: "You said this offhand, but in your heart you felt it was like being knighted by a king." At the dawn of the Thirties, Mencken was monarch of our trade, with George Jean Nathan sharpening arrows at his elbow. If you made the *American Mercury*, you were made. Sandwiched between slices of their "American Credo" and Nathan's "Prejudices," your stuff took on communicated quality. And if you missed but almost hit at *Mercury*, you were sure to sell to *Plain Talk*. I played safe, by shooting at *Plain Talk* first.

G. D. Eaton bought a piece of fiction, "Big Al Came Back" (that became *Gangster's Boy*, starting a second career for a growing-up child star, Jackie Cooper, in Hollywood years later yet years ago), and some other pieces, one of which Smith suggested: a study of the phenomena of the one-day story, a headline sensation for a few hours, then forgotten, because there are no loose ends and hence no follow-ups worth putting on Page One, the only page of today's Final that readers remember tomorrow. When Burton Rascoe, another Schlogl's alumnus, took charge of *Plain Talk* after Eaton's untimely death, I thought the door stood open wide. I sent Rascoe a carefully documented report of youth crimes attributed to the spread of marijuana smoking in Chicago, started by musicians who bought cigarettes they called "muggles" from salesmen opening up a new business for the Syndicate. Rascoe sent this back with a snort. "As an experiment," he informed me, "I once smoked two whole marijuana cigarettes myself, and got no effect out of it whatever. I am therefore returning your article." Indignantly, I re-typed the coffee-spotted pages, and sent the manuscript, Special Delivery, Personal, to Mencken at the *Mercury*.

Then I, too, could mention carelessly at Schlogl's: "By the way, I had a letter today from Henry Mencken." He wrote: DEAR MR. ANDREWS: *This tempts me, but in the end I find myself in doubt, and so I fear I must let it go. Have you anything else in hand or in mind? If so, I'll be delighted to hear of it.* So I banged my typewriter all night, and earned another letter from Mencken. *Let's see some other ideas. The gunmen have been done to death, but there are other oddities in Chicago. Let me know how you look at them, by all means. I'd like very much to get you into* MERCURY. I didn't need to have a check to flourish, when I could show that to Smith. He congratulated me, while Simon the Hunchback grimaced, and was much too kindhearted to tell me what Mencken admitted subsequently: that in those days he made it his business to correspond encouragingly with literally hundreds of unknown beginners, "because postage stamps were cheaper than paying more than twenty-five dollars a page to fill the gaps between Nathan's stuff and mine." I shall continue preferring to believe that like most practising cynics, behind his pose he hid a pitying soul.

I tried again. This time, I imitated Mencken's contempt for the *booboisie*. He wrote: *You know the laws of libel as well as I do. Probably better, with Smith for your instructor. Let's not get us both in trouble.* I tried again, this time with a short story of sorts. Another letter from Mencken: DEAR ANDREWS: *Unfortunately I can't take anything in the form of fiction. I'm using very little of it, and there's an immense amount already in type.* But if I was discouraged by then, apparently he wasn't. He wrote across the bottom of this rejection, in large letters: *I'll be disappointed in you if you don't keep trying.*

« 7 »

Keep on, keep on. Sandburg said it. Smith never stopped saying it, in more than words. Now H. L. Mencken said it, too. Meanwhile *Midweek* rolled along, as well as it ever could, and I had outside markets; not yet the biggest and best, but reasonably reliable. I had a studio, or at least two rooms and a bath, in one of Tower Town's remodeled brownstones. And a dog — a lady chow I christened Rikki-tikki-tavi in memory of Kipling's gallant mongoose — who hated women and barked at me from under the bed if I drank too much; and even a dog-walker, Scrubby Lee, who walked nine dogs for bachelors at three dollars per week per pooch, including baths and bones, and usually had more loose cash to jingle than his employers. I had neighbors who wrote or painted or anyhow talked entertainingly; not many, but enough. I could count on Pablo Katigbak to keep me on my toes, and on Jack Lawson to cover for me if I needed an alibi, and on Claude-Casper-Jordan to fight my battles, even if nobody was mad at me. My credit was good at Schlogl's. I owned two new canes and an extra Homburg, a silver slave-bracelet, two Albrights and a Rouault, stacks of books and records, a radio (almost paid for), and a king-sized bed. I had a few interesting telephone numbers, no more debts than usual, and no problems worrying would cure. In sum, I had attained, as one says, a certain position. But for the first time, that winter, I asked myself: Keep on to what, to where, and why?

I had come down suddenly with a bad case of social conscience. I almost wished I wasn't lucky. Any time, anywhere, I faced down-and-outers. They were not the regulars, beggars by choice, who paid the Syndicate's punks a percentage of what they panhandled, for preferred locations and protection, and spent the rest in the Syndicate's Canal Street deadfalls. These were amateurs, beginners, upstanding men turned derelict through no fault of their own. Gaunt, hot-eyed, muttering, they hated you for having a job and a place to sleep, and themselves for fawning on you. Some wore clothes that cost as much as mine, and were clean and pressed when they started hunting what they knew now they were not going to find. They, like their fathers and grandfathers, believed there was always work for willing hands. This was as sure as the Ten Commandments. Now, all at once, it wasn't so. Some of them sickened while you fumbled in your pockets, and cursed the coins you proffered. *To dig I am not able; to beg I am ashamed*. But pride is a thin thing. The poor devil who spat on my freshly shined shoes in the morning whimpered and pleaded when he was twelve hours hungrier. And Chicago didn't seem to care.

Small stores closed, with bankruptcy notices nailed to their doors and hand-printed signs in the windows: OPENED BY MISTAKE, or BUSTED AND DISGUSTED. Police stopped jailing vagrants. There was no more room in the jails. Rescue missions posted SORRY — No MEALS notices. Soup kitchens opened, ran out of soup and closed, in Bughouse Square where the I. W. W.s ranted, and in the "Slave Market," the two-block stretch of employment agencies for migratory laborers, at Canal and Madison. Much higher up in the social scale, there were startling suicides. But there was no talk about such matters in the World's Greatest Newspaper or in the Paper That Goes Home. Herbert Hoover, the Great Engineer, was confident in the White House. Samuel Insull, forming more holding companies, was confident on his throne. Colonel Mc-Cormick was confident in his Tower. All had to be right with the world.

The city was already starting preparations to celebrate A Century of Progress in 1933. Bad as my mathematics might be, it seemed slightly premature to celebrate so soon, since official announcements said the city was born in 1837. There were whispers here and there that by 1937 there might be nothing left to celebrate with. But Charles G. Dawes said only cowards fear tomorrow, and, three weeks after he resigned as first head of the Reconstruction Finance Corporation, the RFC loaned ninety million dollars to his Chicago bank, which certainly proved something. At 15 North Wells, we were packing up to leave for our fine new home across the bridge from Insull's Opera Building, which as anyone could see was mirror-image of its maker, and, like him, as solid as Gibraltar. Editorially, we agreed with the *Saturday Evening Post* that

"Wall Street may be selling off stocks, but Main Street has more to spend and is spending more of it than ever."

As far as Chicago crime was concerned, there was bated-breath armistice after the Valentine's Day Massacre. Al Capone was comfortably secure in a private cell with connecting bath, in the Eastern Penitentiary in Pennsylvania, where a phone was installed for his convenience and he held meetings in the Warden's office with his brother, Bottles, and Frank Nitti and Greasy Thumb Guzik. He had been behind bars since May 16, 1929, when he and his bodyguard, Frankie Rio, got themselves arrested in Philadelphia and charged with carrying concealed weapons. Arraigned, they grinned and offered no defense, and said "Thanks, Judge" when they were sentenced to serve a year instead of the customary sixty days.

There was something mysterious about this, unless like *Daily News* reporters relaxing at Hy Green's bar you put three and two together.

Three: Albert Anselmi, who got ten thousand dollars for murdering Dion O'Banion in his flower shop in 1926, was accused of being one of the trio that gunned down seven men in one minute at 2122 North Clark Street on February 14, 1929. So was Joseph Scalisi, who boasted after the massacre: "Now I'm the top hood in Chicago." So was Joe Guinta, president of Unione Siciliana. So was Jack McGurn, until he produced a blond alibi, still in her fetching negligee. That left three. Anselmi wasn't arrested. Guinta and Scalisi were jailed, then freed on remarkably low bail. Then, on the night of May 8, 1929, near Gray's Lake in Douglas Park, police acting on a tip whose source was never divulged found the bodies of Anselmi, Guinta and Scalisi in a stolen car overturned in a ditch. They had been beaten to death with baseball bats.

Two: Exactly a week later, in Philadelphia, Capone and his personal executioner went to great pains to get themselves arrested.

178

"I never know when I'll be next," Capone wailed to the Director of Public Safety, at a press conference. "I haven't had peace of mind for years. I'm willing to live and let live from now on." Apparently, the faceless brains behind him in the Syndicate had the same idea. Killings slowed down so noticeably that a college professor's book about them got Page One headlines. His exhaustive statistical surveys had convinced him there was no Syndicate. Chicago, he said, had precisely 1313 separate small neighborhood gangs, with no Big Guy in control. But then, in early 1930, the Citizens' Crime Committee sent a sharply contradictory report to the Police Commissioner, the Cook County Sheriff, the State's Attorney, and all city desks. And Clem Lane, on Police rewrite at 15 North Wells, hummed "Happy Days Are Here Again."

"Our purpose," the Committee's chairman proclaimed, "is to keep the light of publicity shining on Chicago's most prominent and well-known and notorious gangsters to the end that they may be under constant observation by the enforcing authorities and law-abiding citizens apprised of the hazards to be encountered in dealing with those who are constantly in conflict with the law." This preamble introduced a list of twenty-eight names. Al Capone was Abou Ben Adhem. After him came such worthies as George "Bugs" Moran, Ralph "Bottles" Capone, Mike "de Pike" Heitler, and Jack McGurn, "true name Demora." These must, the Committee urged, "be relentlessly pursued in every legal way as aliens, tax evaders, inmates of gambling and disorderly houses, and vagrants." It had all been said before. But a gimmick made all the difference. The Committee came up with a catch-phrase that made headlines clear around the world. The twenty-eight, it said, were Public Enemies.

Poverty wasn't a Public Enemy. Joblessness wasn't, or homelessness, or human desperation. Al Capone was **PUBLIC ENEMY NUMBER ONE**, in bigger type than *ARMISTICE SIGNED!* on November 11, 1918. Not even Smith could play the story any other way. I didn't ask him how he felt about it; I told him how I felt. At twenty-two, you can be bitter and contemptuous easily about the facts of life. I wondered (I still wonder) which I most despised: Capone and all his cohorts, or the enforcing authorities and law-abiding citizens who couldn't or wouldn't act as well as talk. I knew Smith had no control over front-office policy. Still I asked "Why?" when our Financial Section published a "guest editorial," written by a press-agent but signed by a member of the Crime Committee who was also a prominent banker, which explained that Black Friday was really only a gamblers' funeral that actually stabilized the market by eliminating the amateurs, and had only glancing impact on the irresistible up-curve of Chicago prosperity, and which concluded solemnly: "There is nothing wrong with Chicago that eradication of Capone and other Public Enemies will not soon correct."

The day this ran, the bid in the bridge game on the rewrite desk was seven no-trump doubled and redoubled. Even Pablo Katigbak joined the ring of silent spectators. Smith appeared, en route to the Cave of Winds. The World's Oldest Office Boy had just supervised a new recruit in scattering pins where Smith wouldn't miss them. While he added these to the row in his lapel, a telephone rang. He answered quietly: "City desk." Unintelligible chattering shrilled from the receiver. He commanded without raising his voice: "Please catch your breath and start over." He listened briefly, said "Thank you," and hung up. "I'm sorry," he told the bridge players, "but I think we'll have to re-plate for an Extra. Al Capone is back in town."

We re-plated. So did the Opposition. It would be editorializing of the sort Smith detested to suggest that anyone, even on a paper, was pleased by the Big Guy's return from his self-chosen Elba. The fact remained that Public Enemy Number One helped mightily in keeping what I truly believed was the truth about Chicago off of Page One for a period of grace

180

almost as long as Napoleon's Hundred Days. His homecoming pushed far back in the papers a release from the Federal Council of Churches calling for a day of national prayer on "Unemployment Sunday." Flanked by lawyers, escorted by reporters and photographers, he called on the State's Attorney. There was no warrant for his arrest. No criminal charge of any kind had been filed against him. "Then get off my back," he commanded, "and stay off." More headlines.

Statements to the press, not personally to Capone, threatened that if he stayed in Chicago, he'd be haunted and hounded wherever he went by two uniformed policemen. "Roust Big Al, will they?" he demanded. "Like I'm a two-bit punk? What's a matter with these muzzlers? I take a vacation, and while I'm away they forget who I am?" Then he played it for laughs. "Tell you what I'm gonna do," he told Bob Casey and John Drury. "I'll let the cops ride right with me in my new twenty-five-thousand-dollar limousine. They can rest their big flat feet, and I save the price of a couple of bodyguards. That's unless they're scared to be too close to me." The roust failed to materialize. More headlines.

At Hy Green's bar, Clark Rodenbach said, "The one who should be scared is Capone." Other experts chimed in. "He's changed from an asset to a liability. He has become expendable. Everybody knows it but Al. He got the Public Enemy tag hung on the briefcase boys who really run the Syndicate. They don't like it. Bad for big business. They never realized he's yellow behind the bluff and brag, till he ran for cover in the pen in Pennsylvania. Now he's just a loud noise. He was gone too long. The stooges he used to kick around found out it's fun to kick stooges of their own. Now he proves he's dumb as well as yellow by putting on a show that hottens up the heat. The Mob might liquidate him, just to cool things down." *Able was I ere I saw Elba.*

And Capone continued posturing and prancing in the spotlight. Crowds gathered outside the Hawthorne Inn in Cicero to watch him come and go. Then Rodenbach hit Page One ahead of the Opposition with news that Capone had decided, "he says for sentimental reasons," to move back to the South Side Levee District, "where I began my career." Now street urchins fought for the privilege of opening doors for him at the Metropole around the corner from Old St. Mary's Church on South Wabash, or at the Lexington, at State and Twenty-second, to which, the Crime Committee duly reported, the Syndicate had transferred its headquarters.

Catching up with Chicago, I hadn't wasted much money or time on the South Side. It was twenty years since Mike O'Leary, whose mother owned the cow that was accused of kicking over a lantern and setting off the Great Fire in '71, ran the biggest and crookedest gambling hell between New York and San Francisco, on South Halsted Street. It was almost as long since the Everleigh Sisters, Ada and Minna, closed their palace of ill repute at 2131 South Dearborn, where millionaires had charge accounts that ran up to fifty thousand dollars annually, and where on Christmas Days the sisters and their girls sang carols and entertained the press at a decorous turkey dinner, followed by spin-the-plate and blind-man's buff in the parlor. The house rule, by the way, was always NEVER ON SUNDAYS. On the Sabbath, the sisters and their girls sang hymns, and then rode out sedately in the park, and no gentleman offended by accosting them. Old-timers at 15 North Wells spoke of Ada and Minna with fond respect. "They were the kind of Madames you don't meet any more." In Pete Penovich's establishment, I met a fourth-generation sprig from a Founding Family tree, who told of being taken to visit a château in Southern France, where two widowed Baronesses held Sunday salons in the style of the *ancien régime*, attended only by the purest *haut ton*. "I was so impressed," he said, "that I apologized for being from Chicago. They said 'You're very like.' I asked 'Like what?' They said,

'Like your grandfather. He was one of our favorite clients.' You won't believe this, but they were the Everleigh Sisters." I said, "I believe you."

But the South Side was never the same after Gipsy Smith, the bare-knuckle prizefighter turned evangelist, led 20,000 praying followers, men, women and children, down Twenty-second Street into the Levee, which the papers called "Chicago's Little Hell." Lights went out as the paraders passed. In front of the Everleigh Club, they sang "Where Is My Wandering Boy Tonight?" Next morning (as a matter of quite meaningless coincidence, on my second birthday, October 19, 1910), the *Daily News* was the first Chicago paper to declare on Page One: "The Levee must be shut down and kept closed forever." I read this in yellowed clippings Jack Lawson excavated in the Morgue. Then, out of curiosity, I went to see if Al Capone's return made wild ghosts walk again on South Wabash Avenue.

I started my wanderings at Colosimo's restaurant, which was dingy and dull, unless it thrilled you to be shown stains on the floor, regularly renewed with red paint, that marked the spot where Big Jim died, quite possibly shot in the back by Al Capone, who was his trusted bodyguard, employed for this purpose by Colosimo's own nephew, Johnny Torrio. I tried the Four Deuces, down the street, where Capone worked briefly as a bouncer, before the owners vanished and he took over as sole proprietor. It was just another noisy, dirty dive. I tried the Frolics, where the show started after all the other places closed. Sixteen feminine zombies stalked to and fro, mechanically shrilling invitations that the customers ignored. I tried the Casa Granada, where Paul Whiteman had succeeded Guy Lombardo, and was featuring his Rhythm Boys, a so-so trio composed of Harry Barris, who did most of the singing and clowning, with Al Rinker, Mildred Bailey's brother, and a rather amateurish youngster oddly named Bing Crosby. Very late, because no one went there until long after midnight, I joined the milling throng at the black-and-tan Grand Terrace, far out on South Parkway, where Earl Hines (musicians called him "Fatha") played the piano, and Jack Teagarden and Frankie Trumbauer and Red Mackenzie and Peewee Russell and Jimmy and Tommy Dorsey and Randy Hall with his tin whistle, and whoever else chanced to be passing through, joined in jam sessions at sunrise. But this was tourist bait. I had to venture calculated risk, to find what the cabdrivers and joint-steerers left out of their spiels.

Only fools roved alone along the Levee's dark side streets. I did it, asking myself why I wasn't in Tower Town, where I knew the answers and the answerers knew me. Rotting buildings stood vacant, not even worth tearing down. Dark doorways and darker passageways held dregs of down-and-done humanity. I passed an address I had recorded during preliminary research into the Levee's scarlet past. Here Hinky Dink Mike Kenna and Bathhouse John Coughlin held court, as bosses of the Ward. The going price for votes was fifty cents, and a dollar for repeaters. The papers credited Bathhouse John with being the author of such lugubrious lyrics as "Dear Midnight of Love" and "Why Did They Build Lake Michigan So Wide?" A dozen reporters, including a couple who carried press cards like mine, claimed the arguable honor of being Coughlin's literary ghost. That was Chicago. You might as well laugh about the characters who ran the town. They'd go on running it anyhow.

Then I heard angels singing. I looked up, and saw Old St. Mary's Church, on the South Wabash corner where it was built before the Fire in '71. Congregationalists built it, foursquare and so thick-walled that the flames of inferno could not destroy it. They sold out and moved farther south. Catholics took over. Once, for a while, St. Mary's served as temporary Cathedral for the Archdiocese of Chicago. That glory passed. The church had not one single subscribing parishioner

184

when it was assigned to the American order of Paulist Fathers, because of their missionary dedication. And surely if there was ever an asphalt jungle in which missionaries were needed, if not wanted, it was in Chicago's Little Hell just after the turn of the century. That was when Old St. Mary's was first called "Angels' Half-Acre."

My plans for that night in 1930 had definitely not included going to church. But the doors stood open, candles burned inside, and the angelic voices were louder, clearer. Against the sky, I saw glittering lights that advertised the Metropole, where the papers said the Mob used sixty rooms on two floors and probably at that moment Al Capone pranced, postured, bragged, arrogantly unaware of or afraid to turn and face the shadows that inched closer. I went up the stone steps, into an oasis of calm, clean peace. Hours later, I was still trying to convince Father Eugene O'Malley that he and his Paulist choirboys belonged in *Midweek*. Without knowing what I sought in Little Hell, I had found it.

There was more than a physical resemblance between Father O'Malley and Smith. O'Malley, too, was slender, stooped, spectacled, mild, but with steel behind the mildness. He, too, had a dedication to Young Men Going Somewhere. But his were eight and ten and twelve years old — hard-eyed, underfed, suspicious, insolent, ragged, mirthless copies of elder brothers who ranged the Levee District mugging pedestrians, stealing cars, robbing filling stations, ganging up on cops, growing into two-bit punks used by the Syndicate to drive beer trucks and bomb dry cleaners and do minor gun jobs, and die young, or die a day at a time for twenty years in an iron cage. I am not exaggerating. What other future was there for them? Well, Father O'Malley said, there was a step to start from in the Paulist Choir.

He spoke freely, however, only about Father Finn, the founder of the choir, who had been taller, tougher, with large hands almost always balled in fists and a self-sharpening tongue. "Me, train boys to sing?" Father Finn objected when his superiors gave him his assignment. "I'd sooner be sentenced to a cannibal's stew-pot in Senegambia!" But in the black-robed army without banners, soldiers go where they are needed. During the black Depression winter of 1903, traveling on a pass, lacking money for a meal on the train or for streetcar fare when he reached Chicago, Father Finn arrived at Old St. Mary's. "He walked up and down the Levee hunting volunteers for his choir. He got just two. One sang like a nightingale. He attended two rehearsals, then was never seen again. His father had just killed his mother. The other choirboy was eight-year-old Johnny Keeley. He couldn't sing for sour apples, but he had all the rest of the kids on his block buffaloed, so Father Finn made him the Paulist Choristers' peace enforcer." Desperate for more singers, but not at all the man to ask for help from anyone but the Boss Upstairs, finally Father Finn was forced to appeal to priests of another order, at De LaSalle Institute. They helped him enlist recruits. The Good Shepherd Sisters sewed cassocks and surplices. The Paulist Choristers sang publicly for the first time in September, 1904. But it was the great Boy Soprano Battle that set them on the high road.

Episcopal choirboys from prospering Grace Church, bound for a picnic, collided with the Paulist boys, who thought a street brawl was picnic enough for anybody. The ensuing war with fists and stones and barrel-staves stopped streetcars, tied up traffic, and hit Page One in every paper. Father Finn was apologizing to Harrison Wild, Grace Episcopal's organist and choirmaster, when both heard simultaneously that boys from everywhere were besieging their churches, demanding a chance to join their choirs, now that the papers said boy sopranos need not be sissies. Thereafter, Father Finn had all he could handle, in the rehearsal hall next door to McNally's Undertaking Parlors, which was also the polling-place to which

Hinky Dink and Bathhouse John brought their voters on Election Day. Nearby was the biggest gambling dive between New York and California, bossed by Mike O'Leary. Small wonder that St. Mary's began to be known as Angels' Half-Acre.

Eight years after their first concert, the Paulist Choristers sailed for Europe. They were to have been aboard the *Titanic*, but just missed the boat. They won medals in Paris, and sang for the Pope in Rome. President Theodore Roosevelt summoned them to sing in the White House, specifying that they must appear before his Cabinet in executive session, "because I hope you can soften the hearts of some of the members and especially of William Howard Taft." But when the Rough Rider asked the boys to sing his favorite, "Drink to Me Only With Thine Eyes," twelve-year-old Jimmy Kearn (later a priest in Cedar Rapids), declined to sing the solo part because he thought the lyrics were too frivolous. Father Finn always had a stand-in ready. Ralph Summers sang the solo. T. R. shook hands with him, and with Jimmy, too. "I like a man," the Rough Rider said, "who sticks by his principles."

In the great days, the Paulist Choristers made two hundred and forty-one public appearances. Then war and other distractions halted the meteor in its course. Father Finn was needed at the Paulist mother-house in New York. Prohibition, and Repeal, spawned gangsterism. Hoodlums took over at the Metropole, and then at the Lexington. Youngsters stopped coming to Angel's Half-Acre. But in Rome, there was a young priest who had been one of Father Finn's boy sopranos twenty years before.

Recalled to New York, Father O'Malley was told, "Go home, and see what you can do." So he returned to the Levee, as poor as Father Finn was in his generation, as much a stranger, and facing a greater challenge. In Father Finn's days, boys who went wrong turned thief. In 1930, they turned murderer.

The Levee always had a floating population. Rents were paid by the day or week, seldom by the month. Now there was nothing to pay with, unless you took it from somebody else. The only chance to line your pockets was in the Mob or on its fringes. Having no other heroes, ten-year-olds heroized thugs who wore tailored suits and hand-made shoes, and drove big cars, and carried guns. The supply of two-bit punks available to the Syndicate, and totally expendable, exceeded the demand. Yet patiently, indomitably, frail Father O'Malley found a few who wanted to finish school, and play some baseball, and have a decent future. A few, and in fact enough to form a choir. But while they sang, beyond the stained glass windows that pictured the Stations of the Cross, boys like them were three-time losers before they sold their first vote to Hinky Dink and Bathhouse John; and every week, temptation to go and get it with a gun was strengthened, by the spreading spectacle of hunger as the reward for honesty, while Public Enemies rode high and free.

I said this. Father O'Malley didn't. I promised, sure I could count on Smith: "We'll give you two full pages in the magazine, and a color picture of the boys on our cover, for the Easter Edition. That should sell a lot of tickets for your annual concert." The concert paid for shoes and warm underwear and hot meals for the boys, and supported their summer camp in an abandoned icehouse on Crystal Lake. "Well," Father O'Malley granted dubiously, "you may come around if you wish, and see what there is to be seen. But go easy in writing about the boys. They've known sorrow and shame enough already, without it being branded on them for the upper classes to take for proof there's no hope they'll be anything but what their fathers and elder brothers have become."

Some of the story was sure-fire. When the Choristers sang

"The Seven Last Words of Christ," something never done before by a comparable organization, the voice of the boy soloist changed without warning in the middle of an aria. Flawlessly, his stand-in took up the note on which he had begun to fail. None in the audience suspected they heard a solo rendered into a duet. "The change can be heart-stopping," Father O'Malley said. "The boy pours out a pure note, and hears a faltering croak. He thinks he is disgraced, and done. This finishes the first happy years he has had. If he can no longer sing, he is back where we found him. Or so he fears. But God be thanked, it isn't so."

It wasn't so because of the Old Paulist Boys. They were lawyers, storekeepers, dentists, plumbers, Judges, truck drivers, doctors, salesmen, priests, postmen, streetcar conductors, college students. Few were rich, and many were out of work. But each did the best he could for a younger Paulist boy as foster brother. A thousand had made good, and a hundred more were climbing the straight road. Strangely (or perhaps, all things considered, not so strangely), hoodlums wanted to help. Some sent anonymous donations, or bought blocks of tickets for the annual concert. Some even dropped in at St. Mary's, when there was a midnight Mass. A gorilla with a record for brutishness came to Angels' Half-Acre dragging his small son. "Put the fear of God in him. Don't let him turn out damned like his old man." A boy whose dead mother had been Protestant, whose father had asked for a priest before he walked the last mile in Stateville Prison, chose his mother's faith though he sang with the Paulist Choristers. When the Cardinal heard him and praised his voice and the devotion in it, the boy said politely but firmly that he didn't propose to be converted to Catholicism. The Cardinal placed both hands on his head. "It was a very special blessing," Father O'Malley told me, "and it was deserved."

I wrote this and more for *Midweek*. But I left out the story of Solly Levine. He appeared one day in the rehearsal room.

"I decided to join your gang." Father O'Malley asked, "Are you sure you understand about the choir?" Solly said, "If I didn't would I be wasting my time?" Father O'Malley asked, "Are you sure you can sing well enough?" Solly asked, "Am I maybe an amateur? Since I'm knee-high to a lamppost I'm singing for throw-money in saloons." He considered the discussion closed. But Father O'Malley asked, "If you're earning your living as a professional, why do you want to be in a choir for twenty-five cents a rehearsal and fifty cents on Sundays?" Solly said, "They ain't throwing much these days." Then it came out in a rush. His father, unable to find work, had disappeared. His mother scrubbed floors, when her strength permitted. "I gotta get some school," Solly said. "If I have a square meal here, my Mom don't starve herself at home to feed me. If I get free shoes, she don't have to scrub a week to buy me some. Please, Father, let me in!"

Father O'Malley let him in, and held a conference with the other choirboys. Rules they agreed on were never broken. Nobody argued the New Testament against the Old with Solly. Saturdays, when Catholic boys were fined a quarter out of their Sunday half-dollar if they missed rehearsal, Solly was excused. Father O'Malley saw to it that he went to synagogue. But when I said Solly belonged in the *Midweek* piece, Father O'Malley said, "No." I was not to make Solly feel he was separated from the rest, by anything. So I didn't, and was glad I hadn't when on Christmas morning the Paulist Choristers filed into the choir loft at Old St. Mary's, caroling "*Adeste Fideles*." Leading them, singing his soul out, was that Christ-Day's soloist, Solly Levine.

« 8 »

Smith liked being told about Solly. But when my galley proofs came back, I found that for the first time in months he had blocked out whole paragraphs. He was keeping HORROR out of *Midweek*. What he blue-penciled was the ugliness I couldn't help recording, of senseless crime as the deformed off-spring of poverty that needn't be if things were better managed. At my age, somebody had to be guilty. I went to Smith protesting. "How much longer are we supposed to go on shutting our eyes and our ears to what's all around us? I know the paper's for Hoover. I know we're moving into the new building. I know Mr. Strong's backers are having money troubles. But, Mr. Smith, the Depression isn't going to go away. It's getting worse every day." I must have lectured for five minutes before I ran out of breath but not of indignation Then Smith asked himself, as much as he asked me: "What can we do about it?"

He wasn't being patronizing or sardonic. He hated what was going on as much as I did. Worse, because he was wiser, kinder, and so much older. "After a long, long while," he said, "we come to the sad realization that our tears cure nothing." He looked out of the window. "Nor does our disgust. Nor does our anger. Least of all, our anger." Then he said, as I expected, "Shall we smoke on it?" And for almost the last time, we puffed our cigarettes in the Cave of Winds, and talked too casually to deceive each other about day after tomorrow, when we would move out of 15 North Wells, to the new building across the river. Printers and pressmen bought pipes and tobacco at half-price. Reporters settled tabs. The Cave of Winds was closing, after thirty years.

All at once, Smith hurried out. Following, I had sense enough to be silent while he looked up and down along the shabby building fronts. Thus a man looks back along his life, from the Point of No Return. I turned away, and watched an El train thundering overhead.

The next walk we took together was into the new building, where Smith went quite unnoticed in a crowd of Prominent Personages invited to the Grand Opening, lectured by actors hired as guides for the occasion, who declaimed that we were pioneers at the Gateway to the Future. The new building, they said, was the first in Chicago if not in the world built wholly on air-rights. It floated on flying buttresses arching over the Northwestern Railroad tracks. Polished bronze doors in the wing near the Madison Street bridgehead opened on a lofty concourse. Above was a pictorial idealization of the making of a newspaper, almost like something by a Frenchman, though done by John Norton of Chicago. A gradually rising ramp led to the second floor. A wide covered walkway over Canal Street, lined with shops, led on into the Northwestern terminal.

Carl Sandburg hadn't come to the obsequies at 15 North Wells, or to the ceremonies at which Smith, an executive, had to be present. Sandburg hadn't said anything about the move, except to hum "Shall We Gather at the River?" during the last night in our corner at the old homestead. I hadn't heard it since the Indians sang it when my sister was buried in Oklahoma. I nearly asked him to stop singing it. And now I watched Smith, and nearly said things that would have embarrassed both of us, while the guides declaimed through megaphones that scientific studies ruled the building's arrangement, and the force of gravity had been harnessed to speed up production.

Editorial was on the sixth floor, reached by a battery of high-speed elevators. Copy passed downward, through the mechanical departments, until having been efficiently processed into zinc type-plates it reached the presses on the third floor, that spewed out Finals on the floor below, where machinery stacked and counted bundles and loaded them onto delivery trucks in what was called "the basement" though it was suspended forty feet above the trains that chuffed and snorted smoke beneath the building. We were given charts, and needed them, to find the places assigned to us by the efficiency consultants who planned Editorial for maximum use of floor space and minimal confusion.

I followed Mr. MacMillan. His roll-top desk, his fortress

since 1893, was somewhere in a junkyard. Replacing it was a slab of stain-proofed plywood on four spindly metal legs. He recoiled from this, and headed for the men's room. His spectacles were misted, and he couldn't read the cut-out copper letters on a door that spelled out LADIES. He entered, and in a split second came out running. "They've even changed that!" he cried as he passed me. He sat at his new desk only long enough to write his resignation, effective as of that morning.

Still, before he departed, the cold hand of modernity struck one more blow. Somewhere, someone threw the master switches that turned on the air-conditioning. Someone had forgotten a detail. The air-intake ducts were directly over the engines on the railroad tracks below. Soot poured onto the hospital-clean white walls, even in the Victor Lawson Memorial Room where Walter Strong and his partners were entertaining a host of dignitaries. Reddening faces were blackened. Soot covered everyone and everything. The building emptied much faster than it had filled. I am only reasonably superstitious, and not a believer in ill omens. But nautical history is full of ships that were doomed to sink the day they were launched. That day, meeting men and women who were strangers though they had worked for the *Daily News* since they and Victor Lawson were merely middle-aged, I heard them say we never should have moved, and the paper would never be the same again — and I was not at all disposed to disagree.

Soon after, Miss Harriet Dewey retired. We never saw her at the *Daily News* again. Then Walter Strong died, with strange suddenness. Time stood still while we waited to be told which one of fifty rumors might have truth in it. Actually, I was less concerned than most. Without consulting Smith, and assuring myself this was thoughtfulness on my part while he had to fight for the future of a couple of hundred other people, and his own, any way he could, I collected some ragged clothes in a secondhand store on Canal Street and prepared for a one-man investigation. Carl Sandburg came in on me, in our corner that was now a sort of goldfish bowl, all glass and chromium, and caught me practicing how to look and walk like a down-and-outer.

Nothing ever really surprises Sandburg, who has known human beings so long, but he seemed a little startled by my get-up. Then he grinned, while Little Big Mouth held the floor. I said I was going to sleep out, on benches in Grant Park along the lake front, and on the loading platforms under Wacker Drive. I was going to get the drifters to trust me and talk to me. I would come back, if I came back, with documentation to prove my contention that Something Must Be Done. Sandburg asked, straight-faced: "Has anyone gone on record to the contrariwise?" I said bumptiously that all he had to do was read the papers. "I do," he said. "I do." Then for once he offered advice. "When you have to sleep out in this weather," he said, "I learned, at about your age, that the way to keep from freezing is to collect newspapers from the trash cans, and wrap them around you, under your coat. The more, the warmer." I said "I'll try it. Thank you." I started out. He stopped me. "Be sure," he said, "you always put a paper over your heart."

It was already there. If it hadn't been, what ensued would have put it there. I was about to learn that though we had moved out of yesterday into tomorrow, the *ethos* of the Daily News would be the same as long as Smith decided what belonged in the Paper That Goes Home. My teacher was old Patrick Sullivan, who came limping out of the cold dun fog, using a broken broomstick for a cane. He stopped beside my bench, and pitied me. "I've spent my life. All I'm good for is to die, as decently as may be. But you're a sprout just broken off the branch. You oughtn't to be carrying the banner. That's for the has-beens and the never-wasers." He had six tattered newspapers. He insisted on giving me three of them. And he, like Sandburg, said, "Be sure you put one over your heart."

I had money in my pocket. I had a job. A few blocks north, my studio was warm, my chow dog listened for me and barked when the telephone rang. I sat in Grant Park lying to poor old Patrick Sullivan, letting him think I was worse off then he was, digging into him, already enjoying in my mind the round ripe phrases I'd put on paper when I got to my typewriter. It wasn't fair, it wasn't right, but if I gave him a dollar to buy a meal and a bath and a bed I'd rob him of his pride, and that was all he had to go on. I had to let him go on wasting pity on a beginner at the business of being outside looking in.

He is 73 years old, I wrote at dawn that morning. He was born in Galway, the last of eight strong brothers, and all but him at rest beneath the sod. He hasn't had a day's work now in seven months. What does he do when there's work to be had? "At my age you're past picking and choosing." He washes dishes, or tends a garden, or makes himself handy around a farm. "Three meals and a bed, that's all a man should ask for when at last he's worth no more." He hasn't slept in a bed in three weeks. He has one penny, which he keeps for dignity's sake. "As long as I have it, I'm not poor enough to beg." He wears a hat he found in the gutter, with two holes in the crown, and two coats he earned for doing snow-shoveling for a woman who changed her mind about paying him the dollar she promised, because he'd only spend it getting drunk. His trousers are rags held together with bits of string and a safety-pin. His broken shoes have no soles. He walks on pieces of cardboard. "Doesn't it make you hate people to see them going into the big hotels across there on the Drive, seeing them have so much when you have nothing?" "Why should I hate them? They've done no harm to me." "But you're old. Someone should be taking care of you." "My boy, nobody takes care of the old that haven't earned it. Nor have we the right to expect it. We brought ourselves to where we are." He leans back, easing his crippled leg. "I'll sleep a bit now, so to pass the time. But not you. I give you advice, who never heeded any. Stand up and walk, and don't stop walking. That's what the young must do, while the strength of youth is in them. Never stop walking straight ahead. And look ahead, not back." And so he dismisses me, and I owe him his privacy, this brave, kind old man.

So I walked on through the fog. See there? That is the noble, costly statue the city put up in memory of Alexander Hamilton, who founded the Treasury of the United States and set the nation on the path of perpetual prosperity. That is a sleepout on the southwest step of the pedestal. He combs his hair with a broken comb. Now he puts his hat on at a jaunty angle. Then he wraps a newspaper around his torso and buttons his torn shirt over it, and wraps another newspaper around himself, and fastens his vest over it with a safety-pin. He has no coat. Now he spreads three more newspapers on the cement and lies down on them. He turns over once, then straightens on his stomach, his unshaven face on his crooked arm. He pulls another newspaper over his shoulders. He sighs, and unbelievably, he sleeps. But the man on the northeast pedestal can't sleep. This one stands and stares at the slim finger of light from the Lindbergh Beacon on the Palmolive Building, that flicks across storm clouds moving in from Canada. There may be sleet or snow before sunrise. Then no one will sleep, in the hotel called Grant Park. This man wears a hat that cost money, and has a good overcoat, though its buttons are missing. He says he is a carpenter. Has he a family? Lines that were not around his mouth a month ago deepen, but he doesn't answer. How long since he had work? "Nine weeks. No, ten." How long since he ate? "This morning. No. That was yesterday." How long has he been a sleepout? Eight nights. No. Eleven. Suddenly: "What's it to you?" Would he accept a dollar for a meal and a bath and a bed? "Listen, Mister, I didn't panhandle you. I'm not down to that

*yet. Not yet, by God!" Then because he was well brought up
he realizes his rudeness. "Sorry. Thanks. What I get I earn.
I'll stay that way or die trying." As man to man, we say: "Good
night."*

I wrote on and on like that, for five full columns, and put
the pages on Smith's desk defiantly. All he said was, "You
seem to have caught a cold." I sniffled, sneezed, and insisted,
"I feel fine." He said "I'm sure you do." I said, "There's a lot
of sleepouts in Lincoln Park. I thought I'd go up there tonight." He said, "You know nobody asked you to do this." I
said, "Nobody told me not to." He began editing the pages,
making slight corrections to improve the grammar, cutting
nothing. While he did this, he said, "Of course, somebody
might shoot Al Capone and crowd this clear out of the paper."
Then he added wryly: "Or the new publisher may not ap-
prove." That was the first time I heard about Colonel Frank
Knox, who was buying the *Daily News* for twenty-three
million dollars.

Will Irwin wrote, when Victor Lawson owned the paper:
"The *Daily News* is not borrowing money from banks and it
does not need support from trusts or corporations. Even
should it ever change hands, the *News* would go on paying for
a generation by power of its bold honesty." Now Colonel
Knox, who had been a troubleshooter for Hearst, sat in the
Victor Lawson Memorial Room with members of a new
board of directors including Max Epstein of American Trans-
portation, J. E. Otis of Central Illinois Trust, John Stuart of
Quaker Oats and International Harvester, George E. Scott
of American Steel Foundries, and Sewell Avery of U.S. Gyp-
sum and Montgomery Ward. But neither Capone nor new
front-office policy pushed my story off Page One, where it
ran with an Editor's Foreword formally approved by Knox:
*Immediate action to house and feed and find work for hun-
dreds if not thousands of such jobless and homeless men and*

197

women as those described in this factual report from firsthand observation is Chicago's most urgent civic responsibility.

And for once, if never again, the World's Greatest Newspaper voted with the Paper That Goes Home. John T. McCutcheon, the *Tribune's* political cartoonist, did a Page One drawing of the sleepouts I described in the *Daily News*, headed *A Dollar's Worth of Shelter Will Prevent Ten Dollars' Worth of Crime This Winter.* That wasn't exactly what I had in mind, but no matter. Ministers preached sermons and took up charity collections. Committees organized. Five-dollar bills and ten-dollar checks piled up on my desk, "for you to give personally to the neediest person you meet in your wanderings." The solidest satisfaction I got was the only compliment I ever received from the World's Oldest Office Boy. ANDREWS (he wrote): *You surprised me with your "bum" stuff. Sentiment but no sobs. Quite sincere. Quite good. Keep trying.*

There it was again. *Keep on, keep on.* Well, then, what now, young man? I decided the answer lay in a book Carl Sandburg loaned me, in which William Bolitho said:

Journalism leads to everything, but only if you get out of it before too late. No matter how young and energetic and clever you are, there are younger hopefuls crowding up behind you, just as clever and more energetic because they have just begun to fight. Newspaper work should be a stepping-stone. The way to get out is to write a book. Any book, provided it's true to you as its writer, however untrue your truth may be to others.

I asked Carl Sandburg, in our corner: "When you write a book, how do you start?" He said gravely: "I glue the seat of my pants to a chair and put a piece of paper in the machine and pray." I said: "No, seriously." He said "I'm serious." I said: "Well, I've decided to try it." With *The Prairie Years* selling everywhere, and *The War Years* long in work, he was entitled to snort. But he didn't. He asked: "Are you sure you're ready?" I said "I'll never be any readier." Under his

198

gaze, suddenly not so sure, I argued: "If Edgar Wallace could turn out a novel, a light one, in a week, I don't see why I can't." He said "It's possible, it's possible." Pablo Katigbak, however, reported that Bob Casey was the first of a dozen doubters who would happily bet me twenty dollars it wasn't. Not for me. To my amazement more than to Casey's, or Sandburg's, I won that bet, though to this day I haven't had the nerve to try to collect it.

Young Man Becoming a Myth

Tower Town Wonder Boy Bob Andrews sells *Daily News* 80,000-word Chicago story for $500. Grosset & Dunlap publish as book. John Golden dickers for stage rights. Fox Films pays $7500 for movie rights. Nice going, Mr. Andrews. But a very lousy book.

> —*Dirty Dog*
> Chicago
> 1931

Andrews had, on a bet, batted out *Three Girls Lost* in seven days, writing about 15,000 words per night. So he was quite able to turn out a hundred thousand words a week over a period of years, without losing a pound or whitening a hair.

> —JAMES THURBER
> *New Yorker*
> 1948

"Bob Andrews" is a myth. No such actual person exists. The name is a cover for a syndicate of half a dozen writers.

> —*How To Write Radio Drama*
> Chicago
> 1932

GEORGES SIMENON COULD TURN OUT three or four disturbingly competent novels at one time, spending no more than three or four days on the best of them; but he owns Inspector Maigret. Evan Hunter's *alter ego*, Ed McBain, always has an 87th Precinct pot a-boiling; and who but Erle Stanley Gardner can say how many Perry Mason cases he cooks up simultaneously on a single burner? But these prodigies, though they sell packaged merchandise, possess perfected styles and manipulate long-familiar central characters. Furthermore, plot outlines are card-indexed in their capacious and uncluttered minds. This was not so for the amateur author of that fortunately now-forgotten epic, *Three Girls Lost in Chicago*.

There were three girls who dreamed for years about Chicago and what they could find there. They dreamed that in Chicago they could find all the things they longed for, and all the happiness they desired. And that there might be love. And now the three girls were in a big airplane, 3000 feet above the earth, racing toward Chicago, their hearts pounding, their eyes bright, their hopes high. They had left Minneapolis an hour before. They went up through gray mist and suddenly they were above a limitless floor of white clouds like fleecy cotton. The sky had never been as blue before. The sunlight stabbed their eyes. For a frightening moment they could not see the earth at all. But then the clouds parted below them and they saw checkerboards that drifted lazily — farms and roads and towns. They were leaving these behind; they were going to Chicago, at 100 miles an hour;

and in three hours they would be where they had always wanted to be. In three hours, the story would begin.

What story? I had no idea. Crumpling and littering the floor with false starts that led nowhere, I progressed this far finally, during the first of my self-allotted seven days, while Jack Lawson hovered solicitously, filling and emptying wastebaskets, bringing more copy paper. When the sausage factory ground to a full stop, with the next paragraph stuck in it somewhere, he asked sensibly why I didn't just give up. I was tempted. I might have tossed in the towel but for Carl Sandburg sitting across the office, humming and strumming, pointedly paying me no never-mind. I struggled on. I had six days left, including Saturday and Sunday, when finally I hit on allegorical names for my three girls: Marcia Talent, Edna Best, Norene McCann. Respectively from Oregon, South Dakota and Nebraska, they were the girl who might go wrong, the girl who wouldn't mind if she did, and the girl who couldn't if she tried. All cut from the same tinseled cardboard. And what happened to them had to be equally one-dimensional, or I'd never reach the only goal I had: THE END.

I had help, of course. Jack Lawson sorted the pages I finished, and spurred me on by remarking regularly that I'd probably fall apart any minute. Claude Caspar-Jordan made sure that if I did I'd feel no pain, by smuggling in Canal Street gin past the night watchman, in increasing quantities as the week wore on. My chapters ended with cliffhangers, arrived at more by accident than design. The technique, such as it was, was the same I used in writing thirty installments of a circulation contest come-on. It had to be. I knew no other. Scrubby, the dog-walker, reported that Rikki-tikki-tavi was on a hunger strike and might die of loneliness if I didn't come home pretty soon. Carl Sandburg appeared and disappeared, saying absolutely nothing. As for Pablo Katigbak, he encouraged me by listing bets being laid in the newsroom, at eight to one, that no matter how many words I typed Bob Casey would win my twenty dollars because a book is not a book until it's published, and nothing worth publishing was ever written at a hundred words a minute. (I have just clocked this paragraph at a minute and forty seconds. What that proves is problematical.)

Smith, according to the World's Oldest Office Boy, got hourly progress bulletins. Not that what I was up to could have been a secret from anybody. Toward the end of the week, you could hear my typewriter anywhere on the Editorial floor, even in Colonel Knox's office. I was fighting it, punishing it, writing blind. My fingertips puffed. The nail on my space-bar thumb tore to the quick. I gritted my teeth, and communed in spirit with the earlier martyrs. In time to come, I would wonder how I could ever have been such a posturing softy. By then, a hundred thousand words of dialogue a week, with Saturdays and Sundays off, would be pretty much a matter of course. But not yet; not yet.

Halfway through, one of my three lost girls suddenly took command. At least, without warning it became impossible for me to make her talk or act as I was sure she should. This entirely new experience bewildered me, though since it has been repeated on a few occasions over the years, I have come to think that this strange surprise comes more than once to every writer, and that when it does, what follows must improve on whatever went before. In any event, Jack Lawson moaned and Claude Caspar-Jordan went for more gin when they found I was rewriting earlier segments while I piled up more pages, and in turn, rewriting these. *Three Girls Lost* didn't miraculously flower into something to pore over fondly. As a matter of simple fact, I've never read past the first chapter of the finished manuscript. Nor do I ever intend to. But on the morning of the seventh day, I felt I had earned the right, somehow, somewhere along the line, to stop work and look up when Carl Sandburg ambled in, and tell him "I think I've got a book," in the tone of a first-time father announcing at the office: "It's a boy."

He didn't ask for proof. He said "That's fine, that's fine," and gave me some paragraphs for his "Notebook," and went away to do some more research for the fourth of his Lincoln biographies, his thirteenth book in fifteen years. I thundered on, down the home stretch. Pablo Katigbak found Bob Casey, and reported blandly, "I think maybe you owe Bob Andrews twenty dollars." At quitting time for the staff, I had a larger audience than I could see from where I sat. Smith circled the silent spectators so unobtrusively that I didn't know for hours about the note he dropped in my INCOMING basket. The last page tore, and I had to retype it. Then I wrote, in capitals, THE END. My hands stiffened. I couldn't have typed another word if my life depended on it. If anyone had told me I'd do the same thing over and over again, five hundred times and more, I'd have sworn that even I couldn't be an idiot that often.

I heard mild congratulations, and wished I hadn't been quite so stuffy about my requirements for *Midweek*. Someone mentioned odd craftsmen who can engrave the Lord's Prayer on the head of a pin. Granted their perseverance, what does such persevering prove? The World's Oldest Office Boy, departing, said he supposed I could claim I had won my bet. But if it was him and not Bob Casey, who wouldn't miss the twenty dollars and anyhow was too much of a gentleman to quibble, he'd stand pat on the *Century Dictionary* definition, which he had just looked up. BOOK: *A printed work of some length, on sheets fastened or bound together.* I didn't know, and I certainly wasn't going to ask one of our hard-cover authors, how to submit a manuscript to a publisher, even if I cared to put myself on record as sole believer that *Three Girls Lost* was worth publishing, which I didn't. So I started for Hy Green's speakeasy, to tell Bob Casey I was ready to pay off. Jack Lawson stopped me, handing me a note from Smith.

I squinted at the first of two scrawled pages. BOB: *Mr. Dennis has read the first half of your novel.* (That would be Charles H. Dennis, Victor Lawson's biographer, still Colonel Knox's editor in chief, who had given no indication that he saw any promise in *Midweek*, or in me. I thought he read nothing newer than the collected works of Calvin Coolidge. I couldn't picture him going farther than the first few lines in what not even I, but only Smith, had called a novel.) *You may not know,* Smith's note continued, *that Mr. Dennis selects our Daily Serial.* (I not only didn't know it; if Smith hadn't said so I wouldn't have believed it. He must have sent my stuff to Dennis. But how did it get to Smith?) Jack Lawson braced himself, and confessed, "I've been giving Mr. Smith your carbons. I thought I ought to." Why? Jack answered by pointing at Smith's second page: *The DAILY NEWS will buy first serial rights to your novel if you don't want more than $500. That would be the most we ever paid.*

Claude Caspar-Jordan broke the silence. "I sink," he announced judicially, "you catching up like hell on Chicago. I sink we drink to zis." I thanked him for the suggestion, and we headed for Canal Street, picking up Pablo Katigbak at Hy Green's bar. Bob Casey had gone home. Nothing more was said about the bet, then or ever after. My lady chow never barked at me more reprovingly than when I opened the door behind which she slept with one eye open, when the sun was rising cautiously over the *Tribune* Tower. We breakfasted on equal shares of a pound of caviar, a delicacy neither of us had tasted previously. It was presented by Pete Penovich, after Claude Caspar-Jordan ascended Pete's bar, as he had scaled half a dozen others during our *Wandernicht*, shouted for quiet, got it, and declaimed: "Ladies, and what you have bring wiz you; it please' me to present my boss, who have just become papa to a novel. Everybodies will now drink to him. All is on ze house!" You can win a lot of friends that way.

But under cold fluorescent ceiling lights in Editorial, I sensed envy in few pairs of appraising eyes, and reverence in none but Claude's, one of which had run into a door or something. Nobody else had sold the paper a Daily Serial. Nobody else had cared to try. Galley proofs came up in banana-bunches. Nobody pleaded for a sneak preview, not even the Circulation Manager, who rushed out three-color placards for delivery trucks and newsstands: *Awah! Awah! Sho! Sho! THREE GIRLS LOST! New Story Starting Monday In THE DAILY NEWS.* The expletives belonged to Amos 'n' Andy, whose legion of listeners went into spasms of helpless merriment whenever either was uttered on the air. It was quite an honor, to be tied to the tail of Correll and Gosden's comet. And under front-office orders, our elegant photographers (not including Charley Ford, who said he had to draw the line somewhere) asked me to advise and consent while they posed three professionally pretty young women (who were anything but lost in Chicago) for photographic illustrations for my story. This cost more than I collected for the serial rights. Such prodigal expenditure prompted the Promotion Manager to drop into my office for the first time and ask if there was anything he could do for *Midweek.* But Smith changed the subject when I tried to thank him. Carl Sandburg issued no new invitation for pork and beans at Pixley & Ehlers. And definitely, Marcia Talent and Edna Best and Norene McCann would have to get along without a fan club in the newsroom.

On Monday, shortly after they made their bow, my telephone jangled. "Is this," a voice I couldn't place inquired, "the author of *Three Girls Lost?*" I pleaded guilty hopefully. "I would like to invite you," the caller continued, "to address our literary study-group." I said, with a minim of coyness, that I wasn't a public speaker. "Oh, now, Mr. Andrews," the caller remonstrated, "you mustn't be so modest." He set a time and place. Then: "Oh, by the way. The subject on which we'd like you to discourse, regarding which we know you are particularly well informed, is *Should Writers Write Tripe?*" He couldn't wait to chuckle, until after he had hung up. I chuckled, too, in self-defense, while I repeated the conversation to Jack Lawson and Claude. I said I could take a joke even if it wasn't meant to be funny. Jack said maybe the invitation was on the level. I said it couldn't be. Then Claude said owlishly: "Some tripes is better as ozzer tripes." On the outside chance of being able to repeat this and embroider on it, at the scheduled time I appeared, accompanied by Jack and Claude, at the appointed address. It was a vacant lot. So we went to Canal Street, where the bartender had to listen.

Next day, there was another call. "This," an unfamiliar voice declared, "is E. C. Ketcham." I said, "You boys can do better than that." The caller repeated firmly: "My name is E. C. Ketcham. I represent Grosset and Dunlap, the publishers. I am staying at the Sherman Hotel. I would like to have you meet me here for lunch. I want to discuss our publication of your novel, *Three Girls Lost.*" It had to be a hoax. "As a matter of fact," I improvised, "I have a luncheon engagement at the Sherman with Frank Bering, the managing director. Suppose you drop by our table." Frank Bering, a six-goal polo-player and dashing man-about-the-Loop, was also the solid balance wheel in a prosperous partnership whose more flamboyant member, Ernie Byfield, got most of the newspaper space while Frank did most of the work. I had no engagement with him, but Harlan Ware, press agent for the Sherman and its famous College Inn, submitted short stories to *Midweek* now and then, and one good turn deserves another. So Frank, though surprised, was instantly hospitable, when Harlan introduced me to him that noon in the hotel's Oyster Bar (where the Blue Plate Luncheon cost ninety cents, a high price in those days). "Sit down and join us, Bob." So if schemers lurked, to see me gulled again, this laugh was mine; and I listened and learned while Frank gave his recipe for the Original Chicago Cocktail (not recommended for novice drinkers):

Half a gill of brandy, a jigger of Curaçao, one or two dashes of Angostura. Stir well with ice. Strain into preferred glass. Squeeze a lemon peel and drop it in. Pour champagne on top to fill. Frank Bering sold liquor for three quarters of a century, waiting on customers in his father's Ohio store when he was ten years old, still looking out for the comfort of patrons in his Pump Room at Chicago's Ambassador East when he retired at eighty-five, and never drank a drop. He liked to see his guests enjoy themselves, however, and I was happy with my second Original Chicago Cocktail when a portly stranger tapped my shoulder. "Mr. Andrews? I'm E. C. Ketcham."

An hour later, I had a Grosset and Dunlap contract in my pocket, and another five-hundred-dollar check in my hand, and if anyone in Editorial didn't hear about it, that wasn't Jack Lawson's fault, or Claude's, or Pablo Katigbak's. I was busy in Makeup, persuading the printers to pull two fresh sets of galley-proofs, eighty-seven columns each, one for Mr. Ketcham, the other to be stuffed in a large brown envelope which I addressed to *William Fox Film Studios, Hollywood, California.* I mailed this in a hurry, and told myself that if nothing came of it, I'd be the only one to know. But the World's Oldest Office Boy had a cousin working in the postal substation, so the grapevine buzzed. Nobody then on the paper had ever sold a book to the movies. Ben Hecht had, but only after he graduated; and then it wasn't his first-born, or his second, or his third, and it was Literature, not a Daily Serial.

I told Pablo I didn't need him to tell me what was being said. I said, "I can't get ruled off for trying." He asked: "You want to bet?" Little Big Mouth leaped into the vacuum. Dreaming out loud, I said I was all set to start my next book. It wouldn't be another *Three Girls Lost;* it wouldn't be about Chicago. I already had the title: *As If This Flesh*, from Richard II's speech in Shakespeare's tragedy; and my grand plan was Shakespearean, adumbrated by John Donne. I'd tell the true life-story of Francisco Goya y Lucientes, Goya the peerless Spanish painter, who felled brave bulls in the ring at Seville with his bare fist, and fathered more children than he or many horned husbands could count; whose nude *"Maja,"* painted with love, was a goddess unsoiled; whose clothed *"Maja,"* painted to satisfy the Inquisition, was a shameless strumpet; for whom all color died with the Duchess of Alba, so that always thereafter he worked in chiaroscuro, disowning mankind and indicting its masters, whether they brandished swords or breviaries.

I quote this farrago as Pablo recalled it to me, not many months ago, in the Ashoka Hotel in New Delhi. "I remember perfectly though I can see you don't," he said, "because that was the only time I heard you when you had no doubts. You saw that Goya book as if it hung in the air before you. I thought to myself: Could be, could be. So I said something, I forget what, to make you mad enough to stop talking and go write." I wrote. And slowly, now, for me, with long pauses between sentences. Carl Sandburg, humming and strumming across the office, fell silent, and considered me until I was aware of him. He didn't say anything, but he grinned: the way a boss carpenter does when the apprentice who is breaking into the trade beside him suddenly discovers there is more to building a house than driving nails. *Fellowship*, like most portmanteau words, is usually misused. I want to believe I began to comprehend his definition of it at around midnight on July 14, 1930. But next morning, the World's Oldest Office Boy came running from the newsroom. "Long distance for you. Come on." I asked suspiciously: "Why can't I have the call transferred?" He said, "It's on the open line from the New York Bureau. Come on, come on."

All right. I went along with the gag, following him to the open-faced booth in which rewrite men sat when a running story was coming through from Foreign Service. I felt as if I stepped out on a stage. "Hello. Hello." Everything had stopped around me. Everyone was listening. *"Hello!"* A voice came thinly from far off. It was Long Distance, sure enough. *"Andrews? This is Albert Lewis. I'm speaking for Winnie Sheehan."* I wondered who made up those names. *"Listen, Andrews. I'm authorized to close a deal for film rights to your* THREE GIRLS LOST." It had to be another hoax. It had to be. *"Can you hear me, Andrews?* I said "Oh, yes, I can hear you." The mystery voiced asked *"Well, how much?"* All right; no worse for a sheep than for a lamb. Loudly, so no one would miss the best part, I said "I'll sell for forty thousand dollars, not a dime less. Take it or leave it, and I don't care which." Silence, infinitely prolonged. Suddenly I thought, My God, maybe this is on the level, and I've just cut my own fat throat. Then the man in New York barked angrily, asking exactly what the publisher's son had asked when I talked of leaving Minneapolis, *"Who do you think you are? Ben Hecht?"* Then he said: *"Listen, Andrews. Listen good. Seven-five, not a dime more. And you can take that or leave it!"* I yammered, "I'll take it, I'll take it." Then I asked: "How much do you mean by 'seven-five'?" He asked, *"Are you kidding or something?"* I said, "Oh, no. No. No." He said, *"Seven thousand five hundred, what else? We got a deal?"* I said, "We got a deal."

I hung up, and turned to face my audience. Everyone was suddenly busy. Back in my corner, I sat oblivious to Jack and Claude. An hour and forty minutes later, the World's Oldest Office Boy came running again, waving a telegram, minus its envelope, crookedly refolded. "Opened by mistake," he said. I said "Oh, think nothing of it!" and read PLEASE WIRE CONFIRMATION ACCEPTING PRICE SEVEN THOUSAND FIVE HUNDRED DOLLARS FOR YOUR NOVEL THREE GIRLS LOST AS AGREED ON TELEPHONE THIS MORNING. CONTRACTS AND CHECK WILL FOLLOW IMMEDIATELY. ALBERT LEWIS FOX FILMS. Then at last I warwhooped, like a Kiowa and an Arapaho and a Sioux rolled up in one.

2

Carl Sandburg put up with me for four days, during which my head continued to swell while my wallet flattened. No check arrived. Well-wishers, their numbers increasing by the hour, said I mustn't worry. And how about a drink, to celebrate? I paid, with as much off-handedness as I could counterfeit, until I ran out of cash. Then my popularity waned. And Sandburg, having stood my strut and swagger as long as patience was a virtue by his measurement, rose finally and said, "I think the time has come for us to take another walk."

I was due to meet Gene Austin, who had arrived in Chicago to launch a comeback. In his heyday, Gene had sold more records than any other singer before or since. Unlike most entertainers, he stayed out of the market. He was too busy spending to bother about Wall Street. He bought a yacht, and named it *My Blue Heaven* for the song that earned him his first million. Sailing, even on Long Island Sound, made him seasick. So the yacht stayed tied up at the foot of Sutton Place. It was a floating bar, where everything was free to whoever happened to come aboard. Gene had twelve deep pockets built into each of his mink-lined polo coats. Every morning (for Gene, that was one in the afternoon), in his corner suite on the top floor of the Hotel Astor, overlooking Times Square, he donned one of his polo coats, stowed a bottle of the best available bourbon in every pocket, and paraded down Broadway dispensing eye openers and ten-dollar bills to show folk temporarily at liberty, until he had given away all the whiskey and folding money he could carry. On Black Friday in 1929, he was loading up for his share-the-wealth promenade, when his agent and several producers, two ranking comedians and their stooges, three songwriters and a couple of orchestra leaders trooped in, collapsed in chairs, and buried their heads in shaking hands. "We're wiped out," they told Gene. "All gone

213

in the Crash." He hadn't even heard about the Crash. All he read in the papers was Walter Winchell and Ed Sullivan. He didn't own a share of stock. "We ain't got left to eat," his visitors wailed in chorus. "So drink," Gene said, and passed around his bottles. He also handed out cash, picked up tabs, and wrote checks, until he was as flat broke as his friends.

Record sales hit an all-time low. Nightclubs and theaters went dark. Banks closed. For the first time since he left Louisiana with a carney outfit, singing "St. James Infirmary" and playing barrel-house piano for the coochie-dancers, Gene was down to Nickel Number One. But he wouldn't change his way of living. "If I can't go first class, I don't go." He wouldn't cut his asking salary. "I was the highest-unpaid layoff in the business." Finally he had no yacht, no suite, no bourbon to dispense. "People asked me, 'How could you possibly throw away four million bucks?' I said, 'It wasn't easy.'" Then a couple from Chicago passed through New York, bound for their summer home on the Riviera. They had lost only a couple of million in the market, and still had eight or ten million left. Once they had paid Gene two thousand dollars to croon "My Blue Heaven" and "Take Your Shoes Off, Daddy, and Start Running Through My Mind," over long distance from Florida, to help them patch up a lovers' quarrel. Gene told them now that he was so rich he couldn't afford to work. They knew better. Respecting his pride, they asked him, as a favor, to occupy and care for their bijou mansion in Chicago while they were away in Europe. "They talked me into it. I'm a sucker for a sales pitch." It didn't occur to them, however, that a house is not a home unless there are vittles in the kitchen and corn-squeezings in the jug.

Gene stocked the larder, and the bar, by turning the Gold Coast place into a co-operative caravanserai. Any needy passer-by was welcome if he could carry a tune. If money came his way, he put it into the kitty. All contributions were gratefully accepted. The house rule was share and share alike. Nine musicians staked claims in the master's quarters. Six chorus girls set up light housekeeping in milady's chambers. Two sister acts camped in the library. The Mound City Blue-Blowers had the drawing room. Total odd-jobs earnings weren't much, but nobody hungered or thirsted. "Anybody don't enjoy this life," said Gene, "just plain don't deserve home cooking." The moral tone was high. No cat-and-dog fights, no fall-down drinking, no muggles-whiffing, no out-of-bounds romancing. The jam session never stopped. Neighbors gave up complaining to the cops, who came, saw, joined in, and sang Come-All-Ye's until they had to check in to go off-duty — and then were likely to come back, bringing the day shift along. Everybody was hap-hap-happy, in Gene Austin's new Blue Heaven.

I had arranged to meet him and discuss a *Midweek* piece, which I'd write but he'd sign, about Depression victims who couldn't cry for laughing. But Sandburg changed my plans for that evening, without asking if I had any, and I followed where he led.

Silently, Sandburg strode ahead of me through the muggy twilight, along Madison to Michigan, up Michigan to Kroch's big bookstore, open that evening. Inside, there were more clerks than customers. He stepped aside, for me to enter first. He tapped my arm. "Turn around." Wondering, I turned. "Keep turning." The fifth time around, his point got through to me. Wherever I looked, there were books, thousands of them, by men and women, all of whom thought when they wrote THE END, "I have borne a child and everyone will agree how beautiful it is." I faced my judge, who was never more Lincolnian. "Now," he said, "suppose you start trying to learn how to be humble." Then he let me pay for the pork-and-beans at Pixley & Ehlers.

Next morning, the Fox Films check arrived. The first big bite out of my first four-figures bank account bought a rare edition of Goya's *Caprichos*, another of the more expensive and much more revealing *Desastres de la Guerra*, and an 1871 printing of *Extraordinary Popular Delusions and the Madness of Crowds*, because although it is Britishly reticent, it also flays the human foibles that Goya laid bare with such Spanish savagery. The next went for two cases of uncut Old Rarity, and four of Perrier. The one after that got me the first typewriter I ever owned that wasn't secondhand. Now, surely, I was equipped to make words dance. But I couldn't write a hundred words a minute, or even half as much. I tried to convince myself this was because for the first time I wasn't writing for money, and therefore was thinking before I typed. I knew better. I had shadow-boxed with puppets. Now I grappled with Goliath; and I was no little David.

I told Claude Caspar-Jordan, "I could afford to quit the *Daily News* and go to Paris, and then to Spain to see Goya's paintings in the Prado." Claude thought that was a lovely idea. "I go wiz, natural'. To keep you out of troubles." I cogitated, and retreated from decision that must mean good-by to *Midweek*, to fellowship in my corner, to Sandburg, to Smith. "No," I said gallantly, and quoted U. S. Grant. " 'I propose to fight it out on this line if it takes all summer.' " Sandburg heard this, as I hoped he would. It didn't appear to impress him. Perhaps, in his comprehensive collection of folk sayings that sound commonsensical to him, there was one that holds it's no skin off anybody's back if a hungry man takes a bigger bite than he can chew. Anyhow, I saw no castles in Spain, then or ever, except in Goya's searing sketches. Claude retreated to Canal Street, bemoaning the loss of a boon barcompanion. Jack Lawson tiptoed, shooing off authors who hoped to write for *Midweek*. And no one, not even Pablo Katigbak, heard any progress reports from me concerning *As If This Flesh*.

The World's Oldest Office Boy brought in a galley proof headed *Dirty Dog*. "First issue," he announced, "of the new private newspaper for reporters. Collector's item, no doubt." I wasn't interested. Someone, usually someone who isn't much use around the newsroom, is always starting a private scandal-sheet for *sub rosa* circulation. The only reporters' publication I ever saw that was worth reading was published by the New York Newspaper Club and edited by Gene Fowler; and it went downhill rapidly after Gene departed and his nameless successors re-titled it the *Three-Em Dash* and went in for interoffice vendettas. I once published one of my own, in Minneapolis, for a couple of weeks, until I ran out of nasty things to say about the copyreaders. *Dirty Dog,* as it happened, lasted through three editions. I wouldn't have touched the first one, if the World's Oldest Office Boy hadn't insisted. "Marked copy. Look."

My eyes lighted on a segment headed *Poor Old Bill,* which sneered: *The* CHICAGOAN, *as edited by William (Nice Nelly) Weaver, gets worse all the time if that's possible. It isn't even as sophisticated as the* NEW YORKER's *Little Old Lady from Dubuque, which by no coincidence is where Willie hails from.* I wasn't shooting at the *Chicagoan* any more, now I had money in the bank and my Good Book in progress, but for a writer I am pretty loyal to editors who have befriended me. I growled indignantly. "I think I know who wrote this. He's tried for a year to sell something to the *Chicagoan* and can't because he couldn't write his way out of a paper bag." The World's Oldest Office Boy protested: "I didn't mean that. I meant that!" His forefinger stabbed at a paragraph headed GENIUS AT WORK. It capsuled the strange saga of *Three Girls Lost,* quite accurately, and ended *Nice going, Mr. Andrews. But a very lousy book.* I said, "I agree with him. Don't you?" The World's Oldest Office Boy backed away from me uneasily. In the newsroom, he told Pablo Katigbak "If I didn't know Andrews so well, I'd have thought he was sincere."

A memorandum came from Charles H. Dennis: *Your*

Daily Serial is having satisfactory reader reception. I suggest a sequel. Terms as before. Since DAILY NEWS *publication has been your stepping-stone to such remarkable increment, I assume you will feel obligation to deliver sequel earliest feasible.* My typewriter started rattling at top speed, and Jack Lawson told Claude Caspar-Jordan I was acting like my old self again. Then he read what I had written to Mr. Dennis. *Thank you for your kind offer. Unfortunately I am deep into a serious novel which may take months to complete and calls for such total concentration that I am unable to take on any other writing at this time.* I sent this through channels, and the grapevine buzzed anew. "Andrews," the World's Oldest Office Boy announced, "was out on the end of the limb already. Now he has sawed it off." When Pablo Katigbak quoted this, I asked, "What's your opinion?" He shrugged. "For the rich," he said, "birds sing."

I went to Smith, placed a carbon of my note to Mr. Dennis before him, and asked "Was I wrong?" His pencil was poised over a Page One proof of a banner-line story up-dating the wanderings of Public Enemy Number One. South Dakota's Governor had called out the National Guard, to keep Al Capone from settling in the Black Hills, near the historic spot at which Calvin Coolidge had said "I do not choose to run," and waited to be coaxed, and wasn't. Bahama's British-officered police wouldn't let Capone set foot ashore. The Mob claimed connections in Machado's Cuban government, but Havana police gave Capone twenty-four hours to get out and stay out. A hoodlum-rousting detective named Lefty James met Capone on the *Chief* in Pasadena and told him "Los Angeles can't use you." In Florida, the Governor issued orders to sixty-seven Sheriffs: "If Capone shows up in your county, escort him back across the state line." But Capone claimed a taxpayer's rights, as owner of property near Miami. The story Smith shortened while he studied me reported that Capone's lawyers had just won a restraining order. The headline read AL CAPONE

WINS FLORIDA HAVEN. Resignedly, Smith okayed the proof. Then he said "I can't advise you, Bob. I would if I could, but I can't."

He wasn't disowning me. He was simply saying what he told all Young Men Going Somewhere when they, and he, reached a certain milestone. He stood up wearily, and for a moment both of us thought we were going to the Cave of Winds for a smoke to clear the atmosphere. Then he sat down again, took out a cigarette, lighted a match, thoughtfully blew it out, and put the cigarette away although there were no No Smoking signs in the new building. Both of us knew what neither had the heart to say. More than the Cave of Winds was buried back along the road, and there was nothing either of us could do about it. I said something meaningless, and went back to Goya, and was typing steadily though not too fast, because this wasn't a bet I could win in a week (and maybe not in a year), when Jack Lawson interrupted apologetically. "There's a man on the phone, named Gorham. He insists on talking to you in person. He won't say what about."

Expecting anything, I took the call. Not wasting a second, Gorham told me he was speaking for an advertising agency I had never heard of, gave me his office address, and said, "I can see you at 10:10 tomorrow morning, for twenty minutes." I said, "I don't know you, Mr. Gorham, and as far as I know we have nothing to see each other about." He said impatiently: "You wrote *Three Girls Lost*, didn't you?" I admitted it. "Well, Mr. Andrews, we think it's possible you can do some writing for us." I asked "Who is us?" He replied "Blackett-Sample-Hummert," apparently expecting me to stand at salute. "We," he said, "are pioneering in radio." That did it. "We'd be wasting Blackett-Sample-Hummert's time and mine," I said, "discussing radio. I hate radio. Good-by, Mr. Gorham." I hung up on him, slamming that door, only to have Jack Lawson remind me of another one I couldn't close as easily. Tomorrow, in case I'd forgotten, was the *Midweek* deadline. And there were still four empty pages to fill.

All the filler we had in type was stuff we paid for only because Smith, or I, or both of us, had bent without wholly breaking Smith's rule against giving handouts to indigent authors. If I used some of it, Smith would pass the pages without comment. Which made doing this impossible. He allowed me too much leeway already. But the new contributions Jack Lawson had culled from the Unsolicited Manuscripts stack were hopeless. He said so before I could. I hadn't followed through on Gene Austin. First Carl Sandburg, then Goya and *As If This Flesh*, had taken precedence. Now I tried to track Gene by telephone. It took two hours. He was at a used-car lot, negotiating for anything with four wheels that he could afford that would get him out of Chicago. "We have been canceled at the Happy House," he said. "The landlords came home." I asked, "Are you all out in the street?" He said, "We ain't in off of it." Then he added cheerfully: "The act had been on too long anyhow." He explained that he and his Blue Heaven guests had worked up a sort of tab-show. "We're taking it out on the road. It ain't the Follies, but we'll eat. I wouldn't be amazed we even do a little drinking." Then he said he'd appreciate it if I didn't put the Happy House story in *Midweek*. "The landlords ain't happy already." So that canceled out the only possibility I could think of, but I wished Gene luck and said, "Maybe we'll meet again somewhere." (We've been meeting ever since, never by prearrangement. Gene lives in a trailer, now, which of course is called *My Blue Heaven*. The last time our paths crossed, the trailer was parked on a lot in Las Vegas, and he was singing in a cocktail lounge, and running for Governor of Nevada, "just for the exercise.")

I was pretty discouraged, when I heard Dan Fitzgerald guffawing down the hall. A bumbling St. Bernard of a man, always pawing at people with insistent overtures that were

220

almost always rejected, Fitz was a copyreader who wasn't trusted with Page One copy. He didn't count for much after hours, either. A dozen times, at Hy Green's bar, I heard him break in on story-behind-the-storytellers, inquiring with drunken hopefulness: "Did I ever tell you gentlemen how I won my medals?" That was as far as he ever got. Winking at each other, members of the inner circle chorused, "We believe you, Fitz, we believe you!" Then they turned their backs on him and resumed the meeting of the mutual admiration society. Each time, Fitz chuckled sheepishly, then stumbled out, his shoulders sagging, and was docked next morning by the chief of the copy desk for checking in late, still too drunk to work.

Driven by desperation, I buttonholed him at the elevator. "Mind if I join you, Fitz? You know, I never had the chance to hear how you won your medals." Momentarily, his bleared eyes brightened. But the poor foolish dog had been kicked too often. "What would a fat old nothing like me know about medals?" I said, "You weren't old, and you weren't fat, in 1917." He fled from me, to Hy Green's bar, where he gulped three slugs of straight gin, which I paid for. That caused him to drop his guard for an instant. "It wasn't 1917. It was 1915, in the Second Battle of Ypres. With the Ladies From Hell, in their kilts, and the cold steel shining and the bagpipes skirling *Over the Water*." Then, suddenly, he refused another gin, and started out. "You believe me, you believe me. Like all hell, you believe me!" I stopped him at the door, saying honestly: "I do, Fitz. I give you my word: I believe you. And I'll tell you why. If one lie flops, a liar thinks up another one. But you, you're consistent." All at once, I wasn't just trying to fill up a hole in *Midweek*. I said "Fitz, as a personal favor, come on back to the office and tell me about your medals."

I took along two bottles of gin. His hesitance lessened with each drink, until he was walking back and forth, gesticulating, his blurred voice crisp and clear at intervals. He was doing well on a small-city daily in upstate New York when World War I broke out — unmarried, supporting a widowed mother, unable to save any money but pretty much resigned to the onset of middle age. His mother was Scotland-born, and had come to the United States by way of Canada. She didn't think "I Didn't Raise My Boy To Be A Soldier" was a song fit to be sung, and voted against Woodrow Wilson because "He Kept Us Out of War." She had scrimped and gone without, to put her only son through college. Now, with her widow's mite, she bought him a one-way ticket to Montreal. "I looked back from the train and she was waving and smiling, not a tear. She hadn't told me she had cancer. She was gone within the month."

He shipped out for France with the Canadian Division, rated Sergeant, called "Grandpa" by the youngsters in his squad. They tried to protect him, because he was too old to die. Touched by their concern yet determined to prove he belonged in battle, in Flanders Fields he was commissioned lieutenant, for gallantry beyond the call of duty. He got his first medal then. At Ypres, he gathered up the remnants of a broken battalion, all its senior officers being dead, and stormed a hilltop with the steel. From this observation post, he saw the French Zouave and North African battalions disintegrate, leaving the British left flank exposed. Then he saw Duke Albrecht of Württemberg's *Landwehr* Brigades massing for a push through the Steenstrat Gap, and knew this counter-attack could not be met by disorganized Allied detachments scattered over miles behind him.

Wounded, helpless to move, Fitz leveled his Webley side-arm at his youngsters, and ordered them to get out, *sauve qui peut*, leaving him alone. When some said, "No, sir," he fired over their heads. Then, when they were gone, he called for an Allied artillery barrage, aimed at him where he lay bleeding in the mud. Shellbursts zeroed in on Fitz, just as he emptied his Webley blindly at the first wave of the Boche break-through.

He went on shouting aim-corrections until a hundred Allied guns centering on target turned the hilltop into a pyramid of corpses, and the slaughter stopped at stalemate. Three days passed before a graves-detail saw Fitz's shattered hand move slightly, when shoveled mud fell on him in a crowded burial ditch, and stretcher bearers carried him to the first of many medics who were to say, "By every law I know, this man will die." But what was left of Fitz lived.

Fumbling, very drunk by now, he produced dogeared documents no one else had encouraged him to show. I scanned them, and typed: *One lone overage American volunteer, whose act was sacrificial beyond any call of duty, who had no possible hope of surviving the fury he unleashed with his own body as fix-point, unquestionably saved thousands of other lives, and may well have saved the Allies from irreparable defeat, almost three years before the United States at last decided to fight in Europe for freedom for the world, and Black Jack Pershing said in France (or never said, depending on which foreign correspondent gets his think-piece into the history texts) "Lafayette, we are here!"*

Fitz read this over my shoulder, swaying, supporting himself by clutching the back of my chair. "No," he said suddenly. "No. No." I said, "Fitz, it's all here in your citations. Eleven wounds, nine decorations from Allied High Commands." He said, "It's a lie. It's all a lie. I'm a liar." I said, "According to this, you're entitled to the full salute if you walk past the guards at Buckingham Palace." He said, "They saluted me. And I ran. I ran. They saluted my medals, not me, and I had no right to wear them." I said, "Fitz, you're drunk. I'll put you in a cab. Then I'll finish this. It will be the lead in *Midweek*. After the magazine comes out, I think they'll treat you with respect around here. And you deserve it, Fitz. You deserve more than that." He said "No. No. You don't understand. I didn't earn any medals. You have to intend to be a hero, to be one. It never entered my mind. I didn't care about

223

anything but me. I hurt. I hurt so bad I couldn't stand it. I was kicking and bawling like a baby. I was no hero. I was a yellow-bellied coward. All I wanted was to be dead, so the hurting would stop. And for that, I got my medals!" He was sobbing. Tears shone on his gin-reddened flabby cheeks. "I'm not a liar now, but I lied then. Every time they pinned another medal on me, I was a liar!" He reeled against my desk. "Tear up those pages. Let me go on being just a fat old nothing. Please, Bob. Please!"

I said "No, Fitz. You brought me a piece of fiction, and I bought it, and that's that. You're not a liar; you're an author." I started typing again. What I typed was Fitz's confession of cowardice. I made that the lead, and lettered a heading to be worked up in the Art Department: THE TRUTH ABOUT BEING A HERO: A SHORT STORY. *By Major Daniel Graham Fitzgerald, V. C.* "Nobody's expected to believe a piece of fiction. Okay, Fitz?" He stopped sobbing, stared at what I showed him, and chuckled sheepishly. "Somebody else. Not me. Somebody else." I said "Somebody or nobody. Just something you dreamed up." He said "Okay. Okay." We finished the gin, drink for drink. And *Midweek* was taken care of, for that issue, and, if nobody started saluting Fitz, even the head copy-reader called him "Major" occasionally, after the magazine came out, and gave him the Foreign Bureau's war-or-peace correspondence to handle. During World War II, I saw his by-line regularly with *Our Military Expert* under it in bold-face, and understood he had joined Alcoholics Anonymous.

I profited, too. The experience with Fitz set me to tricking up more true tales as fiction, which took care of other holes that yawned in *Midweek* while I applied my creative talents (or so I told myself) to Goya and *As If This Flesh*. Patience and stubbornness wore thin and thinner; but intermittent excursions down dark alleys broke the monotony, and brought in driblets of needed walking-around money.

I remember particularly a roadhouse bartender who had invented a mop you could use without stooping. He did this because he had a bad back from lifting so many beer kegs. Scouts for a stock-promoting combine stumbled onto him, took out a patent on his invention, capitalized a company, floated a stock issue, and staged a telephone sales campaign, working out of what more reputable brokers called a boiler room. Eager buyers begged for more. The promoters obliged, printing batches of Common and Preferred to meet the demand. They never got around to manufacturing many mops. The ex-bartender, listed as president of the company, was allowed to watch the money roll in, and spend the percentage allotted to him. There was a song: "Clap Hands, Here Comes Charlie." His name wasn't Charlie, but whenever an orchestra struck up "Clap Hands," you knew he was in the place, scattering fifty-dollar tips from a roll two inches thick. On Black Friday, the bubble burst. The promoters disappeared. And now there was no "Clap Hands." No headwaiter bowed. No chorus girls came cooing. With his last fifty-dollar bill, he chartered a cab and made his rounds for the last time. At each stop, he brushed past bouncers and, in the Amen Corner, presented the management with a mop. Keeping only one for himself, he shouldered it and walked out of Chicago, back to his old job in the roadhouse.

This really happened, but *Midweek* presented it as another story by Douglas Hardy, who wondered in a final paragraph if its hero whistled "Clap Hands" while he mopped behind the bar.

I told, too, disguised as fiction, the truth about a harmlessly mad old codger, the impressively uniformed doorman at a Gold Coast luxury-apartment tower. Half a dozen tenants or visitors had called or written about him. They found it deliciously amusing that he talked and acted as if the building belonged to him. "If he were Spanish, I'm sure he'd be telling us 'Mi casa es su casa.' He claims he's American, but I think he's really German. He looks like Kris Kringle." The descriptions were accurate. His abundant white whiskers, his twinkling eyes, his jovial "Hoh-hoh!", charmed children and disarmed their nurses and governesses. And it was perfectly true that he believed he owned a sixteen-story structure that represented a multi-million-dollar investment.

He was paid twelve dollars a week, with meals, and a windowless room in the subbasement. Eighty-one years old, he had no living relatives. When he had retired at sixty-five he was board chairman and principal stockholder of a bakery concern that spread over three states, which he had built up from his first small doughnut shop in Little Bavaria. A holding company bought him out, for cash. His money oppressed him. He traveled to his birthplace in Germany. Told once too often that he was pure Aryan, he financed Jews in leaving the country. Denounced for this, ordered to contribute to Hitler's Beer Hall Putsch, he refused, and was called a traitor to the Fatherland. He traveled on around the world. Wherever he stopped, he was lonely for Chicago. So he returned to Little Bavaria, and found he was too wealthy to be liked by the sons of old friends who had died poor. He was ripe and ready when schemers showed him how he might buy neighbors by financing construction of the apartment tower. Before they finished with him, they had all his money, and he had paper and promises. Then they went into what purported to be involuntary bankruptcy, so managed that the bonds he held were rendered valueless. The building he paid for stood, but the title rested with strangers. He might have sued and salvaged something. He chose to settle for the doorman's post. "Money," he told me, "is worthless to a miser and buys nothing for a spendthrift. I have spent my money well."

I couldn't say the same. Where so much of mine had gone so soon puzzled me as much as anyone. A last large bite out of what remained in the bank gave Claude Caspar-Jordan a send-off party, during which we did halova lot catching-up with Chicago. Jack Lawson and Pablo Katigbak helped me load Claude, weeping, onto the *Twentieth Century*. The Army of France was preparing to throw a scare into Hitler. This wouldn't take long, Claude said. "We make a face so, we go *Pouf!* so, and this house painter, he run like he got a Mickey Finn!" He had to report to the colors, but planned to behave so badly in uniform that the Army would kick him out, and his disgusted father would punish him by shipping him back to the home of his heart, Chicago. "I come back quick!" he shouted as the train pulled out. I never saw or heard of him again.

I resumed my unequal struggle with Goya. Gorham, the advertising executive at Blackett-Sample-Hummert, called again. He told Jack Lawson he had heard a rumor that I was writing a sequel to *Three Girls Lost,* called *One Girl Found,* and asked why I wasn't writing it for radio, which didn't call for grammar and punctuation and paid much better. I told Jack, "Tell him you couldn't reach me," and went to Smith, and said I'd like to take a vacation if that was all right with him. I had three *Midweeks* in type, artwork cleared, pages laid out. "I need the time to be by myself while I finish The Book," I said. The capitals were mine. "I think," I went on hurriedly, "I can send the manuscript off to the publishers in about ten days." Smith said, "I heard from someone that you might be going to Europe." I said, "Oh, no. Too far. I'll just go to Canada. I'll be at the Château Laurier in Ottawa." I didn't tell him that was all the trip I could afford, and that, even to manage this, I'd have to write an article for Sir Henry Thornton, the Canadian railroad magnate, to cover part of my expenses. *Three Girls Lost* and what it earned were water under the bridge. Or it's no use crying over spilled milk. Or easy come, easier go. Or something. And Smith was kind. He asked no questions. If he had, I couldn't have answered them.

3

Andrews [James Thurber said in *The Beast in Me And Other Animals*] was a superb example of what Dr. Sheldon has called the mesomorph — big, strong, sanguine, energetic, and inclined more to activity than to contemplation. He was almost six feet tall, weighed two hundred pounds, and boasted a chest measurement of forty-six inches. He dressed better than most reporters, liked to wear rings, and always carried a cane. The cathedral calm of the soundproof office had no allure for Andrews. He could pound a typewriter in a room with a dozen other people pounding typewriters, and he could write in his bedroom while the neighbors' children bawled and radios blared.

We corresponded (*Andrews answered a brief telegraphic query of mine with a letter, no doubt written between teatime and the cocktail hour, that ran to eight thousand words*), and though total blindness was closing in on Thurber he asked me to send him a manuscript of mine that touched on the subject matter of a series of "Profiles" he wrote for the *New Yorker;* on many pages he made thoughtful notes and suggestions in his microscopic handwriting. I never met him, and so was never able to show him how far corporeal substance varies from the myth that so amused him. (*My correspondent advanced an astounding explanation for giving up the writing of radio scripts,* Thurber wrote in 1948. *"I just got tired." Why, Charles Robert Douglas Hardy Andrews!*)

There was a sequence in the story, in 1931, that Thurber might have felt belonged in a soap opera. The setting was the Château Laurier, which looked more like a cathedral than a railroad-owned hotel, and sat in a park overlooking English Upper Town and French Lower Town and the confluence of the Rideau and Ottawa Rivers. My room was high up under the many-chimneyed roof, facing the Parliament buildings on Barrack Hill. I was farther from Goya's Spain than I had been in Tower Town in Chicago, but there was something foreign and in fact European about it; and across the bridge in Hull, in a tiny French restaurant, *Madame la proprietresse* had a neat mustache and a Provençal accent; her husband behind the bar knew many Rabelaisian verses to the tune of *Alouette*; and the red wine was cheap. I was, for the first time in my life, on a literary mission with which nothing mundane interfered. I could roll out of bed when I chose, walk the floor, type for hours at a stretch without interruption, walk along the river and watch rainbows merge in the mist that rose from the Chaudière Falls, return to my room and to *As If This Flesh*, give up and take a taxi to Henri's bar in Hull, come back with no chow named Rikki-tikki-tavi waiting up to scold me for drinking too much, write all night and fall asleep with no alarm clock wound and set. In sum, I was a free soul; and if The Book went badly, there was no one I could blame it on but my lonely and angry self.

I was grateful, not annoyed, when my labors attracted the unfavorable attention of an English Colonel's world-touring widow, whose room was directly under mine. She complained to the manager that the eccentric American had taken to tap-dancing, shaking the ceiling over her bed at five o'clock in the morning. When I demonstrated that the ratta-tat-tat came only from my typewriter, he brought me a thick rubber pad to set it on, and another which he placed beneath my chair. Crumpled balls of paper littering the carpet dismayed him, not from any realization that each represented another chip knocked off my *amour-propre*, but because he was a Scot and thought from my name that I must be the same, and therefore Yankee wastefulness was treason to my heritage. I said he could do me a favor, which I would mention to his employer, Sir Henry Thornton. He could arrange forthwith to have the *Chicago Daily News* delivered every morning at my door. He said it would be easier, and cheaper, to get *The Times* of London, quite fresh, not more than two or three weeks old, borrowed from the Colonel's relict, who was lonely anyhow, and remarkably well preserved for having lived so long in India. I insisted on the *Daily News*. And when the first copy arrived, Goya waited while I caught up with Al Capone.

On October 6, 1931, Public Enemy Number One went on trial in Chicago's old Post Office Building, not for murders most foul but for failing to pay income taxes on his profits from these and lesser felonies. One of his lawyers caused consternation by publicly declaring that there was a Depression going on. "The Government itself is guilty of acts of profligacy," Michael Ahern charged. "It has spent thousands upon thousands in the investigation and prosecution of this case, when it might better have spent the money, in these hard times, for the establishment of breadlines and soup-kitchens." On October 16, the *Daily News* reported further impassioned oratory. "Yes," Capone's defender cried, "this defendant is a gambler. He may even have derived some income from the gambling in Cicero, as the Government contends. But there is no proof that he didn't lose every cent he made in that business, the same as others are losing everything in the stock market, which is also a gambling business." The *Daily News* pointed out editorially that Capone's counsel followed distinguished precedent. America's first Great Mouthpiece, Aaron Burr, laid down the dictum that *Getting a guilty defendant off is purely a science of obfuscation, of beclouding the issues.* Long-respected citizens were being indicted right and left for long-continued dishonesty in financial manipulations. Could Capone's mouthpieces convince the jury that income tax evasion was minor, compared to outright theft? "A tinhorn or a piker may cheat," they told the jurors, "but nobody ever called Big Al Capone a piker." Could the kettle be saved by blackening the pots?

It might have worked, if the kettle's name had not been Capone. On October 17, he was convicted, on three counts of evading income taxes on six hundred and seventy thousand dollars traced to him from 1925 into 1928, and two of further evasions in 1928 and 1929. He had loved newspaper photographers. This time, led out of Federal Court in handcuffs, sentenced to serve eleven years in Federal Prison, he threatened to kill the picture-takers who swarmed around him. He was down and done, and the Opposition said gang-rule was over forever in Chicago. The *Daily News* doubted this. Our calmly factual wrap-up named five much less publicized but much shrewder and more sinister Syndicate bosses, who had probably arranged for and certainly did nothing to prevent the leaks of inside information that convicted the Big Guy and thus relieved them of a loud-mouthed, paresis-poisoned has-been.

Reading this in my cell in the Château Laurier, I wanted to be back in my corner with Carl Sandburg, watching and listening to Chicago, seeing Smith put the lead exactly where it ought to be and tame the Page One banner lines, hearing the story behind the story at Hy Green's bar. And crumpling the paper, I started typing, and didn't stop until I typed THE END. With half an hour to spare, I mailed the bulky manuscript of *As If This Flesh* to the publishers in New York, and caught the night train for Chicago. On the rear platform of the observation car, I lighted a cigarette and negligently tossed the match away in a gesture of farewell to Canada. Only it wasn't a match. It was the solid gold lighter that *Three Girls Lost* bought for me as a symbol of success. Mine no longer, it gleamed and glittered between rails joining in perspective, waiting to be picked up by some track-walking hobo or covered with gravel cast by other passing trains that would come along soon. I discovered I could laugh at myself. I hadn't done that since I started writing *As If This Flesh*.

I laughed again, from the inside out, when I walked into Editorial next morning and the World's Oldest Office Boy greeted me with the line he had been saving for me. "Hi, Bob. Been away?" I said "No, not really." That night, I toured the night spots. Nothing had changed while I was gone. Things were just a little older. Well, so was I. *Life is just a bowl of cherries, Don't take it serious, It's too mysterious.* Everybody sang it; and I joined in. Next morning, I read file copies of the papers I had missed. There were more advertisements of bankruptcy sales. Several brokers had walked out of windows over LaSalle Street. The ugly word "Depression" was no longer *verboten* in the *Daily News*, but it appeared in quotation marks, mostly in reports of speeches by Governor Franklin D. Roosevelt of New York, described in Walter Lippmann's column as "a pleasant man who, without any important qualifications for the office, would like very much to be President." The International Apple Shippers Association was applauded for old-fashioned American Free Enterprise initiative, in selling fruit to the jobless on credit. This made it a matter for congratulation, not concern, that there were ten thousand self-employed small businessmen selling apples on Chicago's streets. A railroad president had declared in an address at the Wharton School Of Finance that "I would steal before I would starve," and Lloyds of London were selling anti-riot insurance; but brightly painted fingernails and Empress Eugénie hats were the rage for women who could afford them, and were described in an article by an eminent psychologist as "manifestations of feminine refusal to let go of the totems of prosperity." Skirts were longer. He said this was a good sign; it meant more women were staying at home. Stenographers' salaries dropped from twenty-five and forty-five dollars a week to an average of sixteen, and girls clerked behind counters in the Loop for twenty-five cents an hour, and less; but the Paul Ash Fan Club had two hundred thousand ticket-buying members, and Balaban & Katz unveiled the mightiest Wurlitzer in all the world. National income, according to our Financial Section, was 81 billions in 1929, less than 68 billions in 1930, only 53 billions in 1931; but since August the President's Organization on Unemployment Relief had been making surveys and drafting recommendations, so not much space was given to a report that the Red Cross was providing emergency relief for more than a million Americans and lacked the funds to care for another half-million applicants. The *Daily News* exhorted both parties to press for early passage of Mr. Hoover's $2,000,000,000 Reconstruction Finance Corporation Bill, which would positively set all wheels spinning full speed ahead.

But a loyal long-time reader of the World's Greatest Newspaper offered a simpler and much cheaper solution. In a Letter to the Editor, he recalled an editorial written by Colonel McCormick's grandfather, Joseph Medill, during another hard-times winter, back in 1875: *If the Communists in this country are counting upon the looseness of our police system and the tendency to proceed against criminals by due process of law, and hope on that account to receive leniency, they have ignored some significant episodes in American history. The Vigilance Committee is a peculiarly American institution. Every lamp post will be decorated with a Communist.* The reader thought this warning should be communicated to the denizens of squalid shack-towns that spoiled his view of Lake Michigan. That their inhabitants called them "Hoovervilles," thus libeling the Great Engineer in the White House who had taken office less than eight months before Black Friday, was in this reader's opinion sufficient to deprive them of any claim for assistance or even sympathy from right-minded citizens.

I wondered and, wondering, went and looked. The Hooverville I visited was a crazy Caligari setting of huts the size of henhouses, built of flattened pieces of tin, splintered boards salvaged from construction debris, strips of tar-paper weighted down with rocks, rusty chicken wire stuffed with rags. Children with sunken eyes and bloated stomachs peered from doorways that had no doors. Pregnant women sat silently on

233

upturned orange crates, staring at mud and pools of stagnant, grease-scummed overflow from the drainage canal. Men muttered together, not plotting revolution, only repeating in bewildered singsong: "I can't figure. I just can't figure." I circled a gully that had been roofed over with sheets of corrugated iron discarded by some building-wrecker. Within this shelter, two large families crouched.

A little farther on, a huge white-enameled truck unloaded garbage and refuge onto one of a string of city barges that would dump their odorous cargo out beyond the city-water intake. I sensed watchers before I saw them. They were children, boys and girls, none more than half my age. Each kept aloof from the others, in mingled shame and greed. The truck pulled away. The children ran pell-mell from shelter. On the barge, they dug with sticks, and with their hands, seizing broken loaves of soggy bread, the green tops chopped from carrot-bunches, some spoiled bananas, beef bones that still had shreds of meat on them. They worked with a weird sort of selectivity, discarding more than they dropped in the paper sacks they carried. One small girl talked softly to herself while she dug and chose. She was planning a stew for supper; and it needed potatoes to give it body. She smiled when she found what she sought: thick peelings cast aside by someone's unthrifty cook. Suddenly, she ran past me, clutching a meal for the whole family. One of the others found a pulpy whole strawberry, and popped it into his mouth; and was ashamed of selfishness. Then the barge-tender came, not too rapidly, ordering them off, not too harshly. They called him bad names, but only in friendliness, and scurried back into Hooverville.

And I knew I couldn't write it, not for the Paper That Goes Home. I couldn't even talk about it, not even to Carl Sandburg, not even to Smith. We continued to print the good news only. The Waldorf-Astoria and the Empire State Building opened in New York, and these gala events got as much space in Chicago as if they had taken place on State Street.

The unemployment total reached fifteen millions, but in *Midweek* we published pages of architectural drawings picturing the Century of Progress World's Fair that would open along the lake front, just about where I visited Hooverville, in 1933, come hell or high water. Anton Cermak, Chicago's new mayor, ordered reassessment of real estate to meet city administration deficits. Harold L. Ickes, already called "the Curmudgeon," asked in the *Daily News* if it wouldn't be a nice idea to begin by finding out why the *Tribune* wasn't paying much higher taxes on its property. Henry Luce launched his *Fortune* magazine, at ten dollars a year. Its immediate success was of course a Page One story. The National Economic League ranked Prohibition Repeal as the nation's paramount problem, with unemployment trailing far behind. This, too, was Page One headline stuff.

I got on Page One myself. Sidney Lanfield, a film director, came from Hollywood to shoot scenes for *Three Girls Lost*, with a cast including three charming young ladies named Loretta Young, Joan Marsh and Joyce Compton. Complete with Homburg hat and cane, I was photographed beside them. No one around the *Daily News*, except Carl Sandburg and Smith, could understand why I stood looking down, not up, as if the whole weight of the world's troubles sat on my shoulders. Nor could I bear to talk about it, even to Sandburg or Smith. The fact was that The Book, which was to prove *Three Girls Lost* was a joke and *One Girl Found* need never follow, had come back with a letter of courteous apology. Two full pages of circuitous tact added up to decision by the publishers I had chosen — who also published Sandburg and Smith — that they wanted nothing whatever to do with *As If This Flesh*.

They suggested obliquely that an obviously ambitious young writer who appeared to have had considerable professional experience should really know better than to waste time and effort on a piece of pornography. That I had written anything of the kind was such stunning news that I read the letter several times before my stomach contracted and sickness welled in my throat. I won't pretend I wept. Mesomorphs swear their tears. I ranted, privately, until the urge to vomit passed. Then I talked to myself reflected in the mirror. The publishers must have made a mistake. Someone had mixed names and manuscripts. But it would hardly be dignified to protest personally. An agent was the answer: an agent who would read The Book and give me his frank and independent comments. Yes, of course; and I knew just the man. I had bought stories from him, for *Midweek*. We had corresponded. He wrote like a writer, not like a manuscript peddler. Surely he would see the truth about The Book.

So I sent it off to him, with an elaborately laconic but lengthy letter, and concentrated rather guiltily on catching up with MIDWEEK while I awaited his verdict. Having something to write that felt worth writing helped. Julius Rosenwald died, and in an article about his life, I did some preaching that Smith let pass, on wealth and its rightful uses.

Young Julius Rosenwald was selling cloaks and suits on the road when he bought a fourth interest in Sears Roebuck in 1895, three years after young Samuel Insull was elected president of the Chicago Edison Company.

Rosenwald was modest about his success. *To say I had vision and foresight in going into Sears is nonsense*, he insisted. *I went in simply because I saw a good chance. I never could understand the popular belief that because a man makes a lot of money he has a lot of brains. Some very rich men who have made their own fortunes have been among the stupidest men I have ever met.* I suspect that actually I used this quotation, and others, more to vent the anger that Smith said did no one any good than in tribute to a truly great Chicagoan.

Philanthropy, Rosenwald had said, *is a sickening word. It is generally looked upon as helping a man who hasn't a cent in the world. What I want to do is to try and cure the things that seem to be wrong.* He told an audience of Negroes, on the South Side in Chicago's Harlem: "I am the inferior of any man whose rights I trample beneath my feet. Men are not superior by the accident of race or color; they are superior who have the best heart, the best brain. Your enemies are also the enemies of liberty, of progress, and of justice." The twenty-million-dollar Julius Rosenwald Fund supported schools and colleges for Negroes, aided Marian Anderson and others of special talent among her people. His Museum of Science and Industry and its permanent endowment cost far more, in his own money, than the Opera Building cost Samuel Insull out of his personal pocket. Yet Insull had criticized him for wastefulness, particularly when he established his Fund for the Well-Being of Mankind with the explicit proviso that all its millions must be expended within twenty-five years after his death. News stories in the Opposition hinted at shocked surprise amongst his peers and contemporaries, that his residual estate was so small: only seventeen million dollars. But our *Midweek* story was headed *HOW TO GIVE AWAY $63,000,000 AND ENJOY EVERY DOLLAR OF IT.*

Smith said it was a fairy tale that couldn't happen in Chicago, and he thanked God it was true. He said Colonel Knox had commented on it. "He calls it 'A lesson in values that will probably be ignored by our malefactors of great wealth,'" Smith smiled, not patronizingly. "Colonel Knox quotes Theodore Roosevelt without quotation marks. But only because their thinking is very much the same. He's a really remarkable businessman. He's determined to make money, but doesn't want to take it away from someone else." He said Knox expected to have the *Daily News* in the black by the end of his first year as publisher. Even if the *Tribune* announced itself as "Chicago's only money-making newspaper," with profits for the last twelve months exceeding two million, nine hundred thousand, and an increase, not a decrease, in syndicate sales of "The Gumps" and "Orphan Annie" and "Gasoline Alley" and

"Dick Tracy," we were weathering the storm well enough to keep the stockholders happy, and *Midweek* seemed safe and secure. He was sure it would be all right with Colonel Knox if we used something, with discretion, about some of my neighbors in Tower Town who were also rising above the Depression in their own odd ways. This allowed me to tell about two elderly ladies who had a studio near mine, where they prepared magnificently photogenic cakes and pies, which they photographed in full color for advertising agencies. Now they had a sign on their door that read LET 'EM EAT CAKE! and, once a week, after they finished their color photographs, hungry painters and sculptors and writers and musicians and students flocked in and feasted on angel-food with whipped cream and maraschino cherries on top, and pumpkin pie covered with pecans.

I told about Scrubby Lee, my dog walker, who had saved his earnings. Now that his clients were penniless, he fed both dogs and their masters out of his savings. And about a certain Mrs. Brown, of a Founding Family, whose whole fortune vanished on Black Friday, and whose unpaid bills piled up until one day she sent engraved invitations to all her creditors, inviting them to be her honored guests, with their wives or sweethearts, at the most superlative cocktail party and ten-course dinner even she, a noted hostess, had ever given even when nobility visited her. And plumbers and carpenters and dry cleaners and grocers and florists and beauticians and butchers and bakers and candlestick makers drank and dined until they could hold no more; and then she said smilingly: "Gentlemen, you have just enjoyed all you will ever collect from me." And, instead of raging emptily "We'll sue!", they stood up and cheered their hostess, then voted unanimously that her credit was good as long as they themselves could stay in business.

All very well, *pour passer le temps*. But at long last I heard from the agent in New York. He chose words more carefully than I ever had except for The Book, regarding which he said very carefully: *I think you are unduly disturbed by suggestions that your book is pornographic. It is too sincere for any such attitude to be taken by truly intelligent people, and the rest do not really matter to a creative artist. I think you have done an artistic piece of writing, and it is regrettable that chances for publication are so slender.* I stopped there for several minutes. Then I managed to read on without further alarming Rikki-tikki-tavi, who was already concerned because I was so sober and so silent. *Your letter troubles me a little, inasmuch as you imply you do not wish to have your manuscript submitted to any but the most respected publishers. There are others who might take a chance on it. Granted, their trend of choice is toward what we may call the provocative type of novel, not advertised in (for example) the* NEW YORK TIMES *Book Section (or the* CHICAGO DAILY NEWS), *and generally (I must admit) stocked for sale "from under the counter" only by certain booksellers. But what you want is to get all you can out of the work you have done, by getting your book published and sold, so let's not be too rigorously fastidious. It's quite possible that word-of-mouth would start things rolling (as it did for Ben Hecht's* FANTASIUS MALAIRE; *banned books sometimes become big sellers in spite of the Watch And Ward Society!). James Branch Cabell was nobody really until* JURGEN *caused a furore, and his is not a bad success story; and actually, I feel you have a touch of the Cabell whimsicality, which excuses the frankness with which you depict the affairs of Goya. So let me have your go-ahead and I'll take this to the proper market. Incidentally, you may want to sign it with a pseudonym, since your future career will be better protected if eventually we can go to a first-line publisher with a "first novel" under your true name.*

So there it was. And I knew what had to be done. I wired the agent. KINDLY RETURN MANUSCRIPT SOONEST POSSIBLE. FORGET THE WHOLE THING. THANKS. When it arrived, I invited Jack Lawson and Pablo Katigbak to a farewell party.

They asked where I was going now. I said, "Nowhere." They came to my place that night expecting almost anything, but unprepared to find me burning the pages of *As If This Flesh* in a Chinese brazier I had borrowed from a neighbor. They asked if I was drunk, or out of my mind, and I said "No, neither, but something can be arranged," and broke out the last two bottles of Old Rarity that *Three Girls Lost* would ever pay for. We had a pleasant evening.

Carl Sandburg had said, "Start learning how to be humble." I told myself that finally I comprehended what he really meant. And things went along, and a story came in from Mac-Kinlay Kantor. I liked it, but I sent it back. *For five months, Mac remembers, I had a total income of $30.20. I wrote stories in sheer desperation, hoping frantically to get a check from somewhere or other.* NEITHER HAND NOR FOOT *was the last I ever sent to Bob Andrews at* MIDWEEK. *I felt like the man in it: bandaged, hog-tied, and helpless; and wasn't even so certain that I had a shotgun under the sheet.* I couldn't help Mac. I couldn't help any author; nor could Smith. Not any more.

Two weeks before Christmas, at the end of 1931, with no advance notice and no indication that he had such a thing in mind, Colonel Knox shot MIDWEEK out from under us. It simply wasn't paying its freight; and Colonel Knox's army-trained efficiency expert, Colonel Visknisski, had convinced him that there was enough literature in the news-sections, without running a soup-kitchen for starving writers in MID-WEEK. It expired so quietly that hardly anyone seemed to notice. Not a single subscriber canceled because the magazine no longer came with his paper on Wednesdays. This, it was hinted quite pointedly at Hy Green's bar, might be inter-preted by some people as confirmation of a suspicion they had long entertained, that MIDWEEK never meant much, anyhow, except to its editor and a few other outsiders. I could blame the death on the Depression if I liked. The fact remained that once more I was on the payroll but without assignment, and once again I sat at my typewriter, pecking out Now IS THE TIME and THE QUICK BROWN FOX, while I waited for word from Smith that didn't come. Only this time, suddenly, I started banging away at something I knew I could write, and finish, and sell, without anyone else telling me what it was and what it wasn't.

I didn't finish *One Girl Found* in seven days. It took almost three times that long. I typed THE END not with exhausted relief but with quiet assurance that the laborer is not only worthy of his hire, but will surely get it, and then some. I waited, and so did Jack Lawson and Pablo Katigbak and the World's Oldest Office Boy, and the crew at Hy Green's bar, for lightning to strike twice. It didn't. *One Girl Found* ran serially in the DAILY NEWS, and Grosset and Dunlap put it between covers, but the new literary agent I had just acquired couldn't stir a ripple of interest in Hollywood. The total take was a thousand dollars, and that was spent before I collected it.

Mac Kantor sent me a clipping. He had a column now in the *Des Moines Register*. It didn't pay much, but anything was an improvement over $30.20 for five months of short-story writing.

While idling over a drink in a local electric-fan and auto-polish emporium, quaintly yclept a drugstore, [he reported] we scanned the rack of popular books and saw two titles by our friend, Bob Andrews: *Three Girls Lost* and *One Girl Found*. And meditating still longer over our drink, we wondered why bright people still think of an author as some long-haired, dirty-faced freak with a holy look in his eyes, scratching out manuscript with a quill pen in some remote attic, preferably in New York or Paris. [Kantor hadn't heard about my brief immurement in the Château Laurier in Ottawa.] Andrews [he romanticized] is as far removed from this conception of an author as one could possibly be. He is full-faced, thick-shouldered, energetic as the volts on a high-tension wire. Within the year that we have known him, he has written probably half a million words, and sold most of them, while working full days at his desk in the office of one of the country's largest newspapers. Altogether, with his polished walking stick, his chow puppy, his luxurious silver-and-green apartment, his rapid intensity of living, he's a far cry from the wraithlike, mooning author of fiction. We don't know when he sleeps, if ever. We've seen him work and eat and drink, in all of which he takes the keenest interest. Perhaps lack of sleep keeps an author healthy and prosperous. Anyhow, he knows there is money in the business of writing; and he goes and gets it.

Kantor insists he was sincere, not satirical. But in fact I wasn't selling any more words than he was. I had run out of markets. *Plain Talk* was dead, *College Humor* reeled, and *Chicagoan* stumbled toward the pit. Mencken's *Mercury* wasn't buying at all. Nor were *Popular Biography* or *Real Detective Tales*. Carl Sandburg opined, in his last "Notebook" for *Midweek*, that even authors were feeling the pinch that had just produced a fine bit of topical poetry: Yip Harburg's "Brother, Can You Spare A Dime?" Smith sent for me, and said the paper could use more pieces by The Previewer, and whatever features I could come in with. This was his way of saying he'd keep me on the payroll as long as he could. But with *Midweek* slain, I felt like an albatross bowing his weary shoulders. Still, I wouldn't leave the *Daily News* if leaving could possibly be avoided.

Just about then, Walter Duranty won the Pulitzer Prize for reporting, conferred because of his pleasant Bolshevik Russia folk stories in the *New York Times*. We thought this did injustice to our own Negley Farson, whose "Seeing Red" dispatches were much less sentimental. According to Duranty, having reached Pulitzer Peak he quit because there were no more heights to scale. Reading between his lines in *I Write As I Please*, I suspected him of whistling in the dark at the top of the stairs. For myself, I had written three books and gotten two of them published, and had a fourth commencing to take shape that was neither another serial nor a second attempt to reach Olympus in one leap; but I was still determined to go on listing my occupation as "newspaperman" as long as the Lord and Colonel Knox would let me. All right. If I couldn't count on staying in my corner with Sandburg, on the *Daily News* with Smith, unless I could afford to work for nothing if needs must, how about removing the seat of my pants from the chair and nailing down an outside income?

So I called Gorham at the advertising agency, and with some difficulty got him on the phone. I hadn't pleased him with my standoffish attitude, and he let me know it. He said he was no longer looking for writers. That problem was now in charge of Mrs. Anne S. Ashenhurst. He spoke this name, new to me yet somehow familiar, with a kind of reluctant reverence. If I'd hold on, he'd check with her. He checked, and came back on the line to say Mrs. Ashenhurst would be interviewing applicants for employment beginning at 9:05 tomorrow. He feared I would have to wait my turn in rather a long line. Apparently, he ventured, there had been some changes in the writing market as well as in LaSalle Street recently. I bristled, but didn't bark, and next morning, with the queasy hesitance of a *penitente* who wishes he had sobered up before he volunteered to scourge himself with cactus thorns, I entered the agency's movie-set offices, twenty stories above the Chicago River, prepared to cast myself with thin-lipped gallantry on the sacrificial altar of the new Ashtoreth, radio. I needn't have been so Shakespearean about it. The supply exceeded the demand.

« 4 »

Mrs. Anne S. Ashenhurst knew exactly what she wanted. She also knew all about newspapermen. She had been married to one, John Ashenhurst, who covered Chicago crime for the

Opposition before I came from Minneapolis, and whose former colleagues wondered why Hecht and MacArthur left him out of *The Front Page*. That was why a bell had rung faintly when I heard her name from Gorham. She herself had been a reporter, on the *Baltimore Sun*, then on the *Paris Herald*. It didn't show on her. Strikingly small, overwhelmingly well-groomed, inflexibly self-possessed, she hadn't been at Blackett-Sample-Hummert long. But there was no doubt her star was on the rise. This, the office story ran, was solely by her own arrangement.

I was told she had been hired as a substitute secretary, but that she never took dictation from anybody. The agency was pouring money into a long-shot gamble, preparing expensive layouts and presentations on the slim chance of getting an oil company account away from a much older and bigger agency. At her desk in the stenographic bull pen, she typed a memorandum to the copy chief, Frank Hummert, whom she had never seen. It said: *I don't know anything about advertising, but I know what women do not like.*

She said that women, out for a Sunday ride in the family car, or being driven to the market or the movies, or penned in the back seat with the children, suffering while John races blithely through STOP signs, think about matters that never occur to men when they slow down at filling stations.

Men, the blunderers, ask "Why?" when women say, "Let's not stop here." No matter who wins the ensuing argument, next time a wise man approaches the filling station where it started, he steps on the accelerator. That oil-company loses a customer. And he passes other filling stations, until he's told "Let's try this one." Because the gasoline is advertised as being better, or cheaper? Not at all. Because the woman in the car likes the look of the LADIES room. Or so said the famous memorandum; and though my knowledge of female idiosyncrasies was limited at the time, this sounded reasonable. In fact, stating the obvious as profundity seemed slightly ridiculous — until I was told that the agency junked its layouts and presentations, submitted nothing but the memorandum, and landed the account and enabled the oil-company to rake in millions before its competitors could catch up with the CERTIFIED COMFORT STATIONS bandwagon.

I never checked this with Mrs. Ashenhurst, whose first indoctrination lecture put me in my place. Frank Hummert, I was given to understand, was also an escaped reporter. The aggressive calling clashed with his recessive temperament. So he invented the idea of writing advertising as if it were feature news. This made him a fifty-thousand-dollar-a-year genius at Albert D. Lasker's monolithic Lord & Thomas agency. Then Hill Blackett and Glenn Sample launched their new agency in the teeth of the Depression, and persuaded him to join them as their principal asset. He wasn't a partner. He bore no responsibility for recruiting clients or keeping them corraled. He attended no brain-picking conferences. It appeared that only Mrs. Ashenhurst had a passkey to the ivory tower in which he sat alone, creating. When she said he was doing this at that very moment, I asked blankly, "Creating what?" Patiently, I was informed he was sole author of "Kodak as you go" and "The skin you love to touch." Clearly, Little Big Mouth was out of order on this reservation. I let Mrs. Ashenhurst do the rest of the talking.

Smith capitalized when he spoke of A Writer. Mrs. Ashenhurst uttered Hummert's name in block letters. He had decided, she said, that radio's daytime hours, then largely empty, should and could be filled with sales messages For Women Only. This contradicted the law and the prophets then honored by advertisers and by the networks — though they were in the business of selling air-time, they declined to believe people would listen to radio except at night when they had nothing else to do. And then it had to be Something Big: Rudy Vallee the Vagabond Lover, or Kate Smith, or Will Rogers, or Lanny Ross and the Maxwell House Showboat, or

Jessica Dragonette, or Amos 'n' Andy, or the Sisters of the Skillet, or Roxy and His Gang from the Capitol Theater, or the Cliquot Club Eskimos, or Floyd Gibbons telling tales at never less than 217 words a minute, or B. A. Rolfe and His Lucky Strike Dance Orchestra playing every tune in three-four time with George Washington Hill directing from the client's booth.

Surveys showed that most men and many working women were out of their homes and away from radios (very few automobiles had radios in those quieter days) from eight or nine in the morning until after 5. P.M. As for housebound wives and mothers, they bustled upstairs and down, indoors and out, engrossed in multifarious petty but demanding tasks, with neither leisure nor the inclination to sit still and be entertained. How, then, could they be induced or compelled to pay attention to radio pitch-men pleading "Buy this" and commanding "Buy that"? Mrs. Ashenhurst said Mr. Hummert would answer this question by inventing a daytime program first, then adjusting it to the ambulant daytime audience. Just possibly, I might be useful in this pioneering adventure.

What they needed, James Thurber summarized when daytime radio and I had grown sixteen years older together, *was a young writer with an indestructible typewriter, strong wrists, a story sense, and the knack of stringing out words. They came up finally with a young man beyond their dreams of stamina and fluency, who was eventually to become one of radio's legendary figures, Charles Robert Douglas Hardy Andrews.*

That first day, there was no suggestion whatever that perhaps daytime radio and I were made for each other. Mrs. Ashenhurst continued her speech, from behind the very wide desk that emphasized her smallness, and her sureness.

"Women," she told me, "are lonely through a third of their waking lives. The average housewife is tied to a schedule that never varies from one day to the next: A set time at which she must feed her husband and send him to his breadwinning job. A set time when the children must be hurried off to school. Then a set time for doing the laundry, for scrubbing the sink, for calling the grocer, for emptying the garbage, and so on and so on. . . ."

Totally feminine, still somehow she set herself apart from women, discussing them as if they formed a strange tribe she studied, or organisms under her microscope. I note this without disrespect. No mere male ever minimized Mrs. Ashenhurst. "The silence throbs," she said. "The empty hours are endless." She wasn't using me for a rehearsal sounding-board, testing phrases already polished. She wrote a memorandum in her mind, and noted what would be retained in the final draft, in cabalistic symbols I couldn't read upside down and backward. "Then," she said, "a friend in need is brought into the room by the turning of a dial. What this invisible guest has to offer may be trivial by man-made tests. But the housewife welcomes it. She knows the voice is being heard by millions of other women. Misery loves company. She isn't called on to stop and ponder and respond, while her work piles up. Her unseen caller never pries or scolds. The voice in the room cares about her; it advises for her good. It discusses what should be, not what is." She stopped, and considered me. She looked at her tiny jeweled wristwatch. Nine minutes of my allotted ten had been used up. She asked, "Can you contribute to this, Mr. Andrews?"

I was sure the same cold potato had been handed to each of the dozen writers who preceded me into her presence, and that it wouldn't be my turn now if they hadn't dropped it, one by one, and walked away not looking back. I was about to do likewise, when Mrs. Ashenhurst mentioned money. She did this delicately. Nobody could accuse her of dangling hay in front of a hungry horse; but she had none of Smith's distaste for financial details. That I stood silent didn't trouble her. She let twenty seconds pass. Then she said "Think about it, Mr. Andrews," and turned to her typewriter. Office typewriters then were all a drab dun-color. Hers was gleaming white. She struck keys crisply, beginning to type what she had noted to herself during my indoctrination. Then, aware I hadn't gone, she asked while still typing: "Is there anything else, Mr. Andrews?" I thought it over, and said "No, Mrs. Ashenhurst," and as fast as I could, got back to a world in which I wasn't a stranger, in my corner at the *Daily News*.

I did my best to push radio out of my calculations. But I couldn't stop thinking about money. An early Rothschild is supposed to have capsuled his business secret, as most important legacy to his heirs, in a cryptic sentence: *Gold has no nationality*. Chicago made it: *The gelt don't care who gets it*. My own experiences with the stuff had been minor, and soon over. But bits and pieces about possessors of it, collected in process of catching up with Chicago, suggested the new book I was trying to put together, which (*Deo adjuvante!*) I might not be ashamed of. I had wondered (as who has not?) how it would feel to own a million dollars. I had written about Julius Rosenwald, who believed his millions belonged to whoever needed them, and about other Chicagoans who said God made the poor, so let God take care of them. I had thumbed through Polk's Chicago directory and discovered that even children were listed with their house addresses. I had read about Samuel Insull on the Financial Page, then met panhandlers and apple vendors on every street. And the new book almost wrote itself. At least for the first few pages.

A mighty multimillionaire lies waiting to die, as unafraid of death as he was of life. Jackals and hyenas whine, waiting to scavenge the old lion's kill. Despising them, he calls for a directory, selects ten names by whim, leaves a million dollars tax-free to each of ten total strangers, and requires in return only that in two years they must tell what unearned fortune did for them, or to them, after a man they never knew played God in the machine. I first called it, with cloudy symbolism, "C. O. D."; then, for a while, the working title was "Glamour"; I don't know why. Then, perhaps more sensibly, I made it "Windfall," playing on the dictionary definition, *Something blown down by the wind; or unexpected good fortune.* Finally, it became what only my intransigence had kept it from being at the start: simply *If I Had a Million.*

I didn't have the cash in hand to pay my next month's rent. Forced to it, I laid *If I Had a Million* aside, and ground out another serial for the *Daily News.* Called "The Stolen Husband," cut from the same cheesecloth as its predecessors, its protagonists were Man, Wife, and Other Woman. The husband was, of course, handsome, not very bright, wrapped up in getting ahead at the office. The wife was lovely, pure, and naturally too much in love to realize soon enough that no man can be trusted if he has a pretty secretary. I finished several chapters, before it struck me that Mrs. Ashenhurst's voice was in my room. What I had on paper pitied self-pitying home-trapped housewives. All that was missing was "Buy this, buy that!" I glared at my pages, stuffed them in my File and Forget box, and once more headed for home at the *Daily News.* But Carl Sandburg was away on a lecture tour, and the World's Oldest Office Boy said Smith was in conference with Colonel Knox.

As much as I could, I typed my way back to where I could show a valid excuse for talking to Smith, when he returned at last, walking slowly with his head bowed, stopping to pick up a pin, straightening and smiling when he saw someone who might not remind him that all things, even the *Daily News,* must change. He asked about *If I Had a Million.* I said evasively "It's growing," and gave him the copy I had written: three long pieces by the Previewer, and a personality sketch of Mei Lin Fang, the marvelous Chinese mime, the highest-paid actor on earth (dollar signs even in this!), then in Chicago on his first and only American tour and unaccountably (I wrote) ignored by Drama columnists. I said that by Monday I'd have a feature with pictures revolving around Smith's fellow member at the Cliff Dwellers Club, Andy Rebori, the playboy architect, who had grandiose plans for "Streets of Paris" at next year's Fair, and was searching high and low for a star as sensational as Little Egypt, who had danced the dance she shouldn't oughter at the Fair in 1893.

I had located Little Egypt. Now a three-hundred-pound great-grandmother, she was Lebanese, not Egyptian, and deeply religious, not weird and wild, and shocked by the muscular gyrations of so-called "ballroom dancers" at the Aragon on the North Side, where Wayne King The Waltz King played diluted Chicago jazz between sets of schmaltz from Vienna. I told all this in a monologue, and stopped finally because Smith shook his head, not saying "No" to the story, just trying to ease things for both of us. "Bob," he said, "I'm not counting column inches on you." I said, "I know you're not, Mr. Smith. That makes it worse." I blurted out what couldn't have surprised him. "I'm lost," I said. "I know that sounds silly, but it's so." He said, "We all get that feeling sooner or later." Then he said, "It helps to be working on a book." I said, "I'm not working very hard on mine." He said, "It's early in the game to stop caring." I said, "That's the point, Mr. Smith. I don't want to stop caring." He understood, and was saddened. "I know there's a waiting list," I said, "and probably I don't belong on it, but is there any hope at all that I could go overseas for the Foreign Bureau?" He said, "I'm sorry, Bob, but Colonel Knox says we have to cut down, not add on." His telephone rang. He answered. "Yes, Colonel. He's in my office now. I'll send him over right away." He hung up and told me "Colonel Knox wants to see you." I waited for more, and wished I hadn't, for I forced him to say, "I don't know what he has in mind." He had never had to say that — until Knox became the publisher.

Unlike Victor Lawson and Walter Strong, Knox set the course for the *Daily News* without consulting Smith, even when he broke Smith's heart by scuttling *Midweek*. With all his being, Knox wanted to be President. Toward that end, he had set up a sort of separate staff, to further his candidacy in advance of the Republican National Convention opening in Chicago in June. I couldn't imagine he'd have any cause to think I might be useful in this effort. He had barked "Hello" at me occasionally, since he took charge. That was the extent of our acquaintance. As far as I knew, to Knox I was high up on Smith's Editorial payroll only because my name began with A. He cut costs as compulsively as he feuded with Colonel McCosmic. The newsroom wondered, and so did I, what my job was these days. So I entered the Lawson Memorial Room, which he had taken for his office, figuring the odds at ten to one that I'd leave no longer entitled to cling to my C. D. N. press card.

He didn't ease my doubts while I marched toward him, thirty full paces across the polished, rugless floor. His desk and a straight-backed chair confronting it were all the furniture in the gymnasium-sized room. I thought he looked tougher than any puff-chested sawdust Caesar on a European balcony. He had been at the first Rough Rider's heels in the charge up San Juan Hill that liberated Cuba in 1898 and made it impossible for Mark Hanna to keep Teddy Roosevelt out of the White House. He was first to follow when T. R. bolted the G. O. P. to launch the Bull Moose crusade in 1912. He went into combat ahead of his men, as colonel of field artillery, in France in 1918. He tore up a long-term contract with William Randolph Hearst in 1929, sacrificing one hundred and fifty thousand dollars a year, announcing "I run errands for no man." Nearing sixty, he still led the strenuous life and found it bully, and was dee-lighted to carry a big stick and swing it with both hands. He was said to count that

251

moment wasted in which he did less than three things simultaneously.

He wasted no time on me. He wrote in barbed-wire longhand, excoriating a mugwump Senator in a personal letter, transferring quotable excerpts to the draft for an editorial, while he said, "I've heard a lot about you, Andrews." He dotted *i*'s and crossed *t*'s while he continued: "I understand you're quite the man-about-town." The week before, John Drury had given me a copy of his first book, *Chicago in Seven Days*, autographed To Bob Andrews, *a real man-about-town*. I had reminded Drury that Richard Harding Davis, in his Van Bibber stories, told of a fellow who roamed Manhattan seeking vainly for someone the catch-phrase fitted, until he got himself fatally shot, and, while dying, heard a reporter telephone his city desk, describing him as "the last of the men-about-town." I didn't think the anecdote would amuse Colonel Knox.

"You must spread yourself pretty thin, getting around to all the sin spots." Now, at last, he gave me undivided scrutiny. "You're well-known, I understand, to the Underworld's upper crust. Apparently you're able to get along with our worst leading citizens." All right; all right. Bending the knee, even to Knox, had its limits. "I think," I said with what I hoped was icy dignity, "that how and where I spend my time and money after working hours is my personal affair." And he didn't explode. He chuckled. "Of course. Of course. We're only young once." Then, finally, he said "Sit down," and leaned forward confidentially. "I have an assignment for you. You're at liberty to say 'No.'"

I didn't say "No," which was why dark rumors spread soon afterward, from Hy Green's bar, that by some subtle machination I had aced myself into the catbird seat as Knox's private and personal reporter. It wasn't so; but it was true I had a secret mission. I promised to tell Pablo Katigbak all about it some day, and am keeping that promise now.

252

Buying the *Daily News* called for a showing of very large cash resources. Knox's own bankroll totaled half a million. He needed three million dollars more to swing a twenty-three-million-dollar deal, and got it from an old and loyal friend in New England who had been merely a pressroom foreman until, weary of breakdowns and delays, he began improvising simple but practical devices that turned out to be patentable, and made him very rich. A simple soul, he found the stock market much too confusing, and let it severely alone. He put his money in safety deposit boxes. So Black Friday and bank closings left him as solvent as ever. He thought Colonel Knox was the best publisher in the business, and told him, "You can have the rest of all I've got if you need it."

I'll call him J. K. Allison. Long a widower, with no near relatives, he came out to Chicago not to watch his money but because he was lonely. Provided with a title of sorts, and a suite of offices, he neither had nor asked for any executive duties, in a vast and complicated shop whose high-speed modernity bewildered him. He roamed here and there, asking underlings "Why?" and "How?" with childlike respect for their, to him, mysterious skills. While *Midweek* still came out, he materialized every so often in Makeup, inquiring naïvely about the color-printing process with which we experimented. As a large stockholder, technically he was my employer. He had a right to resent it, if I answered his questions curtly. But kindliness and shyness made him deferential even to the World's Oldest Office Boy. He was grateful to anyone who talked to him. He lived all alone, at a two-thirds vacant athletic club on Michigan Boulevard where there were no athletes. And Chicago tempted him; and he fell.

Seemingly, he had thought someone should represent the paper in a firsthand study of the city's lower depths. Certainly, he meant no evil and committed no sins. No night rover was ever less a seeker of painted smiles and pinchbeck pleasures. Yet none plunged more blindly into peril. He chartered wild-

253

cat taxis, paying in advance, revealing his wallet stuffed with hundred-dollar bills. "Take me wherever you think it's exciting." In darkest Cicero one night, out on the far South Side the next, down in the Levee District or west beyond Death Avenue or north in some Tower Town *cul-de-sac,* he presented his business card (he had no *C. D. N.* press card) and displayed his bulging wallet. Naturally, no doorman turned him away. He drank soda, not whiskey, but bought the most expensive imitation champagne for the bar girls, and baffled them by asking for nothing but their hard-luck stories. That these were all alike never ceased to amaze Mr. Allison. In the Syndicate's crookedest gambling dives, he bought blue chips and was robbed of them in games beyond his comprehension. He never complained about his losses.

From the Amen Corners, hoodlums eyed him speculatively. At any time, anywhere, he might be slugged and rolled for the contents of his wallet. He might be drugged and carried into some raddled Jezebel's room, to wake with cameras focused on him. He might be snatched, and held for ransom in more than dollars. But who could tell him "You're a fool"? Who had any right to say he couldn't spend his time and money where and as he pleased? The best that could be done was to see that someone went wherever he went and let it be known he wasn't fair prey for the pack. That was my assignment.

All I actually did was tell the management that, for once, I was there as a reporter, but I wouldn't write anything for the paper unless they made it necessary. They asked, "Now why would we do that?" and thanked me for fingering a mustn't-touch, and passed the word: "Treat Mr. Allison real nice so he'll leave happy."

At one stop, there were no other buyers at the bar. Mr. Allison eyed me without a trace of recognition. Was I alone, too? I was. Might he buy me a drink? If I could buy one for him. "My name is Allison." I said "Mine is Andrews." It meant nothing to him. I drank Old Rarity with Perrier. He drank soda. We parted. He walked out. I followed, not too soon. He drove off in his cab. I trailed him in mine. My driver said, "I see that old geezer around alla time. He's a weirdie, that old guy." I said, "It takes all kinds." He said, "Yeah. Yeah. Especially in Chicago." Mr. Allison and I were ships that passed in the night in three more Syndicate spots, before my driver put it on the grapevine. I doubt if I kept Mr. Allison out of trouble, as far as the regulars were concerned. Their code forbade stealing pennies from a blindman's cup. They felt sorry for a weirdie who got nothing but conversation for his gelt. However, there may have been amateurs who needed a "Lay Off" warning. If there were, they had it.

I filed no reports with Colonel Knox regarding Mr. Allison's peregrinations. None were ever asked for. No questions were asked when I turned in expense accounts a war correspondent would have envied.

I had heard nothing from Mrs. Ashenhurst. That was all right with me. Mornings, I worked on *If I Had a Million*. Afternoons, at the *Daily News*, I wrote more Previewer pieces, and more features about the Fair, still eighteen months in the offing. One noon, there were five front-office notes on my desk, time-stamped beginning at 9 A.M., all reading *See Colonel Knox immediately*. Knox greeted me with a Teddy Roosevelt grin, and said, "Night-life appears to agree with you. But you're young." Then he asked if I could line up some free entertainment for a farewell testimonial banquet. "Mr. Allison," he said, "has begun to feel his years. He has decided to go home to New England, where it's restful and quiet."

So I spent my own money that night, for a change, in all the places where my tabs had been much larger while they went on the expense account. As Colonel Knox requested, I asked for volunteers, and so many responded that the free acts honoring Mr. Allison on his last night in Chicago began at

7 P.M. with Eddie South, the Dark Angel of The Violin, and ended at 2 A.M. with Tommy Lyman crooning "Ace in the Hole." Mr. Allison dozed through much of the show, but came looking for me when it was over. He said he'd never forget how friendly everybody was in Chicago. Then he said, "I have a feeling we've met before." I said, "I work for you, Mr. Allison. That is, I'm on the *Daily News*." And suddenly, he nudged my ribs, and winked. "We won't tell Colonel Knox," he whispered, "what a fine time we had while it lasted." Then he let Knox lead him away.

I didn't tell Knox about "The Stolen Husband," either. The day after Mr. Allison departed (he died a few months later, without pain or premonition, between sleeping and waking), Mrs. Ashenhurst telephoned. She said Mr. Hummert had given her a go-ahead directive. I must have something useable in my trunk; all writers had. I said all I had was an unfinished serial. She asked, "Like *Three Girls Lost* and *One Girl Found?*" I said "More or less," and told her briefly about the wife and her husband and the Other Woman. She asked me to bring in whatever I had on paper. It sounded like promising material for the daytime radio experiment Mr. Hummert planned. Women, she said, wonder what their husbands are up to all day long. "Worry, for women, is entertainment." I said I deferred to her superior knowledge, but I couldn't see how "The Stolen Husband" could be put on radio. She indicated that this wasn't my problem.

Next day, in her new office, which adjoined Mr. Hummert's and was almost as elegantly furnished, she said her time checks showed that one three-thousand-word chapter of *Three Girls Lost* took an announcer thirteen minutes to read on the microphone, which left time for two sales messages if superfluous descriptions were eliminated. Thirty chapters would be all right, with virtue triumphant at THE END. Daily installments must, of course, menace that victory with as many delaying complications as we could think of. *We*; not I. She said we would adapt our philosophical approach from Barrie's *What Every Woman Knows*, with a few sage remarks, but not too many, in each day's broadcast. For our story line, we might consider suspense elements suggested by Kipling's *Make him take her and keep her, that's hell for them both*; not too much of this, either, but enough to keep the women worrying. We'd need especially strong cliff-hanger carryovers at the end of each fifth installment, to bring women back after the Saturday-Sunday hiatus. "The Stolen Husband" would be announced on the air as "the first full-length romantic novel ever written especially for women in the radio audience." My fee, in the aggregate, would be four times as much as the *Daily News* paid for a serial. I could retain publication rights. And she would expect me to deliver the first fifteen thousand words by Friday.

This stated, she turned to her white typewriter, and in something of a daze, I headed for my own machine. Originally, I was scheduled to do the reading, too; as if daily batches for the book came hot off the griddle. A studio sound-man tapped keys and yanked a sheet of butcher-paper out of a machine, close to the microphone, to start each chapter. But after a test, it was ruled that my voice was too deep and resonant. Women wouldn't believe an author talked like that. So an announcer with pear-shaped tones impersonated me, but broad-*a*'d himself out of a job in three days. His replacement was a private-parties entertainer who billed himself as The Man With A Hundred Voices. Bobbing up and down and back and forth at the microphone, changing pitch and accents frantically, he carried on hectic crossfire dialogues with himself until, suddenly, he collapsed. Then, although few historians record it, "The Stolen Husband" made history.

Four professionals were called in, to play the characters in a hurried off-the-cuff dramatization of the last twenty installments. Two had never faced a microphone before. The others,

257

Marion and Jim Jordan, happy-go-lucky vaudevillians long at liberty, had done some comedy routines on Station WENR as "The Smith Family," and on WBBM in a show they called "Smackouts." (By 1941, as "Fibber McGee and Mollie," they had the most popular coast-to-coast nighttime show on the networks. In 1961, retired in California, they sold to subdividers, for just under two million dollars, a ranch they began buying when the team earned as much as one hundred dollars a week on "The Stolen Husband," and all of us doubted if we belonged in radio.) There have been other nominees for what may or may not be worth claiming, but James Thurber, for one, held that "The Stolen Husband" was the first true daytime serial, by reason of which he dubbed me (not unkindly) "granddaddy of soap opera."

However, no rockets were sent up at the time by Blackett-Sample-Hummert. No one notified actors or writers of the more or less accidental discovery of a new mother lode, or warned advertisers they'd better join the gold rush before all the claims were staked. None of us guessed that, in less than three years, time buyers would stand in line, with certified checks in their hands, begging to be allowed to add to billings of fifty million dollars annually, for a solid seven hours of soap operas on the networks, five days a week every week of the year. Definitely, I had no suspicion that my personal typewriter output would fill a fifth of those seven hours. Or that a Chicago correspondence school would sell, very successfully, a course in "How To Write Radio Drama" which stated *'Bob Andrews' is a myth. No such actual person exists. The name is a cover for a syndicate of half a dozen writers.* When this appeared, I was much too busy to take time out to prove my existence. But when we were daytime radio's Dawn People, "The Stolen Husband" ran its course and fell off the air with a dull thud.

That didn't disturb Frank Hummert or Mrs. Ashenhurst. They charged the failure to profit and loss, as research experimenters must, never losing sight of the ultimate objective. They already had me writing scripts For Women Only, to be read on the air three mornings a week by an overweight erstwhile lady evangelist from Schenectady, who was introduced by the announcer as the far-famed beauty consultant, Ardis Marvel, direct from her salon in Paris. Actually, Ardis Marvel existed only as brand name for a line of lotions and creams "containing the rare essence of *Asclepias syriaca* (more commonly known as milkweed)," which cost the makers about a dime an ounce and sold for $2.50 per two-ounce jar. I cribbed Ardis Marvel's secrets, "never revealed until now," from a household compendium, *Every Woman's Guide to Health and Charm,* that had been a standard mail-order seller since before I left the Indian reservation. But my cicerone in this second pioneering test of what housewives would listen to, and what it would prompt them to buy, said Ardis Marvel's listeners were not being cheated.

"Men think all women are fools," she explained, "because no woman wants to believe she can't buy beauty in a drugstore. Women starve without lunches for days, if they work for their living, to pay for an expensive lipstick that has just come onto the cosmetic counters, though they know full well that the brand they starved to buy last month, out of fashion now, is for sale in the Five and Ten Cent Store. They'll feed their families on leftovers and use the grocery money to send in for a special facial pack, when the mud in their own back yard might do their complexions just as much good. All women run all their lives after the fool's-fire of beauty. That they're never going to catch it isn't important. What men don't understand is that the search is a substitute for the orchids men have sent and the flattery they invented when such things served their purpose, but which have stopped now. We're restoring lost illusions, encouraging women to dream and hope again. And as long as you can help in this, Mr. Andrews, we'll keep you busy."

Busy, I still found time to go to some of the cocktail parties being staged to bolster flagging interest in the World's Fair, though it was eighteen months away. At one of these, a bustling official hostess who was culling out freeloaders confronted me, demanding, "What do you do?" I said "I write." She dismissed this. "Doesn't almost everyone, these days? I meant: What do you do for a living?" I said "I write for radio." She flounced away in a high-styled huff, and would surely have had me tossed out if I had tried to tell her that while part of my mind wrestled with the lead for a feature story in the *Daily News* about the tug-of-war developing between contestants for the pay-toilets concession at the Fair, the rest of it groped for something new and different I could write for Ardis Marvel to say on the air, about the magical properties of *Asclepias syriaca.*

That a man, especially one who crashed cocktail parties on the strength of a C. D. N. press card, wrote a radio program For Women Only would have been called fantastically incredible. Everybody, or anyhow almost everybody, still thought nobody wrote what was heard on radio. Sixty million loyal listeners believed Eddie Cantor made up his jokes as he went along, and that Amos 'n' Andy said whatever happened to pop into their heads. When a contributor to Gene Morgan's column in the *Daily News* reported "Ben Bernie and Jack Benny met for a battle of wits at the College Inn but not a blow was struck because they forgot to bring their writers," Gene decided not to print it because his readers wouldn't get the point. Nevertheless, the jam on my bread and butter came from writing for Ardis Marvel. . . . until Mrs. Ashenhurst called to tell me that this experiment, like "The Stolen Husband," was leaving the air for oblivion.

"Mr. Hummert is ready now," she said, "to hear your ideas for a continuous serial story, dramatized, to be interpreted by actors and actresses. He hasn't time to read anything. You'll have to tell him about it. If you can come in tomorrow at ten, we'll get your presentation organized." She was ready, when we met, to tell me what the new show must have — what "The Stolen Husband" and Ardis Marvel's beauty lectures had lacked: a strong yet gentle central character, al· ways present, about whom the women listening would care personally, and with whom they could identify in terms of "I knew someone like that" or "That sounds like So-and-so back home." Inspiration Number One: I would write about BACK HOME — in capitals, as she wrote it on her note pad. Had I ever noticed the people who bought home-town papers at the Wrigley Building newsstand? Yes; and had written about some of them in *Midweek*. Alone in the great city, they felt aching nostalgia for what they had left behind — as long as they didn't have to go back to it. Mrs. Ashenhurst ignored my attempt at irony. "Of course," she decided. "Our story is about Main Street America. Everybody's Home Town." Had I ever lived in a little town? Little Big Mouth rode again, but only briefly. Indians, I was informed, are foreigners to most Americans. Well, I said, we had no Indians in Hiawatha, Kansas. How many people in Hiawatha? When I was there, 3969. What sort of people? William Allen White of Emporia, I said, described them in his novels, *In Our Town* and *A Certain Rich Man*: good, bad, and undecided.

I had recently read Helen and Robert Lynd's *Middletown: A Study in Contemporary American Culture*. It analyzed Muncie, Indiana, but made the point that certain likenesses linked all communities in the continental heartland. Mrs. Ashenhurst wrote HEARTLAND on her note pad. I said that although Sinclair Lewis, brought up in Sauk Center, Minnesota, scoffed and satirized in *Main Street* and *Babbitt*, he granted virtues grudgingly to the small-town cult of neighborliness. She wrote down NEIGHBORS. I told some of Carl Sandburg's Lincoln Country anecdotes. She felt they were too backwoodsy for women. I mentioned MacKinlay Kantor's mother, who had written for *Midweek*, and who should be admired by women: strong yet gentle, college-educated but unpretentious in her speech, an editor who exerted much quiet influence in the communities her weeklies served. Mrs. Ashenhurst said "Our lead should be a man. 'A man like many men we all know.' " She wrote that on her note pad. "He can't run a newspaper." Women, she explained, might feel they must pay close attention to an editor. They wouldn't like that, in the long run. "Women hate being lectured by any man."

I said, not too seriously, that our lead could be a barber. Mrs. Ashenhurst's initial reaction was negative. Barbers subscribed to the *Police Gazette* and organized beer-drinking quartets and played pinochle. I said, "Bill was just the opposite." She echoed "Bill?" I said that was the name of a barber I remembered in Hiawatha. She wrote BILL THE BARBER, then added a question mark, then said, "Go on, Mr. Andrews." And I went on and on, and the result was that the next day she was small but not at all inconspicuous in the background, in Frank Hummert's office, making cabalistic notes to herself while Hummert — lean, somber, silent as the Sphinx — sat with his back to me, contemplating the toes of his well-polished London-made shoes silhouetted on the window sill, and I talked for my future.

What I said was no more extemporized than the apparent ad libs between orchestra numbers that charmed the nighttime audience when Ben Bernie, the "Old Maestro," broadcast coast-to-coast from the College Inn with "All the Lads." "There's something special," I said, "about certain men in some small towns. They're both participants in and observers and interpreters of the best as well as the rest, in what is really a microcosm of all we call 'Main Street America.' They may be accused of gossiping, but they never scandalize. They meddle, but no one minds, because they mean so well. They care about people, whom they call 'folks.' They talk a lot, but they think more than they talk." (Six years later, in New York, Frank Craven told me "I'm opening on Broadway in a play that has the same plot, or call it premise, as the soap opera you have on radio. Only, Thornton Wilder calls it *Our Town.*") I paused, but not to frame the sentence that followed. "I remember one like that," I said. "He was the barber in Hiawatha, Kansas. He was always sorry for someone worse off than he was. And one way or another, he did something about it. To him, being neighborly meant worrying about the whole community, and the strangers who passed through, not just about the folks next door." And now for the sell. "Our show," I said, "is centered around a man like that. 'A man like many men we all know.' I'd call him 'Bill The Barber.'" Mrs. Ashenhurst printed JUST PLAIN BILL on her note pad, and added three exclamation marks. I noted this, but proceeded pursuant to instructions. "Bill has a one-chair shop on Main Street near the railroad depot. He has a handyman named Elmer, Elmer Eeps, who plays the banjo and gets in foolish, funny scrapes Bill has to get him out of. Bill is all over town: at the lumberyard, the newspaper office, the livery barn, the hotel where loafers sit on the porch in chairs tipped back against the wall. He's always talking: more *with* than *at*. He's full of pithy sayings — the kind Carl Sandburg collects."

Time for a folk story. I told one my father told me, that he heard from his teacher at Rush Medical. "A doctor's shingle, in the kind of town we'll dramatize, read simply OFFICE UPSTAIRS. When he died, everybody went to his funeral. Somebody marked his grave with his shingle, OFFICE UPSTAIRS." Mrs. Ashenhurst had foreseen correctly. Hummert liked the story. He turned in his swivel chair, looking not at me but at the wall display behind me, of page-ad proofs that called the roll of the agency's clients. "I'd call our town 'Hartville,'" I said. "I'd call our barber, in full, Bill Davidson. He has a daughter, Nancy. Sweet and simple, but not as simple as she seems; no woman ever is. A young lawyer's in love with her. Kerry. Kerry Donovan. Irish but not too Irish." Mrs. Ashenhurst signaled with her eyes. Time to button up the overcoat. "I'd say," I said, "that we start right out in the middle of a personal problem involving and introducing our leads, Bill, Nancy, Kerry, Elmer. We start another problem while Bill is solving the first one, then another one while he solves that one, and so on and so on and so on."

And so on and so on and so on for nearly fifteen years, for me: five shows a week, three thousand words per show, fifty-two weeks a year. Laid end to end, the word-count of at least a dozen novels. Great oaks from little acorns . . . Or, How to become a myth.

"Bill the Barber" went on the air for its test run over WMAQ, the *Daily News* station. No one on the paper but Smith knew I had anything to do with it, until the World's Oldest Office Boy got a tip from his second cousin, an usher in the radio studio, and informed the newsroom "Now Andrews is an actor." I wasn't. I was only trying to explain to actors that we weren't staging "Aaron Slick from Pumpkin Crick." One of them had false teeth that wouldn't stay put. Another told Mrs. Ashenhurst she didn't know anything about acting. The third, she said, would do until we went on the network. (When we did, Frank Craven tried out for the role of Bill. He was turned down. Not the type.) In Carl Sandburg's *Songbag,* I found a theme for which we wouldn't have to pay royalties: . . . *Grasshopper sittin' on a railroad track . . . A-pickin' his teeth with a carpet-tack, Singin' Polly-wolly-doodle all the day!* But the studio organist belonged to Jimmy Petrillo's musicians' union, which made her much too expensive. Radio actors, however, had no union yet. (There weren't enough of them to make organizing them worth while.) We located a nonunion hillbilly troupe, the Pickard Family, and hired Dad Pickard, who had never acted in his life, to play Elmer Eeps, and incidentally to sign the show on and off the air with his jew's-harp and banjo. Other make-does turned out almost as successfully. Before long, we were on the air from coast to coast. And henceforward, for almost a full generation, uncountable millions of housewives and other stay-at-homes solaced daytime loneliness and self-pity by tuning in faithfully and gratefully to hear troubles always worse than their own, infinitely detailed, in a never-ending soap opera that never sold soap: called, as Mrs. Ashenhurst had sensed it must be, "Just Plain Bill."

<h2 style="text-align:center">« 5 »</h2>

There was a rundown old hotel in Tower Town, where show people who never got farther toward Broadway than Chicago lived between engagements. Tent-show stars, Clint and Bessie Robbins and Al Bridges and Moroni Olsen and their peers, occupied the suites. Walking gentlemen and ingenues from riverboat repertory took rooms with private baths. Acrobats, Chautauqua performers and vaudeville teams from the Gus Sun split-week time took what was left. When I first saw the place, the suites were vacant and so were most of the rooms with bath. Even the few tenants who could still pay their rent did their own housekeeping. The hotel wasn't taking in enough money to hire chambermaids. Tenants who couldn't pay, having pawned their flawed yellow diamonds and sleazy fur-pieces and shabby costumes and battered musical instruments and baggage, and all their clothing but what they wore, were likely to be locked out if they left their rooms. So they stayed in them, behind locked doors, cowering if anyone knocked.

How some of these pathetic clowns kept from starving was a mystery in which nobody was particularly interested, until it was solved to some degree by a report in the *Daily News* that bird-loving occupants of luxury apartments across the way had complained to the S. P. C. A. that people were trapping pigeons on the cornices outside the hotel's windows. Checking on this, investigators and reporters accompanying them found that though the hotel had electricity in most of its rooms, there were still gas fixtures on the walls. Over these, hungry troupers had rigged Rube Goldberg contraptions on which they boiled eggs and made hobo coffee, cooking coffee grounds over and over again, and even (if they were lucky and a snare or a mousetrap worked) broiled pigeons. No arrests were made: no ordinance covered pigeon-snatching. But the gas lines were plugged, and evicted offenders joined the apple merchants on windswept corners. Where they found shelter after that was known only to Saint Genesius, patron of jongleurs.

Then word spread that there was work to be had in radio, and actors and actresses swarmed to line up outside of the audition rooms at NBC in the Merchandise Mart and CBS in the Wrigley Building. Names that hadn't been in lights since Otis Skinner played *Kismet* whilst collecting anecdotes for his *Mad Folk of The Theater* were claimed by his contemporaries, gaunt old men as lorn as Banquo's Ghost. Among them was Jefferson De Angelis, who had starred on the road with James O'Neill, father of Eugene; in fact he had played Romeo to Edwin Booth's Mercutio. I gave him a page of "Just Plain Bill" dialogue. He learned his lines in five minutes, and read them with a warmth and authority rare in radio. Hope and pride rekindled, he could hardly wait for his cue. But when it came, he could not, absolutely could not, speak one single word to an eyeless audience, a first-sized blob of metal on a crome-plated stand. I watched him crumble, while I whispered "Do it! Oh, for God's sake do it!" Suddenly, he began to cry. The sound of his shamed sobs, grotesquely amplified over the microphone, was too much to bear. The engineer and I bumped heads, reaching to throw the switch. De Angelis ran blindly out of the studio. When I called the Tower Town hotel, intending to insist he must come back and try it again, I was told "He's not here any more." As far as I know, he kept on running until he fell down and couldn't get up any more.

266

And then came Roger Worthingham: towering, with chiseled Francis X. Bushman profile and a leonine mane of sleek white hair that lay in marceled waves. We were paying bit players five dollars per show, or seven-fifty if they doubled. One of our first regulars appealed in Worthingham's behalf. "I was his understudy when he had his own company under canvas. He hasn't worked in God knows when and God knows when he had his last square meal." I didn't dare propose him for a role in "Just Plain Bill," our show-case show. But more experimenting was going on, and I was writing the words for it. We were exploring potentials of another new daytime audience: children at home after school. The makers of Red Goose Shoes for youngsters were willing to pay the freight. I had mentioned my Indian reservation background, casually. Mrs. Ashenhurst never forgot anything. So I was assigned to write "Red Goose Adventures," a series of half-hour melodramas about Indians, allegedly authentic. I told Worthingham's friend, who was playing a Chippewa chief in a Red Goose Adventure: "I can get him a tryout if you'll help him make it good."

The Chippewa chief would rant for ten seconds, a long speech in a half-hour show. Worthingham would answer with nine words, no more: "I am Sioux. I make no peace with Chippewa." For that, he would earn five dollars, and might be embarked on a new career. And as if life itself were at stake, he rehearsed his speech over and over until we were on the air, with eighty-odd stations taking the broadcast. He chewed his lower lip, stood on one foot and then on the other. His friend declaimed the challenge he must answer. He stood mute. His friend shook clenched fists. He blurted "I am — " and stopped. With rising panic, he repeated "I am — I am — I am — " He couldn't say "Sioux." Thirty seconds ticked off: an eternity to me, helpless in the control booth. Worthingham dropped his page of script, dived for it, banged his skull against the microphone. His friend caught it as it toppled, and thrust it toward him savagely. He howled "I am!" Then his friend bellowed: "You blank-blank-blankety-blank, you're a blank-blank-blankety Sioux!" And eighty-odd stations threw us off the air.

Like Jefferson De Angelis, Roger Worthingham left us for the bourne from which there is no returning. Then we had McKay Morris. He came to Chicago as star in a New York success, playing a Parisian *roué* with a charming accent. The new problem in "Just Plain Bill" called for a tramp found where he had been tossed from a freight train, who turned out to be a White Russian nobleman with emeralds in a pouch inside his tattered shirt. The role was offered to Morris, who came late for rehearsal, scanned my script condescendingly, stepped up to the microphone, and let go with a stentorian reading that set control booth needles spinning. After the broadcast, he refused to consider suggestions from amateurs like us. "I," he said, "was engaged to star in this rigmarole. I shall deliver McKay Morris, as contracted." We brought in a bushel basket filled with part of that day's mail, addressed not to our players but to the characters they played, and asked him to read some letters chosen at random. Puzzled, he complied. He muttered "My God!" and rose. "Gentlemen, I know when I'm out of my territory. I can't work in your show. I don't know how, and it's too late to learn." And he was right.

On the other hand, some of our faceless performers later rose to stardom in front of live audiences. One of these was John Hodiak, who had progressed from villains to heroes, in shows I wrote, before he left for Hollywood and a film career terminated by his early, tragic death. Another was Richard Widmark, whose first steady acting job was in one of my less memorable serials, "Meet the Dixons." Burgess Meredith, not yet nominated by Alexander Woollcott as the new hope of the American theater, was "Red Davis" in a serial written by Elaine Carrington. Robert Walker, slim, spectacled, serious, was thought to lack the looks for leads onstage or in Hollywood. He worked in "Just Plain Bill" and others on my list, while his lovely wife went West, with his blessing, to try her luck in films. She was Jennifer Jones, magnificent in *The Song of Bernadette*. Bob's only screen test, made in New York, had been directed by an assistant talent scout who thought it was ridiculous to waste raw-stock on a fellow who didn't have a chance. The test reached MGM eventually, and was the last of nearly a hundred at which those who then ran that studio looked while seeking a "new face" to be cast with Robert Taylor, Lloyd Nolan, Thomas Mitchell, George Murphy, Desi Arnaz, Barry Nelson, Lee Bowman and others in the all-male cast of a picture I wrote, called *Bataan*. Bob Walker got his chance, and stole the picture, and rose high before he, too, died much too young.

One stage actor got his radio opportunity not because he could act but because he had once written the lyrics for a song Mrs. Ashenhurst remembered, "The World Is Waiting for the Sunrise." He was Gene Lockhart, hired initially to write the announcer's copy introducing selections on the "American Album of Familiar Music." From this, he advanced to roles in "Just Plain Bill," and at length became a regular in our stock company, until he left to play opposite George M. Cohan in *Ah Wilderness*.

But, generally, our regulars had little if any stage experience, and might never have earned a living at the acting trade if soap opera hadn't been invented. Once an electrician who had never read a line was shoved in front of the microphone, a script thrust into his shaking hands, when a professional was taken down drunk between rehearsal and broadcast. The substitute was as wide as he was tall, and had a face as featureless as a cantaloupe, but he was a Barrymore as long as he couldn't be seen. He never fixed fuses again. When television retired him, his radio earnings made him a principal property owner and selectman in a Connecticut village, where he established a dramatic school as a hobby and lectured impressively on the Stanislavsky Method.

A spinster schoolmarm, shelved on an inadequate pension after teaching kindergarten for thirty years, could cry like a baby. Crying babies were always needed in soap operas. We had plenty of work for a dignified scholarly type who had done time for con-game swindles, and whiled away his sentence practicing how to bark like a dog, mew like a cat, coo like a dove, and snarl like a tiger. A paraplegic in a wheel chair played governors and generals. A blind grandmother played Continental adventuresses. And, like all the rest, before long these new careerists told the writer he didn't understand his characters as they interpreted them, and took it as a matter of course that it was they, not the scripts, that kept millions listening. None of them ever got over the unalterable fact that people couldn't look at them, not as they were, but as they envisaged themselves, and compensated by using their voices as if they stood ten feet off listening to themselves. Equally, they resented the phenomenon of all manner of gifts pouring in, addressed not to them but to the characters they portrayed. The sting of this was lessened, however, when the gifts were valuable enough (as they were with increasing frequency) to warrant being taken home.

I have read many patronizing essays on the mentality of adults who knitted socks and sweaters and baked birthday cakes and even sent expensive store-bought presents to Bill and Nancy and Kerry, and to Nancy's baby when in due course I arranged its birth, and to other voices in the room. I think the essayists missed the point entirely. Alec Templeton, the blind pianist entertainer, sent gifts regularly to Bill and Nancy, and told me why, one night at the Chez Paree. "Before my act and between shows, I have nothing to do but sit in my dressing room surrounded by solitude. I can't kill time reading comic strips or writing letters to *Variety* or studying the Racing Form or checking my wardrobe, like other barnstormers. But I can listen. I know Bill isn't real, and Nancy's probably fat and forty. But I make believe she's slim and twenty. The very fact that I can't see the soap opera people lets me tailor them to my own specifications. We can't pick our neighbors in real life, but soap opera gives us friends who make no demands, appear only when we want them to, and go away before they wear out their welcome. So, in simple gratitude, I express my appreciation — not to the actors but to what they've come to represent in my own private world."

There was a corollary to this. It seemed to some who followed where Hummert and Mrs. Ashenhurst blazed trails that comic strips, already possessed of a nationwide daily audience, would transfer easily to daytime serial format. "Orphan Annie" turned out well, but soap operas called "The Gumps" and "Dick Tracy" and "Terry and the Pirates" (even "Mutt and Jeff") were tried and soon abandoned. It appeared that giving live voice to cartooned characters clashed with imagined voices long accepted. Concurrently, we began to believe that soap opera story technique changed comic strips to copies of our cliffhanger problem sequences.

In any case, I never pretended contempt either for our audience or for the soap operas it loved, and do not pretend it in retrospect. *No one but a fool*, quoth Dr. Johnson, *ever wrote but for money*. I wrote for it without apology, no longer hiding behind Douglas Hardy and with no printed pages to be dissected and perhaps regretted. But I wrote as well as I was able, within the limits imposed by the rules of a contest into which no one had dragged me against my will. From my back seat in the Covered Wagon rolling across daytime radio's Great Plains, I played my small role conscientiously. *It takes a mort of words to weigh a minim*, said Daniel Defoe. I wrote many minims, while Hummert and Mrs. Ashenhurst codified the guide from which we never departed.

I wrote, and what I wrote was presented, not for a crowd in a theater, never for "the audience of millions" about which network time salesmen pontificated, but for a housewife alone, or with a couple of her children lying in the living room staring fixedly at a rectangular box, perhaps with Grandma overseeing them; or for a young couple snuggled on a parlor sofa, holding hands with the lights turned low. Our actors were drilled into a special mental attitude. They must think of themselves — and perform — not as stars strutting in the spotlight but as uninvited guests hoping to be asked to stay awhile in some strange small home. We were our own censors. "Bad taste" was defined, in our lexicon, as anything that might embarrass anyone. We were positive that such blush-producing unmentionables as brassières, bathroom staples and specifics for irregularity could never be sold over the air. And there would be no violence for the sake of shock, no Bad Words spoken or implied, and above all, no scarlet-lettered Sex. In sum, we were as respectable as the Paper That Goes Home.

James Thurber summed up soap opera in one long, sardonic sentence: *The recipe for this sandwich is simple although it took years to compound: Between thick slices of advertising spread twelve minutes of dialogue, add predicament, villainy, and female suffering, in equal measure; throw in a dash of nobility, sprinkle with tears, season with organ music, cover with a rich announcer sauce, and serve five times weekly.* (All generalities are debatable, including this one. Many tried the Thurber recipe. On the record, only Blackett-Sample-Hummert soap operas stayed on the air until the agency, not the sponsors or the public, grew tired of them.) Critics clamored that my scripts for these shows were repetitious. They were quite correct: we planned them that way. Under orders, not from laziness or lack of dramatic sense, I had my characters tell what they were about to do, tell that now they were doing it, then tell what they had done. Still our listeners wrote in asking what happened. Not because they were dull-witted, but because they lent us only half an ear while they moved from the washing machine to the ironing board, from the carpet-sweeping to saying "No" to the Fuller Brush man on the door-step. It was easy to trick up a script with attention-compelling, sudden surprises. Then a million women might blame us for holding them spellbound while the biscuits burned, or Tommy fell out of his high chair, or the iron, left turned on, scorched Henry's Sunday shirt. And they would express their anger, next time they went shopping, by not buying what we sold.

They wrote in by thousands, asking, "Does the show always have to be so sad? Can't we hear some happiness once in a while?" We yielded to what we thought was popular demand. Now housewives, fuming because Arthur drank too much beer last night at the bowling alley, storming because Mrs. Jones next door wouldn't keep her chickens penned, fresh from quarreling with the grocery boy, heard joy and laughter on the air, and turned us off, and were unforgiving when the drug-gist said, "We have a two-for-one special on that toothpaste they advertise on 'Just Plain Bill.' " And down went the sales-curve, and the sponsor wired VERY DISTURBED UNFAVORABLE CONSUMER REACTION CURRENT BILL SEQUENCE; and I rewrote all night long, taking out cheer and putting in tears. My con-tract required me to be twenty scripts ahead of broadcast at all times. There was no allowance for extra fees if a whole batch had to be done over because the sponsor's Radio Gift Offer wasn't going over as well as expected. I proposed a standard reply to all who asked for fun and frolics instead of broken legs and breaking hearts. DEAR MRS. ONDERDONK: *We, too, wish everybody could be happy. But if everybody was, there wouldn't be any stories that people would listen to so they can tell themselves smugly: "Oh, well, anyhow, somebody is worse off than I am, so I feel better."* Like my other un-solicited proposals, this was pigeonholed without comment. In fact, I heard little from anyone in authority except when more words were wanted. That was what I was there for: words.

Mr. Hummert had moved to New York, where the agency

was opening new offices, closer to network headquarters and time buyers. Mrs. Ashenhurst traveled back and forth between Chicago and New York. Printer's Ink called Blackett-Sample-Hummert a Depression miracle, the fastest-growing agency in the business, *all based on daytime radio advertising*. Scholarly essayists waked to a new proof of the gullibility of Americans. *However marvelous the mechanics of radio, however unlimited its future, however splendid its potential as a great national talking machine from which Americans could extract sheer disembodied knowledge, the grim fact is that its exploiters are reducing it to the lowest common denominator, and coining millions, because in sorry truth they are right when they tell each other "We are dealing with a universal twelve-year-old mentality."*

We told each other nothing of the sort. We simply adapted a formula for which neither magazines nor newspapers, so loftily critical of their upstart competitor for the advertising dollar, had ever felt need to apologize. H. L. Mencken in the *Mercury* snorted that George Horace Lorimer, who had edited the *Saturday Evening Post* in the years of its glory, let his advertising manager select the stories he published. Lorimer replied sensibly that his magazine would stop showing a profit unless his fiction created an audience for the advertising that paid the bills. The *Daily News* was no more self-conscious than any other newspaper regarding the careful scheduling of "inside–jump" carryovers from Page One alongside preferred-position advertisements. We, too, centered on a target. Women.

Deprived by my typing hours of much opportunity for Little Big Mouth to unburden himself, I took up a now-and-then sideline, lecturing to women about books and authors. I learned almost immediately that I could count on at least one matron to spring up during the question-and-answer period, to interrupt discussion of radio by announcing proudly: "I stop listening the second the commercial starts. I know how long the commercial runs. I don't tune in again till it's over." The first time I heard this, I asked: "Do you also steal magazines from the newsstands?" There was a furore. I explained my meaning: listening to the commercials paid for the free show. This didn't compensate for my impolite inquiry; and I didn't ask the question again. Actually, I held only what the British call a "watching brief" in sales-pitch planning. Otherwise, my conscience might have whimpered now and then. For example, one of the shows I wrote sold a brand-name proprietary product which according to Consumers' Research was nothing but ordinary Epsom salts. The commercials guaranteed that taken according to printed directions enclosed with each bottle, this specific would take off ten pounds in a week. And it would. The directions called for a reducing diet so rigorous that not one person in a hundred would endure it for more than a day. But buoyed up by expectation of magic, armies of women spooned salts into themselves, then starved, and gave all the credit to the stuff that "Just Plain Bill" sold, when pounds disappeared.

Meanwhile our actors lived in a little new private world, untouched by crass commercialism. When I dropped in on a "Just Plain Bill" rehearsal, the Pickard Family surrounded me, complaining in chorus that Dad Pickard, though he had never acted before, was so magnificent as Elmer Eeps that he was entitled to four times as many lines as my scripts gave him. I said that would have to be taken up with Mrs. Ashenhurst. It was; and soon we had another Elmer Eeps. Then Marion and Jim Jordan ("Fibber McGee and Mollie" to be) said confidentially that if I could arrange a deal for them to play all the bits and crowd voices in the shows I wrote, for a fixed team wage of one hundred and fifty dollars a week, they'd hand me twenty-five dollars a week under the table. They were surprised, then touched, when I said I'd do what I could, by writing parts Mrs. Ashenhurst knew they could play better than anyone else, which ought to get them as much as two hundred a week in the long run, but that I didn't take kickbacks. (At about that time, a young singer, married, with four small children, fainted at the microphone in the middle of his fifteen-minute morning songalogue. The doctor diagnosed "acute starvation." His salary was one hundred and seventy-five dollars a week. But his manager and several kickback collectors had been taking 90 per cent of his paycheck.)

As for those who then impersonated Bill, Nancy, and Kerry Donovan, when they were told I wrote the scripts they asked, "That stuff?" (They didn't exactly say "stuff.") They anticipated our countless critics, nicknaming the show "Just Plain Dull," and "Just Plain Bilge." But for them, they said, I'd be out of work. Their personalities, their creative contribution, triumphed over the banality I wrote. Some of my best friends are actors, except when they take my lines and confer their own interpretation. What ensues can be rather grim. But in those early hours of the morning of radio's great daytime, sticks and stones raised no welts, as long as Scrubby Lee, promoted from dog walker to personal courier, picked up another check at the agency each time I sent in another set of scripts.

One Wednesday, with Mrs. Ashenhurst still in New York, "Just Plain Bill" six weeks ahead, and If I Had A Million under control, I felt free to telephone Pablo Katigbak at the Daily News.

We agreed to meet for a quiet alcoholic evening, in a basement hideaway the Syndicate hadn't gotten around to ruining, the Casa De Alex, whose rotund and robustly Rabelaisian proprietor made his own strong red wine and sang "The Gambler's Blues" in Spanish. Pablo said, "It will be my party." I said "Of course not. Hadn't you heard I'm a millionaire? Or would be if I had a million?" He said, "One time, before I go, I push. I push you. I pay. Why? Because today is graduation. Tomorrow, I am on my way to Manila." I said, "You can't walk out on us, Pablo!" He said "In Manila, they will call me 'Mister,' on a paper as big to the Philippines as the *Daily News* to America. Anyhow almost." I said, "Mr. Smith doesn't want you to leave, does he?" Pablo answered obliquely: "Mr. Smith don't ever want anybody to leave." I could wear the shoe if it fitted. "All right," I said. "Eight o'clock at Alex's. I'll do my best to talk you out of it." I didn't mean out of picking up the check.

At seven, Mrs. Ashenhurst telephoned from New York to say a new client wanted to go on the network immediately, with a serial aimed at children. It would be called "The Adventures of Terry and Mary." Title and writing budget had already been okayed. All I had to do was deliver five scripts and a thirteen-week story plan by Monday. Let Longfellow be my inspiration. *Between the dark and the daylight, when the night is beginning to lower,* she quoted, *Comes a pause in the day's occupations, that is known as the Childrens' Hour.* We would, she said, restore this vanished institution to the American Home, for fifteen minutes five days a week at 5:15. Maybe Daddy wouldn't be home that early, unless he was out of a job, but Mama had to be. And while Terry and Mary calmed their rambunctious offspring, women would learn to thank the sponsor, and thus to switch to the kind of aspirin with a cross on the tablets that dissolved in seconds in a glass of water. And would I please start writing immediately? I asked "Don't I always?" But actually, I didn't start until after four the next morning, after Pablo Katigbak shook hands hard, grinned his moon-faced grin, and said, "I bet you we meet some more, some day, some place." (It took twenty-one years for both of us to win that bet, ten thousand miles from Chicago).

In New York, Dr. Lee De Forest burst out at a convention of broadcasting moguls: "What have you done to my child? You have made him the laughingstock to intelligence, surely a stench in the nostrils of the gods of the ionosphere. Murder mysteries rule the waves by night and children are rendered psychopathic by your bedtime stories."

In Chicago, we tried to profit from the mistakes that wrecked the "Red Goose Adventures" series. But before the first week of "Terry and Mary" ended, it was clear we had problems that even Bill the Barber couldn't have solved. Children, it appeared, really have no imagination. Lacking colored illustrations to look at, our little listeners were too lazy or too literal-minded to picture in their brains the stories we put on the air. I dealt with ships and pirates and the sea. Sound-effects conveyed no illusion to the juvenile audience. *Sound and fury signifying nothing.*

Our next decision was that children have absolutely no sense of humor. All then-accredited geniuses in radio dug desperately for tag lines. Jack Pearl's "Vas you dere Sharlie?" and Joe Penner's "Wanta buy a duck?" were as epochal as Hummert's KODAK AS YOU GO and THE SKIN YOU LOVE TO TOUCH or Washburn-Crosby's EVENTUALLY — WHY NOT NOW? But during the hard-pressed day, small shouting imps parroted Pearl and Penner senselessly until their mothers snarled between clenched teeth: "If you say that just once more, I'll murder you!" Sales charts showed conclusively that, on sponsors who gave their imitative tots sayings with which to torture parents, women took immediate vengeance by buying a competitive product. Therefore another pronouncement was graven on tablets of brass: *Don't try to be funny, and avoid all tag lines in Blackett-Sample-Hummert shows.*

As for our child actors in "Terry and Mary," they were juveniles only on their work permits. Fond mothers had caged them in professional schools as soon as they could walk and talk. Their teachers had sedulously stamped out all vestiges of childlike charm. They were all incipient Hamlets and Lady Macbeths. Their diction was offensively precise. They expressed joy as if it were agony. Their tears were turned on and off by the director's pointing finger. No wonder children lis-

278

tening scorned Terry as a stuckup sissy and Mary as a prissy showoff. And no amount of re-casting would ever correct a built-in flaw. We had forgotten, or possibly some of us never knew — having been born so old — that a boy of six hero-worships one of twelve but not one who is merely nine. We had also forgotten that little girls loathe little girls.

Children, new surveys showed, much preferred "Just Plain Bill" to "Terry and Mary." They thought Bill was one of them. And therefore "Terry and Mary" died, between a Friday and a Monday, and very soon afterward the first and forever most successful true soap opera for children burst upon the daytime scene. At General Mills in Minneapolis, it was decided to see if radio advertising could convince mothers that a cold cereal, Wheaties, should be fed to their brood on wintry mornings in place of competitive hot Cream-o'-Wheat or some other traditional porridge. (Myself, I was reared on corn-meal mush and milk.) Mrs. Ashenhurst took the challenge to Hummert in New York, where he now did his creating in an ivory tower overlooking Park Avenue. Clearly, children liked homespun philosophers, so different from short-tempered fathers and easily aggravated mothers. So our strategists sent out for a boy-sized Bill the Barber, and found him in a comic strip called "Skippy."

Percy Crosby, a talented artist turned cartoonist, drew the strip, which was syndicated to many newspapers. Most editors put it on their Childrens' Page. But to Crosby, his diminutive bow-tied hero was himself personified, and spoke with the wisdom of the ages. Skippy's cocky cloth hat and usually neat garb were not a sissy's getup, but the uniform of a born leader, sometimes in baseball games on the sand lot over across the railroad tracks, occasionally in scampish forays against dog catchers and old-clothes peddlers and the iceman, very frequently in dissertations aimed at adults. There were jokes, but these had a deep world-weariness. Skippy's speeches lettered on Crosby's drawings were a mixture of elegant English and what Crosby called Skippyisms. Parents, not their progeny, followed Skippy in the paper. And apparently that was what Crosby wanted. Certainly, he wasn't addressing children when he drew a panorama of rolling hills and unreachable distance, with Skippy in the foreground, dwarfed by Nature's grandeur, pronouncing solemn judgment: "God turns out a pretty nice job of scenery." Nor in the frames within which a ragged tagalong mite he called Sookie declared, "I don't believe in God because I don't believe what I can't see," and Skippy challenged: "Tell me the color of the wind."

To Crosby's shocked surprise, people took Sookie to their hearts. Outraged, he eliminated the interloper from his strips. Editors protested to his syndicate. "Our readers want more Sookie, less Skippy." Wrathfully, Crosby wrote and published a book of illustrated *Skippy Rambles*, climaxed by Sookie's death and burial. Conan Doyle was no more widely castigated for getting rid of Sherlock Holmes by having him thrown off an Alp. Crosby seethed, but surrendered, to a point. Ragged tagalong mites crept into his strips now and then. They were anonymous. He stated firmly, "Sookie is dead and gone." A crusading teetotaler, he used Skippy in a one-man war against strong drink and its defenders. Even the bill then pending, to legalize 3.2 per cent beer, disturbed him. "The Government," he had one of his tagalongs remark wonderingly, "didn't want to horn in on the racketeers, but when the Treasury moved to a tin cup, there was no other way. A very smart Senator found out that makin' beer would bring money into the Treasury." Skippy commented: "The high school kids won't stand for a soft drink when they's used to gin." Skippy also spoke out against advertising. "I looked up at the sky, see, and I was wonderin' if the stars was eyes lookin' down on Nature bein' slowly took away by nothin' but advertisin' an' signboards, an' if the eyes looked at it for a long time, I wondered if it wasn't enough to make 'em cry."

But the agency put Crosby under contract. For one thousand dollars a week, fifty-two weeks a year, he would permit us to dramatize "Skippy." How this could be done had not been discussed, beyond decision to have me start doing it right away. It happened that I was a "Skippy" follower. For that very reason, I doubted that there was anything more than a title to work with, in developing a serial. Crosby's works gave little or no information regarding Skippy's home, his family, his neighborhood (although mention of the Gowanus Canal and other place names such as Vesey Street suggested that Skippy lived either in Brooklyn or in downtown Manhattan). Mrs. Ashenhurst couldn't see why such details presented any difficulty. She said we'd make Skippy the planner and fixer and doer, and Sookie another Elmer Eeps. We wouldn't say it on the air because such literary references would be over the heads of our listeners; but Skippy should be, you might say, an all-American Don Quixote in knee pants, with Sookie for his Sancho Panza. And Crosby sometimes drew a pretty little girl he called Carol; we would use Carol, but not too much; and she must never whine. And in place of "Terry and Mary" piracies and typhoons, we'd have Skippy solve problems regarding which our young listeners would say "Hey, that could happen to me!" but their mothers wouldn't say "It hadn't better!" and stop buying Wheaties if it did. And there was another thing I must watch out for.

To help get the new show off to a good start, Crosby had autographed one of his books *From Skippy's father to the radio writer of "Skippy" in a spirit of peace and good will.* This was written after the contract was signed, but before Crosby heard I was or had been a reporter. He had known a lot of reporters. They were unpredictable, irresponsible, whiskey-drinking fellows. He wasn't at all sure one of them could be trusted to deal righteously with his *alter ego.* As a matter of fact, it concerned the sponsor that I was not only a newspaperman but a writer of books about girls and gangsters. To prevent Crosby from further upsetting the sponsor by sending in criticisms and objections, as he might if given any excuse, I'd have to lean over backward both in my writing and in my personal conduct. I asked, "Isn't getting a thousand dollars a week for doing absolutely nothing too good a deal for him to take a chance on cancellation?" I was told "Creative people are temperamental." As for me, I became "Uncle Bob."

Having learned to our sorrow that professional child actors were a headache and a handicap, we scoured Chicago for small amateurs who might be molded into puppets. There was a plethora of candidates for the role of Skippy. Casting Sookie wasn't as easy, until I noticed that a microphone had vanished from its stand, and a large-eyed, snuffling tyke in his brother's Sunday suit was sidling out of the audition-room with something bulky inside his shirt. Collared, he wept, but turned off the tears when I offered him a candy bar. We had our Sookie. And our Skippy was likable, too, once he realized that he was founder and president of a secret society with a secret code (which I lifted from the "Gold Bug" cryptogram) and a secret handshake (borrowed from a Greek-letter fraternity that once considered admitting me and then decided against it).

Of all the mumbo-jumbo organizations that have flowered in the United States, I doubt if any caught on as quickly, or exerted as much pressure in as many American homes, as Skippy's Secret Society. Writing up the by-laws and other printed paraphernalia took almost as much time and effort as writing scripts for the show. To be eligible for membership, you had to be just like Skippy. So you got your mother to buy *a box of Wheaties like Skippy eats.* You sent in the box-top. Back came a chart. For thirty days, you had to *do like Skippy does:* Brush your teeth morning and night, get plenty of fresh air and exercise and sleep, obey your schoolteacher, run errands for your mother, do your home work, *and eat two heaping bowls of Wheaties.* These duties were checked off daily on your chart. At the end of the month, if all the spaces were marked with an X and your mother signed on the dotted line, you received your membership button, secret codebook, and so on and so forth. After that, of course you'd be loyal to Skippy; you'd make sure your mother went right on buying Wheaties, so *Skippy can stay on the air.*

I was never given accurate figures, which were confidential between executives; but scuttlebutt at the agency gave Skippy's Secret Society a million members before, pursuant to the "Just Plain Bill" formula, Skippy had solved the third among the many problems I thrust upon him. All over America, mothers bought Wheaties and signed charts. But there was no usable theme song for "Skippy" in Sandburg's *Songbag*. Unable to carry a tune or read music, I found an organist who could make sense of some oompah sounds I uttered, and handed in the immortal ballad that was to ask no one knows how many million Americans "Have you tried Wheaties, the best breakfast food in the land?" I was paid fifty dollars for an assignment of copyright. I got the same amount for a slogan: THE BREAKFAST OF CHAMPIONS. I didn't, and don't, bewail such bargain sales, or envy others who got the credit and a lot more cash. I subscribe to a philosophy I knew better than to write into "Just Plain Bill," or "Skippy," or any soap opera that followed. I learned it from a Minneapolis gambler, just before, with a big night's winnings in his pocket, he stepped on the starter of his Pierce-Arrow and was blown sky-high by a bomb placed in the engine by persons still unknown. "Whatever you git," he advised, "don't cry because it ain't any more. Grab it and git, before they git it away from you!"

"Skippy" caught on so quickly that handling the time account started meteoric network careers. Niles Trammell, a soft-spoken Southerner, and Sidney Strotz, who had been a broker and ran the Chicago Stadium before he joined NBC, went on up the ladder until they were running the organization, coast to coast. Everybody, in fact, forgot the Depression outside the studios. "Just Plain Bill" added fifty more stations.

We had to do two daily "Skippy" broadcasts, for networks east and west. To reassure Percy Crosby and General Mills, I was photographed eating Wheaties and drinking milk with Skippy and Sookie and Carol, between the broadcasts. In fact I enjoyed dropping in on the cast. Soberer than some Chicago judges I had known, I told Indian stories, some of them true. Showing how successfully I deceived them, when they heard I was having a birthday Skippy and Sookie gave me two bottles of Scotch and a cocktail shaker.

I could use the sustenance. I was writing "Ma Perkins" now, along with "Just Plain Bill" and "Skippy." Variety, which called itself (and still does, and still with cause) "the Bible of show business," sniffed in its review of my third soap opera: "Ma Perkins" is nothing but "Just Plain Bill" in skirts. This wasn't printed as praise, but no feelings were hurt at Blackett-Sample-Hummert. We knew, before Variety noticed it, that Bill and Ma Perkins were peas from the same pod. Bill was a widower. Ma was a widow. Ma ran a lumberyard, but sold two-by-fours as seldom as Bill gave haircuts. Both meddled joyously, coping with a succession of deceitful promoters, close-fisted bankers, menacing gangsters and designing divorcees. Both were kindly, shrewd, respected, humble, loquacious, concerned, and invincible. In plain truth, some of my earlier scripts for "Just Plain Bill" worked very well on "Ma Perkins," with only slight revisions. The story lines were interchangeable, as machined parts are meant to be. So were our actors and actresses, who played nice folks in one morning show, rotters in the other, and then took both sides at the Children's Hour. Quite often, I wrote the villain out of the last two minutes of "Just Plain Bill," so he could race down two flights of stairs and rush into another studio in the Merchandise Mart, with a minute left in which to catch his breath before beginning a tender love scene as the romantic lead in "Ma Perkins." Duplication, of plot or performers, never seemed to bother the millions of women and children who let nothing keep them from hearing as many as possible of the 45,000 words I ground out every week. My problem was Percy Crosby.

At first, he didn't listen to "Skippy." Then his neighbors, who took it for granted that he was writing "Skippy" on the air, congratulated him on his good sense in exhuming Sookie from the grave. He bought a radio, listened, and let out a howl that carried from his Virginia farm to my corner in Chicago. Memos flew back and forth. Sookie must disappear, or Crosby might cancel his contract. No; we couldn't do without Sookie. Diplomatic agents rushed to Crosby's farm. Eventually, he was induced to swallow Sookie, as long as Skippy didn't call him by name on any of the broadcasts, and if I'd promise to give all the meaningful sayings to Skippy. This called for some emergency rewrites, which stopped my work on *If I Had a Million*. The book had to be finished; I had passed the point of putting it aside. And something had to be delivered to Smith, somewhere within each twenty-four hours. And still I said "I'll try it" when Mrs. Ashenhurst came out from New York to tell me I had another assignment.

This time, my problem was Edna Wallace Hopper.

Hedda Hopper, since then a long-time neighbor in Beverly Hills and enduringly a family friend, says in her autobiographical *From under My Hat:*

I'm always amused when people mix me up with Edna Wallace Hopper. Sure we share the same last name, but she was De Wolfe Hopper's Number Three; I was Number Five, as in Chanel. Edna, a cute bundle, never got any alimony; she didn't need it. I wish I had her knack for finance. In the crash of 1929, instead of losing her shirt as I did, she bought gaudier ones. Edna played Wall Street for a sucker and came out Mrs. Croesus.

(Hedda Hopper, parenthetically, has tenuous connection with the *Daily News*, although, as she is wont to note in her widely published column, she may read it here first. In 1937, Howard Denby, once our Picture Editor, was taken around Hollywood by another *Daily News* alumnus, Jack Lawson, by then the owner operator of a Los Angeles public-relations company. Denby asked, "What's your opinion of Hedda Hopper to write a syndicated daily column from Hollywood?" I said, "If you can get her, you'll have a gold mine to sell." He said, "That's what Cissy Patterson told us. That's why I'm here. We've already signed her." I mention this only to show that sometimes, if not often, I bet on a winner.)

One of Edna Wallace Hopper's minor business ventures had been her sale to a cosmetics firm, for a fine round sum, of the right to use her name on its products. I think she had actually forgotten this long-past deal, when a group of bright opportunists found that Black Friday and the Depression had pushed a number of small concerns into bankruptcy, and for not much cash bought up such assets as there were. Among these was the EDNA WALLACE HOPPER trademark. Blackett-Sample-Hummert took it from there. Edna Wallace Hopper had been touring vaudeville houses, singing, dancing, talking: not denying her age but capitalizing on it. She gave Saturday morning matinees For Women Only, at which she demonstrated the exercises to which she attributed her apparent girlishness. She said with a twinkle: "I'm older than any of you, but when I walk down the street handsome young men try to flirt with me. I'll bet you wish that would happen to you." Now she was placed under contract, EDNA WALLACE HOPPER YOUTH RESTORATIVE CREAM appeared on cosmetic counters, and I began writing pearls of beauty lore for her to scatter on the air.

What I wrote for her, per script, took me eighteen minutes to read aloud. She read it in thirteen, and never missed a word, but her air time was thirty seconds less than that. Her protesting cry — "They're pushing me off the air!" — became the only tag line Blackett-Sample-Hummert didn't frown on.

She wouldn't have dropped it if they had. She didn't own the creams and lotions her employers sold, but they needed her worse than she needed the job, and she let no one forget it. She called women "You lazy girls!", told them "Face yourselves in your mirrors and you'll see why your husband didn't kiss you 'Good-by' this morning!", stirred their desire for emulation by confiding "A strange young man stopped me on my way to the studio and without a word handed me an American Beauty rose!", commanded "Drop whatever you're doing and pay attention while I whisper something I never told anyone before and won't tell you again!"

Seen walking away, she looked sixteen. Seen onstage, artfully lighted, her face marched with her figure. In our crack-of-dawn conferences, she was still doll-like, except for the strained, unnatural tautness of her unwrinkled skin, and the plastic surgeon's sign-off encircling her still youthful throat. She had the dancer's trick of aiding illusion with her hands, which were usually gloved because, as every woman learns (or so I wrote and she said on the air), no woman is ever younger than her knuckles. She effervesced with girlish gaiety, whether she discussed her digestive processes, which she did in elaborate detail on the slightest provocation, or commented with dainty feline distaste on the untrustworthiness of husbands ("Men think women are fools; I say God made 'em so to match the men!").

She spent two full hours making up before she went to the studio, although her masculine audience there consisted only of a carefully cast young announcer who also modeled for collar ads, but who eyed his stopwatch, not her, while he nerved himself to break in with the closing commercial, and an engineer, also chosen for virile handsomeness, who did most of his looking at his dials — because he was never sure, nor was she, when one of her sudden shrill squeals might blast the show right off the air. This possibility amused her. It was also amusing to depart from my scripts, as approved by

287

Mrs. Ashenhurst, whenever a peppery backstage anecdote occurred to her. Titillated listeners asked each other hopefully: "What on earth will she say next?" The papers listed her under TALKS, not DRAMA, but she was a one-woman serial of suspense.

Mrs. Ashenhurst never quarreled with success. A time came, however, when it was felt that Edna Wallace Hopper needed discipline. She got it. I had written some *Midweek* pages under the impressive by-line of a princess, whose actual knowledge of intrigue at the Court of the Czars was somewhat limited, since she was Iowa born and reared, had never been in Europe, and met and married her prince a decade after the Bolshevik Revolution, when he was telling fortunes in a Russian tearoom in Des Moines. Now I was assigned to write beauty talks for the Princess, while a refugee ballerina taught her a Russian accent. She went on the air introduced as Edna Wallace Hopper's long-time friend, imported from Paris to fill in while our star was on vacation. This vacation lasted until the lesson sank in. Then the Princess went back to her job as a stenographer, our chastened star returned to her orbit, I rushed out rewritten scripts, and Mrs. Ashenhurst wired from New York THANKS FOR HOPPER CONTINUITIES THEY ARE VERY GRAND.

I appreciated applause from on high. But more and more, I wanted out. *If I Had a Million* was still unfinished. And Colonel Knox had notified me, through Smith, that he had another special assignment: one that offered the chance to be really a *Daily News* newspaperman again. Oddly, this came about because of a wire story from Oregon, where a jobless cannery manager, Walter Waters, was enlisting veterans of World War I to follow him in a "Bonus March" across the continent to Washington, D.C.

Adjusted compensation payments, voted by Congress in 1924, were not due until 1945. But 272,000 veterans were on relief. They appealed for immediate cash loans against sums not due for thirteen years. President Hoover vetoed this, as obviously unsound financing. Congress overrode his veto. Then the Patman Bill proposed immediate payment of bonuses in full. Waters thought the Bonus Army march to Washington would shame Congress into approving this. Editorially, the *Daily News* doubted if the misguided marchers would ever get as far east as Chicago.

The Opposition said Chicago had troubles enough without opening her gates (nothing was said about her heart) to any more out-of-towners capitalizing on the Depression.

Having concluded comfortably at the end of 1931 that "Gangsterism is over in Chicago," the Opposition now declared that the Employers Association overlooked more than it listed, in its report that a hundred businesses and professions were helpless in the grip of gangsters: *The truth is that conditions are such that any man who dares to oppose extortions, variously veiled, is in dire physical danger, and our agencies entrusted with law enforcement either cannot or will not provide protection.* Frank J. Loesch, chairman of the Chicago Crime Commission, declared: "Fully two thirds of the unions in Chicago are controlled or levied upon, directly or indirectly, by Capone's representatives." Such statements were not discussed at advertising agencies or in radio studios. So I had no one to talk to about anything but more words for the airwaves, until Colonel Knox called me in to start writing about a noble plan that called for the full-time services of Florenz Ziegfeld, P. T. Barnum, and Grover Whalen, none of whom were on the *Daily News* payroll.

Knox thought that if decent citizens could be convinced that Chicago still belonged to them, not to thugs and thieves and bribe-collectors, the city would celebrate A Century of Progress in 1933 with much less embarrassment, and a better chance to keep the World's Fair from becoming what doom-shouters already prophesied it was bound to be: a failure that

289

not even Chicago could live down. Therefore the *Daily News* was going to stage A Carnival of Nations. There were at least forty language groups in Chicago, at least fifty nationalistic and racial societies, some with thousands of members. German and Irish populations were the largest, the most totally organized and politically influential. After them, in order, came Poles, Swedes, Czechs, Italians, and Yiddish-speaking Jews. Cermak, born at Prague in Bohemia, would be our World's Fair mayor, but Ed Kelly, "the man behind the Fair," succeeded marvelously in politics on a three-word platform: ERIN GO BRAGH. (Kelly settled with the United States Treasury for $105,000, having forgotten to pay taxes on $450,000 earned between 1926 and 1928, when his salary as a Sanitary District engineer was $15,000 a year.) Nowhere in America were *Wop* and *Mick* and *Bohunk* and *Polack* and *Heinie* and *Kike* flung back and forth as commonly and cruelly as in Chicago. Boundaries of Little Italy and Little Germany and Little Slovakia were patrolled as belligerently as any borderland in Europe. But, knowing this, Colonel Knox proposed a mammoth program of Old Country music and dancing to be put on within its demesne by each separate hyphenated entity — and that, thereafter, representative features selected from these would be combined in a mammoth all-Chicago, all-American spectacle.

Nothing so ambitious or so complicated had ever been undertaken by a Chicago newspaper. Let the Opposition call it a circulation-building stunt. It had that element. And it wouldn't hurt Knox politically. But of the feuding Chicago Colonels, it was McCormick, not Knox, who made speeches claiming that his paper's promotions were utterly eleemosynary. We were instructed to do no bragging in print about the fact that everything raised by the Carnival of Nations ticket sales would go to charity, with the *Daily News* paying all expenses. My job was feature stories. "What we want," Knox told me, "is names, names, names, and pictures, pictures,

pictures, of people, people, people." I hadn't been handed an opportunity like that since Smith imported me from Minneapolis. But Smith asked with real concern: "Are you sure you can handle it and still keep up with your radio writing?"

I said "It's time I cut down on radio." Smith said, "You haven't asked for my opinion." I said, "I ask for it every time I walk into this office." He said, "You don't owe me that, Bob." I said, "What I owe you, I can't pay." He shook his head. "Bob," he said, "I tried to make a point in *Deadlines*. We tear ourselves apart, on a paper, getting out another Final. Then we get on a bus or a streetcar and there sit people turning to the Sports Page, finding out if the Cubs and the White Sox won or lost, then dropping the paper when they get off. People walk on what was life or death to us. Tomorrow, it's birth and life and death again. We don't call that hack writing. We call it newspapering. Nothing we write remains. That doesn't make it not worth doing, if we do it honestly and capably, to meet a deadline. That's the test: respect for a deadline." He gestured apologetically. "I don't know the first thing about radio, why it's written, what it's aimed at. I only wanted to mention that you must be meeting your deadlines honestly and capably, or they'd get somebody else. So if you'll forgive the advice: I wouldn't feel as if I'd come down in the world." He grinned. "That's the longest speech I ever made to you, Bob. Now what's your plan on Colonel Knox's Carnival?"

A little unsteadily at first, I told him I'd like to start with the Chinese, who weren't on Knox's list of nationalities. He asked if I knew any Chinese. I didn't. So he told me where to start and who to see, and in New Chinatown, on the outskirts of the Levee District, I met grave, prosperous officials of the On Leong Benevolent Association, who were sincerely sorry that they couldn't accept Colonel Knox's proposal to raise funds for charity to destitute Chinese. There weren't any. They hoped I wouldn't interpret as criticism of their Occidental neighbors the fact that since Orientals take care of their own when they're in a foreign country, there were no Chinese selling apples or on relief. However, if the *Daily News* would allot whatever was raised by them to help other foreign-born, unfortunately less well off, they would be happy to show Chicagoans a Chinese opera, and their young people would perform in the costumes and to the music of their honored ancestors. Incidentally, there was a Dixieland Jazz Band composed of young Chinese students in Chicago's colleges. Would I like to have New China as well as Old China on the program? I would; and when Knox read my story, he had an editorial written which suggested that Americans might learn some lessons from Chicago's Chinatown.

I wrote more stories about real people. Writing them cleared my mind's eyes. I saw the people in *If I Had a Million* with more eagerness to know how their stories ended. For the first time, I fell behind schedule on delivery of scripts for "Just Plain Bill" and "Skippy" and "Ma Perkins" and Edna Wallace Hopper, while I wrote not for money but because I couldn't help it. This brought immediate admonition. "Just now especially, Mr. Andrews," Mrs. Ashenhurst said, "we *must* be able to feel we can rely on you." She explained that "Just Plain Bill" was being moved to New York. Not the cast. New actors and actresses had already been engaged. (One of them, Arthur Hughes, had been a dependable but often at liberty character actor, who lived at the Lambs' Club and who made it a part of his contract that his brother Lambs would not be told he had deserted the stage for radio. He played Bill for more than five thousand consecutive performances, but never stopped saying he'd quit in a minute if a good Broadway role came along. When I met him for the first time, after he had been Bill for two years, he echoed "Andrews? Are you connected with the show?")

Since scripts would now have to be mailed, it was more than ever imperative that I must be ahead of deadline at all times. One set of scripts should be sent Air Mail. For protection, two carbon copies should be sent simultaneously by train, Special Delivery. This meant more work for Scrubby Lee, my faithful courier. He missed no mails, but a plane crashed in Pennsylvania, and some post office clerk dropped an envelope in the wrong pouch, and I came home one sunrise and heard Rikki-tikki-tavi barking at the jangling telephone, and, answering it, was told on Long Distance that no script had been received for that day's show, due to go on the air in eleven minutes, New York time. The missing script had been written four weeks before, and promptly forgotten. I hadn't made a file copy. Confessing my stupidity would help no one. All I could do was say, "Hold the phone while I check my file," and stick my head under a cold-water faucet while I checked my memory, and then start dictating, improvising line by line. In New York, stenographers with headphones typed what I dictated, in short takes that were rushed into the studio and seized by actors and actresses who read words they hadn't seen before as realistically as they could, when none knew what was coming next. Neither did I. But I didn't shudder and shake until the ordeal was over, and word was relayed from HQ on Park Avenue that "As usual, Mr. Andrews works best when he has a deadline to meet."

It took some doing, to get back to *If I Had a Million* that same morning. But this, too, had to be done. I was due in Rogers Park that afternoon, to line up the Norwegian show for Colonel Knox's Carnival.

Now there was "Skippy" trouble again. An actor playing a schoolteacher who made life miserable for Sookie had developed a nasty habit of pinching and punching children in the cast, while the show was on the air, if they cut in too soon on one of his speeches, or failed to pick up a cue as quickly as he thought they should. He had a run-of-the-part contract, and also played a running role in "Ma Perkins." Picking up his script one afternoon, he read with amazement that the character he portrayed had suddenly shown symptoms of some mysterious ailment, and must go away at once for treatment that might take days, weeks, or months. His script for the other show had the character he played summoned to California by business that might delay return indefinitely. *Ham,* the vaudeville saying ran, *can be cured; ham actors can't.* But this one became a gentleman overnight. And we had another weapon in the arsenal, for use in case other actors or actresses grew hard to handle — as some did.

All very well. But sixty thousand words a week, plus more for *If I Had a Million,* plus Colonel Knox's Carnival, began to be a bit too much. I drew straws mentally. Then one night I set a bottle of gin beside my typewriter, and arranged with myself that it, and three thousand words that couldn't fail to part me from Edna Wallace Hopper, would be finished concurrently. With malice aforethought, I invented the Edna Wallace Hopper Beauty Bath. "You girls," I said she should say, "have never stopped to realize, I'm sure, how you harm your tender sensibilities by sitting down too suddenly in the bathtub. I learned fifty years ago that it's not the water and bath salts you put in, it's how you put yourself in, that preserves your youth and attractiveness to men. Now drop whatever you're doing, and wherever you are, let's pretend you're in the bathroom. Follow me, girls! Back up, slowly, until your calves touch the rim of the tub. Breathe deeply until you're in a relaxing mood. Now lean backward, arching gracefully. Put your hands back behind you. Rest them firmly on the two sides of the tub. Sag, gently, not too fast, with your hands supporting your weight. Now slide your hands backward, while you drag your heels after you along opposite side of the tub, until you're poised in proper position, with your lowest part four inches above the water. Now dip. Not too deep. Just enough to dampen. Up, quickly. Hold it while I count five and the shock wears off. Now dip again, a little deeper. Up. Down. Up. Down. And let yourself go, girls, splash, splash, splash!"

That had to me my exit script. If it ever even got on the air. But it wasn't. Her Beauty Bath charmed Edna Wallace Hopper. She performed the rather odd acrobatics it called for, without a bathtub, in the studio, and took an encore while she wailed, "They're pushing me off the air!" I was told that literally thousands of postcards and letters rained in. "The rice boiled over and I missed part of your Bath. Please send full written instructions." I shuddered, conjuring visions of melon-shaped matrons balanced insecurely above their tubs, dipping, slipping, bruising bottoms and wrenching sacroiliacs. Nobody sued. Edna Wallace Hopper put the Beauty Bath, complete with portable tub, in her Saturday morning matinees. Far from getting me fired, it got my option picked up.

I might have accepted the inevitable, if Balaban & Katz hadn't just then announced the premiere of the movie version of *Three Girls Lost*. It was opening in competition with Robert Montgomery in *Shipmates*, William Haines in *The Tailor-Made Man*, Wallace Beery and Clark Gable and Jean Harlow in *The Secret Six*, and Pat O'Brien and Adolphe Menjou in *The Front Page*. I could read my reviews already. (Actually, Chicago critics were kind. "*Three Girls Lost* is nothing sensational but it won't ruin your evening. Dick Powell, the singing M. C. on stage, is excellent.") At the *Daily News*, Gene Morgan told me he was going on vacation. He planned to drink his way east across Canada, from Toronto to Montreal, and then sober up while he circled back to Chicago by way of New York.

Some people said Gene's column wasn't very witty. He agreed. Some said he stopped growing up in the days of "Over There" and "Mademoiselle from Armentières." If he did, he was a lot of man by then. Two weeks in some other towns, with Gene for a traveling companion, seemed like a fine idea. I told Gene "Don't you leave without me!" and hurried back to my typewriter. "Skippy," for four hours straight. Some sleep; not much. "Just Plain Bill," five hours. Some more sleep; less than before. "Ma Perkins," five hours. No sleep. *If I Had a Million*, all one night. THE END. All clear. No — Edna Wallace Hopper, two hours more. A cold shower. Scrubby Lee loaded with scripts to mail. Rikki-tikki-tavi assured I wasn't deserting her, but sulkily unconvinced. A taxi to the *Daily News*. A brief talk with Smith. He said of course I was entitled to a vacation. Then he said, "Will you be back?" I said "Of course, Mr. Smith." Then, with my *If I Had A Million* manuscript under my arm, I joined Gene Morgan. Seeing us set off together, Bob Casey told the World's Oldest Office Boy we gave him a dandy idea for a new serial in the *Daily News*. It would be titled *Two Boys Lost*. As Victorian novelists used to say, Little did he know . . .

« 6 »

Hiring a barouche in front of the hotel and riding in it up Mount Royal to see the St. Lawrence at sunset was the thing for Yankee travelers to do before leaving Montreal. Gene Morgan and I did it in style. Which of us decided the Government liquor store might run out of Old Rarity before we returned, and hedged against this catastrophe by putting a case of it in the carriage, we had forgotten by the time we were halfway to the top. He was too considerate to ask why I took my manuscript with me. I couldn't have told him, anyhow. A dozen times since we left Chicago, he had pretended to pay no attention while I leafed its pages with my eyes shut, stopped anywhere, opened my eyes, glared at what I saw, scratched out phrases and scribbled others replacing them. By now, we were three days behind our schedule, and still an overnight sleeper jump from New York. Gene knew I slowed our tour deliberately. He didn't complain. He had told me he meant to write a book sometime; but the more he saw of an author's delivery pangs, the less he felt the product justified the labor. And he wasn't the kind to intrude on a friend by asking, "Why?"

I sat on the stone parapet, my heels dangling over a sheer drop, the manuscript in my lap. Gene went to inspect some monuments. Once more, I closed my eyes and turned pages. Opening them, but not to read, I surveyed the twilight panorama below. I was busy when Gene, returning, yelled in spite of himself. Firmly, he took *If I Had a Million* away from me. All but the last two chapters, completed in Chicago with such sweat and toil — I had folded them, page by page, into paper airplanes, which I sailed down into the shadows. I had no carbon copies, couldn't possibly reproduce what I threw away, and wouldn't have tried to if I could. And I felt fine, just fine, and let Gene take charge, not because I needed being led by the hand but because it was such a pleasure to throw words away before anyone weighed and counted them.

An hour later, we were on the train for New York. Gene insisted that he, not I, should take the manuscript to the agent with whom I'd been corresponding (not the one who found in *As If This Flesh* what I hadn't known was there).

It was my first time in New York. I should have been breathlessly appetent for sights and sounds. I wasn't. I was sleepy. I slept twelve hours, in the Hotel Astor suite that Gene Austin once called home, and would have slept longer if the agent hadn't telephoned, commanding me to meet him for lunch at the Algonquin. That woke me fully. Everybody who was Anybody literarily lunched at the Algonquin. I went there wondering if they'd let me in, a rookie from the Three-Eye League at Schlogl's, and hesitated at the entrance as once I hesitated on the doorstep at 15 North Wells. The agent hailed me, and came bustling, beaming, and walking right on by, to buttonhole people I knew of by name, complimenting them on current triumphs I hadn't read about, having missed the last *New Yorker*.

To prolong one-sided conversation as they passed, he introduced me monosyllabically to Christopher Morley, Cleon Throckmorton, Wolcott Gibbs, Lunt and Fontanne, Dorothy Parker, Robert Benchley, Alexander Woollcott, and others who didn't seem to care who I was, since obviously I wasn't Anybody or I wouldn't be with him. Then he stopped Richard Walsh, the publisher, and told Walsh that John Day could have first look at my new novel. Walsh was courteously unimpressed. We didn't sit at the Round Table, but at a table for two, in the back, near the kitchen. The agent's first words directly to me were, "So you're Andrews. How do you write all those words?" I said, "There isn't much else to do in Chicago." He said, "This soap opera stuff: it's unbelievable." I said that would qualify as understatement. He said, "About this book of yours: I just don't know." I said that was how I felt, too. He said, "That no-warning ending stopped me cold." I heard myself capsuling Vollard's theory that it takes two to make a masterpiece: one to slap on the paint, the other to hit him over the head before he slaps on too much. The agent didn't see the connection. He checked his all-gold wristwatch, mouthed a final bite of boiled beef, and rose. "I'm already late for a meeting. Tell you what. I'll see what I can do with your book. I'll write to you. Care of the *Chicago Daily News?*" I said "Maybe you'd better mark your letter *Please Forward If No Longer There.*" I paid the check, and took a taxi to Park Avenue, and had some difficulty in convincing a gilded young lady in Blackett-Sample-Hummert's reception foyer that Mrs. Ashenhurst would know who I was if my card was sent in.

Mrs. Ashenhurst was just leaving to take the train to Chicago. She hadn't changed outwardly. But she limited meetings to five minutes now, instead of ten. She said Mr. Hummert thought "Skippy" should be more adventurous, and that this would provide foundation for a new contest tied in with a dealer-promotion program on Wheaties. She also indicated that my ideas for this contest might be useful, and that she hoped my New York pleasure trip wouldn't put me behind schedule on scripts. I had mentioned *If I Had a Million,* shyly for me, on several occasions. When I said now that I came east to deliver the manuscript to my agent, Mrs. Ashenhurst asked how I had found time to write a book. I sensed reproof in the question. That I went on working at the *Daily News* was forgiven as a foible I'd outgrow; but, rightly or wrongly, I surmised that any writing that might take me onward and upward was not looked on with approval. So I said I'd be back in Chicago and at my typewriter by day after tomorrow, and didn't force her to ask, "Is there anything else, Mr. Andrews?" — although I had intended to sound out the possibility of breaking in a successor to write for Edna Wallace Hopper.

I went wandering around Manhattan, and dined at Billy Lahiff's Tavern on Forty-eighth Street off Times Square, where I was introduced by Jimmy Cannon, then writing a radio column for the *New York World-Telegram.* They had never heard of me at the more literary Algonquin, but Broadway was all ears about Chicago radio, and the Tavern was Broadway's Camelot, and Billy Lahiff was its King Arthur. Proof of this was in Billy's hamburger-sized solid gold cigarette case, presented to him one Christmas by the Tavern regulars, set with precious stones that spelled out MAYOR OF TIMES SQUARE. He went to great lengths in a continuing effort to lose this Neon-lighted talisman; but someone always found it and brought it back, expecting and collecting a reward. Billy brought up a beautiful niece, Nancy Carroll, who starred on the stage and in films; he gave selfless avuncular aid and counsel to other ambitious young women, including Ruby Stevens, whose name in lights would be Barbara Stanwyck. In fact a hundred actresses, actors, singers, dancers, comedians, columnists, best-selling authors, prizefighters, politicians and other prominent personages owed thanks for a helping hand to the compact, immaculate, wise, kindly former bartender whose Tavern died when he was carried out through its doorway in 1935, refusing to lie down on his stretcher, smiling while he hummed "I'm Headin' for the Last Roundup."

Gene Fowler called Lahiff "A fine man, a quiet man, a friend of all young scribes." He called Lahiff's booming bouncer, Toots Shor, the Night-Blooming Cereus of the Bar-Nothing Ranch. At Lahiff's, it seemed to the country boy from Chicago, everyone had colorful charm. Suddenly I was back in the business of learning stories, not manufacturing them. Every evening, I learned, at precisely 8:05, a certain mounted policeman's horse, on traffic duty at the intersection of Broadway and Seventh Avenue, walked off-post and down the street to the Tavern and planted its forefeet on the curb, and waited for Billy Lahiff to come out, as he did invariably, bearing a silver tray on which there were eight cubes of sugar: the day's payoff to his friend, the horse. But he never paid bribes to Prohibition agents, though his bar was always open.

At nine every night, Billy went for a walk, never farther than six blocks away, to whatever movie palace was showing a movie he hadn't already slept through. In the back row, he dozed peacefully until the film was over. Then he walked quickly back to the Tavern, to greet first-comers in the after-theater rush, and was on the move from table to table until closing time at 2 A.M. Thus it was, they told me, that one night Billy saw a lone woman at a table far back in the place, after everyone else was gone. He went to her, suggesting that she'd better leave so he could turn out the lights. She said she had no money to pay for the meal she had eaten, her first in three days. Her husband had deserted her. She had no one to turn to for help. She stood up, and he saw she was pregnant. "Yes," she said. "My baby will be born in the next few hours." Then she fainted. Billy caught her as she fell.

At three in the morning, at four, at five, telephones rang in bedrooms up and down Manhattan. Billy told regulars who

300

answered sleepily, "You just joined the Broadway Baby Club."
The chief surgeon at French Hospital presided at the accouche-
ment. Wives of a dozen noted husbands provided baby
clothes and other needfuls. A cottage was reserved for mother
and child at the Police Summer Camp up the Hudson. The
Broadway Baby began life with a bank account. The mother
was given funds, a wardrobe, a job. But when she appeared at
the Tavern one night, to thank Lahiff, he hid in the kitchen
until she gave up and went away. It made Lahiff ill to have
anyone tell him "Thank you."

Jack Spooner warned me about this, and when Spooner
gave warning, you harkened. He was The Waiter: in capitals
because if you rated one of his tables, you were in like Flynn.
Spooner wore his Marine's buttons on his waiter's jacket, and
had a Master Sergeant's firmness in maintaining discipline
amongst the customers. If you started to scan the menu, which
never changed, he took it from you, tore it in two, and ordered
what the chef had too much of; and if you wanted to get into
the Tavern again, you ate it and liked it. Spooner, like Richard
Schneider at Schlogl's in Chicago, kept a remarkable autograph album. His had no literary signatures but Gene Fowler's.
The rest were a directory of who was who in sports, show business, and politics. Spooner watched Lahiff, while I explained
that I worked for the *Daily News* in Chicago, and Jimmy
Cannon said it was my first night out in New York. Lahiff
crossed his fingers. I didn't know until hours later that this
meant whatever I ordered was on the house. In fact it meant
more than that.

Lahiff moved on, stopping briefly at one table, then at
another. Where he sat down, those who watched and those he
joined knew he conferred an accolade. You might have been
at liberty for months, you might be a small-timer unable to
get a break at the Palace, but if Billy put his stamp of approval on you, your chance would come sooner or later, and
meanwhile your credit was good at the Tavern, for yourself

and your guests, as long as you needed it. You not only signed your tabs, you signed for large-sized tips, which Billy paid out of his cash register. This was because good waiters were hard to keep happy, even at the Tavern, but also so no one would guess you were temporarily on the cuff. Incidentally, all but a very few of the many who were on the cuff at the Tavern, at one time or another, justified Billy's confidence by hitting the top, and by paying off their tabs in full.

Upstairs, he had three floors of small apartments. You paid your rent if you could, and didn't when you couldn't. George Murphy and his pretty wife, Julie, lived upstairs over the Tavern when they were starting out as a dance team. So did others who became headliners. Gene Fowler was a long-time tenant, and wrote *Trumpet in the Dust* on a typewriter Billy rented for him, on the meat-cutting block in the Tavern's kitchen, while Billy sternly withheld the day's first drinks until Fowler showed him another thousand words on paper. Jimmy Hussey was a special Tavern legend. Irish, he told Jewish stories in an inimitable Yiddish accent, and was equally beloved by Jews and Irish for his gentle goodness. Jimmy was a vaudeville headliner until one night he fainted onstage at the Palace. Doctors said he was dying of tuberculosis, and sent him to Saranac. He couldn't stand the hospital: nobody laughed. He couldn't live if he couldn't tell jokes and get laughs. So Billy established him upstairs at the Tavern, saw to it that he stayed in bed all day, and took his medicine as prescribed, then helped him dress for his performance at the dinner hour. Circulating from table to table, Jimmy told his jokes and got his laughs; and no one laughed out of pity. He was never funnier than while he was dying. He came down one night, stopped the show cold, obediently went back upstairs to bed when Billy said, "Show's over, Jimmy. Leave 'em laughing"; and died in his sleep, smiling as if he were about to ask, "Have you heard this one?"

That was the Tavern. There was nothing like it in Chicago.

Walter Winchell and Ed Sullivan entered, separately because they had a feud, and held forth at separate tables, each to his disciples. A young lawyer who wrote a Broadway column for the *Daily Forward* and aspired to write one for a paper in Manhattan said with outgiving friendliness: "I'm Leonard Lyons." Mark Hellinger joined the select coterie in the Amen Corner, as he did every night, to drink brandy and play backgammon. There went Billy Seeman, who was Jimmy Walker's bosom pal until Jimmy forgot to be on time for the funeral of Billy's mother; and with him Ham Fisher, who drew "Joe Palooka," and Harold Ross, who edited the *New Yorker*. There were Judge Lester Patterson, who bossed the Bronx, and Jim Farley, who led a loyal legion of Democrats; probably they discussed Governor Franklin D. Roosevelt, who wanted the Presidential nomination. Here came young Jerry Wald, who wrote the "Not on the Air" column for the *New York Graphic* and would soon sell Warner Brothers a story, *Twenty Million Sweethearts*, based on the rise of Russ Columbo as managed by Con Conrad, and make Dick Powell a star, and himself shoot up like a comet over Hollywood (and end as a comet ends, consumed by its own fire, but not until there were no further heights to reach).

Jimmy Cannon called the roll, while he jotted notes for a column in the *World-Telegram*, about why and how I wrote soap operas. Coming and going were Bert Lahr, Jack Kearns and Mickey Walker, Damon Runyon, Jack Haley, Eddie Brannick from the New York Giants' front office, Jack Kirkland who was adapting Erskine Caldwell's *Tobacco Road* for the stage (an impossible effort, according to consensus in the Amen Corner). Walter Huston's rambunctious son, John, who had given up prizefighting for revolutionizing in Mexico and given that up to try his hand at writing. Joe Cook, Dave Chasen, Lee Tracy, Monte Brice, Bugs Baer, Rube Goldberg, James Montgomery Flagg, Paul Whiteman, Arthur Tracy, the Street Singer. Phil Regan, the Singing Cop. Morton Downey,

303

the Silver-throated Coca-Cola Tenor. The Marx Brothers, Groucho, Zeppo, Harpo and Chico. Two other Marx brothers, not related to them: Dave and Louis, who manufactured mechanical toys and carried samples which they gave to chorus girls (Dave was known as Spendo, Louis as Makeo). Jimmy McHugh, whose "I Can't Give You Anything but Love, Baby" was called the new theme song of Wall Street brokers romancing Broadway's leading ladies (and how was I to guess that one day Jimmy would be my daughter's godfather?). Johnnie Walker, whose Hollywood stardom began and ended with one film, *Over the Hill*. And, at midnight, we were joined by a large-nosed, mustached, short-coupled aristocrat whom I would have greeted as Dmitri Obolensky if Billy Lahiff hadn't introduced him as Prince Michael Romanoff.

No matter what the tabloids printed about "the phony Prince," Billy liked Mike, and respected him. "I'll tell you," he confided when we knew each other well. "Anybody can be born a prince. But it takes guts to wake up one morning and say 'From now on I'm a prince,' and act and live like one no matter how tough things get. A lot of real princes couldn't cut the buck. It takes what phonies don't have." Mike never forgets a face; and his is unforgettable. I didn't, however, nor did he, mention the James J. Hill Reference Library in St. Paul, or a young reporter who came over from Minneapolis to interview a courtly fugitive from the marital designs of a misguided millionairess. I watched Mike eat and drink extensively, then sign his tab and note *Please add 20 per cent tip for Spooner*. (The same percentage is expected by waiters who work for Mike at Romanoff's in Beverly Hills. You can sign for it, if Mike feels you're not a phony.) Departing, Mike conferred his Imperial blessing. I said, "Thank you, Your Highness."

Altogether, it was a First Night to remember. But Chicago was my beat, and it was high time to get back on it. I hadn't been to bed when I woke Gene Morgan at the hotel and said,

304

"Let's go home." And he didn't ask "What's your sudden hurry?" Nor did he, nor Smith when I reported at the *Daily News*, ask "What happened to *If I Had a Million?*" I delivered, at Blackett-Sample-Hummert, the ideas Mrs. Ashenhurst asked for about a "Skippy" give-away, and sandwiched sets of scripts for "Skippy" and "Just Plain Bill" and "Ma Perkins" and Edna Wallace Hopper between Carnival of Nations pieces with names, names, names, and pictures, pictures, pictures, and people, people, people, for the paper: the mixture as before.

The Norwegian community proposed to mass choral societies — a thousand male voices altogether — with Cesare Formichi of the Chicago Opera as soloist. It was up to me to locate a stage large enough to hold this regiment, in an auditorium in which the singers wouldn't out-number the audience. The Polish committee plumped for a Solemn High Mass to be sung by Adam Didur, the Metropolitan Opera basso, and his dearest rival for acclaim as Poland's gift to music, Jan Kiepura, the tenor who advertised himself in *Musical Courier* with a full-page photograph displaying him costumed in very tight tights for *Peter Ibbetson*, feet planted on a single line of type that read *His voice is pure because his heart is pure.* (When they made their competitive personal appearance, finally, behind the Cathedral altar rail, in the presence of the Cardinal Archbishop, they sang the sacred music as if they dueled with arias. Each in turn stepped down front expecting his claque to unleash applause; and when there was silence, took a big bow nevertheless.)

The Lebanese committee had sent me a carton which contained a gallon jug of moonshine *à la Lebanon*. They called it arrack. It looked like innocent water, but turned milky when water was added, and knocked the ears off the unwary drinker. With this came the committee's report of some minor accidental stabbings, during rehearsal for the sword-dances that would be a part of the Lebanese contribution to Colonel Knox's Carnival. I decided not to inform our readers that several prominent Lebanese merchants were eating their meals from the mantelpiece. As for the Italian contribution, it would be at the other end of the spectrum from Capone and Torrio and Frank Nitti: a full-dress recital in five languages by Italian stars of the Chicago Opera: Tito Schipa, Serafina de Leo and Augusto Bouef. It would open with "My Country, 'Tis of Thee," which Mary Garden was teaching them to sing phonetically.

Second-generation Hungarian-Americans had been hesitant when I first approached them, betraying embarrassment about donning Old Country costumes and learning old-fashioned village dances from their less Americanized parents. Now they told me proudly that they had found Hungary's most famous gipsy fiddler, working as a steel-puddler in the Gary mills. When I went to interview him, he said he couldn't play well enough any more to make people feel like dancing. Pounding noise had dulled his ears. His fingers were callused, bent, and stiff. But I induced him to bring his violin to a rehearsal. He saw the young people in their bright costumes, and remembered his own youth; and years fell from his work-bowed shoulders, and he played hour after hour while old people joined their American-born children, dancing the czardas until they dropped. Smith said that story would rate Page One even if the Colonel's Carnival wasn't a MUST for there.

He didn't ask again, "How about your radio writing?" He said Knox had approved an experiment that shifted Lloyd Lewis from Drama to Sports, to find out if readers would respond to critical reviews, not expertized reports, on baseball and football and boxing and golf. Would I like to do some writing for Lloyd? I would indeed. So I went to the run-down White City arena, and covered a dreary twelve-round bout between Tuffy Griffiths and Kingfish Levinsky, and reported it in a Letter to the Sports Desk that began: "Something must be done to protect the ancient art on which the Marquess of Queensberry placed his stamp and seal. A good beginning would be to match Kingfish Levinsky's sister and manager, Leaping Lena Levinsky, with the little brother of Tuffy Griffiths if he has one. Or a midget would do. Or failing this, to lock these alleged pugilists in any convenient barroom and throw away the key. They wouldn't lay a glove on each other. They proved last night at White City that neither of them could fight his way through the periphery of a cobweb."

Levinsky's sister, in her own Letter to the Sports Desk, announced that her brother would be the next heavyweight champion, and then I would eat my words. Meanwhile, he was booked for a song-and-dance debut on the next Celebrity Night program at the College Inn, and how about some publicity on that? So I headed for Frank Bering and Ernie Byfield's Sherman Hotel, to see if the Kingfish could be worse as an entertainer than he was as a championship contender. But in the Sherman's labyrinthine lobby, I took the wrong short cut, and emerged in a crowded convention hall where General Motors was staging a show of Cars of Tomorrow and the gadgets that would be built into or onto them, as a preview of its exhibit scheduled for the World's Fair. Curiosity added me to the fringe of a silently attentive crowd. Surprised to see such interest focused on a highly technical explanation of the merits of GM's new tubular steel body-frame construction, I looked at the lecturer, and understood.

She was "Miss Chicago World's Fairest," chosen by the Hearst papers as their one-girl challenge to Knox's Carnival of Nations. I had seen her pictures on Page One in the *Examiner*, and her portrait by John Doctoroff, displayed at the Art Institute. Reality outdid them. For once, I voted with the Opposition. Very young, very lovely, in golden crown and jewels and glittering evening gown, she spoke her complicated lines about Cars of Tomorrow with persuasive pertness. Unaware that from this moment she and I were chained by

307

coincidence, I went on about my business in the College Inn, where Ben Bernie, the Old Maestro, had the band and did the talking. The dance floor resembled a backgammon board — which was to be expected, since Andy Rebori, the designer, won so consistently at the ancient game of warriors (which only amateurs think is controlled by the luck of the dice) that it was said he practiced architecture purely as a pastime. John Norton, who did the massive murals in the *Daily News* building, also decorated the walls of the College Inn, to simulate a tropical aquarium. When lights were dimmed for dancing, exotic fish glowed in radium-paint pastels. There were also some very odd fish among the customers.

On Thursdays, Celebrity Nights, all stars and stars-to-be currently appearing in Chicago theaters gladly gave command performances for Ben Bernie. Ashton Stevens, writing for Hearst, reported one morning: *There must have been $75,000 worth of ham on the hoof cavorting in the Old Maestro's not at all impromptu revels last night, at America's most successful supper club; and Frank Bering and Ernie Byfield got it all for free.* The fact was that even the haughtiest headliners welcomed opportunity to invade the new show business, radio, if Bernie presented them on his coast-to-coast broadcast. So it cost Bering and Byfield only the tabs for food and drink to present on a single bill, on this particular Celebrity Night, Helen Morgan, Irene Bordoni, Clark and McCullough, Frank Morgan, Raymond Guion from *Young Sinners* (soon to change his name to Gene Raymond), Buddy Rogers with his trombone, and even Ethel Barrymore, discussing baseball in the same vibrant tones with which, in *Déclassée*, she declaimed "That's all there is, there isn't any more." The cover charge, the highest in Chicago, was two dollars.

Frank Bering said, the last time we talked about Chicago in Palm Springs: "The more business we did at the College Inn, the faster we killed the goose that laid the golden egg." Things were tough all over, for performers. One night, the

308

American Guild of Variety Artists served notice on the Sherman that either their members must be booked at their established salaries, or Ben Bernie's guests had to be paid off at AGVA minimums, not merely in suppers and Scotches. Then there were no more Celebrity Nights, and soon there was no more College Inn. But, like much else in 1932, that was next year's headache.

I buttonholed Ben Bernie. He said Kingfish Levinsky wouldn't be appearing. He had opened in one and closed in the alley — that is, he had showed his wares at rehearsal, and was too awful to be funny. So that took care of that; and it gave me an opening to ask Ben to bring his non-Hibernian musicians to our Irish-American show. He said "Okay," as I had been sure he would. Bernie played benefits so generously that it was said he counted the day a disappointment if there wasn't one to play.

I was leaving, headed for my typewriter and more work on *If I Had a Million,* when Frank Bering stopped me and introduced his pretty dancing partner, Joan Winter, who was starring at the Cort in *The Church Mouse.* I asked if she'd accept some roles in "Just Plain Bill" and "Ma Perkins." She said she'd much rather be in "Skippy," which sounded like a lot of fun. I said she didn't know the half of it, and was prepared to tell her the rest. She was very pretty. But she said she had to hurry back to the theater, for the third act, and, as she departed, Frank told me that as soon as she finished her run-of-the-show contract she would become Mrs. Bering.

I started out again. This time, I stopped because Celebrity Night was starting off with three girls who looked lost. Ben Bernie introduced them as the Gumm Sisters. Some in the crowd thought he called them Gump, and laughed. Sidney Smith's chinless "Andy Gump" was bellwether, then, of Colonel McCormick's flock of *Tribune* comic strips. But laughter died when the littlest Gumm Sister took the spotlight and sang.

Her name was Judy. The sisters were singing their way to Hollywood, where in 1936 she changed her name to Judy Garland. "That child," I informed Frank Bering sagely, "shows promise." He agreed with this remarkable conclusion, and invited me to join the party at his table. I took a look at his guests: Steve Hannagan — Stephen Jerome Hannagan, who had been a newspaperman only long enough to spy out lusher pastures, and now as the only public-relations specialist of his caliber promoted the Indianapolis Speedway and the bathing-suit beauties of Miami Beach — and various Lord & Thomas advertisers; Oscar Serlin, the Broadway talent scout (who subsequently produced *Life with Father*); Jess Krueger, a columnist for Hearst but in spite of that a fine fellow, and a noted cryptologist who might give me some new secret codes for "Skippy"; and Will Rogers, just in from California and just being joined by his look-alike son, Will Jr. There'd be no audience for Little Big Mouth at that table, but it would be a pleasure to sit and listen. And then I saw them all rising gallantly, in deference to the awaited guest of honor. Inevitably, she was Miss Chicago World's Fairest.

Five authentic celebrities as admiring courtiers, or six counting Frank Bering, was too much competition. Much too much. So I told Frank he'd have to excuse me; I must go and write some beauty hints, which quite obviously the real-life *One Girl Found* at his table didn't need. And I didn't see her again until, in Hollywood, newly imported writers were assembled to look at screen tests of promising star material. There on the screen was the former Miss Chicago World's Fairest, robed, jeweled and crowned for the role of the Empress Josephine in *Anthony Adverse*. Her name was Irene Colman. The publicity sheet said she had just been voted "The Girl with the Most Beautiful Eyes." I thought this was understatement.

Jerry Wald and I were working together by then (the mystics say all paths that cross must cross again), on a script we called "I Live for Love." I described our ideal leading lady succinctly: *Irene Colman if we can get her.* We couldn't. They gave us Dolores Del Rio, because the girl from Chicago had a previous engagement at another studio, to appear in "Arise My Love." So we still didn't meet. In fact, a studio executive had told her "You wouldn't be interested in knowing this fellow Andrews. He's an Eastern dude with a cane and a Homburg hat." Eventually, however, California divested me of these drawbacks, and in 1962 we celebrated our twentieth wedding anniversary. Some of my Chicago stories have happy endings.

But in Chicago in 1932, the romance that concerned me was that of two soap opera characters, "Betty and Bob," just carpentered to fit Mrs. Ashenhurst's blueprint, which in turn adapted some Young Marrieds problems I had written into sequences of "Just Plain Bill" and "Ma Perkins." Putting "Betty and Bob" together was a rush order. General Mills had a new packaged mixture ready for market: Bisquick, the first (I believe) of a then-impending spate of kitchen wife-savers. Could women, congenital conformists, be induced to buy and try a patented substitute for measure-and-stir, that eliminated the age-old test of a bride's ability to feed her husband What Mother Used to Bake? Hummert and Mrs. Ashenhurst said a soap opera would do the trick. The client, although not from Missouri, was somewhat dubious. Pros and cons were debated in costly three-way Long Distance telephone conferences, hooking up target in Minneapolis, front-line expendables in Chicago, and Command HQ in New York. I wasn't called in on these. I was already writing scripts and an outline, to be ready for Zero-hour. Premise: Betty and Bob are already married, and the honeymoon is over, when we go on the air.

Plot for first show: Betty burns the biscuits, and cries. Story synopsis: Betty and Bob have one problem after another, most of which are solved by Betty's use of womanly intuition; if the show runs over a year, we may let Betty have a baby; if so, we'll put on a Name-the-Baby contest.

Unless, as began to look probable, Edna Wallace Hopper was about to be canceled, I was committed to deliver a total of seventy-five thousand words a week, including "Betty and Bob." Even sixty thousand words a week called for seven straight hours at the typewriter on Mondays, Tuesdays, Wednesdays and Thursdays, with Friday and Saturday for story conferences, rewrites, and whatever emergencies might arise. At least, I wasn't struggling with another book. Word from the agent in New York was that if he couldn't sell my novel, nobody could; and he was getting pretty discouraged. So much for *If I Had a Million.* I'd write what I knew was already sold. I mailed my "Betty and Bob" portfolio to Mrs. Ashenhurst, and took on some outside writing assignments, just to keep my typing fingers from stiffening.

Thus I had brief encounter with "The Shadow," not a daytime serial but a one-a-week nighttime series of thrillers loosely based on a fictional character whose creator had written mostly for *Black Mask,* a pulp magazine that also published the early works of Raymond Chandler and Dashiell Hammett. A new voice was needed, to inquire sepulchrally at the opening of these ghoulish dramas, "Why was the blood on the stairs?" and answer, with sinister glee, "The Shadow knows!" At an audition that went on for hours, I listened until I could no longer distinguish one basso profundo from another. Then a globular youth with a patriarchal beard that looked false, but wasn't, stepped up to the microphone, spoke the test lines as if he flung them in our faces, and won the job by acclamation, if only because he frightened the audition jury half to death. A week later, he was at the agency announcing he could not only star in the show, but produce and direct it, and also do the writing, for less than the four men doing these jobs were paid, and a whole lot better. And he could, and he did; and that ended my connection with "The Shadow" — and with Orson Welles.

He wasn't interested in "Betty and Bob." Chicago radio had an Underground by now. Whispers that client and agency were not seeing eye to eye, or that initial scripts were too literary — thus violating the immutable principle that soap operas must be planned in such a way that there could never be a final, natural climax — got some shows tabbed APPROACH WITH CAUTION before audition calls were posted. In our case, when word spread that the client insisted on sitting in on the audition, consensus warned "Don't bet on 'Betty and Bob'!" Actually, no one at General Mills questioned scripts or format or sales-hook strategy. The difficulty was that the company owned (and owns) an extremely valuable trade name, Betty Crocker. A succession of estimable ladies, culled from the crowd after rigorous tests, had conveyed the Betty Crocker image temporarily (as others have conveyed it since). Our daytime serial Betty had, therefore, to measure up to standards that were beyond the comprehension of actresses trying out for the role. And even the perfect Betty might be marred if the Bob whose soap opera life she shared and managed wasn't ideally attractive, impressive, and, above all, inoffensive. You couldn't hope to make sense of that, to an actor. One handsome youth, on the call sheet on the strength of limited experience in summer stock, took one look at my mimeographed memorandum describing Bob as well as I could, and turned around and headed for the nearest speakeasy. His name was Tyrone Power.

In the clients' room, two floors above the studio in which actors and actresses paraded past a microphone, the gentlemen from Minneapolis sat silent in a row, while brief snatches of

313

dialogue from my scripts came over a loudspeaker in varying voices and interpretations. This went on for an hour and a half. Then suddenly the chairman of the delegation said, "I think we've heard enough for now." At once, the agency's account executive was on his feet, expostulating. Granted, there might be some bugs in the rug, but those would be shaken out. Why, at that moment, in New York, Mr. Hummert and Mrs. Ashenhurst were running flags up the pole to test the wind, and hauling them down and changing the signal combinations. It was really unfair to burden businessmen with show business details. He'd suggest a late lunch, and some relaxation, while the network production department cleared out the cattle corral and rounded up a new herd. Then his mixed-metaphors hard-sell was interrupted.

By accident or design, someone in the studio two floors below had turned the microphone back on. Over the loudspeaker came an actor's sardonically disgusted voice. "Those so-and-so's up there! We stand and sweat while they cut us up in little pieces with a dull knife. What do they know? Nothing! That agency guy who told us to call him 'Mister' — he couldn't pass the exam for a low-grade moron." That agency guy moved to silence the loudspeaker. The delegation chairman commanded sharply: "Leave it on!" He smiled, for the first time, and his subordinates dutifully did likewise, while the unseen critic took care of us one by one. "That Andrews!" he concluded. "Call him a writer? The stuff he gets away with on 'Just Plain Bilge'! Did you read his publicity? 'The Daniel Defoe of Chicago'! You know what I call him?" He told us, and the chairman (who was also the General Mills vice president in charge of "Skippy") regarded me as if he wished he'd thought of it. "I like that man, whoever he is," the chairman informed us all. "He's sincere. Hire him." So "Betty and Bob" was sold, after all. And until Hollywood called him away to be Alexander Graham Bell, our Bob was Don Ameche.

I never really expected to be much beloved by anyone connected with "Skippy." It was a hard-luck show. No soap opera aimed at mothers through their children ever had a comparable audience, or sold more for its sponsor. That kept it on the network. But hurricane warnings were posted almost every week. And a full-fledged typhoon came close to sinking us when, on a dull news day, the *New York Times* gave Page One prominence to a Parents and Teachers meeting in Scarsdale, at which a young Wellesley-graduated matron rose to protest about what came into her home during the now-crowded Childrens' Hour. Her little ones, she said, were harried and horrified by violence on the air, causing them to up-chuck their suppers and suffer excruciating nightmares. The worst offender, she said, was "Skippy."

The item touched off an amazing chain reaction. Within two days, a dozen newspapers across the continent put similar stories on Page One, all naming "Skippy." Women's clubs trampled each other in a stampede to be counted. And sales curves shot downward. Grocers telegraphed: "Our neighborhood customers are threatening to boycott my store if I don't stop selling the stuff that keeps 'Skippy' on the air." Emissaries from the agency hurried to question the Scarsdale matron who had ignited the prairie fire. She was more amused than embarrassed, while she confessed that she had never listened to "Skippy," nor had her children. She had meant to refer to quite another serial, which she felt it wouldn't be fair to mention under the circumstances. She was sorry for her slight mistake. And I was sorrier. I had worked round the clock writing replacement scripts that were all sugar and no spice. Meanwhile, a committee of renowned child psychologists (including, I was told, Dr. John B. Watson and Dr. Arthur Jersild) was employed to conduct a crash program-

315

survey, determining what was and what was not good for children listening to daytime radio.

Percy Crosby, I heard, was shouting "I told you so!" He was not alone in placing the onus on an erstwhile reporter, a frequenter of Chicago sin spots, a writer of novels, an imbiber of Old Rarity with Perrier. In other entertainment fields (such as motion pictures and television) the classic recourse, when the specter of censorship looms on the horizon, is "Blame it all on the words-merchants." But the psychological doctrinaires disappointed the clamoring critics. Modern children, they said, are deprived of normal and needed stimuli by the nature of modern living. They no longer roam the fields and forests, climbing trees, shooting BB guns at squirrels, fishing in stagnant streams with bent pins for hooks, diving naked into muddy swimming-holes. Nurtured, guarded, spoiled, they become cases for the psychiatrist because they have no outlet for energy and original sinfulness. But, said the scientists, children found a substitute in adventures on the air, which they shared in wish-fulfillment. CONCLUSION: "Skippy" wasn't too violent; it wasn't violent enough.

That enlightening but hardly helpful verdict came in almost simultaneously with a chilling experience for which I have no explanation. Keeping "Skippy" four to six weeks ahead of broadcast, I had written in late January, 1932, a sequence in which it was made to appear that Sookie had been kidnaped. Actually, as the following scripts made clear, Skippy knew Sookie staged his own disappearance to avoid having to act in a school play in which he would have to kiss a girl — a fate, to Sookie, worse than death. Skippy's problem was to arrange for Sookie's apparent escape from kidnapers unknown, in such a way that the schoolteacher, Sookie's enemy, couldn't expel the small schemer for playing hookey once too often. It doesn't sound like much of a plot, and it wasn't. But the script that started the "Skippy" kidnaping

316

sequence got on the air, unbelievably, on March 2, 1932, the day after the Lindbergh baby was kidnaped.

Why no one prevented this, no one could say. I had totally forgotten the sequence, so many more words having come out of my typewriter since I wrote it. I was not in Chicago the night of March 1, but in New York, where I had gone to spend the day at HQ discussing ideas for a give-away offer tied in with a new story line for "Just Plain Bill." Free to spend the night in the Amen Corner at the Tavern, swapping newspaper yarns with Mark Hellinger and Bill Corum and Ted Husing and Billy Lahiff, I told about Charles A. Lindbergh Sr., and his son, as I heard the tale in Minneapolis. Charley Ford from the *Daily News* had scaled a tree outside the guarded fence that surrounded the mansion Charles A. Lindbergh Jr. built at Hopewell, New Jersey, where he sought seclusion with his wife and their infant son. Using telephoto lenses, Charley snapped exclusive pictures of the healthy, laughing Lindbergh baby. We agreed that Lindbergh ought to forgive this invasion of his privacy, on the argument that having made himself the hero of the Great American Success Story he had made his life public property.

However specious this argument may have been, Lindbergh would have heard nothing but honest admiration for the unhappy small-town boy who grew up to fly alone across the Atlantic; to marry Anne Morrow, the daughter of a Morgan partner who was Ambassador to Mexico; to be honored, with his wife and with Mary Pickford, still America's Sweetheart, at the opening of the first transcontinental air service, that took passengers from Los Angeles to New York in only forty-eight hours; to collaborate in research with Dr. Alexis Carrel; to fly the Pacific to Japan with his wife as co-pilot; and to settle finally on a country estate and make great plans for the future of his first-born (which he had outlined only a few days before to Helen Worden, interviewing him for the *New York World*). Joining us, Jimmy Cannon told of a newsroom

317

discussion of what would be the biggest news story that could break. Someone suggested, "If a dirigible should hit the Empire State Building and explode." Someone else hazarded, "If somebody should kidnap the Lindbergh baby." We all said that could never happen.

It was happening that night, but the flash didn't reach the papers until I was on the *Twentieth Century* next morning, bound back to Chicago. Before I got off the train, the "Skippy" kidnaping sequence had gone on the air from coast to coast. The mayor of St. Paul heard the broadcast, and called a newspaper, dictating a proclamation of shock that anyone could be capable of such commercial use of a crime that stunned the nation. And he was right, of course, except that no one ever intended such an incredible breach of decency. No use, however, to ask to be heard in our own defense. Editorialists flayed us. Most of their attacks appeared days after twenty-four "Skippy" scripts had been torn up and replaced by twenty-four new scripts written in less than forty-eight hours, in which there was nothing to which anyone, even Percy Crosby, could take exception. Apparently neither these indignant ones nor the committeewomen and ministers they quoted took the trouble actually to listen to "Skippy." Anyhow, the storm subsided, slowly, and "Skippy" stayed on the air. However, it was hardly coincidental that at about this time I was asked to start writing "Jack Armstrong, the All-American Boy," which was "Skippy" advanced to high school age, with no Crosby to contend with, and which also sold Wheaties, THE BREAKFAST OF CHAMPIONS.

I claim no part in authorship of the "Jack Armstrong" song that exhorted "Wave the flag for Hudson High, boys!" The title itself was mine. It came right off a box of baking soda on my back-bar shelf: the Arm & Hammer brand, trademarked with a mighty biceps flexed for action. As for characters and story lines, these almost wrote themselves. Frank Merriwell would have played second-string to Jack, who threw forward passes the length of the field from behind his own goal line, struck out home-run hitters with the bases loaded, was as peripatetic as the Rover Boys, knew more about electricity than Tom Swift, and was as *sans peur et sans reproche* as Sir Galahad, whether he befriended beggars or defended cripples or out-gamed gangsters. He had a lot of Horatio Alger's heroes in him, too. Not at all surprisingly, he coped successfully with some of the same problems that had previously been solved on "Just Plain Bill" and "Ma Perkins." And when need arose, he was as ready with sententious saws as Bill or Ma — or Skippy.

The "Jack Armstrong" announcer, chosen for strength and sincerity, had given up trying to be a stage actor, refused to be a radio actor, and was convinced that his bulldog physiognomy and line-backer's physique would keep him out of the moives. He was Paul Douglas, who did well afterwards in *Born Yesterday* on Broadway and in *Letter to Three Wives* and many other films in Hollywood, and who used to say (strongly if not too sincerely) when we bumped into each other in Romanoff's: "I owe it all to clean living, fair play, and Wheaties!" It occurred to someone that the show could use some antiseptic sex-appeal. So a mellow-voiced crooner named Art Jarrett, who had been married to Eleanor Holm, was hired to sing and strum his guitar for sign-on and sign-off. Most professionals of high school age sounded like anything but the Hercules of Hudson High. But Don Ameche, dropping over from "Betty and Bob," introduced his younger brother, Jim. And we had the first "Jack Armstrong."

All this activity didn't mean any relaxation regarding "Skippy." On the contrary, we played the shows against each other. It was part of my job to suggest give-aways and promotion contests in a sort of one-two-punch arrangement. So we announced that the American boy who was most like Skippy, and the girl who was most like Carol, and their mothers, would be given free trips to Chicago to see the World's Fair. We promised lavish entertainment for a glorious week, all expenses paid, even to presenting mothers and children with entire new wardrobes and pockets full of spending money. To be most like Skippy or Carol, you had only to send in the most Wheaties boxtops — or reasonable facsimiles thereof, this proviso being required by the Post Office Department.

In a West Coast city, a boy who wouldn't eat Wheaties if he was starving traded two sticks of gum for a boxtop, and set up a facsimile factory in his mother's kitchen. She, and his father, and his three sisters, and several cousins, spent their evenings thereafter as he spent his: marking squares of cardboard in pencil to resemble, reasonably, an actual boxtop. All over the United States, youngsters badgered their mothers into crowding pantry shelves with boxes of Wheaties, the tops torn off, the contents undisturbed. What was done with the hundreds of boxes of Wheaties purchased by the family and relatives of the girl who was finally judged to be most like Carol, I have no idea. A regiment couldn't have consumed that many heaping bowlsful. No Wheaties entered the Little Grey Home out west, but by the rules — for we never cheated in our contests — a boy who was no more like Skippy than I was won a free trip to the Fair. He declared war on sight on the girl who was most like Carol. The mothers didn't cotton to each other, either. The agency's representatives blamed me for seven days and seven nights of misery; and if half of what they told me was true, they had a case. Fortunately for me, I was in New York, not in Chicago, by then.

But not yet; not yet awhile. In 1932 I was sure I'd never leave Chicago. Why should I? I could go and come at the *Daily News*, securely confident that Colonel Knox's Carnival of Nations justified my *C. D. N.* press card. I had "Just Plain Bill" and "Ma Perkins" and "Betty and Bob" and "Jack

Armstrong," even if I lost "Skippy." (I had already lost Edna Wallace Hopper, at long last, without a pang.)

There was no Depression at Blackett-Sample-Hummert, or in my new studio at the Italian Court on North Michigan, where no other newspaperman had ever lived. It was now my home. Mrs. William Vaughn Moody, widow of the poet playwright, had founded the Gourmet Restaurant, which occupied the stone-paved courtyard beneath the authentic New Orleans French Quarter grillework along my balcony. Vachel Lindsay, Edgar Lee Masters, Robert Frost, Rabindranath Tagore, Alfred Kreymborg, Witter Bynner, Harriet Monroe, Margaret Anderson, even Carl Sandburg, came there to speak while tea was served, and departed when the soiree was over.

In my two-story workroom with its murals by a former tenant, Julio De Diego, the Spanish painter who could teach tricks to Salvador Dali, I pounded out dialogue, ten thousand words between cocktails and time for a change of scenery. Now that everything was routine, being a myth was no great chore. I worked with the radio turned on, only because Rikki-tikki-tavi, crouched regally beside my desk, liked having a voice in the room when I was too busy to talk; but I turned it off when one of my soap operas came on. Like the creative geniuses at Blackett-Sample-Hummert, I had developed rules about daytime radio that were never repealed or revised. One was that I listened to nothing I had written. If I did, I might catch flaws and be tempted to attempt improvements. Good enough was good enough.

On April 7, 1932, I stopped typing to listen to a man who reminded Colonel Knox of the first Rough Rider only because the last names were the same, and heard Governor Franklin D. Roosevelt of New York refer for the first time to "the forgotten man at the bottom of the economic pyramid." That wasn't me. According to an editorial in next day's *Daily News*, it wasn't anybody. Frostily, Colonel Knox pointed out

321

that the vote-getting catch-phrase had been plucked out of contrary context by Roosevelt's speech writer, Professor Raymond Moley; its originator, William Graham Sumner, the Yale economist, had actually decried "absurd attempts to make the world over," and held that "the survival of the unfittest," which he said was being advocated by do-gooders pushing the country towards welfare-statism, was "an insult to those who practice industry and frugality."

Knox quoted President Hoover: "While I can make no claim for having introduced the phrase 'rugged individualism,' I should be proud to have invented it. It has been used by American leaders for over half a century in eulogy of those God-fearing men and women of honesty whose stamina and character and fearless assertion of rights led them to make their own way in life." I suppose I could say I had made mine. But I didn't feel rugged or fearless about it. I wrote a speech for Elmer Eeps in "Just Plain Bill" in which Elmer declared himself in favor of "ragged individualism." The agency's show watcher cut it out in rehearsal. Pained puzzlement was indicated, in an immediately subsequent memorandum from HQ, that I of all people should impose liberalism on daytime listeners.

I might have replied that even housewives must be aware that it wasn't presently the best of all possible worlds; that they couldn't help hearing on the radio newscasts, even if they never read a newspaper, about Huey Long howling "SHARE THE WEALTH!" in the Senate and Upton Sinclair's END POVERTY IN CALIFORNIA campaign, and the Townsend Planners demanding two hundred dollars a month for all citizens over sixty; or simply that the individuals any of us could see slouched on park-benches or digging in garbage cans in Chicago were more ragged than rugged. Still complaint would have seemed out of character, coming from me, especially in view of a telegram I had just received from the agent in New York. Reminding me that he had said from the first he'd sell *If I*

Had a Million so fast my head would swim (a statement I found it impossible to recall), he reported a contract for its publication: URGENTLY RECOMMEND YOU PUT FOLLOW-UP ON FRONT BURNER FASTEST FEASIBLE WHILE EVERYTHING GOING YOUR WAY.

That once, I didn't reply "I'll try it" and start another writing job. I wired THANKS. SEE YOU NEXT TIME I'M IN NEW YORK, and stuck to my soap opera knitting. The myth had me merrily monopolizing all the daytime shows that Blackett-Sample-Hummert put on the air; me, or the half-dozen writers who allegedly used my name as their cover. Not so. On radio's Great Plains as much as in Chicago's jungle, the code was *He may keep who can.* The New York office had begun to build a stable of authors: one who knew Dorothy Parker well enough to call her "Dottie," one who had once changed a tire on the ambulance that Hemingway drove in Italy, and others including Charles Jackson (not yet in the mood to write *The Lost Weekend*), who had wandered away from the Algonquin Round Table to slum in radio. Recruited and indoctrinated at the ivory tower on Park Avenue, they were willing (as I was not) to sign agreements certifying that Mrs. Ashenhurst and Frank Hummert were sole authors of the shows for which they provided dialogue. They followed directives from HQ, but had mimeographed copies of my scripts and story lines for ready reference. They referred to Andrews in Chicago, whoever or whatever he might be, as "the Old Pro," with some degree of respect but nonetheless implying clearly that it was high time to change the test from quantity to quality. Concurrently, they perpetuated the thesis that no one man could possibly turn out seventy-five thousand words a week, every week. The proof they offered was that none of them could do it, or would even try to do it.

I note this without malice. Dog-eat-dog was an old established custom on newspapers, too. Sharpshooters had taken aim at me before. Now with uncallused typing-fingers itching to take over wherever I left off, if at any time I announced I was overworked or overbossed, hard-learned strategy made attack the surest defense. Between soap operas, I started writing banana-bunches of scripts not altogether in the Chicago style, for off-network shows beginning to be recorded in New York: "Inspector Stevens of Scotland Yard," which wasn't apt to steal any customers from Agatha Christie or John Dickson Carr, and "Penrod and Sam," credited to Booth Tarkington but resembling his Indiana modernizations of Mark Twain's Tom Sawyer and Huck Finn about as closely as my version of "Skippy" resembled Percy Crosby's drawings. On occasion, I contributed continuities for the first Hummert-Ashenhurst ventures in variety entertainment, "Manhattan Merry-Go-Round" and the "American Album of Familiar Music." I didn't back off when Mrs. Ashenhurst asked me to compete with unnamed rivals in New York, outlining ideas for a new series: "Mr. Keen, Tracer of Lost Persons" — suggested by a forgotten novel she had picked up in a used-books store, and for which she had already chosen the theme song: "Somewhere I'll Find You."

When I recited this list to Smith at the *Daily News*, he couldn't help asking "How?" I was used to the question by now: "How can you possibly juggle seven or eight or more story lines and keep them separated, when you're writing them all at once? Don't you ever get Bill into 'Skippy' by mistake, or find you're letting Jack Armstrong unravel a domestic quarrel in 'Betty and Bob'?" It happened, but not often, and if I caught crossovers in my typed script, little if anything was lost. Dialogue styles presented no difficulty. We never used dialects, never let our soap opera people say "ain't" or drop g's unnecessarily, or stutter, or indulge in other bad habits that would be copied by childish listeners and blamed on our sponsor's product by their mothers. Each soap opera had a practicing philosopher, who disapproved of sin, approved of good deeds, and propounded no epigrams contrary to Aesop, Ben-

324

jamin Franklin, Edgar A. Guest and Dr. Frank Crane. I had only to change the character names, to take care of out-of-place intruders.

Smith took my word regarding such trade secrets, but asked: "What happens when the words won't come?" I said "Filling air-time is like filling Page One. Sometimes it can't be done, but it has to be, so it is." Smith smiled, and said, "You're still a reporter. Still making a game of it: you against the deadline." I said "I learned the game from a champion." He smiled again, then saddened, before he said, "A time comes for some of us when it's not much fun any more." I remembered telling him once what my father told me: *I'm too tired to climb even golden stairs.* Weariness had changed Smith visibly, the last few months. He had stopped looking for Young Men Going Somewhere. He said, "You'll put the bad time off as long as the Lord allows, won't you, Bob?" I could say "Yes, sir" to him without self-consciousness. But then I couldn't think of anything more to say, and left him, hurrying to catch the *Twentieth Century* for New York.

« 8 »

Ben Hecht and Charles MacArthur didn't duplicate their financial success with *The Front Page* when they staged *Twentieth Century* on Broadway in 1933, but they didn't do at all badly. The play made Hollywood aware of Eugénie Leontovich, and of Bill Frawley, my friend since he played Minneapolis in Orpheum vaudeville, caroling "Carolina in the Morning" (as he still does at the drop of a shot of Irish whiskey) in a sweet Killarney tenor that comes startlingly from the dour Far Down face that has stolen laughs on television from such farceurs as Lucille Ball and Fred MacMurray. The play was slapdash comedy, about wildly theatrical characters running up and down Pullman corridors and in and out of drawing rooms. I didn't laugh, when I saw it on opening night, as much as I might have if I hadn't seen so

325

much of the real thing and on occasion had to be a part of the proceedings. This was because, beginning in early 1932, the *Twentieth Century* was my home away from home. I rode it to New York and back again a couple of times a week. My stated reason (which didn't impress the income tax collector) was that I couldn't find any other way to get a full night's sleep occasionally, between sets of scripts.

The evening after my troubling talk with Smith, thinking more than I wanted to about the eventual rewards of being heart and soul a newspaperman, I ordered two double Old Rarity and Perrier thought-quenchers, but I found I didn't feel like drinking and told the porter I wanted nothing else but peace and quiet, and drew my drawing room blinds, and prepared to roll into bed before the train pulled out. Then people started hammering the door down. Opening it, I faced Jack Lait, and Victor Watson (who ranked higher in William Randolph Hearst's executive hierarchy than Walter Howey of *Front Page* immortality). I didn't know them, and they didn't know me, but the porter had told them I must be some kind of newspaperman because I carried a portable typewriter. And you couldn't work on any Chicago paper without hearing tales for or against Jack Lait, or talk with any veteran reporter who didn't agree with Gene Fowler that Victor Watson was Hearst's captain of Cossacks; or, more colloquially, and embellished with appropriate expletives, "Hearst's hatchet man."

As far back as 1913, when Harry K. Thaw had murdered Stanford White for love of Evelyn Nesbit and bought his way out of the electric chair and into the Matteawan hospital for the criminally insane, and then escaped with the greatest of ease and flew to Chicago on a scorching summer's day, Jack Lait had won a bonus direct from the Master at San Simeon for a classsic lead: "Harry Thaw arrived in Chicago last night, as brown as a nut." Lait covered everything from crime to conventions, ghosted the memoirs of ladies who inadvertently slew their lovers, handled top rewrite, wrote on the side for Sime Silverman's *Variety*, turned out vaudeville acts and film stories and hundreds of short-shorts for the Sunday supplement, and (with Lee Mortimer) *Confidential* books about New York and Chicago; and he was never backward about admitting his virtuosity. *I spent the flower of my youth in the Windy Burg,* he wrote in one of his columns. *I knew 10,000 crooks and cops by their first names. My by-line was a household word.*

Hulking, gravel-throated, subtler than he seemed, he wrote and growled and slugged until he reached the top of the heap as editor of Hearst's *New York Mirror*. (He was there at his desk, supposedly retired from on-the-spot reporting, when a Long Distance call came from the son of a Chicago policeman for whom he once did a favor: "Don't ask any questions. Just get on back out here, fast." Lait always played hunches. Playing one then, he became the only newspaperman who saw a bawd he forthwith romanticized into "the Woman in Red" lead John Dillinger out of a Chicago movie theater to be gunned down by Melvin Purvis and his G-men. But that happened in July 1934.) When we met on the *Twentieth Century* pulling out of Chicago in 1932, Lait had been there with Victor Lawson for Hearst-paper conferences on what might be done to save the 1933 World's Fair — which, according to Lait, would take a lot of saving.

I felt that even Lait was wary in the presence of Watson, who was widely and unpopularly known for his habit of memorizing and reporting whatever was said by colleagues whose careers might be terminated without notice if they lost favor with the Master at San Simeon. Watson had worked all his life for Hearst, whose telegraphic code for him was FATBOY. Externally, he was deceptively pudgy-soft and lazy-eyed. But I had heard Bob Casey quote Damon Runyon's verdict: *Vic Watson is the world's worst wrong-o. I wouldn't trust him as far as I could throw the Statue of Liberty.* So there, outside

327

my door, stood two exemplars of success in the newspaper business. What they wanted, and in fact demanded, was my drawing room. Theirs were on either side. The bar for the party would be handier if it was set up in my quarters. What party? The one they were giving, to celebrate. To celebrate what? As it turned out, nothing.

Blondes and other ambiguous guests trooped in, drank, shouted, quarreled, all the way to New York. Nobody slept. Nobody even sat down. Back-slappers performed their pawing ritual. Each time, I expected to see a knife-hilt sticking out from between the shoulderblades they caressed. I watched Jack Lait. His warmest chuckle was wry. At three in the morning, Victor Watson ordered rice pudding topped with whipped cream. I thought he had what the Irish call the look of hell between his eyes. I left the train in the morning, hurrying to reach silence and a cold, cold shower, and wondering more than ever what it was really worth to be called a newspaperman. (In 1937, no longer employed by Hearst, too long with Hearst to be wanted elsewhere, Victor Watson scribbled on the back of an envelope *God forgive me for everything I cannot* and wrote no more, but jumped to his death from the eleventh floor of a third-class hotel in midtown Manhattan.)

My reception at the agency was less than warm. No comment was noted on Mrs. Ashenhurst's memorandum sheet, to which was attached a clipping: the column Jimmy Cannon had written about me in the *World-Telegram.*

Bob Andrews, the Edgar Wallace of radio, drank his favorite potion, Old Rarity with Perrier, in the Amen Corner at Lahiff's watering-hole off Times Square. The agile author, who hammers out more air scenarios than any other writer, chuckled as he tried to remember all the acts he has on the kilocycles. "I have another show, but I can't think of it." He rubbed his tired eyes. Suddenly his fingers snapped like a gambler's when the dice come seven. "I remember now," he said. "It's 'Penrod and Sam.'" Now that this Chicagoan has discovered New York and spends almost as much of his time here as there, anything can happen. He sits at a typewriter, wherever he is, fifteen hours a day, and raps out thirty-two scripts a week, but he's no hermit hiding from life and laughter in a cloistered work cell. He covers a lot of territory after he stops typing for the night. He speaks of his literary labor as if it were a holiday from his true vocation, newspapering. He shuns realism on the radio, and believes stay-at-homes welcome being tricked by make-believe. He heckles highbrows who equate radio with the theater. "Radio isn't show business. Once the theatergoer buys his ticket, he seldom walks out, no matter how bad the play may be. But if he dislikes a radio act, it costs him nothing to turn the dial. If the radio audience had to pay its way in, it would get better shows. But not until." He doesn't think a radio author, employed by a sponsor, has a license to try to manufacture epics for his own delight at the advertiser's expense. "All I try to do," Andrews says candidly, "is soften up the audience for the announcer's sell."

Nobody in the ivory tower on Park Avenue actually complained that Little Big Mouth had talked a little too much, but a memorandum informed me other writers would take on "Penrod and Sam." I wasn't sad about the loss. I set out to do some catching up on New York, with the spare time I had left before returning to Chicago, and at the Stork Club developed rapport of a sort with another of the celebrities I had known only through Walter Winchell's column. That was Sherman Billingsley, who told about being brought up on a farm just off an Indian reservation in Oklahoma. He said his brother bought him a red tin wagon for his birthday, and insisted on hauling him in it, down the road and across the bridge, onto the reservation; and that it took him three trips, because he was still young and hadn't been around much, to realize he was getting his rides on top of a dozen bottles of moonshine smuggled onto the reservation to be sold to the Indians. "That launched me on the road to ruin," Sherman said. Then I told him how long it had taken a member of my

329

family to catch up with him. When Billingsley was riding onto the reservation in his red tin wagon, I explained, my father was the acting Indian Agent, and if the Indian police had caught up with his brother he and I might never have met. We sealed a peace treaty with Old Rarity and Perrier.

When the *Twentieth Century* pulled into Chicago next day, Scrubby Lee was at the station to meet me, with Rikki-tikki-tavi dancing at the end of her leash and a Special Delivery letter in his free hand. It contained a memorandum asking me to start work on a new soap opera, "The Girl Next Door," which was more or less a serialized biography of Norene McCann, the one of my *Three Girls Lost* who couldn't go wrong if she tried. So as it had been in Minneapolis and on the *Daily News*, what was lost on the swings was regained on the roundabouts. More words, and more, and more. Before I knew it, *If I Had a Million* was in the bookstores, and selling steadily. *I noticed* (Carl Sandburg wrote) *a sickly reviewer in the* New York Times *saying Bob Andrews' new novel has a gospel of "futilism." The only trouble with the* Times *reviewer is that he skipped too many paragraphs.* And Walter Winchell wrote in the *New York Mirror: The book would make a grand camera amusement. What a plot!* I didn't know Winchell then, and had never written a fan letter to any newspaperman, but I wrote to him with gratitude I still feel. He answered, "I hope it helps. It is a grand book." I had cared too much about *As If This Flesh.* I had driven myself so far in the opposite direction regarding *If I Had a Million* that if Gene Morgan hadn't intervened all of it would have been paper airplanes sailing down on Montreal. The hardest thing to learn, I decided, and the best if you can also learn not to let it worry you, is that you never know.

Art Arthur, in the *Brooklyn Eagle*, conferred an especially valued crown: *Andrews,* he said, *used to be one of the country's top reporters.* I hadn't realized he was among those pres-

330

ent at Billy Lahiff's when I tried to match newspaper yarns with Mark Hellinger and his coterie. Art told a tale I had told, and made it better. *"I wish to God I was back covering Police tonight,"* he had me say. *"It was great being a reporter, nothing but a reporter. It was great if you didn't let yourself think very much. Sometimes stories come back to me and I wish they wouldn't; they still hurt. . . . There was that night on the Police beat when I was just a fresh kid new from South Dakota and the old-timers got me drunk. And then all the gongs in the world started to ring at once and I heard somebody yell that they'd put over a bandit trap and killed three stickups and I went howling into a car along with the mob. I hammered my head against the side of the car, trying to get sober. I got out of the car somehow with the rest of the reporters and pushed my way through the gawking crowd, feeling important. And I slipped and fell in what was scarlet on the floor, and lay there in a stupid daze, my face alongside what was left of a stickup's head. A big cop had stood behind the screen at the back of the drugstore, ten feet away. Three punks walked in and one of them pulled a mail-order .32 and said 'Put 'em up!' like in the movies. And the big cop laid the barrel of his double-barreled sawed-off shotgun on top of the screen and pulled both triggers. Didn't say anything before he killed the punks, all three of them. And now he was a hero. He stood there bragging about being brave, and kicked one of the corpses, and I called the office and they said, 'Make it a hero case for sure,' and I said 'I'll try.' And then walking out I met a little fat Italian woman, not crying, not speaking, only staring at the youngest of the three dead stickups. 'He was only fifteen,' she said wonderingly. 'He was my baby. He was only fifteen.' And the big cop kicked her dead baby again and called to me: 'Hey, you, be sure you spell my name right so my kid can show it to the kids at school, in the paper, that I'm the one that cut him down.' Then the woman began to scream and I could still hear her when the paper came out."*

331

That story had been adapted in one of the chapters of *If I Had a Million* that I threw away on Mount Royal. I had the mother of a murdered punk given a check for a million dollars. I was glad it wasn't still in the book. As it was, my Aunt Mary wrote to me, from Butler Hall, the hotel for women teachers, near Columbia University, where she lived for thirty years:

DEAR ROBERT:

Your book is interesting, brisk, provocative, in this day of universal belief that money can deliver us from evil. I like its lack of morbid sex messiness, so attractive to some writers. But I do wish it wasn't so grim in spots. I wish you hadn't killed Mark David on the last page. By the way, you would have laughed at your Aunt Mary on study-hall patrol, when no extraneous reading matter is allowed to go unconfiscated. About to pounce on a girl hunched enthralled over a suspicious-looking book, I noticed the title, *One Girl Found*, and, like an Irish cop, flipped my nightstick and walked right on.

A story that was in *If I Had a Million* brought an unexpected caller to my corner at the *Daily News*. He was Frankie Battaglia, a welterweight boxer, whose performance in methodically setting up and chopping down his more experienced and harder-hitting opponent I had reviewed favorably for Lloyd Lewis. I outweighed him by thirty pounds and was three inches taller, but if he had thrown his left hook at me, as I thought he intended to, nothing less than adrenalin could have restored me to locomotion. He had the gracile handsomeness that Hawthorne attributed to Donatello's *Faun*, blurred only a little by blows he had taken. He held a copy of *If I Had a Million*. "Did you write this, Mister?" I said "Yes" and waited. "You have a fighter in it. Dude O'Brien. That right, Mister?" I said "That's right" and asked, "Don't you like the book?" He said, "I don't do the reading. Ernie, he does the reading." Ernie. . .

332

Ernie Fliegel? I knew him in Minneapolis. He was the cleverest lightweight I ever watched. His brother, Joey, was bigger, stronger. They were very poor. Joey brought home five dollars for winning a four-rounder in the amateurs. Ernie took up the same trade. Joey won or lost, and always got hit too often. Ernie avoided solid punches, and always won by a decision. Crowds cheered Joey, whether he knocked out or was knocked out. They booed Ernie. One day in the gymnasium in Minneapolis, Ernie made Joey put the gloves on with him, and told the timekeeper not to ring his bell no matter how long it lasted. Then with thoughtful science he danced and jabbed and chopped until Joey was out on his feet. Then he hugged Joey, and said, "You can fight, but you can't win. I can. So you just retired. From now on, there's only one fighter in the family. Me." And that was how it was.

Ernie went on winning decisions and being booed, and becoming more and more of a draw because the fans went hoping to see him down for the count. He saved his earnings, started Joey in a trucking business, put their sister through nurses' school, bought a house for their mother. Then he spent his savings, twenty-five thousand dollars — to pay the champion for signing to meet him in a title bout. The investment was justified; he knew he would win. For expense money, he boxed a warm-up fight ten days before the championship go. In the first thirty seconds of Round One, he fouled his opponent flagrantly, four times. Fans showered the ring with seat cushions and beer bottles. The referee stopped the fight. The boxing commission began a "fix" investigation.

Then Ernie said quietly, "I'm blind." He had been blind for a week, but thought he could feel his way on instinct, get past the warm-up bout, and then find a doctor to restore his sight — without letting the story get in the papers, which would have given the champion an excuse to cancel their contract and keep Ernie's twenty-five thousand dollars.

Doctors examined Ernie. "It couldn't have been from a

punch," he insisted. "I never let myself get hit that hard." Apparently, ring dust and resin and sweat had worked into his eyes and affected the optic nerve. Whatever the cause, he was finished, blind, and flat broke.

During my last months on the *Journal* in Minneapolis, Ernie lay in a darkened room, bandages covering his eyes. I went to visit him when I could. "They never counted *ten* on me yet," he said, with neither hysteria nor bravado. "They won't now." He asked if I'd mind reading to him. "So I can get some education instead of wasting my time." That was one reason why I drew out so many books at the Minneapolis Public Library. Some I had read before I was on the *Brown County Weekly World* in Kansas. They were new and important to Ernie Fliegel. Even when, finally, the doctors allowed him to get up and walk, with thick black lenses covering his eyes, he asked for more about books. The doctors told him, "You'll have to live with it, Ernie. Any time, you'll step off a curb or bump into a wall, and the nerve will snap. Then you'll be in the dark till you die." Ernie grinned, and said, "I'll see you around."

He began to visit the training gymnasiums. Silence fell when he entered. Young boxers chewed their lips, and slowly took off their gloves. If it could happen to Ernie Fliegel, it could happen to them. He said he was looking for a fighter to manage. "He won't need to think. I'll do the thinking." The fighter he chose was a neanderthalic slugger, boastful, blustering, with streaks of crookedness and cowardice. After I went to the *Daily News*, I saw them fight at the Chicago Stadium. I say "them" because Ernie was in the ring making the moves though physically he sat outside the ropes, black lenses letting in only enough light so he could follow shifting shadows. His puppet won by a knockout, and got such applause as no crowd ever gave to Ernie. He didn't care. Repeating the careful moves that took him to within one step of the title, Ernie took his puppet all the way to Madison Square Garden, to meet the champion. And the slugger sold him out, took a dive, and, in the dressing-room, when Ernie asked "Why?", said, "Because I'm sick of being bossed by a blind has-been!" — and spat in his benefactor's face. He wound up slugging store-keepers for the Syndicate.

Ernie looked for and found another fighter. That was Frankie Battaglia. He had come to me because Ernie had talked about me, and because in *If I Had a Million* I had a blind boxer who said, "They never counted *ten* on me yet. They won't now." That I called my blind boxer Dude O'Brien hadn't fooled Ernie. "He'd be sore," Frankie Battaglia said, "if he thought I made you think he's mad because he's in your book. He says you got the details pretty good for not being a fighter by profession. He said I should bring the book to you and ask you to write your name in it. He said I wasn't to tell you." Tell me what? Battaglia began to cry. "Ernie's back in the hospital. He's blind again. They're going to operate. I heard them tell Ernie 'Don't expect miracles.' "

I went with Battaglia to the hospital at the University of Chicago. Ernie lay quietly, his eyes bandaged, waiting to be wheeled into the operating room. We shook hands. He said, "I told Frankie he shouldn't bother you if you were busy. You didn't need to come all the way down here. I'm fine. I don't need a thing. I'll be out in a week. We fight in the Garden two weeks from Saturday. Frankie's ready. He'll take it all. He's a good boy, Frankie. What he wants to be is a farmer, milking cows and counting chickens. So we've bought him a farm. He'll retire next year. He's all set." The attendants entered. "I'll see you," Ernie said. "I'll see you." We watched until the wheeled stretcher disappeared at the far end of the long hall. Then Frankie said, "Excuse me, Mister." He steadied, choosing his words. "Ernie," he said, "he's a Jew. I'm Catholic. You know how it is. I don't want to do the wrong thing. Not about Ernie. I couldn't ask him, so I'm asking you, Mister. Do you think it would be all right

335

if I talk to a priest about Ernie, if you know a priest I could go to? I mean make my confession and take Communion and offer up a novena for Ernie, that they don't count *ten* on him? Even if we don't go to the same church? I wouldn't do it if Ernie wouldn't like it." I said, "He'll like it. I'll go with you, Frankie."

Ten days later, Ernie came out of the hospital, still condemned to wear thick black lenses, but able to see sufficiently to walk with no one helping him, the way he had before. Frankie Battaglia grinned beside him. They hurried to catch the train to New York, where Frankie didn't win the title for Ernie but was on his feet, still punching, when the fight for the championship ended. Ernie said, "We went all the way. You can't ask for more than that," and told Frankie, "Now let's get you settled on that farm." He managed no more fighters. He opened a restaurant in Minneapolis, which has prospered over the years. His son has just graduated from Navy Officers' Training School. Ernie and I manage to meet somewhere once a year. We talk for hours, not about prizefighting but about our sons, whose first names are the same.

"Jack Armstrong, the All-American Boy" had waited, while I waited for Ernie to beat the knockout timekeeper, so now I had a lot of writing to do. That caused me to miss the first Page One headlines in the *Daily News* foreshadowing collapse of an empire whose Little King wailed self-pityingly, "I wish my day on earth had come." A year and seven months after Black Friday and the opening of his Opera House, six months after Chicago was purged of Al Capone, Samuel Insull left for New York and a showdown with bankers from whom Middle West Utilities, Corporation Securities, and Insull Utility Investments, his holding companies, had borrowed nearly ninety million dollars. The Republican National Convention's decision makers were already gathering in Chicago. Owen D. Young would be a power behind the scenes. Colonel

336

Knox was well aware he would never again have as good a chance to be the dark-horse compromise candidate. But he interfered in no way with *Daily News* coverage of Insull's Waterloo, in which it might be said that Owen D. Young played Wellington, since he spoke for Insull's creditors.

The largest of these were Chicago's financial Gibraltars, Continental Illinois, holding $31,000,000 of Insull's paper, and First National, where his indebtedness was $16,000,000. Commanding the bankers "Stop pushing me!", Insull offered 46,000 shares of Public Service, 110,000 shares of Peoples' Gas, and 180,000 shares of Commonwealth Edison as collateral he said they would have to accept. And for the first time since he began his Chicago conquest, he heard a word he had almost forgotten. Owen D. Young said "No" and our banner line read *INSULL THROWN INTO RECEIVERSHIP*. Chicago trembled on undermined foundations. Corporation Securities dropped to thirteen cents a share, Insull Utility Investments to thirty-seven cents, Middle West to a quarter. In Washington, General Charles G. Dawes resigned as head of President Hoover's Reconstruction Finance Corporation. He had been co-winner of the Nobel Peace Prize in 1925, with Sir Austen Chamberlain of England, and Coolidge's Vice President through 1929. His brother, Rufus C. Dawes, had been assistant to Owen D. Young when Young was agent-general for World War I reparations, and was now president of Chicago's Century of Progress. Three weeks after General Dawes left the R. F. C., it loaned ninety million dollars to what was known in Chicago as "the Dawes bank." But no such fortuitous coincidence rescued Insull.

Two weeks before the Republican Convention opened, he was forced to resign as chairman of Peoples' Gas, Public Service, and Commonwealth Edison. Insull, it was credibly reported, burst into tears. "What did he say? He said 'I've got a melancholy wife,' and that was all he said." Whole soul alone, chin on his chest, the spring gone out of his step,

Insull walked out of the offices where he had reigned autocratically, passing rows of identical desks, closely crowded together, at which clerks of both sexes stood like statues. While his income from salaries alone was $481,000 in 1929, $434,000 in 1930, $486,000 in 1931, his serfs were required to invest sizeable portions of their never generous wages in his promotions. Even the few who dared to hesitate between trusting him with their savings, or being discharged for disloyalty, had given him grudging respect. Now that was gone.

He shrunk as he walked by. Suddenly, he broke into a shuffling dogtrot. There was no sound but the click of his built-up heels until he disappeared from the citadel he never entered again. At the last press conference his public-relations people called, he said,"I have ceased to be newspaper copy." And for a time, that was true. On June 16, the Republican National Convention nominated Herbert Hoover, with Charles Curtis for his running mate, on the first ballot. No votes were cast for Colonel Knox. At Hy Green's bar, it was argued that he had himself to blame. He was too much a newspaperman to be a politician. For myself, I felt he hadn't tried very hard at the convention. The *Daily News*, and Chicago, had come to mean so much to him that he no longer charged toward the White House. I heard him say that Samuel Insull was an object lesson to any man of the poison produced by overweening ambition. (Four years later, the Republicans nominated Alfred M. Landon for President, Knox for Vice President. Howard Vincent O'Brien's column that day in the *Daily News* said citizens would err if they voted for Knox, and Knox and the country would be better off if they didn't. The column ran as written, and with Knox's personal *Okay*.)

Also on June 16, our Page One headlines reported that Congress had overwhelmingly rejected the Patman Bonus Bill, and immediately adjourned. The Bonus Army sang "America" on the steps of the Capitol. Then five thousand Bonus Marchers left Washington, most of them hitchhiking because almost all were penniless. Thousands remained, squatting on the steps of Federal buildings or camped in a Hooverville of tents and shacks on the Anacostia mud flats along the Potomac. Next, while the *Tribune* called it treason, the *Daily News* reported without editorial comment that Harold L. Ickes had quit the Republican Party to head the League for Roosevelt and Garner. Then on June 24, our Paris Bureau cabled: SAMUEL INSULL IS HERE CLAIMING HE ISN'T INSULL. He hurried on — to Florence, to Turin, then to Athens, and there was arrested at request of the American Ambassador but quickly released because no extradition treaty covered his case. "I should not be bothered by the police," he complained. "I have just been unfortunate and lost lots of money, over a hundred million dollars of my own." This hit Page One just when Democrats were pouring into Chicago for their National Convention, and anything that made the *status quo*, defended by the Ins, look less than perfect was ammunition for the Outs.

I wrote some features about the Democratic Convention, sitting in the press box next to Will Rogers, whose new contract to write a syndicate column reputedly paid him five thousand dollars a week. His *Political Follies* was a best seller, and he said it would sell twice as well if it included the craziness he watched that July in Chicago. I watched him write sentences in perfectly grammatical English, every word correctly spelled, and then go through his copy, meticulously inserting *ain'ts* and Oklahoma cowboy quaintness. He ate popcorn omnivorously, and dozed through Convention speeches. Someone in the throng cast one vote for Will Rogers for President. He opened one eye, commented, "Not all the fools are dead yet," and went back to sleep. On the third ballot, California and Texas touched off pandemonium by swinging over to Franklin D. Roosevelt. Somebody told the police to lock all doors, to prevent anyone from entering or leaving the

Chicago Stadium. Photographers were trapped inside, with their papers waiting for Page One pictures. The Associated Press claimed it was one of their photographers, un-named — but we claimed it was Charley Ford of the *Daily News* — who darted into a telephone booth and called for a private ambulance to come to the Stadium, park outside, and send in a stretcher and attendants to carry out a delegate who had just suffered a heart attack. The ambulance arrived. Police ushered the stretcher bearers to the phone booth. Exclusive pictures were carried out on the bosom of an apparent corpse that revived miraculously once the ambulance was speeding toward the *Daily News* building, stopping for no traffic lights. On July 2, the *Daily News* printed the full text of Roosevelt's acceptance speech, in which he called for "a new deal for the American people." Then on July 28, the *Daily News* was the only avowed Republican newspaper that headlined WAR THREATENED IN WASHINGTON.

That day, the *Bonus Expeditionary Force News*, published on the Anacostia flats in sight of the Washington Monument, began its Page One editorial: *Historians of the future will record that the collapse of American democracy reached its final stage in 1932 and that thereupon dictatorship began. The sly man in the White House prepares to strike at our liberty.* That afternoon, President Hoover ordered his chief-of-staff, General Douglas MacArthur, to evict the Bonus Army from the capital. General MacArthur executed his orders. Delayed action, he told reporters, including Paul R. Leach of the *Daily News*, might have "threatened the institutions of our country" and led to "insurgency and insurrection." The men in the Bonus Army camps, he said, had become "a bad-looking mob animated by the spirit of revolution." The *Daily News* didn't think use of military force was justified. This stand was referred to later by party leaders in the Senate who objected when Knox accepted appointment as Roosevelt's Secretary of the Navy. His answer, published in the *Daily News* in 1940, said, "I am American first and Republican afterward."

It wasn't my business then, nor is it my intention now, to pontificate about politics. It is probably bad manners to look behind the record on Samuel Insull, which reads that when he was finally returned to Chicago in 1934, and tried on charges of embezzlement and using the mails to defraud, the juries acquitted him. I discussed this at the time with Steve Hannagan, to whom newspapermen gave credit personally, though not in print, for getting Insull off scot-free. Hannagan had Insull wear hand-me-downs, and wait on the street for a bus, and speak gently to reporters. His skill created Insull in a new image: that of a well-meaning little old man who had made some mistakes which could happen to anybody. I liked Steve Hannagan, and drank Ave to him when he died, alone, in Kenya, where he had gone to develop a Coca-Cola franchise. But I never pitied Samuel Insull, nor can I apologize for my prejudice. I think I had good cause to wish him bad cess, though I never saw him closer than from among reporters watching on the day when he went to and from the execution block, six years before he dropped dead in Paris leaving one thousand dollars in cash and fourteen million dollars in debts.

He wouldn't have been caught in the same grave with Dollie Wedburg. But Dollie did what Insull didn't: he died all square. And he taught me other odd ideas that would have baffled Insull. One was that you're ahead if you wind up with the morning paper, an apple, and a bottle of milk. Drinking my milk and eating my apple one sunrise, and reading Hearst's *Examiner*, I turned to Louella Parsons's column as I have every day since she started writing it. Smith called Louella a first-rate reporter, and I concur. She possesses, uniquely in her field, the quality Smith said good reporters never lose. She never stops being excited about the news she has to tell. And she excited me, that morning. Her Hollywood

341

news was headlined *"IF I HAD A MILLION"* PUR-CHASED BY PARAMOUNT FOR ALL-STAR SPECIAL. The agent in New York had written intermittently since the book came out. Each letter was more discouraging than the last. If he couldn't sell the book to Hollywood, he had said, nobody could; and he couldn't. Now, in her first Exclusive, Louella Parsons said Paramount was assigning ten teams of writers, ten directors, and all of the studio's players — Charles Laughton, George Raft, Jack Oakie, Gene Raymond, Carole Lombard, Gary Cooper, W. C. Fields, Allison Skipworth, Wynne Gibson, Charles Ruggles, Mary Boland, Richard Bennett, Bob Burns, and a dozen more — to put *If I Had A Million* on the screen. I wired the agent. No reply. I called him on Long Distance. No answer. At the *Daily News*, the World's Oldest Office Boy snapped to salute. "I guess," he said, "you were just born with a golden horseshoe in your Little Big Mouth." I told him he was very funny. Gene Morgan said "I think we need a drink," and bought it, and said nothing whatever about rescuing *If I Had a Million* from me on Mount Royal.

For four interminable days, only faith in Louella Parsons sustained me. Then at long last the agent got around to confirming her Exclusive. He had been too busy, until then, collecting the check from Paramount and making sure it cleared the bank so he could deduct his commission. He sent me his personal check for the balance. It cleared on the second bounce. Then well wishers descended on me. Recalling what became of my loot from Fox for *Three Girls Lost*, they said it mustn't happen to my easy money from Paramount. Clearly, I didn't know the value of money. Weakly, I said I thought it was to buy things with. They said that could wait. What I must do was let them invest my windfall for me. Then I could watch my nest egg grow. I said this sounded rather dull. But finally, because they meant so well, I surrendered. That left me with a sheaf of facsimile checks for a million dollars which the publisher had printed to advertise the book.

Thirty years later, in Hollywood, an actor named Marvin Miller presented my wife and myself with a million-dollar facsimile check which he autographed. Thus he let us know that he played Michael Anthony in "The Millionaire" — a series on CBS Television — distributing million-dollar gifts to strangers as emissary of one John Beresford Tipton. When another guest at the party jogged his memory, he recalled having seen me mentioned in small print, after hair-stylists and set-dressers, as writer-consultant for "The Millionaire." But he was amazed to hear I had autographed identical million-dollar checks in 1932. Mine were worthless, too. But so was the Insull stock my kind friends bought for me, with all the cash I got for *If I Had a Million*, just before his financial crash. Ah, well. I still had my typewriter. And in 1932, still a long, long way to go.

Young Man in a Rubber-tired Rickshaw

DEAR BOB: What you have written about me for Walter Winchell, and what I believe you really feel, is greatly exaggerated. Thank you.

—HENRY JUSTIN SMITH
office memorandum
1933

It isn't a thing Chicago writers want, any more than writers from anywhere else want it or willingly accept it. But once you're writing in Hollywood and dining at Chasen's, it seems necessary not to have been anywhere before you were here.

—ROBERT HARDY ANDREWS
Chicago Daily News
1941

While the Hollywood party went on around them, Carl Sandburg and Bob Andrews sat in a corner talking about old but unforgotten days on the *Chicago Daily News*. They had more fun than anyone there.

—VINCENT X. FLAHERTY
Los Angeles Examiner
1961

AT MIDNIGHT ON NEW YEAR'S EVE, 1932, Lady
Godiva rode a white horse across Michigan Boulevard, clad
only in a snowstorm. She was expected at the Artists' Ball,
and would have been there on time if there was any way to
ride a horse through a revolving door. There wasn't, and none
of us knew how to get the door off of its hinges. The wind
howled in from the lake. Lady Godiva turned blue, to match
the color of her comments. Her horse, tired of capering
costumed celebrants, headed for his warm barn in Lincoln
Park. Lady Godiva fell off, but was caught by willing hands.
There was a lot of pull-and-haul, before her victorious bearers
carried her, above their heads, into the hotel ballroom. *Auld
Lang Syne* was drowned by the roar of a spontaneous stampede from which Lady Godiva fled, breaking the world's
record for the high-hurdles dash to the powder room. And to
me, the calendar to the contrary, that was the opening event
of Chicago's Century of Progress World's Fair of 1933.

On New Year's Day, there were rumors that Lady Godiva
might sue everyone concerned, for damages to her dignity and
so forth. These were quickly quashed by Andy Rebori. He
said that the night before, in a flash of realization, he saw that
while he hunted everywhere for the sensational attraction he
needed for his Streets of Paris at the Fair, here she stood (or
rather, ran) before his very eyes. Her name, he told me, was
Helen Gould Beck. She was an artist's model, an actress, and
a dancer. There was, he reminded me, a Depression in 1893,
though then it was called a Panic. Chicagoans had feared

then that their Columbian Exposition was foredoomed. Not so: fairgoers came from everywhere. Not, he said, to be awed by art and thrilled by science, but to see Little Egypt dance the dance her mother never taught her. All right. Andy Rebori would bet his bottom dollar, and as many more of the same as he could raise, on a little lady whose costume would consist of openwork sandals and two large ostrich-plume fans. She would be billed as Sally Rand.

And soon after this promising announcement, on the argument that I was Colonel Knox's official World's Fair worrier, the World's Oldest Office Boy presented me with a calling card four inches square. The name on it was H. E. Man. Just that. I said, "Show him in whatever he is," and surveyed a mountainous version of Erskine Caldwell's Jeeter Lester, who said he was mighty thankful he finally found somebody who could tell him how to go about putting on his act at the Fair. I asked what his act consisted of. He said "I lift my bull." He had heard somewhere, just possibly in school, where he went as high as the Fourth Grade, about some foreigner, it might have been a Greek, who started lifting a bull calf, and got stronger while the calf grew bigger, until he was the only he-man on earth who could balance a full-grown bull on his shoulders and tip his hat while he was doing it. My caller said he could do the same, and whistle *Dixie* meanwhile. Hence H. E. Man on his card.

He had his bull in a truck he'd borrowed from his Down South neighbor, a well-off moonshiner, and asked how much I figured the folks at the Fair would pay him every time he lifted the critter, which he would do right now to show me something I never saw before. I said "This I wouldn't miss" — and asked Charley Ford to bring his camera, and called a press agent, an ambitious beginner who was looking for something that would land a client, and himself, on Page One. He came hurrying to join us in the parking lot, where H. E. Man unloaded a bull the size of a buffalo from a rattletrap Model

348

A pickup, then stripped to the waist and bulged his muscles in a Lionel Strongfort pose, then crouched under the bull's belly, crooning reassuring sounds, and began to grunt and lift. The bull wasn't used to an audience. It bawled and kicked, while H. E. Man straightened up an inch at a heave. The press agent thought the bull was falling. Helpfully, he grabbed its tail and yanked. Frightened, the bull forgot its company manners. He jumped backward, just too late.

Charley Ford got a picture that would never do in the Paper That Goes Home. With regret, we told H. E. Man we just didn't think the Fair could use him. For all I know, he butchered and ate his bull. In any event, the experience was highly educational for the press agent, whose own calling card brandished the professional name he had just adopted: MIKE TODD. From then on, he said, he'd stick to entertainment that could be controlled. The next week, he signed up a rival for Sally Rand: Faith Bacon, who danced amidst flames that burned off her draperies, and sometimes scorched Bacon. From that to *The Hot Mikado* was a natural upward step. From there on, nothing stopped Mike Todd, until a chartered plane that shouldn't have been in the air that night smashed into a mountain the pilot should have been able to miss, and he died in an accident that needn't have happened. ("It wouldn't have," a friend of his told me one night at Chasen's, "if Mike was doing the flying." I said, "But he didn't know how to fly a plane." His friend said, "Not knowing how never stopped Mike Todd." Men have had worse epitaphs.)

So much went on in Chicago early in 1933 that even New Yorkers talked about Chicago's Fair. In the Amen Corner at Lahiff's, Ted Husing said he doubted if many Easterners would go to it, since New York would be having a Fair in 1939. I said "Six years is a long time to wait." Ted said "Not if it gets you to the Big Town." I said the trouble with New Yorkers was that secretly they envied Chicagoans. I almost believed it. But not quite; nowhere near as much as I had a year before. Shows opened in New York. They played Chicago when actors were as used-up as their costumes, and the jokes were two years out of date. John Drury had to dig deep, and pad elaborately, to fill his *Dining in Chicago*. On my brief visits I had dined around the world in Manhattan, and never tipped the same headwaiter twice. Some of New York's Old Rarity was really right off the boat from Scotland. Ted Husing diagrammed last season's games on the tablecloth at "21," to teach me what the Big Ten didn't know about football. At the Stork Club, annoyed by a butter-and-egg man from Milwaukee, Peggy Hopkins Joyce rapped him over the head with a magnum of Veuve Clicquot '27, and said sweetly as he fell: "Consider yourself launched." In Chicago, it would have been a beer bottle; but she wouldn't have wielded it. Having married a couple of Chicagoans, she said she would never go there any more. And where in Chicago was there a Prince who would borrow my Irish blackthorn walking stick, as Mike Romanoff did at Peppy D'Albrew's Chapeau Rouge, to complete his wardrobe for the role of an impecunious impostor, making his stage debut with Harry Richman in *Say When?* We had lost Al Capone. New York still had Dutch Schultz and Legs Diamond and Owney Madden and Vincent Baby-Killer Coll.

Mark Hellinger and Walter Winchell and Bill Corum and Jimmy Cannon and John O'Hara and Quentin Reynolds and Louis Sobol and James Kilgallen and Stanley Walker and Ed Sullivan told New York newspaper tales I couldn't top. (They respected the *Daily News*, but, after all, it was in Chicago.) Summing up, New York was the Big Time: still a new world to me, but one around which nobody put up NO TRESPASSING signs.

Even in radio, we were losing our early lead. Staged in New York, written by and for New Yorkers, the rise of "The Goldbergs" surrounded the inimitable Gertrude Berg with such stars in the making as Joseph Cotten, Van Heflin, and

350

Everett Sloane. When Norman Brokenshire ran out of script with air time still to fill, he was so sure of his coast-to-coast audience that he held the microphone out of a studio window and commanded, "Ladies and gentlemen, listen to the heartbeat of New York!" and was unanimously obeyed. Listeners clear to Hawaii and Alaska got their foreign-affairs information from Walter Winchell, a vocal Gatling gun, and their conversation pieces from Alexander Woollcott, the Town Crier. Half of my own shows, written in Chicago, were broadcast from New York. More would probably be moving there. Chicago had a tight little island of radio actors. New York had the Lambs Club and the Friars and the Players to draw on; and every Broadway closing released more actors and actresses eager and able to work in daytime serials. Such things and more considered, I stayed a little longer each time I took the *Twentieth Century* east from Chicago, and returned each time a little less loyally. (Romance is over, according to Ovid, when delusion dies and analysis sets in.)

Chicago dignitaries were interviewed and photographed before departing for Europe to solicit loan of Old Masters for an international exhibition at the Fair. I asked Smith why nobody bothered to ask Chicago artists if they might have pictures that visitors to the Fair would look at, and maybe even buy, and persuaded him to let me write Previewer pieces that were frank publicity for an outdoor art show in Grant Park, picnic and circus and challenge combined. Most of the paintings were nudes. That, I hinted broadly, was in keeping with the real *ethos* of the Fair. True or false, nobody wrote indignant Letters to the Editor or called on the police to put a stop to public strip-teasing.

Three exhibitors in the outdoor show shared an attic in Tower Town, and ownership of a savage, one-eyed, black alley cat named Georgeous Technicolor. Surprisingly, one of them sold a figure study for a whole thirty dollars. He ran as fast as he could to buy three bottles of gin and four steaks weighing

351

two pounds each. His partners hurried to join him at their first square meal in months. When I dropped in, they were letting their own food grow cold while they pleaded with the cat: "Attack the steak! Attack the steak!" Gorgeous Technicolor wouldn't move. Square meals were so rare and far between, in Chicago's art colony, that the poor animal had forgotten what a steak was for.

As for me, I moved from "The Girl Next Door" to a new soap opera called "Judy and Jane," which might be described as a continuation of the adventures of the other two girls in *Three Girls Lost*. And "Just Plain Bill" and "Ma Perkins" and "Betty and Bob" and "Jack Armstrong, the All-American Boy" were renewed. And even "Skippy" boomed, because of the contest for free trips to the Fair. There were some brief mentions in the press of a "Dust Bowl" developing in Oklahoma, Kansas, Texas, Colorado, and New Mexico. No dust blew in Chicago. *Esquire: The Magazine for Men* began publication, opening a new market for some writers and illustrators. Brewers planned vast *bierstubes*, at the Fair; 3.2 per cent beer would be legal, and Prohibition was sure to be repealed, by year's end.

Twelve million wage earners were out of work, and five million families, a seventh of the nation's population, were on relief or supported by charity. President Hoover, about to vacate the White House, warned Americans not to rest their hopes on "false gods arrayed in the rainbow colors of promises." Chicago, that toddling town, was undismayed. The *Daily News* announced that a fleet of Ford trimotor planes capable of carrying twelve passengers each as fast as one hundred and twenty-five miles an hour was ready to bring big spenders to the Fair. Westinghouse was building an experimental atom-smasher, whatever that might be, and would exhibit working models "as another milestone in A Century of Progress." Never mind about Samuel Insull and the Depression. Forget bank closings and J. P. Morgan being questioned by Congress

352

with a midget perched on his knee. *Throw away your hammer and get a horn!*

From Berlin, John Gunther filed a story whose ultimate implications were not yet conceivable. We headlined *GERMAN REICHSTAG BURNING. Police,* Gunther reported, *dragged an incoherent, hysterical, half-naked Dutchman named Marinus van der Lubbe out of the burning building. Herman, Goering, Nazi Number Two, blandly announced that the Communists had set the fire as a signal for World Revolution. Adolf Hitler, about to be confirmed as Chancellor, piously proclaimed the burning as "a sign from heaven."* For the same Final, I wrote five columns with pictures about the German-American contribution to Colonel Knox's Carnival of Nations. Then I took the speedboat up the river from the *Daily News* to the Wrigley Building, to supervise the first broadcast of a show entirely my own, called "Captain Jack": an adventure serial for children that took a sort of Chicago Swiss Family Robinson on an archaeological expedition to the City of the Sacred Well in Yucatán. The opening script built up to a plane crash in the jungle, which our sound-man simulated by smashing orange crates and spilling water from washtubs. When this was over, the studio was a shambles. The cleanup porter, looking in, wailed, "Oh, my goodness, Mr. Andrews got another show! Ain't nobody messes up a studio like him!"

"Captain Jack" didn't last past the first thirteen weeks, and I wasn't sorry when the contract ran out. Writing radio was enough; coping with radio sponsors was something I wasn't geared for. Officially, I wasn't concerned with other shows now coming out of the Blackett-Sample-Hummert mill: "Stella Dallas," "Young Widder Brown," "Lorenzo Jones," "Our Gal Sunday." But people acting in them told me, when I visited New York, "We're doing the same 'honeymoon in California' routine you did last month in 'Betty and Bob' " or

353

"I picked up my script and there was the identical dialogue you gave me in 'Just Plain Bill.'" That figured as par for the course. Some soap opera writers, and especially Irma Phillips and Elaine Carrington, creators respectively of "The Guiding Light" and "Pepper Young's Family," were widely publicized. I have never hired a press agent. This may be why Irving Settel, the author of such classics as *The Ad-Viser* and *How To Write Television Comedy*, presented me in his *Pictorial History of Radio* (published in 1960) under a label I never used even in pulp magazines: *Between the two of them,* said Settel, *Elaine Carrington and Charles D. Andrews turned out a prodigiously large proportion of the serials that saturated the air waves over twenty-five years. Charles D. Andrews created "Just Plain Bill." He was also, while employed by Frank Hummert, the Sol Hurok of soap opera, responsible for "Ma Perkins" and "Backstage Wife."*

I never knew two men less like each other, physically, mentally, and in their philosophy regarding entertainment, than Hummert and Hurok, and I give all responsibility for "Backstage Wife" to Mrs. Ashenhurst. The plot came straight from her white typewriter: *A nice girl marries an international matinee idol; we dramatize her womanly problems, with touches of Broadway and Hollywood glamour; how can she hold her husband and protect her happiness?* Given all that to work with, anyone could write the scripts; and the show ran longer and sold more for its sponsors than competing serials, out of other shops, that won Peabody Awards. But the classic soap opera was still to be put together on the assembly line.

"Women wonder," Mrs. Ashenhurst told me in the ivory tower on Park Avenue, "what would happen if, after they've been married for ten or fifteen years, they should lose their husbands, through death or divorce. Will they have to go out and earn their own living again? Can they? After being out of practice so long, devoting themselves entirely to a man,

354

is there still a place for them as stenographers or teachers or beauty operators, competing with other younger women? Will they have to marry again in order to have a home? Have they lost their charm, sacrificed their youth and looks, for the sake of the husband who is gone? Will they be too old to find new romance, yet not old enough to be content without it?" She told me very seriously: "This is a very serious problem, Mr. Andrews. Exploring it will touch on doubts and fears every woman feels though few of them admit it openly. We must answer the questions every woman asks, at one time or another, in her secret heart." I knew, by now, why I had been summoned suddenly from Chicago. It no longer occurred to Mrs. Ashenhurst, or to me, to discuss How or When or Why. And we would get to Who in a minute.

"Can a woman," Mrs. Ashenhurst asked while she noted her question on a pad, "find new romance after thirty-five?" I said, "Some of them seem to." She didn't hear me. "Can it possibly be real and forever?" she asked. "Or will it be only second-best?" I said, "I don't know, Mrs. Ashenhurst." Nor were her rhetorical questions ever answered conclusively by the woman over thirty-five to whom we gave a name and a goal that day. Twenty-five years after I wrote the first script for "The Romance of Helen Trent," and hurried back to Chicago, with Mrs. Ashenhurst ahead of me, to cast the show and start testing it (of all places, over the *Tribune* station, WGN), our ageless Helen still searched for true love the second time around, and still hadn't found it. If she had, the show would have vanished from the network, instead of becoming, as it was, the most listened-to and longest-running soap opera of them all.

I had come full circle, back to For Women Only. *You ride all day on the merry-go-round and where have you been?* I didn't have to go on riding around and around and going nowhere. I wasn't irreplaceable. All I had to do was step off and

355

out. And then? I pondered probabilities, and liked the look of none of them, while I took Helen Trent through the divorce that of course she didn't want, and out into a new life filled with men she couldn't trust. More enthusiastically, I did some writing for Smith, about a less romantic seeker regarding whom there were also some questions, most of them still unanswered. This had to do with Mayor Anton Joseph Cermak, "last of the Bohemian bosses."

From Chicago's Little Prague, bounded by Eighteenth and Twenty-sixth Streets and Halsted Street and Pulaski Road, Cermak had moved up, step by step, finally into what amounted to Chicago's Executive Mansion: a triplex penthouse on North Sheridan Road, with a fine view of Pete Penovich's flourishing rooftop gambling establishment just down the road apiece. There were those at the *Daily News*, beginning with Colonel Knox and most definitely including Smith, who remained unimpressed when Cermak proclaimed that he had given a solemn pledge to President-elect Franklin D. Roosevelt (while proclaiming also that he had carried Chicago for Roosevelt): "As Mayor, I will clean up Chicago or die trying." However, an obscure policeman took Cermak's New Deal vow so seriously that he shot Frankie Nitti, "the Enforcer," in the neck. This act of startling *lèse-majesté* set off a stunning chain-reaction.

On February 15, 1933, Cermak went to Florida to see Mr. Roosevelt, announcing that the sole purpose of his trip was to invite the incoming President to open the World's Fair on May 27, "when a beam of light that has traveled through space from the far-off star, Arcturus, will activate an electrical impulse and set in progress our Century of Progress commemoration." Newsroom rumor had it that, in fact, Cermak had decided to place himself on the side of the angels by providing information that would warrant action by the new Administration against the corruption and coercion that had made the Syndicate a law unto itself. This might have been printed, if

356

at Miami one Giuseppi Zangara had not burst from a crowd, firing a pistol purchased in Chicago, narrowly missing Roosevelt and mortally wounding Cermak.

The officially accepted explanation of the crime was that Zangara's insane hatred of constituted authority prompted his attempt to assassinate Roosevelt, and that Cermak became his victim purely by accident. Walter Winchell, for one, disputed this theory. Demonstrating why he classes himself amongst all-time top newspapermen, the former song-and-dance vaudevillian scooped every reporter on the scene, including those who represented the *Daily News*, by getting the only interview with the assassin. "I'm Walter Winchell," he informed an awestruck sheriff. "Let me in there and I'll put your name in every paper in the world." Since Winchell worked for Hearst, the wide coverage he delivered didn't include the *Daily News*. Nor would Smith print, because it couldn't be proved, a home-grown Exclusive alleging that actually Zangara was hired and trained to miss the President-elect and murder the mayor who was about to talk too much, and that if Zangara had failed in Florida, a more experienced triggerman was on standby call to finish the job on Opening Day at the World's Fair.

An earlier mayor who had also sworn to clean up Chicago, Carter Harrison Sr., had been assassinated at the Columbian Exposition forty years before. The result was a notable increase in attendance at that Chicago Fair. As for Cermak, he lingered on for ten days after Roosevelt, taking the oath of office, declared: *This great nation will endure as it has endured, will revive and prosper. The only thing we have to fear is fear itself: nameless, unreasonable, unjustified terror which paralyzes needed efforts to convert retreat into advance.* Nobody showed fear in Chicago; nobody, that is, who mattered. Only the people who didn't know if they'd have a bed to sleep in tomorrow night.

Forty-one per cent of all Chicago city taxes were delinquent.

357

Teachers and other public employees hadn't been paid in months. In the farm country on which Chicagoans depended for their daily bread, two hundred million dollars in mortgages stood defaulted. But in Rome, Mussolini ordered Italo Balbo to mass an armada of Fascist Italy's new air power for a good-will flight to Chicago and the Fair. And *From 1933 onward*, according to one authority, *Chicago gangsters enjoyed their most complete immunity from prosecution, and by far their greatest prosperity*. I did no writing about this. My stuff would have been down-beat, and that wasn't wanted, even in the *Daily News*. Crusaders were out of style in Chicago, for the duration of the Fair. Anyhow, I had enough to handle in the cleaner, greener Never-Never Land of soap opera. Especially now that "The Romance of Helen Trent" was on my list.

If it was true, as James Thurber has recorded, that "Just Plain Bill" was daytime radio's *Les Miserables*, then surely "Helen Trent" was its never-consummated *Lysistrata*. And making the trick of always-almost-but-never-quite work, and keep on working, was a major assignment even for Mrs. Ashenhurst and a Myth. Still, I stole time between sets of scripts to go on the town one night with Thornton Wilder. Passing through, he had called to ask diffidently if I might know where Miss Texas Guinan was appearing. I said she was at the Planet Mars, a New York-style club just opened to catch the expense-account trade of exhibitors and entrepreneurs arriving ahead of the opening of the Fair. Luckily, I didn't add that I wouldn't recommend the food, the liquor, the prices, or the place. This unwonted reticence saved me from feeling foolish when Wilder invited me to join him at supper, while he paid his respects to an old and valued friend.

We entered the Planet Mars while the midnight show was shaping up. Time had blurred Texas Guinan's brassy ebullience, but it hadn't weakened her onstage voice. "Hello, suckers!" rang across the sparsely populated room, while coryphees did languid calisthenics and counted unattached customers. Suddenly, Guinan spied Wilder. Leaving the spotlight, she came to him instantly, and led the way to a ringside table, meanwhile discussing his books and his plays in preparation with quiet intelligence that told me why Wilder treasured her friendship. Then she got around to noticing me. Wilder introduced us. "Andrews? You wrote *If I Had a Million*. Winchell sent me a copy. It's good. Kept me up all night." Suddenly, she was back in the spotlight, halting the chorus-girl walk-about, demanding and getting full attention while she gave a chapter-by-chapter resumé of *If I Had a Million*, and commanding: "You suckers be sure you buy it. Take old Tex's word: You won't be wasting your money." Smiling, Wilder murmured: "Members of the same club." And I felt that, after all, I had arrived somewhere, though I couldn't have said just where.

That dawn, I walked again in Grant Park, through drifting fog. Angular buildings and towers, none of them quite completed, rose from new acres dredged out of the lake. There, in a few more days, throngs would file through turnstiles, and Sally Rand would preen between her fans, while Chicago notified the universe: "Whatever you've read and heard, it's only the half of it." The homeless and jobless, huddled on benches and sprawled on pallets of old newspapers, might, just might, find work or at least get handouts when the Fair got under way. An Opposition editorialist found encouragement in the fact that the Panic of 1893 came after the Fair, not before. This time, we had our Depression first. Logically, then, brighter days were soon to come.

I doubted it. I doubted it even more when, in our corner at the *Daily News*, I found a copy of Carl Sandburg's *Rootabaga Stories* on my desk. He sat studying a paragraph he had written, while I studied his gift and wondered why it was given. *Rootabaga Stories*, published while I was still on the

Aberdeen American in South Dakota, was dedicated to Spink and Skabootch, Sandburg's daughters, who read the book when they were children and wrote their proper names, Margaret and Janet, on its flyleaf. Beneath these, in his neat rounded script, Sandburg had penned: R. A. *We girls have used this but you won't mind.* I minded. Because this was Sandburg's good-by.

He said he wasn't actually leaving the *Daily News*. That was something nobody who ever worked there ever really did, as far as feelings were concerned. But he wouldn't be humming and strumming in our corner from now on. He had books to finish and poems to put on paper, and lectures to give and traveling planned, and an urge to be off away from people more — far enough to see them clearer — now that he was nearly an old man. He was fifty-four.

He was eighty-two, and going strong, when Vincent X. Flaherty wrote in the *Los Angeles Examiner:*

Sometimes in brooding moments I mourn the loss of my old school-kid verve when I became goggle-eyed in the presence of a famous person. I recaptured a bit of that lost stimulus when I was privileged to meet a great man, a gentle giant of literature, Carl Sandburg, at the cocktail party Milton Berle gave for him at the Beverly Hills Hotel. It was the only cocktail party I ever attended where much attention was paid to the honored guest. If I acted slightly cub-reporterish around the gentleman, so did Louella Parsons. She knew him when she was a teen-age reporter in Chicago. While the Hollywood party went on around them, Sandburg and Bob Andrews sat in a corner talking about old but unforgotten days on the *Chicago Daily News*. They had more fun than anybody there. Bob brought with him one of Sandburg's first books.

I had brought *Rootabaga Stories,* and Sandburg wrote a second autograph on its flyleaf. This one was addressed to my daughter. MERRY ANDREWS: *Time has been so kind to your*

father and to me. God love you. CARL SANDBURG. But it takes
time to learn how to be thankful to Time.

« 2 »

Claude Caspar-Jordan was gone. Jack Lawson was gone. Pablo
Katigbak was gone. Now Sandburg was gone. And Smith was
no longer the Smith who wrote *Deadlines*. Before Jake Lingle,
Smith could not have believed newspapermen could sell out
their papers, and themselves. Since Lingle, Smith wondered
increasingly if all his life he had been self-deceived. It angered
Colonel Knox, but it bewildered Smith, when Heywood Broun
bombarded the *Daily News* with accusations of resistance to
formation of a chapter of the Newspaper Guild. Smith never
opposed anything that would give more pride and dignity to
reporters. But he simply couldn't understand what had
changed: why they must organize to demand what he had
given every man an equal chance to earn for himself. SALARY
INADEQUATE IF THAT MATTERS was his hesitant way of asking,
"How much does it really mean to you to carry a C. D. N.
press card?" Knowing this, I knew, too, that if he brought
himself to ask me that question point-blank, I would have to
answer honestly "Not as much as it did four years ago or
even a month ago"; and when I did that, a curtain would fall,
and never rise again. Smith was a sentimentalist. I was, and
am, a sentimentalist about him. He would edit this out of
my copy, if he could. And I am glad there was one other time
when he couldn't.

Walter Winchell told me, at Lahiff's in New York, that
he could use a guest column. I said the only story I wanted to
see in print just then was one I knew I couldn't get into the
Daily News, and I didn't think he would publish it, either,
or could, since it would be about Smith. I had never heard
of the Hearst papers publishing anything that praised a rep-
resentative of the Opposition. Besides, Smith worked for
Knox, whose name was anathema to the Master at San

361

Simeon. But Winchell said "Write it," so I did. And for the first time ever (and I believe, the last), *Daily News* reporters cut a column out of the *Examiner* and posted it in the newsroom, because it was all about Smith. He didn't mention the piece, nor did I. But I found on my desk, in a sealed envelope, a note he had penciled on copy paper. DEAR BOB: *What you have written about me for Walter Winchell, and what I believe you really feel, is greatly exaggerated. Thank you.* HENRY JUSTIN SMITH. He hadn't signed his full name to any message since he sent the telegram that started me from Minneapolis to Chicago and 15 North Wells. And it was the last office memorandum I ever received from him.

I had an odd arrangement with a onetime prizefighter, Mickey Eulo, who operated the cigar store in a Tower Town hotel that was home for Machine-gun Jack McGurn and others of his tribe. Out of his whole Eighth Grade graduating class in school out on Death Avenue, Mickey was the only one who had no jail time marked against him in police make-files. He sold very few cigars. Profits he turned over to the Syndicate came from bookmaking and bootlegging; you could lay a bet on anything, in the back room behind Mickey's counter, and another door led to a storeroom filled with bottled whiskey and gin, some of it safe to drink. But Mickey mixed into nothing that might get him arrested and booked. His personal racket was a twenty-six game, old style, played with five dice which you rolled to form a poker hand. Since then, twenty-six game parlors have proliferated all over Chicago. Most of them are run by girls, and beating the house is very bad form, not to say impossible. Rolling dice with Mickey, I almost always won. How this could be was baffling; I am a dedicated loser at any game of skill or chance. But I had beaten Mickey consistently, and had piled up merchandise credits which I hadn't cashed, on the principle that tomorrow's needs might well be more urgent than today's.

362

Now I cashed my chits — for whiskey: twelve bottles each of Scotch and bourbon. I arranged with the proprietor of the Casa De Alex, where Pablo Katigbak and I had said "See you again some day some place," to let me give a private party on a Monday night, when customarily the place was closed. Then I invited eleven guests from the *Daily News,* including the World's Oldest Office Boy and Hal O'Flaherty and Gene Morgan and John Drury and Bob Casey and others who had put up with me long-sufferingly, and even on occasion made me feel I was still a newspaperman though I wrote radio for my living. They came. So did an uninvited thirteenth guest, who shall be nameless since through all the years he has gone out of his way to deny that he was there. My friends saw two bottles at each drinking station. The freeloader said I was showing off my wealth. I wasn't; at least not intentionally. The Irish rule for a wake is that no mourner shall go thirsty. Nor shall he spoil the fun with tears. So everybody told stories with snappers; everybody but the thirteenth at the table. He asked if this was a secret meeting to form a cell of the Newspaper Guild. Was that why Smith wasn't present? When he was ignored, he sulked, and soon announced that he was leaving. Nobody pleaded "Stay." He was just going out the door when a bottle fell from under his coat and broke on the floor. He had four others, appropriated surreptitiously. I asked him to keep them, with my compliments. But none of us could think of anything to laugh about after he departed saying we were phonies and so was Smith. The party broke up soon.

I stayed on the move, postponing sleep while more important things were taken care of, writing batches of "Helen Trent" and "Just Plain Bill" and "Skippy" and "Betty and Bob" and "Backstage Wife" and "Jack Armstrong" and "Judy and Jane" and "Ma Perkins," starting new story lines that were carefully complicated to make sure no one else could step in and solve them — thus building a backlog that ought to

363

keep my home fires burning, wherever home might be, for several months to come. Rikki-tikki-tavi allowed Scrubby the dog-walker to think she was now his dog. Meanwhile I got "Meet the Dixons" ready, and discussed by mail and telephone a show called "Aunt Jenny's True Life Stories," for a New York agency whose president had told his clients "Anything Blackett-Sample-Hummert can do, we can do better." I had shut my eyes and crossed my fingers and jumped into open space when I left Minneapolis. I was older and less reckless now.

And suddenly it was May, 1933. *WORLD'S FAIR OPENS GATES. . . . DILLINGER NAMED PUBLIC ENEMY NUMBER ONE.* On the Chicago lakefront, crowds, confusion, and conquest. . . . Bursting out of Indiana, declaring war on the United States, John Dillinger: robbing banks, killing policemen, raiding police arsenals, altering his face and fingerprints, reveling in his Mad Dog notoriety. I read only the headlines about him. In fact, I hardly looked at the papers. Not even at the *Daily News.* If I did, I might be tempted to tear up the bill of divorcement. *Whatever you git, don't cry because it ain't any more. Grab it and git, before they git it away from you.* I went to the Fair at last, and wandered, bumping and being bumped, lonely among sightseers who thought they were in Chicago. They weren't; not in my Chicago. That was gone with the wind.

One thing I couldn't do. I couldn't face Smith and say "Good-by." He wouldn't want me to. So I hired a rubber-tired rickshaw drawn by a Phys. Ed. major from Northwestern, who resented being called away from research for a thesis on ecdysis as exemplified by Sally Rand, and I bribed a gate guard to let me make my exit in style. I caught the *Twentieth Century* for New York, looking into the future over a double Old Rarity with Perrier, cherishing no fond illusion that I left lost Eden behind. Smith brought me to Chicago and put me in a corner with Carl Sandburg and let me see a fine show free on my C. D. N. press card. From here on, it would be PAY AS YOU ENTER. That didn't mean it wouldn't be worth seeing. I am pretty sure it will go on being that until

THE END